DATE DUE

			PRINTED IN U.S.A.

Authors & Artists for Young Adults

ISSN 1040-5682

Authors & Artists for Young Adults

VOLUME 4

**Agnes Garrett and Helga P. McCue,
Editors**

 Gale Research Inc. · *DETROIT · NEW YORK · LONDON*

Managing Editor: Anne Commire

Editors: Agnes Garrett, Helga P. McCue
Associate Editor: Elisa Ann Ferraro

Assistant Editors: Marc Caplan,
Eunice L. Petrini, Linda Shedd

Sketchwriters: Dianne H. Anderson, Catherine Coray,
Johanna Cypis, Marguerite Feitlowitz, Mimi H. Hutson,
Deborah Klezmer, Dieter Miller, Beatrice Smedley

Researcher: Catherine Ruello

Editorial Assistants: Marja Hiltunen, June Lee, Susan Pfanner

Production Manager: Mary Beth Trimper
External Production Assistant: Marilyn Jackman

Art Director: Arthur Chartow
Keyliner: C. J. Jonik

Production Supervisor: Laura Bryant
Internal Production Associate: Louise Gagné
Internal Production Assistant: Wayne A. Jalava

Library of Congress Catalog Card Number
ISBN 0-8103-5053-X
ISSN 1040-5682

Printed in the United States of America

Contents

Introduction vii

Acknowledgments xi

Douglas Adams 1

C. S. Adler.. 11

V. C. Andrews 19

James Baldwin.................................... 29

Bruce Chatwin 45

Arthur C. Clarke 55

Paula Danziger..................................... 73

Lois Duncan 81

Russell Freedman................................ 95

Carlos Fuentes 107

Rosa Guy 121

Lynn Hall.. 131

Nat Hentoff.................................... 141

Bel Kaufman................................... 155

Spike Lee 165

Mark Mathabane.......................... 181

Robin McKinley 193

Walter Dean Myers....................... 203

Phyllis Reynolds Naylor................ 215

Jane Yolen..................................... 229

Author/Artist Index..................... 245

Introduction

"[Today's youth] is a generation whose grade-school years were informed and enlivened by Betsy Byars, who teaches the basic lesson to the next generation of book buyers: that a novel must entertain first before it can do anything else. But I don't get these readers until they hit puberty. They haven't even budded, and already the Blume is off. I don't get them till puberty, and it's the darkest moment of life. For while puberty is the death of childhood, it isn't the birth of reason.

"Puberty is the same gulag we all once did time in, robbed of the certainties of grade school and still years away from a driver's license. Puberty is waking up every morning wondering which sex you are, if any. Puberty is the practice of strict sexual segregation with all the girls on one side of an invisible line and all the boys on the other: big women, little men. Like a Shaker meeting but without the hope of eternal life. Puberty is no fun, and changing the name of the junior high to the middle school has fooled nobody. In America puberty is deciding at the age of twelve or so to divorce your own parents, charging irreconcilable differences. The children of the underclass hit the streets then and are thereafter out of reach of home and school and books. The children of the middle class recede to their rooms and lock themselves into elaborate sound systems, paid for by parents, that eliminate the possibility of a parental voice. They are free of us at twelve.

"I write for these people whose own parents haven't seen them for days. In our impotence we've reasoned that children must be given freedoms in order to learn how to handle them. But it doesn't work that way. The prematurely emancipated young transfer all their need for a dominating, problem-solving authority from weak adults at home and school to the peer group. The only government they recognize is the vengeful law-giving of each other.

"That's what I write: counterculture literature of individuality to a conformist readership. I write books for the knapsacks of young soldiers of both sexes going forth every school day hoping to survive the 'Chocolate War.' I write for the inmates of schools where you cannot win a letter sweater for literacy. You can win a letter sweater only for mindless conformity, for listening to language from the coach that would get the librarian into big trouble. I write for a generation of young people who don't have to drop by the library, even on the way to the Gifted Program. They don't have to drop by anywhere except, perhaps, the shopping mall."

—Richard Peck

"The time of adolescence is in itself a wonderful age to write about. It combines an idealism and honesty and a wily sophistication that no other time of life enjoys. The teenager has vitality and enjoys life although he sees the ugliness and absurdities as well as the joys.

"Adolescents are also engaged in some of the most important 'work' they will ever do. It is the time when one establishes one's identity and comes of age in a number of critical areas—social, political, cultural, sexual. Conflict prevails during these years with one's parents, teachers, peers and, most painfully, with oneself."

—Hila Colman

Authors and Artists for Young Adults is a new reference series designed to bridge the gap between Gale's *Something about the Author*, designed for children, and *Contemporary Authors*, intended for adults. This new series is aimed entirely at the needs and interests of the often overlooked young adults. We share the concerns of librarians who must send young readers to the adult reference shelves for which they may not be ready. *Authors and Artists for Young Adults* will give high school and junior high school students information about the life and work of their favorite creative artists—the people behind the books, movies, television programs, plays, lyrics, cartoon and animated features that they most enjoy. Although most of these will be present-day artists, the series is open to people of all time periods and all countries whose work has a special appeal to young adults today. Some of these artists may also be profiled in *Something about the Author* or *Contemporary Authors*, but their entries in *Authors and Artists for Young Adults* are completely updated and tailored to the information needs of the young adult user.

Entry Format

Authors and Artists for Young Adults will be published in two volumes each year. Each volume in the series will furnish in-depth coverage of about twenty authors and artists. The typical entry consists of:

—A personal section that includes date and place of birth, marriage, children, and education.

—A comprehensive bibliography or film-ography including publishers, producers, and years.

—Adaptations into other media forms.

—Works in progress.

—A distinctive sidelights section where secondary sources and exclusive interviews concentrate on an artist's craft, artistic intentions, career, world views, thematic discussions, and controversies.

—A "For More Information See" section arranged in chronological order to increase the scope of this reference work.

While the textual information in *Authors and Artists for Young Adults* is its primary reason for existing, entries are complemented by illustrations, photographs, movie stills, manuscript samples, dust jackets, book covers, and other relevant visual material.

A cumulative Author/Artist Index appears at the back of this volume.

Highlights of This Volume

A sampling of the variety of creative artists featured in this volume includes:

DOUGLAS ADAMS......decided along with a couple of fellow graduates from Cambridge University to pursue a writing career. "We then had an argument about what sort of jobs we ought to take to support us in the meantime. They argued for a second career to fall back on. I argued for the minimum job necessary for survival so that there would be no fall-back position, you would have to become a writer." Adams then worked as a hospital reporter, barn builder, chicken-shed cleaner, and bodyguard for an Arab royal family before the enormous success of *The Hitchhiker's Guide to the Galaxy*. "...I remember lying drunk in a field in Innsbruck one night. I sort of laid down on the ground and stared up at the stars and it occurred to me then that somebody ought to write a hitch hiker's guide to the galaxy....When I was writing the first of *Hitchhiker*'s down in Dorset, I would leave notes to myself to find later, saying, 'If you ever get the chance to do a proper, regular job—take it. This is not the occupation for a growing healthy lad.' "

PAULA DANZIGER......was inspired to begin her first book after being injured in a serious car accident. "I lost the ability to read....I could write backwards—a perfect mirror image of normal writing. I had recurring nightmares...and functioned with a great deal of difficulty. My feelings of helplessness and terror dredged up a lot of material from my childhood....I wrote [*The Cat Ate My Gymsuit*] in therapy, bringing newly-drafted pages to many appointments." Since that time, Danziger's writing has been dedicated exclusively to young adult literature. "I get so tired of the question, 'So when are you going to do your adult book?' As though I've just been practicing all these years to become 'good enough' to write for grown-ups....There is widespread misconception that it is easier to write for young people than for adults. It is not....Children are arguably the most important members of society—they are the future." Danziger has yet to fulfill her second ambition "to be a stand-up comic. But I have trick knees and can't stay up too late."

LOIS DUNCAN......showed the makings of a writer by the age of three. "...I was dictating stories to my parents, and as soon as I learned to print, I was writing them down myself." She made use of her story-telling techniques in order to terrorize her younger brother. "I shared a room with [him], and at night I would lie in bed inventing tales to give him nightmares. I would pretend to be the 'Moon Fairy,' come to deliver the message that the moon was falling toward the earth. 'And what will happen to *me*?' Billy would ask in his quavering little voice. 'You'll be blown up into the sky,' the Moon Fairy would tell him. 'By the time you come down the world will be gone, so you'll just keep falling forever.' Eventually our parents had the good sense to put us in separate rooms." Duncan was a published author by the age of thirteen and has since written over thirty books. "People ask, 'Are you going to keep writing?' They might as well ask if I plan to continue breathing. I expect to do both just as long as I possibly can."

MARK MATHABANE......was raised in Alexandra, South Africa, where growing up Black under apartheid "meant hate, bitterness, hunger, pain, terror, violence, fear, dashed hopes and dreams." When informed that Blacks couldn't "read, speak, or write English like white people because they have smaller brains," Mathabane vowed "that whatever the cost, I would master English....Finally, I had something to aspire to." He came to America after tennis champion Stan Smith helped him secure a scholarship to Limestone College in South Carolina. When a librarian led him "to the treasure," a world of books by Black authors, Mathabane's life took a turn. "Here were Black men and women...wrestling with fate itself in an heroic attempt to make the incomprehensible—man's inhumanity to man—comprehensible." Awed by the power of the word, Mathabane authored *Kaffir Boy*, the story of his childhood in South Africa. "It is a shame that by far most of what the outside world knows about apartheid comes from writers who are white. The world will not fully understand the complexities of South African society until more Black writers are heard from."

WALTER DEAN MYERS......spent his childhood in the "bright sun of Harlem streets, the easy rhythms of black and brown bodies moving along the tar and asphalt pavement, the sounds of hundreds of children streaming in and out of red brick tenements....I write to give hope to those kids who are like the ones I knew—poor, troubled, treated indifferently by society....I was a high-school dropout, and I know how easy it is for them to lose their brightness." Myers traces the story-telling tradition back to his foster father. "There were stories of ghosts and of rabbits that came through walls and of strange creatures that rose from the sea (the sea being the Hudson River) in the still of night....Sometimes, when the stories were *really* scary, he would act as if he were scared himself. I remember one Saturday [he] told me a story about a huge bunny that escaped from a farm and went around looking for bad children....When Dad got to the part about the bunny coming up the fire escape...he glanced toward the window, put on his best startled face, and took off running down the hallways of our apartment with me in close and screaming pursuit. We didn't stop until we reached Morningside Park."

Forthcoming Volumes

Among the artists planned for future volumes are:

Maya Angelou	Annie Dillard	Harry Mazer
Jean Auel	Bob Dylan	Norma Fox Mazer
Avi	Loren Eiseley	Milton Meltzer
Richard Bach	Amy Ehrlich	Gloria Naylor
Toni Cade Bambara	Louise Erdrich	Joan Lowry Nixon
Berke Breathed	William Faulkner	Zibby O'Neal
Bianca Bradbury	Dick Francis	Gene Roddenberry
Robin Brancato	Eileen Goudge	Ntozake Shange
Sue Ellen Bridgers	Chester Gould	Aranka Siegal
Bruce Brooks	Bette Greene	Stephen Sondheim
Eve Bunting	Judith Guest	Steven Spielberg
Edgar Rice Burroughs	Ann Head	Mary Stolz
Tracy Chapman	Hermann Hesse	Mildred D. Taylor
Agatha Christie	Marjorie Holmes	Julian Thompson
Christopher Collier	John Hughes	J. R. R. Tolkien
Caroline B. Cooney	Victor Hugo	Garry Trudeau
Cameron Crowe	Barry Lopez	Bill Watterson
Jim Davis	Ann M. Martin	Meg Wolitzer

The editors of *Authors and Artists for Young Adults* welcome any suggestions for additional biographees to be included in this series. Please write and give us your opinions and suggestions for making our series more helpful to you.

Acknowledgments

Grateful acknowledgment is made to the following
publishers, authors, and artists whose works appear in this volume.

ALADDIN BOOKS. Cover illustration by Jeanette Adams from *The Solomon System* by Phyllis Reynolds. Cover illustration © 1987 by Jeanette Adams. Cover design © 1987 by Lisa Hollander. Reprinted by permission of Aladdin Books, an imprint of Macmillan Publishing Company.

ATHENEUM. Sidelight excerpts from *How I Came to Be a Writer* by P.R. Naylor. Copyright © 1978, 1987 by Phyllis Reynolds Naylor./ Jacket illustration by John Steven Gurney from *The Year of the Gopher* by Phyllis Reynolds Naylor. Jacket illustration © 1987 by John Steven Gurney./ Jacket illustration by Melodye Rosales from *Beetles, Lightly Toasted* by Phyllis Reynolds Naylor. Jacket illustration © 1987 by Melodye Rosales. All reprinted by permission of Atheneum Publishers, an imprint of Macmillan Publishing Company.

AVON BOOKS. Cover illustration from *The Bodies in the Bessledorf Hotel* by Phyllis Reynolds Naylor. Copyright © 1986 by Phyllis Reynolds Naylor. Reprinted by permission of Avon Books, New York.

BALLANTINE BOOKS. Cover illustration from *A String of Chances* by Phyllis Reynolds Naylor. Copyright © 1982 by Phyllis Reynolds Naylor./ Cover illustration from *The Shell Lady's Daughter* by C.S. Adler. Copyright © 1983 by C.S. Adler./ Cover painting by Michael Whelan from *The Songs of Distant Earth* by Arthur C. Clarke. Copyright © 1986 by Serendib BV./ Cover painting by Michael Whelan from *2061: Odyssey Three* by Arthur C. Clarke. Copyright © 1987 by Serendib BV. All reprinted by permission of Ballantine Books, a division of Random House, Inc.

BANTAM BOOKS. Cover illustration by Max Ginsburg from *The Friends* by Rosa Guy. Illustrations © 1983 by Max Ginsburg./ Cover illustration from *The Keeper* by Phyllis Reynolds Naylor. Cover © 1987 by Bantam Books, Inc. All reprinted by permission of Bantam Books, a division of Bantam, Doubleday, Dell Publishing Group, Inc.

BEACON PRESS. Sidelight excerpts from *Notes of a Native Son* by James Baldwin. Copyright 1955, renewed 1983 by James Baldwin. Reprinted by permission of Beacon Press.

BERKELEY PUBLISHING GROUP. Jacket illustration by Darrell Sweet from *The Outlaws of Sherwood* by Robin McKinley. Copyright © 1988 by Robin McKinley. Reprinted by permission of The Berkeley Publishing Group.

CLARION BOOKS. Cover photograph from the Chicago Historical Society from *Lincoln: A Photobiography* by Russell Freedman./ Jacket illustration by Darryl Zudeck from *Kiss the Clown* by C.S. Adler. Jacket illustration © 1986 by Darryl Zudeck. Both reprinted by permission of Clarion Books, a division of Houghton Mifflin Company.

DEL REY. Sidelight excerpts from *The View from Serendip* by Arthur C. Clarke. Copyright © 1977 by Arthur C. Clarke./ Sidelight excerpts from *1984: Spring. A Choice of Futures* by Arthur C. Clarke. Copyright © 1972, 1984 by Fawcett Publications, Inc. Both reprinted by permission of Del Rey, a division of Random House, Inc.

DELACORTE PRESS. Jacket painting by Peter Caras from *The Pistachio Prescription* by Paula Danziger. Copyright ©1978 by Paula Danziger./ Cover illustration from *Does This School Have Capital Punishment?* by Nat Hentoff. Copyright © 1981 by Marnate Productions, Ltd./ Jacket illustration by Allan Manham from *The Day They Came to Arrest the Book* by Nat Hentoff. Jacket illustration © 1982 by Allan Manham./ Jacket illustration by Richard Lauter from *The Divorce Express* by Paula Danziger. Jacket illustration © 1982 by Richard Lauter./ Jacket illustration by Richard Lauter from *It's an Aardvark-Eat-Turtle World* by Paula Danziger. Jacket illustration © 1985 by Richard Lauter./ Jacket illustration by Joe Csatari from *This Place Has No Atmosphere* by Paula Danziger. Jacket illustration © 1986 by Joe Csatari./ Jacket illustration by Hiram Richardson from *American Heroes: In and Out of School* by Nat Hentoff. Jacket illustration © 1987 by Hiram Richardson. All reprinted by permission of Delacorte Press, a division of Bantam, Doubleday, Dell Publishing Group, Inc.

DELL PUBLISHING. Cover photograph by H. Armstrong Roberts from *Giovanni's Room* by James Baldwin. Copyright 1956 by James Baldwin./ Cover photograph from *The Fire Next Time* by James Baldwin. Copyright © 1962, 1963 by James Baldwin. Cover photograph © 1985 by Stephen Shames/Visions./ Cover illustration from *Jazz Country* by Nat Hentoff. Copyright © 1965 by Nat Hentoff./ Cover illustration from *This School is Driving Me Crazy* by Nat Hentoff. Copyright © 1976 by Nat Hentoff./ Cover illustration from *Summer of Fear* by Lois Duncan. Copyright © 1976 by Lois Duncan./ Cover illustration from *The Disappearance* by Rosa Guy. Copyright © 1979 by Rosa Guy./ Cover illustration from *Can You Sue Your Parents for Malpractice?* by Paula Danziger. Copyright © 1979 by Paula Danziger./ Cover illustration from *Hoops* by Walter Dean Myers. Copyright © 1981 by John Ballard./

Cover illustration from *Dragon's Blood* by Jane Yolen. Copyright © 1982 by Jane Yolen./ Cover illustration from *Heart's Blood* by Jane Yolen. Copyright © by Jane Yolen./ Cover illustration from *New Guys Around the Block* by Rosa Guy. Copyright © 1983 by Rosa Guy./ Cover illustration from *The Outside Shot* by Walter Dean Myers. Copyright © 1984 by John Ballard./ Cover illustration from *Locked in Time* by Lois Duncan. Copyright © 1985 by Lois Duncan./ Cover illustration from *Binding Ties* by C.S. Adler. Copyright © 1985 by C.S. Adler./ Cover illustration from *Remember Me to Harold Square* by Paula Danziger. Copyright © 1987 by Paula Danziger./ Cover from *The Twisted Window* by Lois Duncan. Copyright © 1987 by Lois Duncan./ Cover illustration from *And I Heard a Bird Sing* by Rosa Guy. Copyright © 1987 by Rosa Guy. All reprinted by permission of Dell Publishing, a division of Bantam, Doubleday, Dell Publishing Group, Inc.

DIAL PRESS. Sidelight excerpts from *The Fire Next Time* by James Baldwin. Copyright © 1962, 1963 by James Baldwin./ Sidelight excerpts from *The Devil Finds Work* by James Baldwin. Copyright © 1976 by James Baldwin. Both reprinted by permission of Dial Press, a division of Bantam, Doubleday, Dell Publishing Group, Inc.

FARRAR, STRAUS & GIROUX. Cover design by Honi Werner from *The Hydra Head* by Carlos Fuentes. Translation © 1978 by Farrar, Straus and Giroux, Inc. Reprinted by permission of Farrar, Straus and Giroux, Inc.

DONALD I. FINE. Sidelight excerpts from *James Baldwin: Artist on Fire* by W.J. Weatherby. Copyright © 1989 by W.J. Weatherby. Reprinted by permission of Donald I. Fine, Inc.

FIRESIDE PRESS. Cover illustration from *Spike Lee's Gotta Have It* by Spike Lee. Copyright © 1987 by Spike Lee./ Sidelight excerpts from *Uplift the Race: The Construction of "School Daze"* by Spike Lee with Lisa Jones. Copyright © 1988 by Spike Lee./ Sidelight excerpts and cover illustration from *Do the Right Thing* by Spike Lee with Lisa Jones. Copyright © 1989 by Spike Lee. All reprinted by permission of Fireside Press, a division of Simon & Schuster, Inc.

HARMONY BOOKS. Jacket illustration by Peter Cross from *So Long, And Thanks for All the Fish* by Douglas Adams. Jacket painting © 1984 by Peter Cross. Reprinted by permission of Harmony Books, a division of Random House, Inc.

HARPER & ROW. Jacket illustration by David Palladini from *Beauty: A Retelling of the Story of Beauty & The Beast* by Robin McKinley. Copyright © 1978 by Robin McKinley./ Jacket illustration by Deborah Healy from *Spaceships & Spells* by Jane Yolen, Martin H. Greenberg, and Charles G. Waugh. Jacket art © 1987 by Deborah Healy. Copyright © 1987 by Jane Yolen, Martin H. Greenberg, and Charles G. Waugh./ Jacket illustration by Gary Lippincott from *Werewolves: A Collection of Original Stories* by Jane Yolen and Martin H. Greenberg. Jacket art © 1988 by Gary Lippincott. Copyright © 1988 by Jane Yolen and Martin H. Greenberg./ Jacket illustration by Bradford Brown from *Scorpions* by Walter Dean Myers. Jacket art © 1988 by Bradford Brown. Copyright © 1988 by Walter Dean Myers. All reprinted by permission of Harper & Row, Publishers, Inc.

HOLT, RINEHART & WINSTON. Jacket illustration by Sara Schwartz from *My Love, My Love or The Peasant Girl* by Rosa Guy. Copyright © 1985 by Rosa Guy. Reprinted by permission of Holt, Rinehart & Winston.

ALFRED A. KNOPF. Sidelight excerpts from *Boston Boy* by Nat Hentoff. Copyright © 1986 by Common Sense Productions, Inc. Reprinted by permission of Alfred A. Knopf, Inc.

J. B. LIPPINCOTT. Sidelight excerpts from *A Dialogue* by James Baldwin and Nikki Giovanni. Copyright © 1973 by James Baldwin and Nikki Giovanni. Reprinted by permission of J. B. Lippincott, a division of Harper & Row, Publishers, Inc.

LITTLE, BROWN. Jacket painting by Gary Watson from *Stranger With My Face* by Lois Duncan. Copyright © 1981 by Lois Duncan./ Sidelight excerpts from *Chapters: My Growth as a Writer* by Lois Duncan. Copyright © 1982 by Lois Duncan./ Jacket illustration by Derek James from *The Third Eye* by Lois Duncan. Copyright © 1984 by Lois Duncan. All reprinted by permission of Little, Brown and Company.

MACMILLAN. Sidelight excerpts from *Kaffir Boy* by Mark Mathabane. Copyright © 1986 by Mark Mathabane. Reprinted by permission of Macmillan Publishing Company.

NEW AMERICAN LIBRARY. Cover illustration from *Kaffir Boy* by Mark Mathabane. Copyright © 1986 by Mark Mathabane. Reprinted by permission of New American Library, a division of Penguin Books USA Inc., New York.

ORCHARD BOOKS. Cover illustration by Trina Schart Hyman from *The Faery Flag: Stories and Poems of Fantasy and the Supernatural* by Jane Yolen. Text © 1978, 1984, 1987, 1988, 1989 by Jane Yolen. Illustrations © 1989 by Trina Schart Hyman. Reprinted by permission of Orchard Books.

PENGUIN BOOKS. Sidelight excerpts from *The Songlines* by Bruce Chatwin. Copyright © 1987 by Bruce Chatwin. Reprinted by permission of Viking Penguin, a division of Penguin Books USA, Inc. In Canada by the Literary Estate of Bruce Chatwin.

POCKET BOOKS. Cover illustration by Boris Vallejo from *Beauty* by Robin McKinley. Cover artwork © 1985 by Boris Vallejo./ Sidelight excerpts from *Prologue to Flowers in the Attic* by V.C. Andrews. Copyright © 1979 by Virginia Andrews./ Cover illustration from the boxed set of the Dollanger novels by V.C. Andrews./ Cover illustration from *Seeds of Yesterday* by V.C. Andrews. Copyright © 1984 by Vanda Productions, Ltd./ Cover illustration by Steve Huston from *Garden of Shadows* by V.C. Andrews. Cover artwork © 1987 by Steve Huston./ Cover illustration by Richard Newton from *Gates of Paradise* by V.C. Andrews. Cover artwork © 1989 by Richard Newton. All reprinted by permission of Pocket Books, a division of Simon & Schuster, Inc.

PRENTICE HALL. Jacket illustration from *Up the Down Staircase*, 25th Anniversary Edition by Bel Kaufman. Copyright © 1964,

1988 by Bel Kaufman. Reprinted by permission of Prentice Hall Press, New York.

PUFFIN BOOKS. Cover illustration by Diane de Groat from *The Young Landlords* by Walter Dean Myers. Cover © 1979 by Viking Penguin Inc., 1979. Reprinted by permission of Puffin Books and Viking Penguin, a division of Penguin Books USA, Inc.

G. P. PUTNAM'S SONS. Jacket illustration by Troy Howell from *Fly Free* by C.S. Adler. Copyright © 1984 by C.S. Adler. Reprinted by permission of G.P. Putnam's Sons.

RANDOM HOUSE. Sidelight excerpts from *Who Speaks for the Negro?* by Robert Penn Warren. Copyright © 1965 by Robert Penn Warren. Reprinted by permission of Random House, Inc.

SCHOLASTIC. Jacket painting by Jim Dietz from *Fallen Angels* by Walter Dean Myers. Copyright © 1988 by Jim Dietz. Jacket painting © 1988 by Jim Dietz. Reprinted by permission of Scholastic, Inc.

CHARLES SCRIBNER'S SONS. Jacket illustration by Lloyd Bloom from *The Loving* by Lynn Hall. Copyright © 1980 by Lynn Hall./ Jacket illustration by Toby Gowing from *Just One Friend* by Lynn Hall. Copyright © 1985 by Lynn Hall./ Jacket illustration by Toby Gowing from *The Solitary* by Lynn Hall. Jacket illustration © 1986 by Toby Gowing./ Sidelight excerpts and jacket illustration from *Kaffir Boy in America* by Mark Mathabane. Jacket design by Jack Ribik. Copyright © 1989 by Mark Mathabane. Jacket © 1989 by Macmillan Publishing Company. All reprinted by permission of Charles Scribner's Sons, an imprint of Macmillan Publishing Company.

SIMON & SCHUSTER. Sidelight excerpts from *Spike Lee's Gotta Have It: Inside Guerilla Filmmaking* by Spike Lee. Copyright © 1987 by Spike Lee./ Jacket illustration by Wilson McLean from *The Long Dark Tea-Time of the Soul* by Douglas Adams. Jacket © 1989 by Simon & Schuster, Inc. Both reprinted by permission of Simon & Schuster, Inc.

TWAYNE. Sidelight excerpts from *Presenting Rosa Guy* by Jerrie Norris. Copyright © 1988 by Twayne Publishers. Reprinted by permission of Twayne, a division of G.K. Hall & Co., Boston.

VIKING. Jacket illustration by Tony Eubanks from *Mojo and the Russians* by Walter Dean Myers. Copyright © 1977 by Walter Dean Myers./ Jacket illustration by James Griffin from *It Ain't All for Nothing* by Walter Dean Myers. Copyright © 1978 by Walter Dean Myers./ Jacket illustration by Rockwell Kent from *In Patagonia* by Bruce Chatwin./ Jacket painting by Thomas Jones from *On the Black Hill* by Bruce Chatwin. Copyright © 1982 by Bruce Chatwin. Jacket reproduced courtesy of Birmingham Museums and Art Gallery. Jacket design by R. Adelson./ Jacket illustration from a drawing by Philip Gidley King from *The Songlines* by Bruce Chatwin. Copyright © 1987 by Bruce Chatwin. Jacket design by Neil Stuart. All reprinted by permission of Viking Penguin, a division of Penguin Books USA, Inc.

Sidelight excerpts from "Interview with Phyllis Naylor," by Kay Bonetti, number 7036, February, 1987, in *American Audio Prose Library*. Reprinted by permission of *American Audio Prose Library*./ Sidelight excerpts from "The Saturday Library Matinee," by Nat Hentoff, April, 1976, in *American Libraries*. Copyright © 1976 by Nat Hentoff. Reprinted by permission of Nat Hentoff./ Sidelight excerpts from "Bird At My Window," by Thomas L. Vince, volume 25, number 20, January 15, 1966, in *Best Sellers*. Copyright © 1966 by The University of Scranton./ Sidelight excerpts from "A review of 'Down by the River'," by Hildagarde Gray, volume 41, January, 1982, in *Best Sellers*. Copyright © 1982 by The University of Scranton./ Sidelight excerpts from "An Interview with Carlos Fuentes," by Alfred MacAdam and Alexander Coleman, volume IV, no. 4, 1979, in *Book Forum*. Copyright © 1979 by The Hudson River Press. Reprinted by special permission of Brandt & Brandt Literary Agents, Inc./ Sidelight excerpts from "Children's Writing Today for Tomorrow's Adults," by Rosa Guy, November 4, 1984, in *The Boston Globe*. Copyright © 1984 by Globe Newspaper Company./ Sidelight excerpts from "Twenty One: Douglas Adams," by D.C. Denison, January 20, 1985, in *The Boston Globe*. Copyright © 1985 by Globe Newspaper Company. Reprinted by permission of D.C. Denison./ Sidelight excerpts from "Edith Jackson," by Zena Sutherland, volume 32, number 7, March, 1979, in *Bulletin of the Center for Children's Books*. Copyright © 1979 by The University of Chicago./ Sidelight excerpts from *Bulletin of the Center for Children's Books*, April, 1985./ Sidelight excerpts from "Exploring the Cosmos with Arthur C. Clarke," by Roger Ebert, December 2, 1984, in *Chicago Sun-Times*./ Sidelight excerpts from " 'Hitchhiker' Author Along for the Ride," by Eric Zorn, October 28, 1982, in *Chicago Tribune*. Copyright © 1982 by Chicago Tribune Company. Used by permission./ Sidelight excerpts from "Author Takes His Fans on a Galactic Joyride," by Peter Kobel, March 13, 1985, in *Chicago Tribune*. Copyright © 1985 by Chicago Tribune Company./ Sidelight excerpts from "How Typical Children Read Typical Books," by Perry Nodelman, Winter, 1981, in *Children's Literature in Education*. Copyright © 1981 by Agathon Press, Inc. Reprinted by permission of the publisher and the author./ Sidelight excerpts from "Prolife Leaders Say 1986 Has Been a Very Good Year," by Randy Frame, November 21, 1986, in *Christianity Today*. Copyright © 1986 by Christianity Today, Inc./ Sidelight excerpts from "Lois Duncan on the Twisted Window," by Lois Duncan, Spring/Summer, 1987, in *Dell Carousel*./ Sidelight excerpts from "Mistress of the Macabre," October 11, 1981, in *The Detroit News*. Copyright © 1981 by *The Detroit News*, a Gannett Corporation./ Sidelight excerpts from "Interview with Carlos Fuentes," by Jonathan Tittler, September, 1980, in *Diacritics*. Copyright © 1980 by Diacritics, Inc. Reprinted by permission of The Johns Hopkins University Press.

Sidelight excerpts from "Rosa Guy: Writing With Bold Vision," October, 1977, in *Essence*. Copyright © 1977 by Essence Communications Inc./Sidelight excerpts from "The Most Touching of All Gifts," by Bel Kaufman, December, 1985, in *50 Plus*./ Sidelight excerpts from "The Beauty of Being a Late Bloomer," by Bel Kaufman, June, 1986, in *50 Plus*. Reprinted by permission of the author./ Sidelight excerpts from "From Russia with Hope," by Bel Kaufman, July, 1987, in *50 Plus*. Reprinted by permission of the author./ Sidelight excerpts from "When Eternity Moves," by C. Dreifus, May-June, 1986, in *Film Comment*. Copyright © 1986 by C. Dreifus. Reprinted by permission of the author./ Sidelight excerpts from "Bed-Stay BBQ," by Marlaine Glicksman, July/August, 1989, in *Film Comment*. Copyright © 1989 by Marlaine Glicksman. Reprinted by permission of the

Sidelight excerpts from "The Friends," by Alice Walker, November 4, 1973, in *The New York Times Book Review*. Copyright © 1973 by The New York Times Company. Reprinted by permission of the publisher./ Sidelight excerpts from "A Talk with Carlos Fuentes," by Frank MacShane, November 7, 1976, in *The New York Times Book Review*. Copyright © 1976 by The New York Times Company. Reprinted by permission of the publisher./ Sidelight excerpts from "Bruce Chatwin, Passing Through," by John Russell, December 14, 1980, in *The New York Times Book Review*. Copyright © 1980 by The New York Times Company. Reprinted by permission of the publisher./ Sidelight excerpts from "In the Beginning was Jupiter," by Arthur C. Clarke, March 6, 1983, in *The New York Times Book Review*. Copyright © 1983 by The New York Times Company. Reprinted by permission of the author and the author's agents, Scott Meredith Literary Agency, Inc., 845 Third Avenue, New York./ Sidelight excerpts from "I Actually Thought We Would Revolutionize the Industry," by Walter Dean Myers, November 9, 1986, in *The New York Times Book Review*. Copyright © 1986 by The New York Times Company. Reprinted by permission of the publisher./ Sidelight excerpts from "Fallen Angels," by Mel Watkins, January 22, 1989, in *The New York Times Book Review*. Copyright © 1989 by The New York Times Company./ Sidelight excerpts from "Astounding Story! About a Science Fiction Writer!" by Godfrey Smith, March 6, 1966, in *New York Times Magazine*. Copyright © 1966 by The New York Times Company./ Sidelight excerpts from "Three Writers, Recalling Favorites, Urge Wide Choice of Literature," May 29, 1977, in *New York Times Magazine*. Amended by Bel Kaufman. Copyright © 1977 by The New York Times Company./ Sidelight excerpts from "Brave New Tales of 2019," by Dick Teresi, September, 1986, in *Omni*. Copyright © 1986 by *Saturday Review* Magazine./ Sidelight excerpts from "The Voice of Youth," by Nat Hentoff, January, 1972, in *Parents' Magazine*. Reprinted by permission of the author./ Sidelight excerpts from "Writing for Children," by Paula Danziger, September, 1988, in *PEN Newsletter*. Reprinted by permission of the author./ Sidelight excerpts from "Carlos Fuentes Conquers the Land of the Gringos with a Haunting Tale from South of the Border," by Harriet Shapiro, March 3, 1986, in *People Weekly*. Copyright © 1986 by Time, Inc./ Sidelight excerpts from "Playboy Interview: Arthur C. Clarke," by Ken Kelly, July, 1978, in *Playboy*. Copyright © 1986 by *Playboy*. Reprinted with permission./ Sidelight excerpts from *The Hitchhiker's Guide to the Galaxy* by Douglas Adams. Copyright © 1979 by Douglas Adams. Pocket Books.

Sidelight excerpts from "Children's Books," November 15, 1985, in *Publisher's Weekly*. Copyright © 1985 by Reed Publishing USA./ Sidelight excerpts from "Books and the First Amendment," by Kenneth Davis, April 11, 1986, in *Publisher's Weekly*. Copyright © 1986 by Reed Publishing USA. Reprinted from *Publisher's Weekly*, published by the Bowker Magazine Group of Cahners Publishing Co., a division of Reed Publishing USA./ Sidelight excerpts from "Walter Dean Myers," by K.O.F., February 26, 1988, in *Publisher's Weekly*. Copyright © 1988 by Reed Publishing USA. Reprinted from *Publisher's Weekly*, published by the Bowker Magazine Group of Cahners Publishing Co., a division of Reed Publishing USA./ Sidelight excerpts from "Conversation With a Blue Novelist," by John P. Dwyer, Fall, 1974, in *Review: Latin American Literature and Arts*. Copyright © 1974 by the Center for Inter-American Relations, Inc. Reprinted by permission of the publisher./ Sidelight excerpts from *20th Century Science Fiction Writers* by Curtis Smith. St. James Press./ Sidelight excerpts from "No More Interviews, a Conversation with Carlos Fuentes," by Regina Janes, Winter, 1979, in *Salmagundi*. Copyright © 1979 by Skidmore College./ Sidelight excerpts from "Teaching in Triplicate," by Bel Kaufman, April 10, 1965, in *Saturday Review*, Copyright © 1965 by *Saturday Review* Magazine./ Sidelight excerpts from "Plea for Professional Dignity," by Bel Kaufman, October 14, 1966, in *Scholastic Teacher*. Copyright © 1966 by Scholastic, Inc. Reprinted by permission of the publisher./ Sidelight excerpts from "Innocence, Betrayal, and History," by Rosa Guy, November, 1985, in *School Library Journal*. Copyright © 1985. Reprinted from *School Library Journal*, a Cahners/R.R. Bowker Publication, by permission./ Sidelight excerpts from *Literature for Today's Young Adults*, second edition, by Alleen Pace Nilsen and Kenneth Donelson. Scott, Foresman./ Sidelight excerpts from "Letters I'm Glad I Got (and a few I could have done without)," by Lois Duncan, September/October, 1988, in *Society of Children's Bookwriters Bulletin*./ Sidelight excerpts from "Douglas Adams," by Susan Adamo, June, 1981, in *Starlog*. Copyright © 1981 by O'Quinn Studios, Inc. Reprinted by permission of the publisher./ Sidelight excerpts from "Arthur C. Clarke Beyond 2010," by David Hutchison, January, 1984, in *Starlog*. Copyright © 1984 by O'Quinn Studios, Inc. Reprinted by permission of the publisher./ Sidelight excerpts from "Douglas Adams; You Can Get There From Here," by Robert Greenberger, January, 1986, in *Starlog*. Copyright © 1986 by O'Quinn Studios, Inc. Reprinted by permission of the publisher.

Sidelight excerpts from "An Adams Guide to a Galaxy of Games," by Mike Gerrard, March 12, 1985, in *The Times*, London. Copyright © 1985 by Times Newspapers Limited./ Sidelight excerpts from "Creator of Cosmic Spin-off," by Bryan Appleyard, January 11, 1986, in *The Times*, London. Copyright © 1986 by Times Newspapers Limited./ Sidelight excerpts from "Here's to Children," by Bel Kaufman, February-March, 1978, in *Today's Education*. Reprinted by permission of the publisher and the author./ Sidelight excerpts from "First Day of School," by Bel Kaufman, September-October, 1981, in *Today's Education*. Reprinted by permission of the author./ Sidelight excerpts from "Storytelling That Inspires Laughter, Tears, Reflection," by Bel Kaufman, December, 1973, in *Today's Health*, New York. Reprinted by permission of the author./ Sidelight excerpts from "Inspire a Love of Learning," by Bel Kaufman, September, 1974, in *Today's Health*, New York./ Sidelight excerpts from " 'Go Tell It on the Mountain': Belatedly, the Fear Turned to Love for His Father," by James Baldwin, January 12, 1985, in *TV Guide* Magazine. Copyright © 1985 by News America Publications, Inc., Radnor, PA. Reprinted by permission of *TV Guide* Magazine and the Literary Estate of James Baldwin./ Cover photograph by UPI/Bettmann Newsphotos from *Going to Meet the Man* by James Baldwin./ Publicity on Walter Dean Myers from Viking Press Junior Books./ Sidelight excerpts from "A Gothic Million in the Attic," by William Ruehlmann, November 8, 1981, in *The Virginia Pilot and The Ledger-Star*. Copyright © 1981 by *The Virginia Pilot and The Ledger-Star*. Reprinted by permission of the publisher./ Sidelight excerpts from "A Nomadic Heart, Bruce Chatwin, Like a Modern Oscar Wilde, Weaves Amazing Tales," by Edmund White, August, 1987, in *Vogue*. Copyright © 1987 by The Conde Nast Publications, Inc. Courtesy *Vogue*./ Sidelight excerpts from "Clarke, Arthur Charles," by Stanley J. Kunitz, in *Twentieth Century Authors*. H.W. Wilson./ Sidelight excerpts from "Looking Backwards - and Ahead - with 'Alice'," by Nat Hentoff, October, 1970, in *Wilson Library Bulletin*. Copyright © 1970 by the H.W. Wilson Company./ Sidelight excerpts from "Hearing from the Teen-age Reader," by Nat Hentoff, September, 1972, in *Wilson Library Bulletin*. Copyright © 1972 by the H.W. Wilson Company. Reprinted by permission of the publisher./ Sidelight excerpts from "The Young Adult Perplex," by Patty Campbell, February, 1986, in *Wilson Library Bulletin*. Copyright © 1986 by the H.W. Wilson Company. Reprinted by permission of the publisher./ Sidelight excerpts from "Turning a Profit from Memories," by V.C. Andrews, November, 1982, in *The Writer*.

Photo Credits

Authors & Artists for Young Adults

Douglas Adams

Born March 11, 1952, in Cambridge, England; son of Christopher Douglas (a theology teacher and management consultant) and Janet (a nurse; maiden name, Donovan) Adams. *Education:* St. John's College, Cambridge, B.A. (with honors), 1974. *Agent:* Ed Victor Ltd., 162 Wardour St., London W1V 4AT, England.

■ Career

Writer, 1978—; British Broadcasting Corporation (BBC), London, England, radio producer and scriptwriter for "Hitchhiker's Guide to the Galaxy" radio and television series, 1978—, script editor for television series "Doctor Who," 1978-80.

■ Awards, Honors

Golden Pen Award, 1983, for *The Hitchhiker's Guide to the Galaxy.*

■ Writings

The Hitchhiker's Guide to the Galaxy (novel; adaptation of radio play), Pan Books, 1979, Harmony, 1980.

The Restaurant at the End of the Universe (novel), Pan Books, 1980, Harmony, 1982.
Life, the Universe and Everything (novel), Harmony, 1982.
(With John Lloyd) *The Meaning of Liff,* Harmony, 1984.
So Long, and Thanks for All the Fish, Crown, 1984.
The Hitchhiker's Trilogy: Omnibus Edition, Harmony, 1984.
The Original Hitchhiker's Radio Scripts, Harmony, 1985.
The Hitchhiker's Quartet, Harmony, 1986.
Dirk Gently's Holistic Detective Agency, Simon & Schuster, 1987.
The Long Dark Tea-Time of the Soul, Simon & Schuster, 1989.

Radio Plays:

"The Hitchhiker's Guide to the Galaxy" (two series), BBC-Radio, 1978, KCRW-FM, 1987.

Plays:

"The Hitchhiker's Guide to the Galaxy," first produced in 1979.

Also author of episodes of "Doctor Who" for BBC-TV.

■ Adaptations

"The Hitchhiker's Guide to the Galaxy" (television series), BBC-TV, PBS-TV, 1983, (computer game), Infocom, 1984, (cassette; abridged), Listen for Pleasure, 1986, (unabridged) Minds Eye, 1988.

"The Restaurant at the End of the Universe"
    (cassette), Listen for Pleasure.
"Life, the Universe and Everything" (cassette),
    Listen for Pleasure.
"So Long, and Thanks for All the Fish"
    (cassette), Listen for Pleasure, 1985.
"Dirk Gently's Holistic Detective Agency"
    (cassette), Simon & Schuster, 1987.

■ Work In Progress

First nonfiction book, about exotic and endangered animals, tentatively titled *Last Chance to See.*

■ Sidelights

The son of a theology teacher/management consultant and a nurse, Douglas Adams attended Cambridge University, studying English literature. While at school, he spent much of his time writing sketches for Cambridge Footlights, a theatrical club which provided early training for comedians such as John Cleese, Eric Idle, and Graham Chapman. "It's not so much that being a member of Footlights gives you a guaranteed entree into show business, which a lot of people kind of assume simply because so many people have come out of it. The reason why so many people of that type have come out of it is because they've gone into it. Certainly in my experience, when I was deciding on what kind of university career I was going to have, I wanted to go to Cambridge because I wanted to do Footlights—mainly because I knew I had a reasonable opportunity to meet people of like mind....It's just sort of a rallying flag."[1]

After university Adams and "a couple of guys" decided to make a go of writing together. "We then had an argument about what sort of jobs we ought to take to support us in the meantime. They argued for a sound career to fall back on. I argued for the minimum job necessary for survival so that there would be no fall-back position, you would have to become a writer."[2]

Adams held a number of minimum jobs after graduation, including hospital reporter, barn builder, chicken-shed cleaner, and bodyguard for an Arab's royal family. "I sat outside their hotel room for twelve hours a night while they watched television. It wasn't difficult—you stand up, sit down, open a door, close a door, you bow. And if someone comes along with a gun or a hand grenade, you run away."[1]

He also worked with Monty Python's Graham Chapman for a year, "mostly on projects that never saw the light of day. The Pythons go through regular periods where they're not talking to each other and say they'll never work together again. This was one such period. Graham [Chapman] is not the least weird person in the world."[3]

"We were once commissioned to write a one-hour American TV special for Ringo Starr...and the working title was, rather originally I thought, 'The Ringo Starr Show.' Yes, it took us some time to come up with *that* one."[4]

He scraped by for a time writing radio and television comedy until he sold an idea which had come to him even before entering the university. "I had a copy of a book called *Hitch Hiker's Guide to Europe* which I'd carry around with me,...[it] was a useful book. And I remember lying drunk in a field in Innsbruck one night.

"I sort of laid down on the ground and stared up at the stars and it occurred to me then that somebody ought to write a hitch hiker's guide to the galaxy. The thought didn't come back to me for years afterward.

"I suppose for some time after I became a writer, I just thought that science fiction would be a good vehicle for comedy. It took me a long time actually to convince anybody else of this and I tried it in all sorts of forms and guises. It wasn't until I suddenly remembered...[*Hitch Hiker's Guide*] and put it together with the more general aspects of the idea that the thing actually started to come together. It started out in radio."[4]

Adams presented BBC Radio 4 with a pilot script for the "Hitchhiker's Guide to the Universe." While waiting to hear from the BBC, he sent the script to Bob Holmes who was then the story editor of "Dr. Who." "Writing 'Hitchhiker' was a do-or-die proposition for me. I was in a terrible state financially. I couldn't pay the rent. I'd moved back in with my parents. I basically retreated from everything."[5]

"I was getting pretty nervous and suddenly, in the same week, I was commissioned for the whole series of 'Hitchhikers' plus a commission to write four episodes for 'Dr. Who (Pirate Planet).'

"Really, from that moment, which must have been late 76-77 until the end of 1980, I didn't have a day off. I mean, it was sort of panic-time continually."[4]

Adams was warned to expect universal silence from the "Hitchhiker's" series and was paid a minimal 1,000 pounds for six months work. "I was the only person who knew actually what I intended and what it was meant to sound like so I was very heavily involved in the production. The producer (Geoffrey Perkins) was very tolerant from that point of view which not all producers would be. Some producers tend to be very defensive, protective of their jobs.

"The first two shows took an *immensely* long time to make because we were dealing with techniques that none of us knew about or how to set about making. Then, this sort of system evolved on how to make it. After a while, I took more and more of a backseat simply because now everyone knew how to do it. But, I was still always there just sort of putting my own in and making trouble."[4]

"There was a long sound effect in episode two [of the 'Heart of Gold' going into Improbability Drive] which took us two days to do...which is totally unheard of at the BBC because, at the BBC on the whole, a standard radio comedy show will tend to be rehearsed in an afternoon, recorded in front of an audience that evening and edited the next day and that's it.

"There were questions delicately being asked about *what in the hell we thought we were doing* taking over studio after studio; editing channel after editing channel; hours and hours and hours; days and days. If we hadn't come up with the goods at the end of it, our heads would be rolling. But luckily, it turned out okay."[4]

"It took a long time to get it on, because it was very different from the comedy that was being done at that time. People weren't recording in stereo. They insisted on a studio audience. They wanted sparse use of sound effects. And we came along and wanted to do things completely different. We wanted the sound to be the verbal equivalent of a rock album."[5]

"Hitchhiker's Guide" aired in 1978. "It premiered in a blaze of silence. There were no special announcements—we were just on! Gradually, though, word of mouth spread."[5]

The show became so popular that the BBC rebroadcast the series four more times and approved production of a second series.

Meanwhile Adams also accepted the job as "Dr. Who" story editor. "The crazy thing about the show, one of the things which led to my feelings of frustration, was basically doing twenty-six episodes a year with one producer and one script editor. It's one hell of a workload. . . .It's not like any other drama series. Say, you're doing a police drama

Drawing for the jacket of Adams' first book.

series. You know what a police car looks like and you know what the police station in the area looks like; you know what the streets look like, what burglars, criminals do. With 'Dr. Who,' with every new story, you have to reinvent totally but be consistent with what's gone before. Doing twenty-six shows in one year, when each one has to be totally new in some extraordinary way, was a major problem. And there's no money to do it with. I mean, in real terms, 'Dr. Who's' budget has been shrinking. Somehow or another, you have to come up with the goods. Twenty-six a year is *too many*."[4]

Simultaneously, he was asked to novelize "Hitchhiker." "I never set out to be a novelist, because I thought I was just a scriptwriter. When I was asked by Pan Books to turn my radio scripts of 'The Hitchhiker's Guide to the Galaxy' into a book, I thought that there were two ways of doing it. I could either do the normal script-novelization hack job, which involves going through the script putting 'he said' or 'she said' (and in the case of my books, 'it said' as well) at the end of each line, or I could have a go at doing it properly. I decided to see if I could do it properly."[6]

"When I was writing the first of 'Hitchhiker's' down in Dorset, I would leave notes to myself to find later, saying, 'If you ever get the chance to do a proper, regular job—take it. This is not the occupation for a growing healthy lad.' I'd find another note under that saying, 'This is not written after a bad day. It is written after an *average* day.'"[4]

1979. *The Hitchhiker's Guide to the Galaxy* published. In less than a month it sold 100,000 copies and went on to sell two million copies in England, reaching the top of the London *Sunday Times* bestseller list. The story begins when planet Earth is destroyed to make room for a new hyper-space bypass. The only survivor, Arthur Dent, is rescued by his friend Ford Prefect who turns out to be from the planet Betelgeuse (pronounced Beetlejuice). Ford is a researcher for *The Hitchhiker's Guide to the Galaxy*, a book designed to assist space travelers.

Arthur and Ford manage to hitch up with Zaphod Beeblebrox (the two-headed ex-president of the universe), his girlfriend Trillian, and their chronically depressed robot, Marvin. Having discovered the answer to the universe, the crew sets off to find the question. "Arthur Dent is to a certain extent autobiographical. He moves from one astonishing event to another without fully comprehending what's going on. He's the Everyman character—an ordinary person caught up in some extraordinary events.

"Marvin was based on a friend of mine—his wife recognized him instantly—and he's the sort of person who's on the one hand brilliant, and on the other leaves a dark cloud wherever he goes. Zaphod is a character of the '60s. He's relentlessly relaxed. As for Ford Prefect—well, he's the sort of guy who, when faced with saving the world from destruction or going to a good party, will choose the party every time."[5]

"*The Hitchhiker's Guide to the Galaxy* was originally intended to consist of a lot of things that I associated with real hitchhiking transferred up on the cosmic scale, but somehow that never materialized, and there is very little about hitching in it in the end. Still, what you end up with tends to be a by-product of your failure to write whatever it was you set out to write."[6]

Peter Kemp, reviewer for the *Listener*, said of the *Guide*: "What makes this book almost unputdownable is its surreal, comic creativity."

Gerald Jonas for the *New York Times Book Review* added: "Humorous science-fiction novels have notoriously limited audiences; they tend to be full of 'in' jokes understandable only to those who read everything from Jules Verne to Harlan Elison. The *Hitchhiker's Guide* is a delightful exception."

The fact that Adam's work appeals to a much broader audience, than is typically reached by science fiction, may be attributed to his own lack of enthusiasm for traditional sci-fi genre. "I'm not a science-fiction writer, but a comedy writer who happens to be using the conventions of science fiction for this particular thing."[6]

"I think *Hitchhiker's* has been so popular because in the long run it's not really a parody of science fiction at all. It's a parody of everything else."[7]

Though Adams' satirical approach has earned him comparisons with Jonathan Swift and Kurt Vonnegut, he maintains that P. G. Wodehouse has been the primary influence on his work. "While Wodehouse didn't write about robots and spaceships, the structure of comedy—achieving surprise by setting up expectations and defeating them—is somewhat the same."[8]

"I don't want to write seriously. My aspirations are much higher. I aspire to write 1/100th as well as P. G. Wodehouse."[3]

The second book in the "Hitchhiker" series, *The Restaurant at the End of the Universe*, proved to be as well received as the first, but by the time Adams finished the third in the trilogy, the response to the series was mixed.

"I wrote the third book, *Life, the Universe and Everything*, not enjoying myself at all. When I was three-quarters through I reread it and saw it was absolutely terrible. It did not work.

"So I started again, this time rather desperate. Only four pages of the original still stand, and what I've got now seems to be pretty good. [It] entered at No. 1 on the bestseller charts back home and [sold] in *bananas* numbers."[7]

Tom Hutchinson for the *London Times* commented: "Humour is not that rare a quality in science fiction, but Douglas Adams's contribution to future mock must surely be unique: he violates SF taboos while at the same time and quite obviously regarding them with deep affection: you only hurt the genre you love. He is a treasure and science

Dust jacket from the 1984 novel in which Arthur Dent falls in love.

fictioneers should place a preservation order upon him.''

Whereas Brian Stableford for *Science Fiction and Fantasy Book Review* said, ''It is probable that no one will enjoy *Life, the Universe and Everything* as much as its predecessors. Once you expect the unexpected, it is no longer unexpected, and that which is startling and amusing only as long as it remains surprising cannot endure being spun out into trilogies.''

Regardless of what reviewers had to say about Adams' work, by the time *Life, the Universe, and Everything* was published, the *Guide* had developed a devoted following which seemed to insure his success. ''Somebody once said that a cult is what happens when everybody goes out to buy a book, each of them thinking that they're the only one who knows about it. But the 'Hitchhiker' books have sold about seven million copies. And that ain't a cult.''[1]

As a result Adams' lifestyle changed considerably. ''I used to hitch a lot when I was a student and loved it. You can't take the slow boat to China anymore as people with wanderlust and no money used to do. So you hitch. Unfortunately it's something you can only do for real, you can't do it as an affectation. I occasionally think it would be great to do some hitching again, but since I can afford to go by car or plane or whatever, it would not work. I'd feel a complete fraud.''[6]

1984. *The Meaning of Liff*, by Adams and John Lloyd published. ''It goes back to when I was twelve. One day, the English teacher walked into class, gave us each a town name and asked us to come up with a meaning for that word. Think of the name as an ordinary word and what it would mean. So, we each created something. I enjoyed that session very much.

''In 1978, myself, John Lloyd, and other people were in Greece playing charades. As the afternoon wore on, we drank more and more and we wanted to find another game that required slightly less standing up. Then, I suddenly remembered this thing we had done at school and we began tossing some of these around. There are all kinds of situations and experiences that we have all been through which aren't properly identified because there isn't a name for them. So, we started doing these words. A whole pile of them ended up on sheets of paper which ended up in John Lloyd's

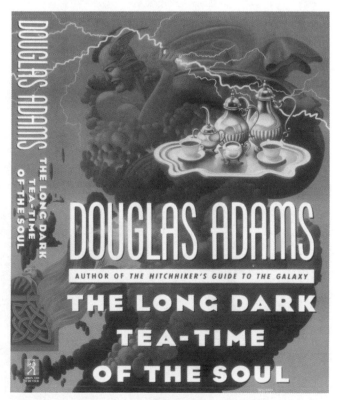

Adams' 1989 hardcover novel.

Cover for the computer game that takes the player on a cosmic jaunt into outer reaches.

bottom drawer and were forgotten about. Then, he was the progenitor of a successful TV show in Britain called 'Not the Nine O'Clock News.' When he was assembling a book based on the show, he was looking for extra little goodies to use, remembered the stuff in the bottom drawer, pulled it out and began peppering it through the book. It turned out to be the book's most popular part, or so I am told. It seemed like a good idea to do more as a book."[9]

"It's a dictionary, sort of. What we've done is come up with a whole bunch of concepts that have no words for them, and matched them with perfectly delightful British place names that otherwise have no meaning.

"An Ely is the first, tiniest inkling you get that something, somewhere has gone terribly wrong.

"A Wembly is the moment of shock and realization that it has happened and you're going to be in court for the next five years.

"Papple: What a baby does to soup with his spoon.

"Ulingswick: A grossly overdeveloped epiglottis."[7]

Also in 1984, Adams published *So Long, and Thanks for All the Fish*, which continues to chronicle the adventures of Arthur Dent, but with two changes: he's back on earth and he's in love. "Arthur Dent falling in love was actually in response to people telling me, 'There's a whole area of your books that you never touch.' I thought I would have a go at it. I was always a bit nervous about it, I still feel nervous about it and it was part of a deliberate attempt to do things differently. To be honest, I created this problem: going back into a familiar environment and then striving to do things differently means all kinds of archings of the back."[9]

"I tried to change direction while writing this book. Everyone wanted another 'Hitchhiker' book—and that wasn't what I wanted to do.

"It's easy to lapse into self-mimicry. In this one, I was too concerned with what not to do rather than what to do....Style should be determined by content. When style determines content, you've got trouble. There was perhaps a mismatch of medium and content here."[10]

The novel is set in Han Dold City. Adams got the idea for the rather unpleasant place on his way out of a movie. "It was one night in New York and I was coming out of 'Gandhi.' The first thing one couldn't help noticing was a pile of mattresses burning in the middle of the street. Then I saw a group of young men obviously stealing a car....Then a man walked up to me and asked if I wanted my picture taken with his llama."[11]

Though the book sold well, some critics felt the serial was wearing thin. Robert Reilly said in *Twentieth Century Science Fiction Writers*: "*So Long, and Thanks for All the Fish*, although it includes a number of details clearly intended to wrap up some of the loose ends from the previous volumes, proves to be too much of the same thing. The freshness which lent such force to *Hitchhiker* is gone; the joke has been carried too far."

"One of the strange things about having your first book be successful is that you must learn your craft in public. For months and months after writing each book, I can hardly bear to think about them. I *never* feel comfortable and happy at all. I felt that particularly about the second book and even more particularly about the third. And again about the fourth. After I wrote the third book, I loved the second. Now that I've written the fourth, I suddenly discovered all this stuff I loved about the third one.

Videocassette cover from the BBC-TV series.

"Nobody could say anything bad about my writing that I haven't already thought ten times worse. I'm a professional at this job and I do *not* want to have my ego massaged."[9]

Adams is doubtful about writing further books in the trilogy. "I'm a little superstitious about saying never, like Sean Connery, but absolutely *not*...for the moment. I feel written out about 'Hitchhiker's' and I don't think I have anything new to say in that particular medium. There are other things I want to do....The important thing is to find a whole new set of characters and a whole new environment."[9]

"Hitchhiker's Guide" computer game released. "I really enjoyed working on this game so much. I feel that it has sort of given me a whole new lease on life. There was a stage...when I felt that, well, I've had all these successful books, and I was going to have to write more books—which is good, let's not knock it—and then maybe movies or TV. I had all of these things to do. But still, I kind of felt like the six-year-old kid who says, 'Mommy, I don't know what to do.' Then I got involved with computers, which suddenly seemed to be one of the most extraordinary resources for imagination. I've just become totally engrossed, and now there seem to be more things to do than I could possibly encompass."[1]

"The game requires you to start out being Arthur Dent and begins as if it's going to be a fairly straightforward trek through the story, which is precisely what I *didn't* want it to be. It gets the player going and lulled into a sense of false security. Also, we move quickly to the point where the Earth gets demolished. And then, all hell breaks loose and it goes through the most extraordinary number of directions. Largely, the game just glances at events which were a major part of the books, while things which were one line throwaways are those I used for the game's big set pieces. The reason was to keep *me* interested in doing it. I also wanted to make it fair for people who haven't read the books. So, readers and nonreaders were, as much as possible, on equal footing and the game was equally difficult for both."[9]

"It's not shooting down spaceships or chasing maidens through dungeons. You have options. It asks you what you want to do, and you type it in. It has a vocabulary of 600 words."[3]

Adams describes the world of computer games as "kind of like working in the movies in 1905. It's not quite respectable, and no one is taking it seriously."[3]

"I'm fascinated by it. While setting up the software, I can go days without writing."[12]

Adams has started his own software company and plans to author more games. His "Hitchhiker's Guide" has already earned him a strong reputation and was reviewed in the *London Times.* "The arrival of 'Hitch-Hiker's Guide to the Galaxy' as a computer adventure has been greeted with justifiable glee by those lucky enough to get a copy, but the main reason why this is without doubt the best adventure ever seen on a computer has been overlooked—it is the first time an honest-to-goodness real author, rather than a computer programmer-author, has been directly involved in the writing of an adventure.

"In the future the writing of an adventure game may be as valid to an author as the writing of a radio play or short story."[13]

Prophetically, in 1979, Adams addressed the future of new computer technologies. "'I speak of none but the computer that is to come after me,' intoned Deep Thought, his voice regaining its accustomed declamatory tones. 'A computer whose merest operational parameters I am not worthy to calculate—and yet I will design it for you. A computer that can calculate the Question to the Ultimate Answer, a computer of such infinite and subtle complexity that organic life itself shall form part of its operational matrix. And you yourselves shall take on new forms and go down into the computer to navigate its ten-million-year program! Yes! I shall design this computer for you. And I shall name it also unto you. And it shall be called...the Earth.'"[14]

1987-1989. Adams published *Dirk Gently's Holistic Detective Agency* and *The Long Dark Tea-Time of the Soul,* both of which feature the detective Dirk Gently and his encounters with bizarre supernatural forces.

"[Writing is] a terrible business....You're sort of stuck in a room by yourself for hours on end, just trying to believe you're not hopeless, actually....I've done it so far and it's worked so far. People have liked it and it's been alright. But, you look at the piece of paper and you can't think of anything to put on it and—You've got something! Then you read it, say 'God, that's *awful!*' And you cross it out and you sort of keep this up for hours and it's pretty demoralizing until, suddenly, you get on a streak. And, that doesn't happen very often. Pathetic business. It really is."[4]

Footnote Sources:

1 D. C. Denison, "Twenty One: Douglas Adams," *Boston Globe*, January 20, 1985.
2 Bryan Appleyard, "Creator of Cosmic Spin-Off," *London Times*, January 11, 1986.
3 Peter Kobel, "Author Takes His Fans on a Galactic Joyride," *Chicago Tribune*, March 13, 1985.
4 Susan Adamo, "Douglas Adams," *Starlog*, June, 1981.
5 James Brown, "Thumbs Up for 'The Hitchhiker,'" *Los Angeles Times*, April 4, 1982.
6 *Contemporary Authors*, Volume 106, Gale, 1982.
7 Eric Zorn, "'Hitchhiker' Author Along for the Ride," *Chicago Tribune*, October 28, 1982.
8 *Dictionary of Literary Biography Yearbook 1983*, Gale, 1984.
9 Robert Greenberger, "Douglas Adams: You *Can* Get There from Here," *Starlog*, January, 1986.
10 Jon D. Markman, "'Hitchhiker' Has a Life of Its Own," *Los Angeles Times*, April 19, 1985.
11 Deborah Zabarenko, "Galactic Hitchhiker Returns to Planet Earth," *Houston Post*, January 27, 1985.
12 Peter C. Wyckoff, "A 'Hitchhiker's Guide' to Douglas Adams," *Houston Post*, April 21, 1985.
13 Mike Gerrard, "An Adams Guide to a Galaxy of Games," *London Times*, March 23, 1985.
14 Douglas Adams, *The Hitchhiker's Guide to the Galaxy*, Pocket Books, 1979.

■ For More Information See

Stage and Television Today (London), August 9, 1979 (p. 17).
London Times, December 2, 1979 (p. 39), October 23, 1988 (p. G6).
Chicago Tribune Book World, October 12, 1980.
Washington Post Book World, November 23, 1980 (p. 6), December 27, 1981.
Los Angeles Times Book Review, December 7, 1980.
New York Times Book Review, January 25, 1981.
Times Literary Supplement, September 24, 1982 (p. 1032).
Newsweek, November 15, 1982 (p. 119).
People Weekly, January 10, 1983 (p. 33ff).
Publishers Weekly, January 14, 1983 (p. 47ff).
Contemporary Literary Criticism, Volume 27, Gale, 1984.
Chicago Tribune, January 3, 1985.
Curtis C. Smith, editor, *Twentieth-Century Science-Fiction Writers*, St. James Press, 1986.
Los Angeles Times, June 13, 1987 (section 6, p. 71ff).

C. S. Adler

Born Carole Schwerdtfeger, February 23, 1932, in Long Island, N.Y.; daughter of Oscar Edward (a car mechanic and chief petty officer in the Naval Reserve) and Clarice (an office manager; maiden name, Landsberg) Schwerdtfeger; married Arnold R. Adler (an engineer), June, 1952; children: Steven and Clifford (twins), Kenneth. *Education:* Hunter College (now Hunter College of the City University of New York), B.A. (cum laude), 1953; Russell Sage College, M.S., 1967. *Home:* 1350 Ruffner Rd., Schenectady, N.Y. 12309.

■ Career

Worthington Corp., Harrison, N.J., advertising assistant, 1952-54; Niskayuna Middle Schools, Niskayuna, N.Y., English teacher, 1968-77; writer, 1977—. Volunteer worker in child abuse and protection program, at local children's shelter, and as tutor of foster children. *Member:* Society of Children's Book Writers, Author's Guild, Phi Beta Kappa.

■ Awards, Honors

Golden Kite Award for Fiction from the Society of Children's Book Writers, Children's Choice from the International Reading Association and the Children's Book Council, and selected one of Child Study Association of America's Children's Books of the Year, all 1979, and William Allen White Children's Book Award, 1982, all for *The Magic of the Glits; The Shell Lady's Daughter* was selected one of American Library Association's Best Young Adult Books of the Year, 1983; Child Study Children's Book Award from the Child Study Children's Book Committee at Bank St. College of Education (N.Y.), 1985, for *With Westie and the Tin Man.*

■ Writings

The Magic of the Glits (illustrated by Ati Forberg), Macmillan, 1979.
The Silver Coach (Junior Literary Guild selection), Coward, 1979.
In Our House Scott Is My Brother, Macmillan, 1980.
Shelter on Blue Barns Road, Macmillan, 1981.
The Cat That Was Left Behind (Junior Literary Guild selection), Clarion Books, 1981.
Down by the River, Coward, 1981.
Footsteps on the Stairs, Delacorte, 1982.
Some Other Summer, Macmillan, 1982.
The Evidence That Wasn't There, Clarion Books, 1982.
The Once in a While Hero, Coward, 1982.
Binding Ties, Delacorte, 1983.

Get Lost, Little Brother, Clarion Books, 1983.
Roadside Valentine, Macmillan, 1983.
The Shell Lady's Daughter, Coward, 1983.
Fly Free, Coward, 1984.
Good-bye, Pink Pig, Putnam, 1985.
Shadows on Little Reef Bay, Clarion Books, 1985.
With Westie and the Tin Man (Junior Literary Guild selection), Macmillan, 1985.
Split Sisters (illustrated by Mike Wimmer), Macmillan, 1986.
Kiss the Clown, Clarion Books, 1986.
If You Need Me, Macmillan, 1987.
Carly's Buck (Junior Literary Guild selection), Clarion Books, 1987.
Eddie's Blue-Winged Dragon, Putnam, 1988.
Always and Forever Friends, Clarion Books, 1988.
One Sister Too Many: A Sequel to Split Sisters, Macmillan, 1989.
The Lump in the Middle, Clarion Books, 1989.
Ghost Brother, Clarion Books, 1990.
Help, Pink Pig (sequel to *Good-Bye Pink Pig*), Putnam, 1990.

Contributor of articles and stories to periodicals, including *American Girl*, *Co-Ed*, and *Ingenue*.

■ Sidelights

Born in Rockaway Beach, Long Island, C. S. Adler has lived all over New York City. "I had a restless father, so we moved every couple of years; I saw all the boroughs. New York City was filled with empty lots I used to explore. I was fascinated with with the interesting weeds, bugs, wee beasties and flowers like honeysuckle, roses, and morning glory. And there was the zoo and the park. Manhattan's park at Riverside Drive was a teenage hangout and a great place to sunbathe.

"An only child, my family consisted of my mother, father, grandmother, and an aunt. My father was a chief petty officer in the Naval Reserve and a car mechanic; my mother was an office manager; and my grandmother was in charge of me. I roamed around a lot on my own and usually had friends to roam with. New York City in those days was pretty safe, so when I got to be ten or eleven, I used the subways to prowl museums and parks. The city offered many options; it was a good place for a poor kid to grow up. We didn't have a lot of money, but you didn't need a lot of money when I was young.

"Moving around so much was probably good experience for becoming a children's author, because one of the most traumatic things in a child's life is moving and being new in a new school. I was a very shy child who didn't make friends easily, yet friends were very important. So it was difficult. That experience made me sympathetic to that particular aspect of a child's problems."[1]

Adler's father left the family when she was twelve. "That was another experience that made me comfortable writing about divorce and separation.

"I was very close to my mother. She was understanding, liberal, and tolerant of all people. She taught me to treat everybody as an individual, evaluating a person on his character rather than anything else. All those good values have stuck with me, I think. My mother had the advantage of being a working mother. My grandmother took the brunt of the nagging business of child raising. I never stopped being close to my mother. I also was, and am, very close to my aunt.

"My mother and aunt encouraged me to think well of myself. They also pointed out my negative aspects—reminding me that I wasn't perfect—but basically, I knew they loved me and thought I was wonderful. Having someone who thinks that is just what you need when you're a child.

"As a youngster, I was boring. Reading and writing were the only things that interested me. I was an omnivorous reader. I went to libraries and read just about everything I could get my hands on: adult books, fairy tales, the Alcott books—anything that was there. I'd get excited about one book and two weeks later, I'd be excited about another.

"I remember reading about the Nazi concentration camps in the newspaper. Although I was brought up with no religion, I empathized tremendously. I am half Jewish and half Lutheran. I identified strongly with the Jewish half during that period.

"The writing came almost immediately after I'd learned to read. By age seven, I'd begun writing stories for myself. I remember writing a book about a boy in China. I had no idea what China or Chinese boys were like, but it seemed exotic. I'd write little stories and put them together with cardboard covers and rubber bands to make them look like a book. Every once in awhile, I would con a friend into listening to one. I never showed them to teachers. It was just something I liked to do for fun. Even if nobody had published my books, I'd still be writing. Some people talk a lot; I write a lot."[1] At thirteen, Adler sent her first story to a professional magazine. "Thereafter, I got the proverbial drawer full of rejection slips.[1]

Other than reading, writing, nature, and people, not much else interested her. "I wasn't much of an athlete. As a matter of fact I had asthma and a heart condition. So I had sort of a restricted youth, first by my family, and then because I had to stay out of gym classes. My family thought I was delicate. I imagined that I had no physical ability. As it turns out, I have plenty; I'm as strong as a horse. (My husband calls me a middle-aged jock.)

"As a student, I was a well-behaved, dutiful child who sat quietly, listened, did her homework, and got good marks—the kind of student teachers like. I always managed a friend or two, but I never felt popular. After my father left, we stayed put in Manhattan. I went to Hunter High School which was a very stimulating school, very challenging. I had a number of friends and those were good years.

"I met my husband, Arnold, when I was sixteen by crashing one of the dances at City College where he was a veteran who'd returned to school. I was a New York girl, a sophisticated dresser, and very tall, so I looked about twenty. We dated, but I never told him how old I was. I did tell him I went to Hunter, but he thought I meant Hunter College. My mother liked him as soon as she met him; she thought he was charming. Besides, she trusted my judgment."[1]

Legitimizing the misunderstanding, Adler attended Hunter College. "I always wanted to be a writer, but my mother informed me that I shouldn't just take English and psychology courses because I'd probably have to earn a living. So I nearly lost my Phi Beta Kappa key by taking typing and stenography, at which I was terrible. Unfortunately, I was most interested in getting home, speaking to Arnold over the phone, going out weekends, and getting my degree so that he would marry me. I raced through college, and finished in three years.

"I can't say that there were any particularly influential professors for me. Actually, Arnold was much more influential because he was a great deal older. An engineer, he was also interested in literature. At sixteen, he had me reading the *Partisan Review*. I would say that he helped develop my cultural interests."[1]

Completing course work at Hunter in 1952, Adler married at twenty. "My husband worked for General Electric, so for the first nine years of our married life, we moved every two or three years. I got used to that; it didn't bother me. We lived in Cincinnati, Ohio and parts of New York State and New Jersey. We finally settled in Schenectady,

where we've lived for twenty-five years. I love having a sense of belonging and having people know who I am. If I go to the theater, I say hello to a dozen different people. That's exciting for someone who comes from New York City.

"I had never had much interest in children before I married, although I knew I wanted them. Everyone in my generation did. Once I had them, three sons—two were twins, I fell madly in love with them and became a very happy homemaker. I emulated my mother as well as I could because I admired her tremendously. I tried to be as loving, understanding, open-minded, and encouraging of independence as she was. I had no desire to go out and work. I wanted to stay home with the children, so I continued writing and getting rejection slips. But my main interest in life was raising the kids until they were all in school.

"By then, I had figured that I was never going to make it as a writer and began to think in terms of a more sensible career. I went back to get my

Softcover edition of Adler's multi-award winning novel.

masters degree and began teaching, an alternative that allowed me to stay home summers with the children."[1]

Adler taught sixth- and eighth-grade English for nearly ten years. "The experiences I had teaching were what made me a writer, and that's the age I write about. I was fascinated by my students; I thought they were the most interesting people around. Teenagers are up front with their problems and emotions. You have to know adults a long time before you know what they are about. Many of us wear facades—children don't. Watching them, I empathized and got into emotional relationships with them, all very useful in my writing as it turned out. Many of the kids I taught appear in my books, not their particular problems or lives—I don't do that—but their personalities.

"The discipline, however, was very difficult. Eighth-graders are not easy to deal with in groups of thirty, and the amount of paper work was gigantic. I was working seventy hours a week, taking 150 papers home a night. It became too much. I decided that if I was ever going to be a writer, it was then."[1]

Her first book, *The Magic of the Glits*, was published in 1979. "My husband and I were in Wellfleet, Cape Cod. He was surf-casting and I was up in the dunes doing what I do, which is writing to entertain myself. I wrote a fifty-page story about fairies and the ocean. The boy, Jeremy, was based on a boy I had once had in class. When I got home, I developed the story and sent it out. It didn't sell right away. It got rejected and had to be rewritten, but eventually it sold. That was a marvelous, marvelous day. I invited everyone over and we had wine and cheese to celebrate.

"Ever since that first book, I've sold most everything I've written. I've been able to indulge my passion, producing more than two books a year."[1]

Besides *The Magic of the Glits*, several of Adler's books have contained some element of magic. "*The Silver Coach*, my second book, was suggested by an anniversary gift given by my son, Steven, to my husband and me, a silver filagree coach the size of a fist with doors that open and wheels that turn, so charming it seemed to demand to be put into a book."[2]

"About a quarter to a third of my books have some magical influence. Don't ask me where it comes from. Not only was I *not* interested in magic, I'm *still* not interested in it. I have absolutely no idea why I have it in my books."[1]

But "family is a common theme. Divorce is not. If you look at the thirty books that I have now written, only about a third of them have anything to do with divorce or separated parents. That's a fair match to what is true in society today.

"Writing about families very different from mine is more interesting than writing about my own. In fact, I'm least successful when writing about someone most like my own relatives or myself. I try not to duplicate my own life in my books. The fun of being an author is projecting yourself into other people's lives. That is particularly enjoyable when the person is very different from you. I'm not a very funny person, but I love getting into the character of a funny girl. I find other people fascinating.

"My interests are basically personal: emotional problems and family relationships. Those things fascinate me most. I'm not a very political or cause-minded person. When I look at the newspaper, I'm not worrying about nuclear war; I'm looking for things about child abuse or latch-key children. Those issues would stick in my mind and probably become the theme of another story.

"I don't really worry about keeping up with the pace of the world or whether I'm totally capable of adjusting to the times. I don't think of myself as a chameleon. I pretty much stay who I am and write the kind of thing I write, doing my best to understand people around me.

"We live in a fast-paced society. Living and living well becomes more difficult as things change faster and faster. We have all these environmental concerns and world problems, and this pile-up of problems puts pressure on everyone, kids and adults. Although we have huge pockets of the country where the child is still the most important thing in town, I think what we have is a tendency to be less child-oriented as a society. I know a great many families who haven't changed over the years, where the main concern of the parents is still their children. But I know other families where parents seem more concerned with their own careers and children become secondary.

"I note from my fan mail that children find bits and pieces of their own problems and themselves in my books. Kids claim that my books are realistic and that they see their friends in some of my characters. Maybe they'll also see ways of dealing with life that they hadn't thought of before. Hopefully, I'm transmitting good values. At least they're my values, and I think they're good. In a sense I'm still teaching. Since I am an optimist, I think things

Jacket for the 1984 Coward edition.

Cover from the 1985 paperback.

work out well for *most* people. Children tend to despair because they have no idea that tomorrow could bring a sunny day. I can remind them of that."[1]

Adler has worked as a volunteer in a child abuse and neglect program. "That was during the few years I spent at home. I gained some important relationships from that experience. It was very satisfying. I suppose I learned a lot from it. *Fly Free* and *The Cat That Was Left Behind* had to do with foster children."[1]

Down by the River, Adler's first book for older young adults was published in 1981. "A fifteen- or sixteen-year-old girl will have different interests and concerns than a twelve-year-old: boys, her future, college, and the world around her. The twelve-year-old might also be interested in boys, but it would be at a different degree of intensity. She wouldn't possibly be concerned only about sexual contact as the older girl might be. Things would be lighter. A twelve-year-old girl might be

more interested in friendships, things smaller and closer to home."[1]

Reviews of the book tended to characterize the critical response to Adler's work in general. Reviewer Hildagarde Gray wrote: "It has arrived! A love story in which the man and woman learn to need and like each other and have concern for each other long, long before the meeting of the bodies in delicate heart-felt, better than heat-felt, physical love....The nest-building urge *is* more common among women than feminists may acknowledge. Here it is given a dignity and status of a career choice acted upon by a heroine neither simple nor saccharine, but rather ordinary and appealing."[3]

To this consideration, Adler responded: "The woman's movement was very good for those of us who come from a previous generation that never even considered how debased women had been in a society where a housewife, working on full batteries, was considered less than her husband who had the unquestionable right to rule the roost. It is a positive thing that women should have a chance to use their talents and abilities as fully as men, and that a little girl be raised to consider a career as very important in her life.

"However, there were also negative aspects to the women's movement. It's very difficult to make everything perfectly equal in any relationship. By setting up expectations of total equality—that a woman needs to have a successful career and shouldn't stay home and have children at all—that makes marriage and babies very hard to fit into a life. So many people fail at it because they can't commit to another human being, they don't want to be tied down and they can't compromise.

"Children do suffer from the uneasy relationships their parents have with each other. Where both parents are demanding, the child is caught in between. In the old relationships the woman would sacrifice, stay home, and take care of the child, maybe even stay with a man who was terrible. I don't think that was right either, but good and bad come with change. To some extent, children might be better off if somebody *did* sacrifice and stay home, whether the man or the woman. There is no

Softcover edition of the 1983 novel.

Dust jacket from Adler's 1986 novel.

question that there is extra stress on the single parent who tries to do both things."[1]

Some critics have ventured to call Adler's sensitive handling of her characters and family relationships "classy." "That's the nicest compliment I could get. I suspect that sensitivity comes from being an only child and a listener when I was young. When you are an only child, you are so lonely and interested in the outside world that you absorb a great many subtleties of life. Then you understand people better as you get older.

"I strongly believe in listening to other people's criticisms. I'm very grateful for them. I have a critiquing group and I rarely protest my editor's criticisms. I use and enjoy them. As for reviewers, since there isn't anything I can do about the book after it's published except grieve if they don't like it, I can't say that I'm thrilled when I get a negative review. I don't learn much from it. I just feel bad.

"My career is a very positive thing in my life. I have the cottage in Cape Cod because I'm a writer. I love what I'm doing. My husband and kids are proud of me. I feel comfortable, successful, and happy that my dreams actually came true. That makes me feel very, very lucky."[1]

Adler adheres to a fairly strict schedule. "In the summertime, I get up about 5:30 and work for three hours. Then I play or take care of household concerns and friends who come to visit. I have a tremendous amount of company—overnight guests. That for me is a great pleasure. In the winter I work six hours a day, usually from twelve to six. I get up a little later, play tennis or clean house in the morning, and then sit down at the computer to work all afternoon. In the summertime, I usually finish five pages a day. In the winter, ten pages a day. That may be an original or a rewrite, or a rewrite of a rewrite, or the fourth or fifth draft. I never send things out until I've gone through four or five drafts. Then an editor will usually ask for another draft and possibly another one after that. Then we go back and forth to copyediting and galleys.

"As soon as I finish one book, I sit down and start another, which I've probably been thinking about for a while. I've never been blocked and I work very quickly. I have a passion for not wasting time.

"I get inspiration wherever I can find it. I read the newspapers to pick up issues and concerns. I listen to conversations on beaches and buses and steal from them whatever I can. I listen to my friends and their stories of themselves, their childhood, and their children. Anyone who tells me a story must be aware that they may find that story used in a book. Most people don't mind. They're glad to contribute bits and pieces of their life. They're amused when it shows up in a book of mine.

"I do a fair amount of research for my books. Some require a lot, some don't require any. If I'm writing about something which I already know, I don't research. I didn't for Magic of the Glits. *Good-bye, Pink Pig* was another one. But very frequently, I end up going to the library. I check out a stack of books and take a bunch of notes from them. Then I get hold of whatever local experts I can find. Usually there are people in Schenectady who can answer my questions, whether about police procedure, environmental concerns, dyslexia, or whatever.

"One of my young-adult books, *Kiss the Clown*, dealt with dyslexia and had to do with a girl who came from Guatemala. I don't remember why she

LAUREL-LEAF CONTEMPORARY FICTION

Binding Ties
C.S. Adler

Anne fought to get away from her family of women, but some links are not easy to break.

DELL-20413-5 U.S. $2.95 CAN. $3.95

Adler's 1985 novel explores the difficulties of adolescent love.

came from Guatemala, but she did. There were also horses and a boy who worked in a stable. I had to read a pile of books about Guatemala because I had never been there and I had to go down to the local stable because I don't know a great deal about horses. That book took more research than most. Right now I'm working on a book that deals with children looking for some Indians. So I've had to research Indians.

"In *Ghost Brother*, the children were interested in skateboarding which I know nothing about. I had to research skateboarding both from books and kids themselves."[1]

Ghost Brother also draws on a highly personal subject for Adler, the 1988 death of one of her twin sons. "My son, who was married, died in a car accident. I've done a lot of writing about it. The ghost who appears to the little brother is my son as he was at fifteen. It's a brother relationship story. All three of my sons were pretty close to each other. They still are. They live in different parts of the country, but we see each other as often as possible."[1]

This was a second blow. Adler's mother had died in December of 1986. "I was there with her when she died of multiple problems in the hospital. They were three terrible, painful months for her. She wanted to die and I wanted to see her out of her misery. It was a relief when she finally let go. I had loved her very much. I keep all her things around me. She will always be part of my life as my son will be.

"A child once asked from an audience where I was speaking, 'Have you ever written about death?' I said, 'No, I'm very fortunate. I'm a middle-aged lady and I've never had any experience with death, so I don't feel confident to write about it.' Well, now I'm confident.

"I hope that my books will make kids more positive about life as well as more sympathetic to others. I also hope that I can entertain them. I'd like them to feel good about themselves when they finish one of my books."[1]

Footnote Sources:

[1] Based on an interview with Dieter Miller for *Authors and Artists for Young Adults.*

[2] C. S. Adler, *Something about the Author,* Volume 26, Gale, 1982.

[3] Hildagarde Gray, "*Down by the River*" (review), *Best Sellers,*, January, 1982.

V. C. Andrews

Born Virginia Cleo Andrews, June 6, in Portsmouth, Va.; died of cancer, December 19, 1986, in Virginia Beach, Va.; daughter of William Henry (a tool and die maker) and Lillian Lilnora (a telephone operator; maiden name, Parker) Andrews. *Education:* Educated in Portsmouth, Va. *Home:* Virginia Beach, Va. *Agent:* Anita Diamant, The Writers' Workshop, 310 Madison Ave., New York, N.Y. 10017.

■ Career

Writer. Formerly worked as a fashion illustrator, commercial artist, portrait artist, and gallery exhibitor.

■ Awards, Honors

Professional Woman of the Year from the City of Norfolk, Virginia, 1984.

■ Writings

Novels:

Flowers in the Attic, Pocket Books (paperback), 1979, Simon & Schuster (hardcover), 1980.

Petals on the Wind, Simon & Schuster, 1980, large print edition, G. K. Hall, 1983.
If There Be Thorns, Simon & Schuster, 1981, large print edition, G. K. Hall, 1983.
My Sweet Audrina, Poseidon Press, 1982.
Seeds of Yesterday, Poseidon Press, 1984.
Heaven, Poseidon Press, 1985, large print edition, G. K. Hall, 1986.
Dark Angel, Poseidon Press, 1986.
Garden of Shadows, Pocket Books, 1987.
Fallen Hearts, Pocket Books, 1988.
Gates of Paradise, Pocket Books, 1989.

■ Adaptations

Motion Pictures:

"Flowers in the Attic," New World Pictures, 1987.

■ Work In Progress

A novel based in thirteenth-century France.

■ Sidelights

Born Virginia Cleo Andrews in Portsmouth, Virginia, the third child and first daughter to William Henry, a tool and dye maker, and Lillian Lilnora Parker, a telephone operator. "I was brought up in a working-class environment, with a father who loved to read as much as I did. When I was seven he took me to the public library and signed me up for my first library card. He went home with two books. I went home with nine.

"Books opened doors I hadn't even realized were there. They took me up and out of myself, back into the past, forward into the future; put me on the moon, placed me in palaces, in jungles, everywhere. When finally I did reach London and Paris—I'd been there before."[1]

"I loved Jules Verne and Edgar Allan Poe...moody books, *Jane Eyre, Wuthering Heights,* Thomas Hardy, books with atmosphere; Russian novels with rain and stormy weather."[2]

"I never had the conscious thought of wanting to escape into another world; it's just that I didn't see fairies dancing on the lawn, I didn't see giants and witches, and I wanted to."[3]

Although Andrew's father was an avid reader, the family kept only three books in their home. "They were the Bible, *Tarzan and the Jewels of Opar,* and *The Navy Man's Journal.* The Tarzan got me really turned on to fiction—a man living in the trees with apes! From the *Journal* I learned to send signals across the water."[3]

"I was happy until I became an adolescent. Then life comes at you too fast. People think that when you mature physically, you mature mentally as well, but you don't. Then you get confused. I was very pretty, and some fathers of my little girlfriends made advances. This threw me. But I was always wise enough to get out, to run away. I did a lot of running away, disappearing suddenly."[2]

"I never wanted to be an ordinary housewife in the kitchen. I used to look at my mother and her sisters and all the pretty young girls who got married. All of a sudden, they were drudges. 'I'm not going to let this happen to me!' I said. I had no intention of getting married till after thirty, but life kinda threw me a little curve."[2]

During her late teens, Andrews developed orthopedic problems that eventually left her an invalid, having to rely on the care of her mother and the use of crutches and a wheelchair. "I had a bout of growing bone which threw my body out of alignment. But the doctors would not believe me when I said my hip hurt. They said, 'You walk too gracefully; you can't possibly hurt; you look too good.' I found out that looking too good is a terrible way to go into a doctor's office. They don't take you seriously. They think women are vain anyway.

"When it finally became obvious that the bone spur had thrown my spine out of alignment, it led me into a bout with arthritis, which I needn't have had if they had taken the bone spur off immediately. This went on for four years, starting when I was about eighteen. Then they began to correct the damage with operations. I have had four major ones and have one more coming up. I can have corrective surgery, but I'm a little leery of doctors because they made mistakes with me. One doctor had a small stroke while he was operating. The saw slipped and he cut off the socket of my right hip."[4]

Psychic experiences played an important role in Andrew's life. A firm believer of ESP and reincarnation, she claimed to have known, because of psychic flashes, that she was going to be crippled. "As a child, I really felt in my bones that I was not going to lead an ordinary life. I had psychic moments which showed me I was going to have trouble, and that eventually I was going to end up using crutches. I was very angry at the time. These visions occurred often, like fate preparing me so that I'd be able to cope, a sort of kindness to get me ready.

"I have adjusted to my way of living. I really don't think I'm missing out on too much. I think I'm happier than a lot of people who walk perfectly normal."[4]

"It's not that I'm a hostage. That would mean that someone is deliberately holding me a prisoner. I can go out. I don't feel like a hostage. In fact, sometimes I rather like it.

"I always have a wonderful excuse not to see people I don't want to see. I find my characters much more interesting than the ones I meet."[2]

With the assistance of tutors, Andrews graduated from high school, then completed a four-year art course. After her father's death, when she was twenty, the family moved to St. Louis, then to Arizona where Andrews supported herself without much enthusiasm as a commercial artist. "I was a professional artist—painting oils, acrylics, watercolors and portraits. I never liked it as much as I like writing, but it was easy.

"We needed the extra income....And I sold everything I painted.

"In order to sell paintings today you've got to paint in a way I didn't like. I felt I wasn't being true to myself....

"So I stopped painting and picked up a book on writing and started writing."[5]

"When I was a child I thought it boring to be only me for a whole lifetime, and so I thought the perfect thing for me to be would be an actress who would play many parts, and be many people. Since life often has a way of diverting you from your

Victoria Tennant (right) starred in the film adaptation of Andrews' novel, *Flowers in the Attic.* (Copyright © 1987 by New World Pictures.)

chosen path, I became an artist, and was still unsatisfied, for an artist is an artist, doing the same thing every day. Then I began to write, and discovered to my delight, in writing of my characters, I assumed their bodies, and their minds, and literally, I became what they were, and so in a way, when I write, I am on stage, speaking the lines, directing, producing, etc.

"It takes about fifty pages before I can begin to really identify with my characters, so they do take me up and out of myself to such a degree my own life becomes secondary. As in *Flowers in the Attic*, the situation was not pleasant, but there is no beauty without ugliness, and no enjoyment without suffering, we have to have the shade in order to see the light, and that is all I do in a story, put my characters in the shade—and try before the ending, to have them in the sunlight."[6]

Andrews produced from thirty to forty pages a night, usually typing in bed, but often writing while standing up in a body brace. "I'm a very self-driven person, motivated by what is within me. I only begin to write a story when it has to come out of me. I trust my instinct."[7]

Her output was prodigious, completing nine books in seven years; each of them was turned down. A major breakthrough was achieved when she submitted a novel called *The Obsessed* and was told by editors that her 290,000 word story—two boxes of manuscript pages—showed promise but was simply too long. Encouraged, Andrews began revising extensively and came up with a ninety-eight page version she titled *Flowers in the Attic*. Early readers responded favorably but agreed that she should get "more gutsy." "[I began to] deal with all those unspeakable things my mother didn't want me to write about, which was exactly what I wanted to do in the first place."[2]

"I stopped avoiding confrontation and all the things that made me feel uncomfortable."[8]

1979. A tale of child abuse and incest, V. C. Andrews' *Flowers in the Attic* rocketed to the best-seller list only two weeks after it was published. It is the story of the four Dollanganger children. The offspring of an incestuous union, the children are locked up in an attic because if their grandfather learns of their existence, he will cut their mother out of his will. Forgotten by their unfeeling mother, physically beaten by their sadistic grandmother, the children turn to each other for love. Andrews sold the novel to Pocket Books for $7,500 and dedicated it to her mother. "She hasn't even read the books. She never reads any. She thinks they're all lies anyway."[8]

"It is so appropriate to color hope yellow," she wrote in the prologue. "Like that sun we seldom saw. And as I begin to copy from the old memorandum journals that I kept for so long, a title comes as if inspired, *Open the Window and Stand in the Sunshine*. Yet, I hesitate to name our story that. For I think of us more as flowers in the attic. Paper flowers. Born so brightly colored, and fading duller through all those long, grim, dreary, nightmarish days when we were held prisoners of hope, and kept captives by greed. But, we were never to color even one of our paper blossoms yellow.

"Charles Dickens would often start his novels with the birth of the protagonist and, being a favorite author of. . .mine, I would duplicate his style—if I could. But he was a genius born to write without difficulty while I find every word I put down, I put down with tears, with bitter blood, with sour gall, well mixed and blended with shame and guilt. I thought I would never feel ashamed or guilty, that these were burdens for others to bear. Years have passed and I am older and wiser now, accepting, too. The tempest of rage that once stormed within me has simmered down so I can write, I hope, with truth and with less hatred and prejudice than would have been the case a few years ago.

"So, like Charles Dickens, in this work of 'fiction' I will hide myself away behind a false name, and live in fake places, and I will pray to God that those who should will hurt when they read what I have to say. Certainly God in his infinite mercy will see that some understanding publisher will put my words in a book, and help grind the knife that I hope to wield."[1]

The sequel, *Petals on the Wind*, also became an instant success, rising to the number one position and remaining on the *New York Times* best-seller list for nineteen weeks. *Petals'* popularity was so great that it even caused *Flowers* to reappear on the list for a brief stint. *If There Be Thorns*, the third part of the Dollanganger trilogy, continued Andrews' impressive track record, attaining the number two slot on most best-seller list, the second week after its release. While the books' themes of incest, misogyny, rape, and revenge have outraged some readers, others, particlarly adolescent girls who constitute the major proportion of Andrews' readership, have found the mixture irresistible. In fact, all three of the Dollanganger novels have been record breakers for Pocket Books, the first

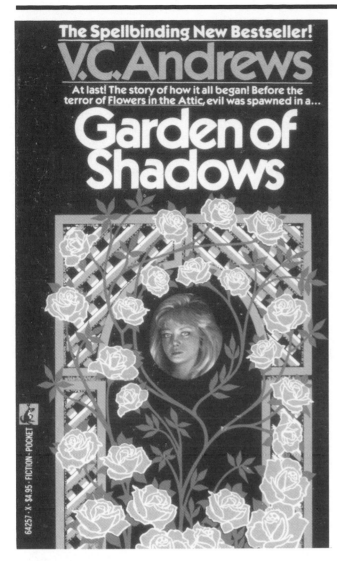

Cover from the paperbound edition of Andrews' 1987 novel.

two alone selling over seven million copies within two years.

In order to promote the sales of a first novel by an unknown author, her editor, Ann Patty, then associated with Pocket Books, instituted a massive publicity campaign, complete with complimentary preview editions, haunting radio advertisement, and aggressive in-store merchandising. The boost combined with the book's chilling cover graphics and controversial themes.

"Not long after my first novel, *Flowers in the Attic*, was published, many letters came to fill my mailbox, clearly indicating that most of my readers think I am writing about my own life. Only in some ways is this true. Cathy Dollanganger's persona is not mine, but her way of responding to the traumatic events in her life reflects what mine would have been in the same situation. Her emotions are my emotions. Her dilemmas are somewhat similar to mine, but not precisely.

"It's difficult to say where a writer leaves off and the character takes over. One could hope to be as verbal as Cathy, and say all the right things at the right time, but in real life that seldom happens. Dialogue can move the action along speedily. When you construct a good strong character, often he or she will take off and lead the way, surprising you. Shout hooray when your characters do this for you.

"When I look back and try to understand why I write as I do, and why so many of my readers are convinced that only an autobiography can be written as emotionally and powerfully, I realize that I do put a great deal of myself into my stories. I suffer when my characters suffer. I lose weight when they do. (Take notice, all of you writers who are overweight—starve your characters.)

Cover from the paperback edition of the 1984 novel.

"In formulating situations and characters, I take bits and pieces from my life, from the lives of my friends, and from the tales told to me by older family members, and I weave them into my novels. I use my dreams, too. It seems my dreams are the most powerful imaginative force I have going for me, but for memories. Yet, somewhere in my chest, near my heart, lives that force I draw upon for ideas, too. The more I trust it, the more willing it is to give. It seems I have a warehouse of memories—my own, and those belonging to others—to draw upon. If you don't have that kind of retentive memory, keep a journal.

"There is the magic of memories…they do not have to be inhibited by the strict truth. A writer can, and a writer *must,* embroider and embellish what might be a simple tale without all the imaginative trappings. To take one's own life story and tell it exactly as it happened (unless you've led one very exciting life), usually makes for a less than suspenseful story. A novel has to be paced so it has peaks of excitement that grow ever higher as it approaches the climax. Life just doesn't move along speedily enough, as a novel must. Dialogue in reality can be so mundane as to be absolutely boring.

"One of my most effective methods of finding story ideas is to take one situation from my life and ask, What if I hadn't run as fast as I had? What if I had been caught? What then? Would I have suffered? — been kidnapped? — raped? — then killed?"[9]

"Why do I write about such oddball situations? Why have an imagination if you don't go that way? I guess I'm just drawn to that sort of thing. I don't like everything to be explained by scientists who say there are no little green men from Mars. I don't like that, I want them to be there."[2]

"I don't think those people creating the stew over incest have read the books. They think I'm going to have brothers and sisters all over the country looking at each other with lust. That's not it at all.

"It was just a natural event in the story that came out, and it was referred to specifically only in one paragraph that was not that explicit.

"After all, there's incest in the Bible!"[3]

"It takes a certain amount of loneliness to get kinky. You cannot be kinky when there are a lot of people around. They normalize you. But a writer can build on these odd notions."[10]

Despite the overwhelming popularity, Andrews' novels have not met with proportionate critical acclaim. In her *Washington Post Book World* review of *Flowers in the Attic,* Carolyn Banks says it "may well be the worst book I have ever read." She calls the book's plot "unbelievable" and its dialogue "indigestible." She adds, "The principle of selection does not seem to have entered the author's head, nor her editor's."

1982-1984. *My Sweet Audrina* and *Seeds of Yesterday* proved to be two more smashing commercial successes. "For a certainty, in my novels, the worst is bound to happen. My characters are clever enough, and fast enough, but by playing God, I always trip them up in some way and allow what I escaped to happen to them. Then the fun—or terror—begins.

"In…*My Sweet Audrina* my main character, Audrina, meets her fate in the woods. In the incident that I experienced, the memory of which was the basis of what happens to Audrina, I *could* have met my fate in the valley between a ring of low hills that swallowed my screams for help. *I* was lucky enough to escape. Pity my poor character who didn't."[9]

Reviewing *My Sweet Audrina* in the *New York Times Book Review,* Eden Ross Lipson finds the storyline difficult to follow, claiming: "Most of the brief sexual passages involve third parties watching in fascination, which gives things a little spin, I suppose. Nothing else makes much sense." However, not all the reviews of Andrews' novels have been so negative. Without dismissing the criticism leveled by other reviewers, some critics have found praiseworthy elements in her works. While, she acknowledges that certain situations in *Petals on the Wind* tax credibility, Bea Maxwell, writing in the *Los Angeles Times Book Review,* praises Andrews' storytelling ability, particularly her skill in ensnaring her audience. "Andrews lulls the reader, she shocks and awakens," she says.

Dale Pollock, another *Los Angeles Times Book Review* critic, sees weak spots in *If There Be Thorns,* namely the ending, but finds the book "an absorbing narrative" in which the two speakers "emerge as credible (if pitiable) characters." Pollock also sees considerable merit in Andrews' ability to tell the story through the eyes of two adolescent boys. "Andrews excels at re-creating the confusion and frustration of being old enough to grasp the pieces of a family mystery, but too young to assemble the puzzle." London *Times* reviewer Patricia Miller seems to sum up the attitude of many of those who find themselves attracted to Andrews' books when she writes:

Cover for Pocket Books boxed set of the Dollanganger novels.

"Virginia Andrews' writing is embarrassingly crude and naive, especially in her first books, though she has improved greatly in the course of writing four."

Ruth Piepgras in the *Chicago Tribune*'s "Point of View" feels that "the question that author Andrews fails to answer, and the one that possibly makes these books so enticing to youngsters, is whether incest is wrong. It seems to be a question with which the author herself is struggling." Piepgras' response to that question is "Yes, Virginia, incest is wrong. Incest needs to be made an open subject, but it must be done in such a way that little girls will know they are not alone. They need to know that it happens to others, too, and they need to know that it's all right to tell some-

one....Virginia C. Andrews and publisher Pocket Books could have used their skill in marketing to youngsters to help open up this subject in a way that helped, not hurt, children. When kids read these books and come to the conclusion that incest is okay, that's not helping. That's hurting. Perhaps a more direct question to Andrews would be in order: 'Why don't you properly research the subject of incest and present it as the crime against children that it is? Or are you afraid that if you don't titillate the curiosity of youngsters in this fanciful way, you won't be filling your bank account so rapidly?'" And so it goes. Andrews' books are wildly successful, but always seems to stir great controversy, sometimes bordering on anger.

"I don't think anything that appears wonderful and shiny on its surface doesn't have a dark side to it. I never write a scene with a sunny day that there isn't a little cloud up there. I think that's realism."[2]

The city of Norfolk, Virginia named Andrews "Professional Woman of the Year." "You bet I'm glad. I know I'm a celebrity and like it. I like the attention I get and I like the money. I like the things I can buy. It takes the worry off. But being a celebrity can sometimes be pesty.

"The fans are kind, loving and understanding. The sales people aren't. They have an expensive product to sell and they chase you out into the mall. But I can go pretty fast in my motorized chair."[5]

"I used to be very bitter. I think if I had failed at writing, maybe I would be bitter now. I always wanted to be somebody exceptional, somebody different, who did something on her own, some creative things...."[2]

1984-1986. *Heaven* and *Dark Angel,* which chronicle the saga of the Casteel family, published. With six novels, and over twenty-four million books in print, Andrews was named #1 Best Selling Author in a survey by the American Booksellers' Association's list of America's Top Ten Paperbacks in the horror/occult category. It showed that she held five spots, topping Stephen King.

Andrews sold the movie rights of *Flowers in the Attic* to Fries Entertainment—New World Pictures, retaining final script and cast approval. "I did picture the movie in the back of my mind when I was writing it.

"It's thrilling to see my characters come alive, to see actors and actresses playing them.

"I turned down five scripts before...[the final] one. I was upset at the beginning, when there were changes from the book, till I began to see their point. They changed everything I objected to. They had really horrible things in there. I kept thinking, 'You idiots, you don't know what you're doing.'

"But my film agent told me, 'Virginia, you say that in such a nice way, they want to do what you say.' I kept writing them letters, blasting away at all the gross things they had in there. Like when Cathy [the oldest child] is kissing Bart [her mother's second husband] they had him wake up and go into action, and I said, 'You can't have him do that!'

"They wanted to make it more gothic—they even had Dobermans nipping at the escaping children's heels."[11]

"Right after [the producers] met me they said they would give me a cameo role. I thought they would conveniently forget it, so it surprised me when they invited me to Ipswich, Mass. to do my little bit. I was a maid. They had me cleaning windows."[5]

December 19, 1986. Andrews died of cancer at her home in Virginia Beach. She continued to write up to the time of her death. *Garden of Shadows* and *Fallen Hearts,* which continue the saga of the Casteel family, were published posthumously.

Footnote Sources:

1 V. C. Andrews, "Prologue" *Flowers in the Attic,* Pocket Books, 1987.
2 Stephen Rubin, "Blooms of Darkness," *Washington Post,* September 20, 1981.
3 William Ruehlmann, "A Gothic Million in the Attic," *Virginia-Pilot and Ledger-Star,* November 8, 1981.
4 S. Rubin, "Mistress of the Macabre," *Detroit News,* October 11, 1981.
5 Jim Lewis, "Is Life a Bore? Then Take Up Writing," *Houston Post,* December 21, 1986.

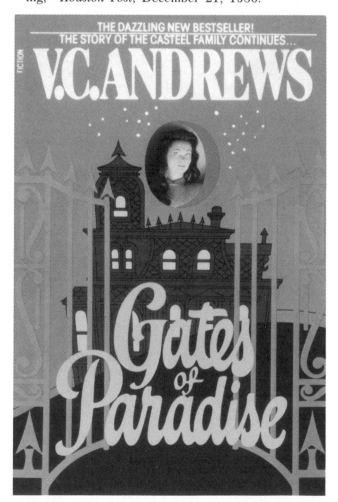

Hardcover edition of Andrews' final novel.

6 "V. C. Andrews," *Contemporary Authors*, Volumes 97-100, Gale, 1981.

7 Nikki Janas, "Portsmouth Author Colors Hope Yellow," *Panorama*, November 4, 1979.

8 Patricia Miller, "Courage, Tragedy, Romance, Mystery: That's the Author—the Books Are Somewhat Different," *London Times*, September 15, 1982.

9 V. C. Andrews, "Turning a Profit from Memories," *Writer*, November, 1982.

10 "Obituaries," *San Francisco Examiner and Chronicle*, December 21, 1986.

11 William Goldstein, "On Location with 'Flowers in the Attic,'" *Publishers Weekly*, November 14, 1986.

■ For More Information See

Washington Post Book World, November 4, 1979.

Norfolk Ledger-Star, November 29, 1979 (p. B1), May 30, 1980 (p. B1).

New York Times Biographical Service, July, 1980 (p. 934ff).

Los Angeles Times Book Review, October 5, 1980, August 30, 1981, April 29, 1984.

People Weekly, October 6, 1980 (p. 51ff).

New York Times, June 14, 1981 (section VII, p. 34).

Chicago Tribune, June 28, 1981 P. 17ff).

Los Angeles Times, August 30, 1981 (p. 13).

New York Times Book Review, October 3, 1982.

New York Post, March 23, 1986.

Detroit Free Press, January 18, 1987.

Cinefantastique, December, 1987 (p. 38ff).

Obituaries:

Norfolk Ledger-Star, December 20, 1986.

Detroit Free Press, December 20, 1986.

Detroit News, December 20, 1986.

Houston Post, December 20, 1986.

San Francisco Chronicle, December 20, 1986 (p. 16).

New York Times, December 21, 1986 (p. 44).

Los Angeles Times, December 21, 1986.

Washington Post, December 21, 1986.

St. Louis Post Dispatch, December 21, 1986.

Chicago Tribune, December 21, 1986 (section 2, p. 13).

Variety, December 24, 1986.

Time, January 5, 1987.

Publishers Weekly, January 9, 1987 (p. 30).

School Library Journal, March, 1987.

James Baldwin

Born August 2, 1924, in New York, N.Y.; died of stomach cancer, December 1 (some sources say November 30), 1987, in St. Paul de Vence, France; son of David (a clergyman and factory worker) and Emma Berdis (Jones) Baldwin. *Education:* Graduate of De Witt Clinton High School, New York, N.Y., 1942. *Home:* St. Paul de Vence, France. *Agent:* Edward Acton, Inc., 17 Grove St., New York, N.Y. 10014.

■ Career

Writer, 1944-87. Youth minister at Fireside Pentecostal Assembly, New York, N.Y., 1938-42; variously employed as meat packer, porter, handyman, factory worker, elevator operator, dishwasher, waiter, and office boy in New York City, and in defense work in Belle Meade, N.J., 1942-46. Lecturer on racial issues at universities in the United States and Europe, 1957-87. Director of play, "Fortune and Men's Eyes," in Istanbul, Turkey, 1970, and film, "The Inheritance," 1973. *Member:* Congress on Racial Equality (member of national advisory board), American Academy and Institute of Arts and Letters, Authors' League, International PEN, Dramatists Guild, Actors' Studio, National Committee for a Sane Nuclear Policy.

■ Awards, Honors

Eugene F. Saxton Fellowship, 1945; Rosenwald Fellowship, 1948; Guggenheim Fellowship, 1954; National Institute of Arts and Letters Grant for Literature, 1956; *Partisan Review* Fellowship, 1956; Ford Foundation Grant, 1959; *Nobody Knows My Name* was selected one of American Library Association's Outstanding Books of the Year, 1961; National Conference of Christians and Jews Brotherhood Certificate of Recognition, 1962, for *Nobody Knows My Name;* George Polk Memorial Award from Long Island University Department of Journalism, 1962, for magazine reporting; Foreign Drama Critics Award, 1964, for "Blues for Mister Charlie"; D.Litt. from the University of British Columbia, Vancouver, 1964; National Association of Independent Schools Award, 1964, for *The Fire Next Time; If Beale Street Could Talk* was selected one of American Library Association's Best Young Adult Books, 1974, and one of New York Public Library's Books for the Teen Age, 1980, 1981, and 1982; Honorary Doctor of Letters, Morehouse College, 1976; American Book Award nomination, 1980, for *Just above My Head;* Honorary Degree, City University of New York, 1982; named Literary Lion by the New York Public Library, 1983; named Commander of the Legion of Honor (France), 1986; French-American Friendship Prize, for *Harlem Quartet.*

■ Writings

Fiction:

Go Tell It on the Mountain (novel), Knopf, 1953.

Giovanni's Room (novel), Dial, 1956, reissued, Transworld, 1977.

Another Country (novel), Dial, 1962.

Going to Meet the Man (short stories), Dial, 1965.

(Contributor) John Henrik Clarke, editor, *American Negro Short Stories*, Hill & Wang, 1966.

This Morning, This Evening, So Soon (short story), Diesterweg, 1967.

Tell Me How Long the Train's Been Gone (novel), Dial, 1968.

If Beale Street Could Talk (novel), Dial, 1974.

Little Man, Little Man: A Story of Childhood (juvenile; illustrated by Yoran Cazac), Dial, 1976.

Just above My Head (novel), Dial, 1979.

Also author of *Harlem Quartet* (novel), 1987.

Nonfiction:

Autobiographical Notes, Knopf, 1953.

Notes of a Native Son (essays), Beacon Press, 1955.

Nobody Knows My Name: More Notes of a Native Son (essays), Dial, 1961.

The Fire Next Time (essays), Dial, 1963.

(Author of text) Richard Avedon, *Nothing Personal* (photographic portraits), Atheneum, 1964.

(With others) *Black Anti-Semitism and Jewish Racism* (essays), R. W. Baron, 1969.

(With Kenneth Kaunda) Carl Ordung, editor, *Menschenwuerde und Gerechtigkeit* (essays delivered at the fourth assembly of the World Council of Churches), Union-Verlag, 1969.

(With Margaret Mead) *A Rap on Race* (transcribed conversation), Lippincott, 1971.

No Name in the Street (essays), Dial, 1972.

(With Francoise Giroud) *Cesar: Compressions d'or*, Hachette, 1973.

(With Nikki Giovanni) *A Dialogue* (transcribed conversation), Lippincott, 1973.

The Devil Finds Work (essay), Dial, 1976.

(With others) John Henrik Clarke, editor, *Harlem, U.S.A.: The Story of a City within a City*, Seven Seas [Berlin], 1976.

The Evidence of Things Not Seen (essay), Holt, 1985.

The Price of the Ticket: Collected Nonfiction 1948-1985, St. Martin's, 1985.

(With others) Michael J. Weber, editor, *Perspectives: Angles on African Art*, Center for African Art, 1987.

Plays:

"Giovanni's Room" (based on novel), first produced in New York City at Actors' Studio, 1957.

Blues for Mister Charlie (first produced on Broadway at ANTA Theatre, April 23, 1964), Dial, 1964.

The Amen Corner (first produced in Washington, D.C. at Howard University, 1955; produced on Broadway at Ethel Barrymore Theatre, April 5, 1965), Dial, 1968.

One Day, When I Was Lost: A Scenario (screenplay; based on *The Autobiography of Malcolm X*, by Alex Haley), M. Joseph, 1972, Dial, 1973.

"A Deed from the King of Spain," first produced in New York City at American Center for Stanislavski Theatre Art, January 24, 1974.

Also author of "The Welcome Table," 1987.

Other:

Jimmy's Blues: Selected Poems, M. Joseph, 1983, St. Martin's, 1985.

Contributor of book reviews and essays to numerous periodicals in the United States and abroad, including *Harper's, Nation, Esquire, Playboy, Time, Life, Saturday Review, Negro Digest, Look, New York Times, Partisan Review, Mademoiselle,* and *New Yorker.*

■ Adaptations

"Amen Corner" (musical stage play), adapted by Garry Sherman, Peter Udell and Philip Rose, produced on Broadway at the Nederlander Theater, November 10, 1983, also produced at Tricycle, January 20, 1987.

"Go Tell It on the Mountain" (television drama), "American Playhouse" series, PBS-TV, January 14, 1985.

■ Sidelights

James Baldwin was a novelist, playwright and essayist, but to many Americans he was known as a spokesman for blacks who grew up during the civil rights movement of the 1960s and 1970s. Baldwin rejected the title of "spokesman," preferring to be called a "witness," or one who speaks the truth. Throughout his life he turned away from anger and hatred and spoke eloquently for the human heart, urging black and white, male and female, oppressor and oppressed to recognize their similarities in the human condition.

Many famous writers and actors, both black and white were friends of Baldwin. Hailed by many as a prophet and visionary, he is most often praised for his essays, while controversy surrounds the quality of his novels and plays.

James Baldwin was born James Arthur Jones on August 2, 1924 in Harlem Hospital to Emma Bertis Jones, father unknown. Three years later, his mother married David Baldwin, a preacher from New Orleans. Baldwin grew up assuming he was his father. "We grew up—first house I remember was on Park Avenue—not the American Park Avenue, or maybe it is the American uptown Park Avenue where the railroad tracks are. We used to play on the roof and in the—I can't call it an alley—but near the river—it was a kind of garbage dump. Those were the first scenes I remember. My father had trouble keeping us alive—there were nine of us. I was the oldest so I took care of the kids and dealt with Daddy....Part of his problem was he couldn't feed his kids, but I was a kid and I didn't know that. He was very religious and very rigid."[1]

"He was righteous in the pulpit and a monster in the house. Maybe he saved all kinds of souls, but he lost all his children, every single one of them. And it wasn't so much a matter of punishment with him: he was trying to kill us. I've hated a few people, but actually I've hated only one person, and that was my father.

"He didn't like me. But he'd had a terrible time, too. And of course, I was not his son. I was a bastard. What he wanted for his children was what, in fact, I became. I was the brightest boy in the house because I was the eldest, and because I loved my mother and I really loved those kids. And I was necessary: I changed all the diapers and I knew where the kids were, and I could take some of the pressures off my mother, and in a way stand between him and her—which is a strange role to play. I had to learn to stand up to my father, and, in learning that, I became precisely what he wanted his other children to become, and he couldn't take that and I couldn't either maybe."[2]

"You know, you always take your estimate of yourself from what the world says about you.

"I guess the one thing my father *did* do for me was that he taught me how to *fight*. I had to know how to fight because I *fought* him so hard. He taught me—what my real *weapons* were. Which were patience. And a kind of ruthless determination. Because I had to endure whatever it was: to *endure* it; to go under and come back *up*; to *wait*.

"He taught me everything I *know* about hate. Which means he taught me everything I know about *love,* too."[3]

"My father said, during all the years I lived with him, that I was the ugliest boy he had ever seen, and I had absolutely no reason to doubt him. But it was not my father's hatred of *my* frog-eyes which hurt me, this hatred proving, in time, to be rather resounding than real: I have my mother's eyes. When my father called me ugly, he was not attacking me so much as he was attacking my

A 1965 volume of Baldwin's simple movingly-written short stories.

mother. (No doubt, he was also attacking my real, and unknown, father.) And I loved my mother. I knew that she loved me, and I sensed that she was paying an enormous price for me. I was a boy, and so I didn't really too much care that my father thought me hideous. (So I said to myself—this judgment, nevertheless, was to have a decidedly terrifying effect on my life.) But I thought that he must have been stricken blind (or was as mysteriously wicked as white people, a paralyzing thought) if he was unable to see that my mother was absolutely beyond any question the most beautiful woman in the world."[4]

"I had to watch my father and what my father had to endure to raise nine children on twenty-seven dollars and fifty cents a week—when he was working. Now, when I was a kid I didn't know at all what the man was going through; I didn't know why he was always in a rage; I didn't know why he was impossible to live with. But I had not yet had to go through his working day. And he couldn't quit his twenty-seven-dollars-and-fifty-cents-a-week job *because* he had nine kids to feed. He couldn't say, as our kids can, 'I don't like white people.' He couldn't say anything. He lived his whole life in silence except in the church. And he couldn't explain—how can you explain to a five-year-old kid?—'My boss called me a nigger and I quit.' The kid's belly's empty and you see it and you've got to raise the kid.

"My father finally went mad, and when I became a man I understood how that could happen. It wasn't that he didn't love us; he loved his wife and his children, but he couldn't take, day after day, hour after hour, being treated like a nigger on that job and in the streets and on the subways—everywhere he went. And of course when he came home he didn't understand his children at all. They were moving further and further away from him because they were afraid of him, and also, which is even worse, afraid of the situation and the condition which he represented. You know, when you're called a nigger you look at your father because you think your father can rule the world—every kid thinks that—and then you discover that your father cannot do anything about it. So you begin to despise your father and you realize, Oh, that's what a nigger is. But it's not your father's fault and it's not your fault; it's the fault of the people who hold the power because they have deliberately trained your father to be a slave, and they have deliberately calculated that if he is a slave you will be a slave, you will also accept it and it'll go on forever."[5]

Baldwin's father may have been incapable of giving him love, but his mother compensated for this lack by loving and nurturing him. "I think she saved us all. She was the only person in the world we could turn to, yet she couldn't protect us.

"She was a very tough little woman, and she must have been scared to death all the years she was raising us.

"Those streets! There it is at the door, *at* the door. It hasn't changed either, by the way. That's what it means to be raised in a ghetto. I think of what a woman like my mother knows, instinctively has to know. . .; that there is no safety, that no one is safe, none of her children would ever be safe. . . .You can't call the cops."[2]

"I was considered by everyone to be 'strange,' including my poor mother, who didn't, however, beat me for it. Well, if I was 'strange'—and I knew that I must be, otherwise people would not have treated me so strangely, and I would not have been so miserable—perhaps I could find a way to use my strangeness. A 'strange' child, anyway, dimly and fearfully apprehends that the years are not likely to make him less strange. Therefore, if he wishes to live, he must calculate, and I knew that I had to live. I very much wanted my mother to be happy and to be proud of me, and I very much loved my brothers and my sisters, who, in a sense, were all I had. My father showed no favoritism, he did not beat me worse than the others because I was not his son. (I didn't know this then, anyway, none of the children did, and by the time we all found out, it became just one more detail of the peculiar journey we had made in company with each other.) I knew, too, that my mother depended on me. I was not always dependable, for no child can be, but I tried: and I knew that I might have to prepare myself to be, one day, the actual head of my family. I did not actually do this, either, for we were all forced to take on our responsibilities each for the other, and to discharge them in our different ways. The eldest can be, God knows, as much a burden as a help, and is doomed to be something of a mystery for those growing up behind him—a mystery when not, indeed, an intolerable exasperation. *I*, nevertheless, was the eldest, a responsibility I did not intend to fail."[4]

Taking this sense of responsibility seriously, young Baldwin started school. "At the point I was going to P.S. 24 the only Negro school principal as far as I know in the entire history of New York was a principal named Mrs. Ayer, and she liked me. In a way I guess she proved to me that I didn't have to

Olivia Cole and Paul Winfield as they appeared in *The American Playhouse* series' "Go Tell It on the Mountain." Broadcast on PBS-TV, 1985.

be entirely defined by my circumstances, because you know that every Negro child knows what his circumstances are but he cannot articulate them, because he is born into a republic which assures him in as many ways as it knows how, and has got great force, that he has a certain place and he can never rise above it.

"She was a living proof that I was not necessarily what the country said I was."[1]

He then moved on to P.S. 139, Frederick Douglass Junior High School, where he studied with the black poet Countee Cullen and became serious about writing. "I began plotting novels at about the time I learned to read. The story of my childhood is the usual bleak fantasy, and. . .I certainly would not consider living it again. In those days my mother was given to the exasperating and mysterious habit of having babies. As they were born, I took them over with one hand and held a book with the other. The children probably suffered, though they have since been kind enough to deny it, and in this way I read *Uncle Tom's Cabin* and *A Tale of Two Cities* over and over and over again; in this way, in fact, I read just about everything I could get my hands

on—except the Bible, probably because it was the only book I was encouraged to read. I must also confess that I wrote—a great deal—and my first professional triumph, in any case, the first effort of mine to be seen in print, occurred at the age of twelve or thereabouts, when a short story I had written about the Spanish revolution won some sort of prize in an extremely short-lived church newspaper. I remember the story was censored by the lady editor, though I don't remember why, and I was outraged.

"[I] also wrote plays, and songs, for one of which I received a letter of congratulations from Mayor La Guardia, and poetry, about which the less said, the better. My mother was delighted by all these goings-on, but my father wasn't; he wanted me to be a preacher."[6]

Paper was so expensive during the Depression days that he often wrote his stories on paper bags. More and more, school became torture. "I was physically a target. It worked *against* me, y'know, to be the brightest boy in class and the smallest boy in class. And I suffered. So I really *loathed* it."[3] On the other hand, writing was his salvation. "[It] was an act of love. It was an attempt—not to get the world's attention—it was an attempt to be loved. It seemed a way to save myself and to save my family. It came out of despair."[7]

"By this time, I had been taken in hand by a young white schoolteacher, a beautiful woman, very important to me. I was between ten and eleven. She had directed my first play and endured my first theatrical tantrums and had then decided to escort me into the world. She gave me books to read and talked to me about the books, and about the world: about Spain, for example, and Ethiopia, and Italy, and the German Third Reich; and took me to see plays and films, plays and films to which no one else would have dreamed of taking a ten-year-old boy. I loved her, of course, and absolutely, with a child's love; didn't understand half of what she said, but remembered it; and it stood me in good stead later. It is certainly partly because of her, who arrived in my terrifying life so soon, that I never really managed to hate white people— though, God knows, I have often wished to murder more than one or two....I never felt her pity, either, in spite of the fact that she sometimes brought us old clothes (because she worried about our winters) and cod-liver oil, especially for me, because I seemed destined, then, to be carried away by whooping cough.

"I was a child, of course, and, therefore, unsophist-icated. I don't seem ever to have had any innate need (or, indeed, any innate ability) to distrust people: and so I took Bill Miller as she was, or as she appeared to be to me. Yet, the difference between Miss Miller and other white people, white people as they lived in my imagination, and also as they were in life, had to have had a profound and bewildering effect on my mind. Bill Miller was not at all like the cops who had already beaten me up, she was not like the landlords who called me nigger, she was not like the storekeepers who laughed at me. I had found white people to be unutterably menacing, terrifying, mysterious— wicked: and they were mysterious, in fact, to the extent that they were wicked: the unfathomable question being, precisely, this one: what, under heaven, or beneath the sea, or in the catacombs of hell, could cause any people to act as white people acted? From Miss Miller, therefore, I began to suspect that white people did not act as they did because they were white, but for some other reason, and I began to try to locate and understand the reason. She, too, anyway, was treated like a nigger, especially by the cops, and she had no love for landlords."[4]

Baldwin was accepted into the predominately white De Witt Clinton High School in The Bronx, where he contributed to the school literary maga-zine, *Magpie*, becoming co-editor along with his life-long friend, Richard Avedon. About this time he began his career as a youth minister at Harlem's Fireside Pentacostal Church. This religious conver-sion ended his relationship with Bill Miller, for he could no longer go to sinful plays and movies. She, in great disappointment, told him she had lost respect for him, a remark he never forgot. "I underwent, during the summer that I became fourteen, a prolonged religious crisis. I use the word 'religious' in the common, and arbitrary, sense, meaning that I then discovered God, His saints and angels, and His blazing Hell. And since I had been born in a Christian nation, I accepted this Deity as the only one. I supposed Him to exist only within the walls of a church—in fact, of *our* church—and I also supposed that God and safety were synonymous. The word 'safety' brings us to the real meaning of the word 'religious' as we use it. Therefore, to state it in another, more accurate way, I became, during my fourteenth year, for the first time in my life, afraid—afraid of the evil within me and afraid of the evil without....Many of my comrades were clearly headed for the Avenue, and my father said that I was headed that way, too. My friends began to drink and smoke, and embarked—at first avid, then groaning—on their sexual careers."[8]

Also beginning to question his sexual identity, he fell in love with an older man, a Harlem racketeer, at age sixteen. "I will be grateful to that man until the day I die.

"Even now, I sometimes wonder what on earth his friends could have been thinking, confronted with stingy-brimmed, mustachioed, razor-toting Poppa and skinny, pop-eyed Me when he walked me (rarely) into various shady joints, I drinking ginger ale, he drinking brandy. I think I was supposed to be his nephew, some nonsense like that, though he was Spanish and Irish, with curly black hair. But I know that he was showing me off and wanted his friends to be happy for him."[9]

By seventeen, Baldwin had become disillusioned with the church. "Being in the pulpit was like being in the theatre; I was behind the scenes and knew how the illusion was worked. I knew the other ministers and knew the quality of their lives. And I don't mean to suggest by this the 'Elmer Gantry' sort of hypocrisy concerning sensuality; it was a deeper, deadlier, and more subtle hypocrisy than that, and a little honest sensuality, or a lot,

Baldwin at the onset of his writing career, 1953.

of the Lamb had not cleansed me in any way whatever. I was just as black as I had been the day that I was born. Therefore, when I faced a congregation, it began to take all the strength I had not to stammer, not to curse, not to tell them to throw away their Bibles and get off their knees and go home and organize, for example, a rent strike."[8]

With the help of his friend Emile Capouya, Baldwin abandoned the church, but he was forced to leave home. His father's mental state was deteriorating rapidly, and he needed to support the family. After graduating six months later than the rest of his class from De Witt Clinton High School, he went to work in Belle Meade, New Jersey, laying railroad track with Emile.

Belle Meade proved to be his first exposure to racism. "I was working with a whole gang of Southerners, and I caught hell. It was a great

would have been like water in an extremely bitter desert. I knew how to work on a congregation until the last dime was surrendered—it was not very hard to do—and I knew where the money for the 'the Lord's work' went. I knew, though I did not wish to know it, that I had no respect for the people with whom I worked. I could not have said it then, but I also knew that if I continued I would soon have no respect for myself.

"And the fact that I was 'the young Brother Baldwin' increased my value with those same pimps and racketeers who had helped to stampede me into the church in the first place. They still saw the little boy they intended to take over. They were waiting for me to come to my senses and realize that I was in a very lucrative business. They knew that I did not yet realize this, and also that I had not yet begun to suspect where my own needs, *coming up* (they were very patient), could drive me. They themselves did know the score, and they knew that the odds were in their favor. And, really, I knew it, too. I was even lonelier and more vulnerable than I had been before. And the blood

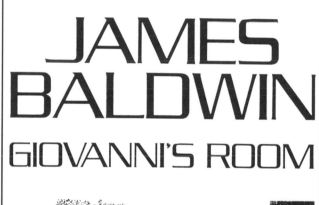

"VIOLENT, EXCRUCIATING BEAUTY."
—*San Francisco Chronicle*

DELL• 32881-0 •U.S. $4.95
CAN. $6.50

Paperback edition of the controversial novel in which Baldwin discusses his own ambiguous sexuality.

revelation that people could be so—so *monstrous.* My childhood was awful, but it was awful in another way. I hadn't made any clear connection between the fact of my color and the fact of my childhood. It seemed not possible for me to think of myself as 'a nigger,' you know. I fought back. So I spent more than a year out there, fighting my co-workers, fighting my bosses, fighting the *town.*"[3]

After being fired several times, and unsuccessfully trying to get served in local segregated restaurants, he was forced to return home after the death of his father, who had been committed to Central Islip Mental Hospital. His mother, pregnant with her ninth child, delivered Paula Maria a few hours after her husband died. David Baldwin was buried on James Baldwin's nineteenth birthday. "I had forgotten, in the rage of my growing up, how proud my father had been of me when I was little. Apparently, I had had a voice and my father had liked to show me off before the members of the church. I had forgotten what he had looked like when he was pleased but now I remembered that he had always been grinning with pleasure when my solos ended. I even remembered certain expressions on his face when he teased my mother—had he loved her? I would never know. And when had it all begun to change? For now it seemed that he had not always been cruel. I remembered being taken for a haircut and scraping my knee on the footrest of the barber's chair and I remembered my father's face as he soothed my crying and applied the stinging iodine. Then I remembered our fights, fights which had been of the worst possible kind because my technique had been silence.

"I remembered the one time in all our life together when we had really spoken to each other.

"It was on a Sunday and it must have been shortly before I left home. We were walking, just the two of us, in our usual silence, to or from church.

"My father asked me abruptly, 'You'd rather write than preach, wouldn't you?'

"I was astonished at his question—because it was a real question. I answered, 'Yes.'

"That was all we said. It was awful to remember that that was all we had *ever* said."[6]

After the death of his father, Baldwin returned home for a while, supporting the family with a variety of jobs: meatpacker, porter, dishwasher, waiter, office boy, handy man, factory worker and elevator operator. Soon, however, he had to get away. "I figured out that by the time the youngest kid would be able to take care of herself, I'd be 36.

And it would be harder to begin a career then. I'd seen a lot of brilliant, unhappy, *miserable* and *evil* people—*trapped* in Harlem, in various basements, being janitors. And they really *were* brilliant. That's why they became so monstrous.

"And I could see it happen to me. It *would* happen to me—if I stayed. And I was ready to take a very long shot: the shot was simply that I would turn into a writer before my mother died and before the children were all put in jail—or became junkies or whores. But I knew I had to jump *then.*"[10]

He moved to Greenwich Village and began working seriously on his first novel. While working as a waiter at a West Indian restaurant called Calypso, he began to explore the themes of race and sexuality and tried to deal with his emotions about his stepfather.

A critical moment came when he met his idol, Richard Wright, who reviewed his manuscript called "In My Father's House" and recommended him for a Eugene F. Saxton Fellowship. With this five hundred dollars he was able to keep working, but he was unable to finish the work and was ashamed to face Wright. He tried, in vain, to imitate Wright's style. "Instinctively I knew that wasn't the direction to go in. Richard and I were two very different people, two very different writers. I knew I had to find myself as a writer even if it cost me this book. I became paralyzed. I couldn't go on with it. I felt it was irreparably ruined—and I with it."[9]

Wright went abroad, to Paris, while Baldwin stayed in Greenwich Village, writing essays and reviews for *Nation, New Leader, Commentary* and *Partisan Review.* His first published work was a review of Maxim Gorki's *Best Short Stories* in *Nation* in 1947, which received favorable comments. It was followed by a controversial article on black anti-Semitism entitled "The Harlem Ghetto" in *Commentary.* His editor, Robert Warshow, helped him develop as a writer. "He made me feel like a real writer in the end. He kept turning it back to me saying I had avoided something or left something out and he was right. He kept pushing me and I literally sweated it out. Anti-Semitism in Harlem was particularly difficult for me to deal with. Although I'd grown up with Jewish boys in high school, I hadn't consciously explored anti-Semitism. It was too delicate. And Robert Warshow forced me to deal with it. He was a marvelous editor. He taught me a lot at the right time. I learned you had to force from your experience the last drop, sweet or bitter, it could possibly give."[9]

Rip Torn and Ann Wedgeworth in a scene from the 1964 stage production of "Blues for Mister Charlie."

During this time he made life-long friendships with the painter Beauford Delaney and the actor Marlon Brando. Delaney, in particular, influenced his writing. He became for him, "the first walking, living proof, for me, that a black man could be an artist. He became, for me, an example of courage and integrity, humility and passion. An absolute integrity: I saw him shaken many times and I lived to see him broken, but I never saw him bow."[9]

In 1948, Baldwin won a Rosenwald Fellowship, and tried to write *Ignorant Armies,* in which he grappled with the issue of bisexuality. For a while he lived with a black woman and considered marriage. Instead, he threw the wedding ring he had bought into the Hudson River, where a boyhood friend, Eugene, had committed suicide by jumping off a bridge.

The book did not work, and Baldwin began to struggle with his failure and his anger and his sexuality. "I no longer felt I knew who I really was, whether I was really black or really white, really male or really female, really talented or a fraud, really strong or merely stubborn. I had become a crazy oddball. I had to get my head together to survive and my only hope of doing that was to leave America."[9]

With the rest of his Rosenwald Fellowship money, he went to Paris, where Beauford Delaney and Richard Wright were living. "But I was past caring. My whole life had become a gamble. I wasn't really choosing France, I was getting out of America. I had no idea what might happen to me in France, but I was very clear as to what would happen if I remained in New York. I would go under like Eugene."[9]

Years later he described his departure, a moment he never forgot. "It was raining—naturally. My mother had come downstairs, and stood silently, arms folded, on the stoop. My baby sister was upstairs, weeping, I got into the cab, waved, and drove away.

"It may be impossible for anyone to tell the truth about his past. You drag your past with you everywhere, or it drags you. Therefore, the simplest thing for me to say concerning that first departure from America is that I had no choice. It was not the heroic departure of a prodigy. Time was to prove (and how!) that I was a prodigal son indeed, but, by the time the fatted calf came my way, intimacy with too many dubious hamburgers had caused me to lose my appetite. I *did* want the people I loved to know how much I loved them, especially that little girl weeping on the top floor of that tenement: I will say that. And my departure, which, especially in my own eyes, stank of betrayal, was my only means of providing, or redeeming, that love, my only hope. Or, in other words, I knew then that I was a writer, but did not know if I could last long enough to prove it. And, if I loved the people I loved, I also knew that they loved me, did not deserve and could scarcely afford the spectacle of the firstborn as a disaster.

"This was quite an assignment for a black, defenseless-looking high school graduate who—to remain within the confines of the mentionable—had had feet, fists, tables, clubs, and chairs bounced off his only head, and who, by the time of November, 1948, trusted no one, and knew that he trusted no one, knew that this distrust was suicidal, and also knew that there was no question any longer of his *life* in America: his violent destruction could be taken as given; it was a matter of time. By the time I was twenty-two, I was a survivor—a survivor, furthermore, with murder in his heart.

"A man with murder in his heart will murder, or be murdered—it comes to the same thing—and so I knew I had to leave. Somewhere else, anywhere else, the question of my life might still be open, but in my own country that question was closed."[11]

Baldwin spent the next ten years in Paris; he arrived penniless and spoke no French. Arested for stealing a bed sheet, he even had to sell his clothes and his typewriter, but he kept on working on a new version of "In My Father's House," which he had retitled *Go Tell It On the Mountain.* "I became committed to the book when I left home, when I was seventeen. I finished it, many versions and eternities later, in Switzerland, when I was twenty-seven. I had been carried to Switzerland, to the mountains, by a Swiss friend I had met in Paris. Those early Paris years were rough—so rough that my friend's decision to kidnap me was a literal attempt to save my life. Something in the nature of a kidnaping was indicated since I had visited Switzerland once and wasn't likely to leap at the notion of visiting it again—and the journey actually resembled a kidnaping in that I was too weak and tired to protest, or, if memory serves, to have any real reaction at all. I didn't even feel gratitude, although Lucien had ruthlessly blackmailed his parents into allowing him to take back the family chalet; he claimed that the mountain air was necessary if he were not to perish of tuberculosis, and that, furthermore, he needed so many pounds of milk, meat and butter a week.

"So there I was, in the mountains, a long way from home—me, Bessie Smith, Fats Waller, and the Swiss—a kind of breathtaking historical conjunction. And I actually climbed a mountain, to the great wonder of the village (and me).

"After nearly ten years, the book was finished in three months. The title comes out of a kind of wonder of gratitude. I took it home, to my baby sister, who had been born the day our father died. And I sold it...a great moment in my life."[12]

In 1952 Baldwin returned briefly to the United States for the publication of *Go Tell It on the Mountain.* Then he returned to Paris and wrote "Amen Corner," his first play, a book of essays titled *Notes of a Native Son,* and his second novel, *Giovanni's Room.* The homosexual theme of *Giovanni's Room* made it difficult to publish. His American publisher, Knopf, rejected it. "They told me to burn it! They said it would ruin me if I tried to get it published. I had turndowns because they treated it like pornography. But I wouldn't accept such treatment! I took it over to England and my publisher there, Michael Joseph, said if his lawyers passed it, he'd love to publish it. And there were no problems. None at all! The Book got good reviews. And once the English accepted it so well, the cowards here took it. Never talk to me about the *courage* of American publishers. You're stupid if you let their rejections worry you—and I say that as one who was stupid. Always make up your own mind. You just can't afford to let people give you your evaluation of your own book. Certainly not if you're a Negro. If I've learned one thing from life, that's it."[9]

About this time Baldwin became good friends with Norman Mailer, although they argued frequently. Baldwin was becoming well known. "One of the reasons I had fought so hard after all was to wrest from the world fame and money and love. And here I was at thirty-two finding my notoriety hard to bear, since its principal effect was to make me more lonely; money, it turned out, was exactly like sex, you thought of nothing else if you didn't have it and thought of other things if you did."[9]

The 1965 stage production of "The Amen Corner," starred Frank Rivera and Bea Richards.

Based in America from 1957 to 1970, Baldwin overcame his fear of the American South to become involved with the civil rights movement. "The thing to do, y'know, if you're really terribly occupied with—with *yourself!*, the thing to do is to, at any price whatever, get in touch with something which is *more* than you. Throw yourself into a situation where you won't have time to weep. So I went South. Because I was *afraid* to go South."[13]

He met and worked with Martin Luther King, James Meredith, Medgar Evers, Harry Belafonte, Roy Innis, Bayard Rustin and many other prominent civil rights workers. "This was the point where I meant something in their lives. And they began to *depend* on me more. And—it turned out that money could be raised on my *name*, y'know. And they needed money to pay all those terrible court costs. To get people out of jail....And so I began donating my time to *do* that!"[13]

Flying back and forth to Paris, trying to finish his new novel, *Another Country* while working on a new book of essays called *Nobody Knows My Name*, he also apprenticed himself to the director Elia Kazin in order to learn more about play writing. While dramatizing *Giovanni's Room* he met the playwright Lorraine Hansberry and they became fast friends. Finally, he fled to Istanbul, to the home of an actor friend, where he was able to finish *Another Country*. "I couldn't find the peace of mind—the space free of other people—to write anywhere in America. People always seemed to know where I was hiding with my typewriter and they were always dropping by at all times of the day and night. Consequently I was drinking far too much and getting hardly any sleep. I was too exhausted to write. I *had* to get away."[9]

In 1962 *Another Country* was published. An important scene in the book is the suicide of Rufus, who killed himself like Baldwin's friend Eugene. He described it as "the hardest thing I ever wrote because that was the key to the book. But I kept putting it off. It had to do, of course, with reliving the suicide of my friend who jumped off the bridge. Also, it was very dangerous to do from the technical point of view because this central character dies in the first hundred pages, with a couple of hundred pages still to go. The point up to the suicide is like a long prologue, and it is the only light on Ida. You never go into her mind, but I had to make you see what is happening to this girl by making you feel the blow of her brother's death—the key to her relationship with everybody. She tries to make everybody pay for it. You cannot do

that, life is not like that, you only destroy yourself."[9]

During 1962 Baldwin visited Africa and began working on a new book of essays, *The Fire Next Time*, while staying at the guest cottage of his friend, novelist William Styron. The book was published in 1963 to wide critical acclaim.

The next year he collaborated with his friend, Richard Avedon, producing *Nothing Personal*, a collection of photographs with commentary by Baldwin. He also completed his third play, "Blues for Mr. Charlie."

Then, 1965 saw the publication of *Going to Meet the Man*, and his now-famous debate with William F. Buckley at Harvard titled "The American Dream Is at the Expense of the American Negro."

Baldwin completed *Tell Me How Long the Train's Been Gone* in 1968 and then suffered through a long, dry spell. Distraught over the assassinations of Martin Luther King, Jr., Malcolm X and Medgar Evers, he was unable to write. "I just reeled after King's death. We had been young together, we had tramped all over the South together. I was never the Christian that Martin was, but I sat behind him and was awed by his faith and I believed in him. There was a certain logic in Malcolm X's death, but Martin getting his head blown off in Memphis trying to get a raise for garbage men...."[14]

After falling ill and spending several months in seclusion, Baldwin re-emerged. "The tangible thing that happened to me—and to blacks in America—during that whole terrible time was the realization that our destinies are in our hands, black hands, and no one else's.

"I decided I have no right nor reason to be despairing. But I do not believe in the promise of America in the same ways. There will be no moral appeals on my part to this country's moral conscience. It has none."[15]

In 1971 Baldwin bought a French farmhouse in St. Paul de Vence, which would become his permanent home. He also owned an apartment house in New York, which provided a home for his mother.

The seventies were productive for Baldwin. He published *A Dialogue* with poet Nikki Giovanni in 1973 and *If Beale Street Could Talk* in 1974. And in *The Devil Finds Work*, he wrote about the frustrations of working with Hollywood, based on his experience of trying to write a screenplay of Malcolm X's life. "Cinema is propaganda, no less. It is a racist tool, a heterosexist tool, enhancing the mindless majority, punishing the misfit. Behavior is shaped through what kids—what we all—watch, on screen, on TV, on commercials, now in music video. New technologies support and abet old prejudices and forms. The minority world of same-sex love, of non-stereotypes, is deliberately unexplored and minimized—by invisibility.''[16]

In 1985 he published *The Price of the Ticket*, a collection of all his essays. He was also working on *No Papers for Muhammed* when he fell ill from stomach cancer at his home in St. Paul de Vence. He died there, surrounded by friends and survived by his mother and all his brothers and sisters, on December 1, 1987, at the age of sixty-three. Five thousand people attended his memorial service at The Cathedral of St. John the Divine on Amsterdam Avenue, at the edge of Harlem. "This is life's aim. To remove barriers in others, in oneself. When the barriers of youth end, the barriers of age begin. So I keep in touch with youth, in myself and in the young. Not to avoid death. No. To sail through life on at least one smooth tide of unity.''[16]

Footnote Sources:

1 Kenneth B. Clark, "A Conversation with James Baldwin," *Freedomways*, summer, 1963.
2 Robert Penn Warren, *Who Speaks for the Negro?*, Random House, 1965.
3 Fern Marja Eckman, "James Baldwin," *New York Post*, January 15, 1964.
4 James Baldwin, *The Devil Finds Work*, Dial, 1976.
5 J. Baldwin and Nikki Giovanni, *A Dialogue*, Lippincott, 1973.
6 J. Baldwin, *Notes of a Native Son*, Bantam, 1955.
7 John W. Roberts, "James Baldwin," *Dictionary of Literary Biography*, Volume 33, Gale, 1984.
8 J. Baldwin, *The Fire Next Time*, Bantam, 1963.
9 W. J. Weatherby, *James Baldwin: Artist on Fire*, Donald I. Fine, 1989.
10 F. M. Eckman, "James Baldwin," *New York Post*, January 16, 1964.
11 J. Baldwin, "Every Good-bye Ain't Gone," *New York*, December 19, 1977.
12 J. Baldwin, "*Go Tell It on the Mountain*: Belatedly, the Fear Turned to Love for His Father," *TV Guide*, January 12, 1985.
13 F. M. Eckman, "James Baldwin," *New York Post*, January 19, 1964.
14 William A. McWhirter, "Parting Shots: After Years of Futility Baldwin Explodes Again," *Life*, July 30, 1971.
15 George Goodman, Jr., "For James Baldwin, a Rap on Baldwin," *New York Times*, June 26, 1972.
16 George Hadley-Garcia, "Removing Barriers," *New York Native*, October 14-20, 1985.

■ For More Information See

Culture for the Millions, Van Nostrand, 1959.
Current Biography 1959, H. W. Wilson, 1960.
Alfred Kazin, *Contemporaries*, Little, Brown, 1962.

Nona Balakian and Charles Simmons, editors, *The Creative Present: Notes on Contemporary American Fiction*, Doubleday, 1963.
Irving Howe, *A World More Attractive: A View of Modern Literature and Politics*, Horizon Press, 1963.
Marcus Klein, *After Alienation: American Novels in Mid-Century*, World, 1964.
Harry T. Moore, editor, *Contemporary American Novelists*, Southern Illinois University Press, 1964.
Norman Podhoretz, *Doings and Undoings*, Farrar, Straus, 1964.
Current Biography 1964, H. W. Wilson, 1965.
Robert Bone, *The Negro Novel in America*, Yale University Press, 1965.
Robert Brustein, *Seasons of Discontent: Dramatic Opinions 1959-1965*, Simon & Schuster, 1965.
David Littlejohn, *Black on White: A Critical Survey of Writing by American Negroes*, Viking, 1966.
Fern Marja Eckman, *The Furious Passage of James Baldwin*, M. Evans, 1966.
Stanley Edgar Hyman, *Standards: A Chronicle of Books for Our Time*, Horizon Press, 1966.

DELL • 32542-0 • **U.S. $4.95** CAN. $6.50

JAMES BALDWIN
THE FIRE NEXT TIME

"GREAT...EXTRAORDINARY....A COMPASSIONATE AND ELOQUENT SERMON FOR OUR TIME, DEMANDING THE MOST AGONIZING SELF-EXAMINATION FROM ANYONE WHO READS IT."
—*Harper's*

Baldwin's ground-breaking 1963 commentary on emerging black consciousness.

Herbert Hill, editor, *Anger and Beyond*, Harper, 1966.

Susan Sontag, *Against Interpretation and Other Essays*, Farrar, Strauss, 1966.

C. W. E. Bigsby, *Confrontation and Commitment: A Study of Contemporary American Drama*, University of Missouri Press, 1967.

Frederick Lumley, *New Trends in Twentieth-Century Drama: A Survey since Ibsen and Shaw*, Oxford University Press, 1967.

Anthony Burgess, *The Novel Now: A Guide to Contemporary Fiction*, Norton, 1967.

Abraham Chapman, editor, *Black Voices: An Anthology of Afro-American Literature*, New American Library, 1968.

Eldridge Cleaver, *Soul on Ice*, McGraw-Hill, 1968.

C. W. E. Bigsby, editor, *The Black American Writer*, Volume I: *Fiction*, Volume II: *Poetry and Drama*, Everett/Edwards, 1969.

Warren French, editor, *The Fifties: Fiction, Poetry, Drama*, Everett/Edwards, 1970.

Donald B. Gibson, editor, *Five Black Writers: Essays on Wright, Ellison, Baldwin, Hughes, and LeRoi Jones*, New York University Press, 1970.

David Frost, *The Americans*, Stein & Day, 1970.

Darwin T. Turner, *Afro-American Writers*, Appleton, 1970.

John A. Williams and Charles F. Harris, editors, *Amistad I: Writings on Black History and Culture*, Random House, 1970.

Ruby Cohn, *Dialogue in American Drama*, Indiana University Press, 1971.

George A. Panichas, *The Politics of Twentieth-Century Novelists*, Hawthorn, 1971.

M. G. Cook, editor, *Modern Black Novelists: A Collection of Critical Essays*, Prentice-Hall, 1971.

Wilfrid Sheed, *The Morning After*, Farrar, Straus, 1971.

Sherley Anne Williams, *Give Birth to Brightness: A Thematic Study in Neo-Black Literature*, Dial, 1972.

New York Times Biographical Edition, Arno Press, 1972.

Abraham Chapman, editor, *New Black Voices*, New American Library, 1972.

Contemporary Literary Criticism, Gale, Volume I, 1973, Volume II, 1974, Volume III, 1975, Volume IV, 1975, Volume V, 1976, Volume VIII, 1978, Volume XIII, 1980, Volume XV, 1980, Volume XVII, 1981, Volume XLII, 1987.

A. Kazin, *Bright Book of Life: American Novelists and Storytellers from Hemingway to Mailer*, Little, Brown, 1973.

Stanley Macebuh, *James Baldwin: A Critical Study*, Joseph Okpaku, 1973.

Kenneth Kinnamon, editor, *James Baldwin: A Collection of Critical Essays*, Prentice-Hall, 1974.

Roger Rosenblatt, *Black Fiction*, Harvard University Press, 1974.

Clarence Major, *The Dark and Feeling: Black American Writers and Their Work*, Joseph Okpaku, 1974.

Addison Gayle, Jr., *The Way of the World: The Black Novel in America*, Anchor Press, 1975.

John Simon, *Uneasy Stages: Chronicle of the New York Theatre*, Random House, 1975.

Theressa Gunnels Rush and others, *Black American Writers Past and Present: A Biographical and Bibliographical Dictionary*, Scarecrow, 1975.

Karin Moeller, *The Theme of Identity in the Essays of James Baldwin*, Acta Universitatis Gotoburgensis, 1975.

H. Ober Hesse, editor, *The Nature of a Humane Society*, Fortress, 1976.

Therman B. O'Daniel, *James Baldwin: A Critical Evaluation*, Howard University Press, 1977.

William J. Weatherby, *Squaring Off: Mailer vs. Baldwin*, Mason/Charter, 1977.

Daryl Dance, *Black American Writers: Bibliographical Essays*, St. Martin's, 1978.

Louis Hill Pratt, *James Baldwin*, Twayne, 1978.

Dictionary of Literary Biography, Gale, Volume II: *American Novelists since World War II*, 1978, Volume VII: *Twentieth-Century American Dramatists*, 1981, Volume XXXIII: *Afro-American Fiction Writers after 1955*, 1984.

Carolyn Wedin Sylvander, *James Baldwin*, Frederick Ungar, 1980.

Fred Standley and Nancy Standley, *James Baldwin: A Reference Guide*, G. K. Hall, 1980.

F. Standley and N. Standley, editors, *Critical Essays on James Baldwin*, G. K. Hall, 1981.

Malcolm King, *Baldwin: Three Interviews*, Wesleyan University Press, 1985.

Contemporary Authors Bibliographical Series, Volume I: *American Novelists*, Gale, 1986.

Harold Bloom, editor, *James Baldwin*, Chelsea House, 1986.

Concise Dictionary of American Literary Biography: The New Consciousness 1941-1968, Gale, 1987.

Periodicals:

New Yorker, June 20, 1953, November 25, 1961, August 4, 1962, July 8, 1974, November 26, 1979, December 21, 1987 (p. 31).

New York Times Book Review, February 26, 1956, July 2, 1961, June 24, 1962, December 12, 1965, June 2, 1968, June 28, 1968, May 28, 1972 (p. 17ff), May 19, 1974 (p. 2), May 2, 1976 (p. 7), July 31, 1977 (p. 1ff), September 23, 1979 (p. 35ff), May 24, 1984, December 20, 1987 (p. 1).

Time, June 30, 1961, June 29, 1962, November 6, 1964, June 7, 1968, June 10, 1974, December 14, 1987.

Atlantic, July, 1961, July, 1962, March, 1963, July, 1968, June, 1972.

Ebony, October, 1961 (p. 23ff).

Newsweek, February 4, 1963, June 3, 1969, May 27, 1974 (p. 82).

Mademoiselle, May, 1963 (p. 174ff).

Life, May 24, 1963 (p. 81ff), June 7, 1968, June 4, 1971.

Negro Digest, June, 1963 (p. 54ff), October, 1966 (p. 37ff), April, 1967.

New York Times, June 3, 1963 (p. 1ff), May 31, 1964, April 11, 1965, May 31, 1968, February 2, 1969 (section 2, p. D-9), May 21, 1971, May 17, 1974, June 4, 1976, September 4, 1977, September 21, 1979, September 23, 1979, November 11, 1983, January 10, 1985, January 14, 1985.

New York Herald Tribune, June 16, 1963 (section 6, p. 1ff).

Encounter, August, 1963 (p. 22ff), July, 1965 (p. 55ff), September, 1972 (p. 27ff).

Midcontinent American Studies Journal, fall, 1963.

New York Post Daily Magazine, January 13, 1964 (p. 21), January 14, 1964 (p. 21), January 17, 1964 (p. 39), May 3, 1964 (p. 23).

Vogue, July, 1964.

Esquire, August, 1964 (p. 59ff), July, 1968 (p. 49ff).

New York Times Magazine, March 7, 1965 (p. 32ff).

New York Post, November 9, 1965 (p. 8), June 8, 1974 (p. 35).

Arts in Society, summer, 1966 (p. 550ff).

Atlas, March, 1967 (p. 47ff).

New York, July 8, 1968 (p. 39ff).

Look, July 23, 1968 (p. 50ff).

Black World. June, 1972, December, 1974.

Intellectual Digest, July, 1972 (p. 67ff).

Muhammad Speaks, September 8, 1973 (p. 13ff), September 15, 1973 (p. 29), September 29, 1973 (p. 29ff) , October 6, 1973 (p. 30ff).

Black Scholar, December, 1973-January, 1974 (p. 33ff).

Listener, July 25, 1974.

Publishers Weekly, January 19, 1976 (p. 58).

New York Amsterdam News, May 22, 1976 (p. D-9ff). October 8, 1977 (p. D-12), March 25, 1978 (p. D-10), June 12, 1982 (p. 25).

Essence, June, 1976 (p. 54ff), December, 1984 (p. 72ff), March, 1988 (p. 51ff).

Village Voice, October 29, 1979, January 12, 1988 (p. 35ff).

London Magazine, December, 1979-January, 1980.

Black Collegian, January, 1980 (p. 105ff).

People Weekly, January 7, 1980, December 21, 1987 (p. 89).

Jet, March 25, 1985 (p. 22), July 7, 1986 (p. 4), June 20, 1988 (p. 27).

Times (London), May 15, 1986, January 19, 1987, January 22, 1987.

New York Native, December 21, 1987 (p. 20ff).

Gentlemen's Quarterly, August, 1988 (p. 214ff).

Obituaries:

Chicago Tribune, December 2, 1987.

Daily News, December 2, 1987 (p. 4ff).

Newsday, December 2, 1987 (part 2, p. 2ff).

Detroit Free Press, Decemember 2, 1987, December 8, 1987.

Los Angeles Times, December 2, 1987.

Variety, December 2, 1987 (p. 110).

New York Times, December 2, 1987 (p. A1ff), December 9, 1987 (p. B1ff).

Philadelphia Inquirer, December 2, 1987, December 9, 1987, December 14, 1987.

Times (London), December 2, 1987.

Washington Post, December 2, 1987.

Time, December 14, 1987 (p. 80).

Newsweek, December 14, 1987 (p. 86).

Jet, December 21, 1987 (p. 18), December 28, 1987 (p. 14).

Current Biography, January, 1988 (p. 80).

New York Review of Books, January 21, 1988 (p. 8).

School Library Journal, February, 1988.

Bruce Chatwin

B orn May 13, 1940, in Sheffield, Yorkshire, England; died of a rare bone marrow disease in Nice, France, January, 1989; son of Charles Leslie (a lawyer) and Margharita (Turnell) Chatwin; married Elizabeth Chanler (a writer), 1965. *Education:* Attended private secondary school in Marlborough, England, and University of Edinburgh. *Residence:* Gloucestershire, England.

■ Career

Sotheby & Co. (art auctioneers), London, England, porter, became picture expert and art auctioneer, 1959-65, director of the impressionism department, 1965-66. Writer.

■ Awards, Honors

Hawthornden Prize, 1978, and E. M. Forster Award, 1979, both for *In Patagonia*; Whitbread Book of the Year Award for First Novel and James Tait Black Memorial Prize for Fiction from the University of Edinburgh, both 1982, both for *On the Black Hill.*

■ Writings

In Patagonia (travel adventure), J. Cape, 1977, Summit Books, 1979.
The Viceroy of Ouidah (novel), Summit Books, 1980.
On the Black Hill (novel), J. Cape, 1982, Viking, 1983.
The Songlines, Viking, 1987.
Utz, Viking, 1989.
What Am I Doing Here?, Viking, 1989.

Contributor to periodicals.

■ Adaptations

"Cobra Verde" (motion picture; based on *The Viceroy of Ouidah*), adapted and directed by Werner Herzog, Union Generale Cinematographique/DeLaurentis Entertainment Group, 1987.
"On the Black Hill" (motion picture), directed by Andrew Grieve, British Film Institute, 1988.
"The Songlines Quartet" (musical adaption of *The Songlines*), adapted by Kevin Volans, first produced at Lincoln Center, N.Y., November, 1988.
"In Patagonia" (cassette), Books on Tape, 1988.
"On the Black Hill" (cassette), Books on Tape.

■ Sidelights

Chatwin was born in England into a family of "...professional people, architects and lawyers, who did not go in for trade. There were, however,

The 1987 novel that explores the hopes and dreams of two companions.

scattered among my forebears and relatives, a number of legendary figures whose histories inflamed my imagination."[1]

"[They were] horizon-struck wanderers who had scattered their bones in every corner of the earth: Cousin Charlie in Patagonia; Uncle Victor in a Yukon gold camp; Uncle Robert in an oriental port; Uncle Desmond, of the long fair hair, who vanished without trace in Paris; Uncle Walter who died, chanting the suras of the Glorious Koran, in a hospital for holy men in Cairo.

"[The name Chatwin] had once been 'Chettewynde,' which meant 'the winding path' in Anglo-Saxon; and the suggestion took root in my head [as a young boy] that poetry, my own name and the road were, all three, mysteriously connected."[2]

From 1940 to 1945 Europe was consumed with World War II. "I remember the fantastic homelessness of my first five years. My father [a lawyer in civilian life] was in the Navy, at sea. My mother and I would shuttle back and forth, on the railways of wartime England, on visits to family and friends.

"All the frenzied agitation of the times communicated itself to me: the hiss of steam on a fogbound station; the double clu-unk of carriage doors closing; the drone of aircraft, the searchlights, the sirens; the sound of a mouth-organ along a platform of sleeping soldiers.

"Home, if we had one, was a solid black suitcase called the Rev-Robe, in which there was a corner for my clothes and my Mickey Mouse gas-mask. I knew that, once the bombs began to fall, I could curl up inside the Rev-Robe, and be safe."[2]

"My earliest recollections date from 1942 and are of the sea. I was two years old. We were staying with my grandmother in furnished rooms on the seafront at Filey in Yorkshire. In the house next door lived the Free French, and the men of a Scottish regiment were stationed in dugouts across the street. I watched the convoys of gray ships as they passed to and fro along the horizon. Beyond the sea, I was told, lay Germany. My father was away at sea, fighting the Germans. I would wave at the ships as they vanished behind Flamborough Head, a long wall of cliffs.

"My first job, while staying in Stratford-on-Avon with my great-aunts, Janie and Gracie, in 1944, was to be the self-appointed guide to Shakespeare's monument and tomb in the church. The price was threepence a go. Most of my customers were G.I.'s. Not that I knew who Shakespeare was, except that he was somehow associated with the red brick theater from whose balcony I would chuck old crusts to the swans. Yet, long before I could read, Aunt Gracie had taught me to recite the lines engraved on the tombslab:

> "'Bleste be ye man yet spares thes stones And curst be he yt moves my bones.'"[1]

"I lost teddy bears without a whimper, yet clung tenaciously to three precious possessions: a wooden camel known as Laura, brought by my father from the Cairo bazaar; a West Indian conch shell called Mona, in whose glorious pink mouth I could hear the wish-wash of the ocean; and a book.

"The book was *The Fisherman's Saint*, an account of Sir Wilfred Grenfell's mission work on the coast of Labrador. I still have it. On the title page is written: 'To Bruce on his 3rd Birthday from the postman at Filey. For when he grows up.' I imagined the book must contain some wonderful secret (which it did not), and it maddened me to have to wait all those years. The usual run of children's books left me cold, and at six I decided to write a book of my own. I managed the first line, 'I am a swallow.' Then I looked up and asked, 'How do you spell telegraph wires?'

"Once, we visited my father on his minesweeper in Cardiff Harbor. He carried me up to the crow's nest and let me yell down the intercom to the ward-room. Perhaps, during those heady months before the Normandy landings, I caught a case of what Baudelaire calls 'La Grande Maladie: horreur du domicile.'

"Certainly, when we moved into the grim-gabled house of our own in Birmingham, I grew sick and thin, and people wondered if I was going to be tubercular. One morning, when I had measles, my mother rushed upstairs with the newspaper and said, jubilantly, that Japan had surrendered and my father would be coming home. I glanced at the photo of the mushroom cloud and knew something dreadful had happened. The curtains of my bed-room were woven with tongues of orange flame. That night, and for years to come, I dreamed of walking over a charred black landscape with my hair on fire."[1]

After the war, the family made a trip into the Welsh black hills. The experience made a deep impression on Chatwin and he would write about that area in later life. He also made voyages on the family-owned, "...*Sunquest*, an 18-ton Bermudian sloop built in the 30s to sail around the world. We only sailed as far as Brittany, and once to Spain. I hated the actual sailing, for I was always horribly seasick—and yet I persevered. After reading an account of the effect of the H-Bomb on Britain, my 'life-plan' was to sail away to a South Sea island and never come back."[1] The Chatwins then toured Italy, Greece, and the Middle East. At thirteen the boy was sent to spend the summer in Sweden, with a family that wanted to practice English conversation.

Chatwin was educated at exclusive private schools. "At boarding school I was an addict of atlases and was always being ostracized for telling tall stories. Every boy had to be a 'little Conservative,' though I never understood—then as now—the motivations of the English class system.

"The first grown-up book I read from cover to cover was Capt. Joshua Slocum's *Sailing Alone Around the World*. This was followed by John C.

Voss's *The Venturesome Voyages of Captain Voss*, by Melville's *Omoo* and *Typee*, then Richard Henry Dana and Jack London. Perhaps from these writers I got a taste for Yankee plain style? I never liked Jules Verne, believing that the real was always more fantastic than the fantastical.

"The great English novelists were left unread, but were heard, very much heard—*Oliver Twist*, *Wuthering Heights*, *Pride and Prejudice*—on gra-mophone records, in plummy English voices, as I lay in the Birmingham eye hospital with partial paralysis of the optic nerve—a psychosomatic condition probably brought on by Marlborough College, where I was considered to be a dimwit and dreamer.

"I tried to learn Latin and Greek and was bottom of every class. There was, however, an excellent school library, and I seem in retrospect to have come away quite well read. I loved everything French—painting, furniture, poetry, history, food—and, of course, I was haunted by the career of Paul Gauguin. For my seventeenth birthday the owner of the town bookshop gave me a copy of Edith Sitwell's anthology, *Planet and Glow-worm*, a collection of texts for insomniacs, to which I can trace a number of literary fixtures.

"Yet the idea of becoming a writer never entered my head.

"For a time I went along with the suggestion that I follow the family tradition and train as an architect; but, because I was innumerate, my chances of passing the exams were remote. My parents gently squashed my ambition to go on the stage. Finally, in December 1958, since my talents were so obviously 'visual,' I started work as a porter at Messrs. Sotheby and Co., Fine Art Auctioneers, of Bond Street [London], at wages of six pounds a week.

"I learned about Chinese ceramics and African sculpture. I aired my scanty knowledge of the French Impressionists, and I prospered. Before long, I was an instant expert, flying here and there to pronounce, with unbelieveable arrogance, on the value or authenticity of works of art. I particu-larly enjoyed telling people that their paintings were fake."[1]

By 1965, Chatwin was director of that great auction house, the youngest-ever. "But something was wrong. I began to feel that things, however beautiful, can also be malign. The atmosphere of the Art World reminded me of the morgue. 'All those lovely things passing thrugh your hands,' they'd say—and I'd look at my hands and think of Lady Macbeth. Or people would compliment me on my 'eye,' and my eyes, in rebellion, gave out....I woke one morning half-blind."[1]

"During the course of the day, the sight returned to the left eye, but the right one stayed sluggish and clouded. The eye specialist who examined me said there was nothing wrong organically, and diagnosed the nature of the trouble.

"'You've been looking too closely at pictures,' he said. 'Why don't you swap them for some long horizons?'

"'Why not?' I said.

"'Where would you like to go?'

"'Africa.'

"The chairman of the company said he was sure there was something the matter with my eyes, yet couldn't think why I had to go to Africa.

"I went to Africa, to the Sudan. My eyes had recovered by the time I reached the airport.

"I sailed down the Dongola Reach in a trading felucca. I went to the 'Ethiopians,' which was a euphemism for brothel. I had a narrow escape from a rabid dog. At an understaffed clinic, I acted the role of anaesthetist for a Caesarean birth. I next joined up with a geologist who was surveying for minerals in the Red Sea Hills.

"This was nomad country—the nomads being the Beja: Kipling's 'fuzzy-wuzzies,' who didn't give a damn: for the Pharaohs of Egypt or the British cavalry at Omdurman.

"Our camel-man was a joker called Mahmoud.

"When the geologist went back to Khartoum, Mahmoud took me off into the desert to look for rock-paintings.

"At night, lying awake under the stars, the cities of the West seemed sad and alien—and the pretensions of the 'art world' idiotic. Yet here I had a sense of homecoming.

"Mahmoud instructed me in the art of reading footprints in the sand: gazelles, jackals, foxes, women. We tracked and sighted a herd of wild asses. One night, we heard the cough of a leopard close by. One morning, he lopped off the head of a puff-adder which had curled up under my sleeping-bag and presented me with its body on the tip of his sword blade. I never felt safer with anyone or, at the same time, more inadequate.

"We had two camels, two for riding and one for waterskins, yet usually we preferred to walk. He went barefoot; I was in boots. I never saw anything like the lightness of his step and, as he walked, he sang: a song, usually, about a girl from the Wadi Hammamat who was lovely as a green parakeet. The camels were his only property. He had no flocks and wanted none. He was immune to everything we would call 'progress.'

"Later, when I went back to England, I found a photo of a 'fuzzy-wuzzy' carved in relief on an Egyptian tomb of the Twelfth Dynasty at Beni Hassan: a pitiful, emaciated figure, like the pictures of victims in the Sahel drought, and recognisably the same as Mahmoud.

"The Pharaohs had vanished: Mahmoud and his people had lasted. I felt I had to know the secret of their timeless and irreverent vitality.

"I quit my job in the 'art world.'"[2]

Chatwin then enrolled as a student of archaeology at the University of Edinburgh, paying tuition and supporting himself by selling off, piece by piece, the art collection he had amassed while working at Sotheby's, where he had been a "voracious collector."

At the University, Chatwin spent more time in fieldwork, particularly in Afghanistan and Africa, than in classroom study. "When I left Sotheby's I thought I could exorcise my horror of things—things to be assessed, sent for, put up and said—by going into a world of pure scholarship. But I found that archaeology is just as much dominated by things as any auction house. So I began to study nomads—people who by definition leave nothing behind them. The best thing that happened to me in archaeology was that I found a nomadic people in Africa called the Peuls. The Peuls have an esthetic of personal beauty and an esthetic of the beauty of the cow. They breed more and more beautiful people and more and more beautiful cows, and that's absolutely all they care about, except that when they move on from one place to another they leave a garland of straw in a thorn bush, just to show they've been there. [They were] my kind of people."[3]

"The more I read, the more convinced I became that nomads had been the crankhandle of history, if for no other reason than that the great monotheisms had, all of them, surfaced from the pastoral milieu."[2]

"Archaeology seemed a dismal discipline—a story of technical glories interrupted by catastrophe, whereas the great figures of history were invisible. In the Cairo Museum you could find statues of pharaohs by the million. But where was the face of Moses? One day, while excavating a Bronze Age burial, I was about to brush the earth off a skeleton, and the old line came back to haunt me:

"'*And curst be he yt moves my bones.*'

"For the second time I quit.

"Gradually the idea for a book began to take shape. It was to be a wildly ambitious and intolerant work, a kind of 'Anatomy of Restlessness' that would enlarge on Pascal's dictum about the man sitting quietly in a room. The argument, roughly, was as follows: that in becoming human, man had acquired, together with his straight legs and striding walk, a migratory 'drive' or instinct to walk long distances through the seasons; that this 'drive' was inseparable from his central nervous system; and that, when warped in conditions of settlement, it found outlets in violence, greed, status-seeking or a mania for the new. This would explain why mobile societies such as the gypsies were egalitarian, thing-free and resistant to change; also why, to reestablish the harmony of the First State, all the great teachers—Christ, Buddha, Lao-tse, St. Francis—had set the perpetual pilgrimage at the heart of their message and told their disciples, literally, to follow The Way.

"The book grew and grew; and as it grew it became less and less intelligible to its author. It even contained a diatribe against the act of writing itself. Finally, when the manuscript was typed, it was so obviously unpublishable that for the third time, I gave up.

"Penniless, depressed, a total failure at the age of thirty-three, I had a phone call from Francis Wyndham of the *Sunday Times* of London's magazine, a man of outstanding literary judgment, whom I hardly knew. Would I, he asked, like a small job as an adviser on the arts? 'Yes,' I said.

"We soon forgot about the arts, and under Francis's guidance I took on every kind of article. I

Klaus Kinski starred in the Werner Herzog film, "Cobra Verde."

wrote about Algerian migrant workers, the couturier Madeleine Vionnet and the Great Wall of China. I interviewed Andre Malraux on what General de Gaulle thought of England; and in Moscow I visited Nadezhda Mandelstam.

"Each time I came back with a story, Francis Wyndham encouraged, criticized, edited and managed to convince me that I should, after all, try my hand at another book. His greatest gift was permission to continue.

"One afternoon in the early 70's, in Paris, I went to see the architect and designer Eileen Gray, who at the age of ninety-three thought nothing of a fourteen-hour working day. She lived in the Rue Bonaparte, and in her salon hung a map of Patagonia [the southern tip of South America—a region that includes Chile and Argentina], which she had painted in gouache.

"'I've always wanted to go there,' I said.

"'So have I,' she added. 'Go there for me.'

"I went. I cabled the *Sunday Times* of London: 'Have Gone to Patagonia.' In my rucksack I took Mandelstam's *Journey to Armenia* and Hemingway's *In Our Time.* Six months later I came back with the bones of a book that, this time, did get published. While stringing its sentences together, I thought that telling stories was the only conceivable occupation for a superfluous person such as myself."[2]

Chatwin's travel book *In Patagonia* was published in 1977 and became an instant success. It is a series of short sketches and stories culled from his personal observations and the accounts of others.

During his six months of travel, Chatwin was able to truly exercise his life long passion for walking. "I haven't got any special religion....My God is the God of Walkers. If you walk hard enough, you probably don't need any other God."[4] "Walking is not simply therapeutic for oneself but is a poetic activity that can cure the world of its ills."[5]

Chatwin's first novel, *The Viceroy of Ouidah,* is about the nineteenth-century Brazilian gaucho, Francisco De Souza, who became a powerful slave trader in Dahomey, West Africa (now The People's Republic of Benin).

The novel was originally intended to be a biography, but while in Dahomey in 1978, doing research, Chatwin found himself one morning "arrested as a mercenary, stripped to my underpants, and forced to stand against a wall in the searing sun while vultures wheeled overhead and the crowd outside the barracks chanted '*Mort au mercenaire!*'

"After this interruption I lost the stamina to pursue my researches, though I had acquired ripe material for a novel. Since it was impossible to fathom the alien mentality of my characters, my only hope was to advance the narrative in a sequence of cinematographic images, and here I was strongly influenced by the films of Werner Herzog."[5] "Especially his way of replacing psychological probing with disturbing *tableaux vivants.*"[6]

"I remember saying, 'If this were ever made into a movie, only Herzog could do it.' But that was a pipe dream. The novel, *The Viceroy of Ouidah,* appeared in 1980 to the bemusement of reviewers, some of whom found its cruelties and baroque prose unstomachable."[5]

Chatwin's dream came true when his novel was made into a film by the German director Werner Herzog. It was shot in Ghana. "Klaus Kinski is in it and the King of Dahomey is played by the paramount ruler of Ghana, who like all kings wants to be a movie star.

"Herzog had read and liked my book *In Patagonia* when he was filming 'Fitzcarraldo.'...I know the scenario for his *Viceroy* scarcely resembles my novel in any literal way, but he's cast the authentic descendants of the very people I was writing about. And the sets! He found an Italian architect who took three hundred men and four months to build an absolutely whopping African palace out of mud, all covered with skulls."[6] The film was released in 1987 with the title "Cobra Verde."

For his next work, *On the Black Hill,* Chatwin wrote more in the form of pure novel. The brooding, pastoral book chronicles the eight-year life-span of identical-twin Welsh farmers, and explores the mystical bond these bachelors shared.

While writing the novel, Chatwin "...spent a lot of time on the border between England and Wales....I try to make each of my books completely unlike all the others. The Welsh border country is as far as you could get from either Patagonia or the Kingdom of Dahomey, but in its way it's equally remote. Radnor—the county in question—is one of the least populated places in England. It once had a traffic light, I believe, but they've got rid of it now.

"The people who live there identify the outer world with the Cities of the Plain. 'The road to Hell is the road to Hereford,' they say. When I read the files of the local newspaper I found that they put the end of World War II on column five of the front page. Column one was headed '53-pound Salmon Landed on Local Estate.' I've known that countryside since my childhood, but some of the people are very secretive. To get into one house, I offered my services as a chimneysweep. They were accepted. The chimneys hadn't been swept since World War I. Half way through the job I remembered that I'd been living on Park Avenue the week before. There's nothing to beat juxtaposition!"[3]

This book too was a great success and Chatwin now had a loyal and enthusiastic following. It was released as a film in 1988, directed by Andrew Grieve and starring the Welsh actors and brothers Mike and Robert Gwilym. "I went to a few days of shooting. The director has been astonishingly faithful to the book—just the opposite of Herzog. In the Welsh town where he's set it, all the locals are quite hipped up. The nativity play he's staged has children speaking with the *exact* intonations I heard in my head."[6]

In the early 1980s Chatwin went to the most remote place he could find—Central Australia—intending to develop a novel from notebooks he had compiled on the nomadic way of life while traveling in Africa in the late 1970s. "I wanted to get right away from other men's books, from libraries and references, to see whether I could organize them."[7]

"I had a presentiment that the 'travelling' phase of my life might be passing. I felt, before the malaise of settlement crept over me, that I should reopen those notebooks. I should set down on paper a resume of the ideas, quotations and encounters which had amused and obsessed me; and which I hoped would shed light on what is, for me, the question of questions: the nature of human restlessness.

"Could it be, I wondered, that our need for distraction, our mania for the new, was, in essence, an instinctive migratory urge akin to that of birds in autumn?"[2]

While in Australia, Chatwin became interested in "Songlines." "The labyrinth of invisible pathways which Australian Aboriginals call the 'Footprints of the Ancestors' or 'The Way of the Law.' Europeans know them as 'Songlines' or 'Dreaming Tracks.'

"Aboriginals believe that the totemic ancestor of each species creates himself from the mud of his primordial water hole. He takes a step forward and sings his name, which is the opening line of a song. He takes a second step which is a gloss on the first

line and completes the linked couplet. He then sets off on a journey across the land, footfall after footfall, signing the world into existence: rocks, escarpments, sand dunes, gum trees, and so on."[8]

Making two trips to Australia, he socialized with the Aboriginals and researched their method of defining the world through melody, what a songline was and how it worked. "What I learned [in Africa]—together with what I now knew about the Songlines—seemed to confirm the conjecture I had toyed with for so long: that Natural Selection has designed us—from the structure of our braincells to the structure of our big toe—for a career of seasonal journeys *on foot* through a blistering land of thorn-scrub or desert.

"If this were so; if the desert were 'home'; if our instincts were forged in the desert; to survive the rigours of the desert—then it is easier to understand why greener pastures pall on us; why possessions exhaust us, and why Pascal's imaginary man found his comfortable lodgings a prison."[2]

Softcover edition of Chatwin's first book.

Twin brothers, Mike and Robert Gwilym, play twin bachelors in the 1987 British film "On the Black Hill."

"In the summer of 1986 I completed my book, *The Songlines* under difficult conditions. I had in fact picked up a very rare fungus of the bone marrow in China. Certain I was going to die, I decided to finish the text and put myself into the hands of doctors. My work would then be done. The last third of the manuscript was a commonplace book of quotations and vignettes intended to back up the main line of argument. I put this into shape on sweltering summer days, wrapped in shawls, shivering with cold in front of the kitchen stove. It was a race for time.

"I made a miraculous recovery. The book came out in June 1987....I promised myself *not* to buy the newspapers and read the reviews. I relented and bought the London *Independent*. I think I am quoting the reviewer correctly by saying he found my work 'unbearably pretentious.'

"The book did well. When it appeared on top of the best-seller list, I had a crisis of confidence. Had I at last joined the trash artists?

"Early on I saw it was useless to lay down the law on a subject so tenuous and decided to write an imaginary dialogue in which both narrator and interlocutor had the liberty to be wrong. This was a difficult concept for English-speaking readers. I had a running battle over whether the book should be classified as fiction or nonfiction. 'Fiction,' I insisted. 'I made it up.' A Spanish reviewer had no such difficulty. A *libro de viaje* was a travel book and a *novela de viaje*...there was *Don Quixote*.

"Understandably, the academics were cautious. But I refused to budge from the basic tenets I aired in the book:

"—As a South African paleontologist, Dr. Elizabeth Vruba, said to me, 'Man was born in adversity. Adversity, in this case, is aridity.' Homo sapiens evolved once and once only, in southern Africa sometime after the first northern glaciation (circa 2,600,000 years ago) when the North Pole formed, the sea level fell, the mediterranean became a salt lake, and the mixed South African forest gave way to open savannah scrub.

"—Homo sapiens were migratory. He made long seasonal journeys interrupted by a phase of settlement, a 'lean season' like Lent.

"—The males of Homo sapiens were hunters and the women were gatherers of vegetable food and small game. But the function of their journeys was to make friendly contact with neighbors near and far. Men talk their way through the problem of inbreeding. Animals fight to achieve this.

"—Man is 'naturally good' in Rousseau's sense and the sense of the New Testament. There is no place for evil in evolution. The fighting impulse in men and women was designed as a protection from wild beasts and other terrors of the primeval bush. In settlement these impulses tend to get thrown out of gear. Compare the story of Cain the settler and Abel the wanderer.

"—Man is a talking creature, a singing creature. He sings and his song echoes up and down the world. The first language was in song. Music is the highest of the arts."

Though *The Songlines* reads like an autobiography and the main character is named "Bruce," Chatwin has stated that, "There is nothing attached to that 'Bruce' which is made up from somewhere else, but whether it happened to me then and there is another thing."[7]

"[The book] is itself a trip and a succession of discoveries—it's influenced by Denis Diderot's *Supplement to the Voyage of Bougainville.*"[6]

Chatwin always wrote in longhand on yellow legal pads and was a stickler for how words were placed on a printed page. "I love the texture of nineteenth-century French writing as it sits on the page. I especially love the one-line paragraph for certain effects, and Flaubert was the total master of that."[7]

"Those of us who presume to write books would appear to fall into two categories: the ones who 'dig in' and the ones who move. There are writers who can only function 'at home,' with the right chair, the shelves of dictionaries and encyclopedias, and now perhaps the word processor. And there are those, like myself, who are paralyzed by 'home,' for whom home is synonymous with the proverbial writer's block, and who believe naively that all would be well if only they were somewhere else....I have tried to write in such places as an African mud hut (with a wet towel tied around my head), an Athonite monastery, a writers' colony, a moorland cottage, even a tent. But whenever the dust storms come, the rainy season sets in, or a

Dust jacket from Chatwin's 1982 novel.

pneumatic drill destroys all hopes of concentration, I curse myself and ask, 'What am I doing here?'"[9]

"I hate to be typed as a travel writer, but I do have one or two masterpieces of that sort continually in mind. One is Osip Mandelstam's account of his journey to Armenis....Another is the memoirs of Babur, the Indian whom E. M. Forster once wrote about....I love to shop around the literatures. But I hope that...all my new books, if I get to write them—will be full of surprises."[4]

Rarely having a place he called "home," Chatwin owned very few possessions. "In our century where there is this mania for possessions, the thing is to travel light, to be unencumbered. You need your freedom in which to think. Your head is freer if you don't have things. I don't believe all this hoo-ha about 'travel' as such. I think the whole mystique about the traveler is rather over-stretched."[7] "I just think of the world as the place on which I move."[10]

Once while traveling in the Sudan, Chatwin met an ancient nomadic woman whose smile burned a lasting impression on him. "I live with that old woman's smile. The smile...was like a message from the Golden Age. It had taught me to reject out of hand all arguments for the nastiness of human nature. The idea of returning to an 'original simplicity' was not naive or unscientific or out of touch with reality.

"Renunciation, even at this late date, can work."[2]

In January of 1989, *Utz* was published. It tells the story of an old Eastern European art collector whose collection is confiscated by the government. It was inspired by a chance conversation he had had with an old man in Prague in 1967.

That same month, Chatwin died. Succumbing to the debilitating illness he had contracted in China in the early '80s. He was survived by his wife, Elizabeth Chanler, also a writer, whom he had married in 1965. "My life has been a search for the miraculous. Yet at the first faint flavor of the uncanny, I turn rational and scientific. Shouldn't there always be an explanation?

"But then you don't travel in order to find explanations. You travel in order to find things that defy explanations."[11]

Footnote Sources:

[1] Bruce Chatwin, "I Always Wanted to Go to Patagonia," *New York Times Biographical Service,* February, 1983.
[2] B. Chatwin, *The Songlines,* Penguin, 1988.
[3] John Russell, "Bruce Chatwin, Passing Through," *New York Times Book Review,* December 14, 1980.
[4] B. Chatwin, *In Patagonia,* Penguin, 1988.
[5] B. Chatwin, "On Location. Gone to Ghana: The Making of Werner Herzog's 'Cobra Verde,'" *Interview,* March, 1988.
[6] Edmund White, "A Nomadic Heart, Bruce Chatwin, Like a Modern Oscar Wilde, Weaves Amazing Tales," *Vogue,* August, 1987.
[7] Michele Field, "Bruce Chatwin," *Publishers Weekly,* August 7, 1987.
[8] B. Chatwin, "The Songlines Quartet," *New York Review of Books,* January 19, 1989.
[9] B. Chatwin, "A Tower in Tuscany," *House and Garden,* January, 1987.
[10] Erik Eckholm, "Have Speculations, Will Travel," *New York Times Book Review,* August 2, 1987.
[11] B. Chatwin, "An Unexpected Encounter in Nepal," *Esquire,* October, 1983.

■ For More Information See

Washington Post Book World, July 26, 1978, December 23, 1978 (p. E14), January 4, 1981 (p. 4).
House and Garden, June, 1984 (p. 140ff), January, 1988 (p. 122ff).
New York Times Magazine, March 16, 1986 (p. 34ff).
New York Times Book Review, August 2, 1987 (p. 1ff), January 15, 1989 (p. 3).
Interview, December, 1988 (p. 138ff).
Current Biography Yearbook 1988, H. W. Wilson, 1989.
Contemporary Literary Criticism, Volume 28, Gale, 1984.
Vogue, August, 1989 (p. 326).

Obituaries:

Time, January 30, 1989 (p. 59).

Arthur C. Clarke

Born December 16, 1917, in Minehead, Somersetshire, England; son of Charles Wright (a farmer) and Mary Nora (a post office employee; maiden name, Willis) Clarke; married Marilyn Mayfield, June, 1953 (divorced, December 17, 1964). *Education:* King's College, University of London, B.Sc. (first class honors), 1948. *Home and office:* 25 Barnes Pl., Colombo 7, Sri Lanka. *Agent:* Scott Meredith Literary Agency, Inc., 845 Third Ave., New York, N.Y. 10022; and David Higham Associates Ltd., 5-8 Lower John St., London W1R 4HA, England.

■ Career

British Civil Service, His Majesty's Exchequer and Audit Department, London, England, auditor, 1936-41; Institute of Electrical Engineers, London, assistant editor of *Science Abstracts*, 1949-51; free-lance writer, 1952—. Underwater explorer and photographer, in partnership with Mike Wilson, on Great Barrier Reef of Australia and coast of Ceylon, 1954—. Lecturer, touring United States and Great Britain, 1957-74. Chairman, Second International Astronautics Congress, London, 1951, and Symposium on Space Flight, Hayden Planetarium, New York, 1953; moderator, "Space Flight Report

to the Nation," New York, 1961; Has appeared on television and radio numerous times, including as commentator with Walter Cronkite on Apollo missions, CBS-TV, 1968-70. Acted role of Leonard Woolf in Lester James Peries' film "Beddagama," 1979.

Director, Rocket Publishing Co., London, and Underwater Safaris, Colombo, Sri Lanka; trustee, Institute of Integral Education, Sri Lanka. Fellow, Franklin Institute, 1971, King's College, 1977, Institute of Robotics, Carnegie-Mellon University, 1981; Chancellor, University of Moratuwa, 1979—, and International Space University, 1989—; Vikram Sarabhai Professor, Physical Research Laboratory, Ahmedabad, 1980; founder and patron, Arthur C. Clark Centre for Modern Technologies, Sri Lanka, 1984—. Board member, National Space Institute (United States), Space Generation Foundation (United States), International Astronomical Union (Search for ExtraTerrestrial Intelligence) Commission 51, Institute of Fundamental Studies (Sri Lanka), and Planetary Society (United States). *Military service:* Royal Air Force, 1941-46, radar instructor, became flight lieutenant.

■ Member

British Interplanetary Society (honorary fellow; chairman, 1946-47, 1950-53), British Astronomical Association (council member, 1949-52), International Academy of Astronautics (honorary fellow), American Institute of Aeronautics and Astronautics (honorary fellow), American Astronautical

Society (honorary fellow), Royal Astronomical Society (fellow), Sri Lanka Astronomical Society (patron), Association of British Science Writers (life member), British Sub-Aqua Club, Society of Authors (council member), International Science Writers Association, International Council for Integrative Studies, World Academy of Art and Science (academician), British Science Fiction Association (patron), Royal Society of Arts (fellow), American Association for the Advancement of Science, National Academy of Engineering (United States; foreign associate), Science Fiction Writers of America, Science Fiction Foundation, H. G. Wells Society (honorary vice-president), Third World Academy of Sciences (associate fellow), Institute of Engineers (Sri Lanka; honorary fellow), Sri Landa Animal Welfare Association (patron).

■ Awards, Honors

International Fantasy Award, 1952, for *The Exploration of Space;* Hugo Award from the World Science Fiction Convention, 1956, for best short story "The Star," 1969, for screenplay "2001," and 1974, for novel *Rendezvous with Rama;* Guest of Honor at the World Science Fiction Convention, 1956; Kalinga Prize from UNESCO, 1961, for science writing; Boys' Club of America Junior Book Award, 1961, for *The Challenge of the Sea;* Stuart Ballantine Gold Medal from the Franklin Institute, 1963, for originating concept of communications satellites; Robert Ball Award from the Aviation-Space Writers Association, 1965, for best aerospace reporting of the year in any medium; Westinghouse Science Writing Award from the American Association for the Advancement of Science, 1969; Second International Film Festival Special Award, and Academy Award co-nomination from the Academy of Motion Picture Arts and Sciences for Best Screenplay, both 1969, both for "2001."

Playboy Editorial Award, 1971; D.Sc., Beaver College, 1971, and University of Moratuwa, 1979; Nebula Award from the Science Fiction Writers of America, 1973, for novella "A Meeting with Medusa," 1974, for novel *Rendezvous with Rama,* and 1980, for novel *The Fountains of Paradise; Rendezvous with Rama* was selected one of American Library Association's Best Books for Young Adults, 1973, *2001,* 1975, and *Imperial Earth,* 1976; Aerospace Communications Award from the American Institute of Aeronautics and Astronautics, 1974; John W. Campbell Memorial Award from the Science Fiction Research Association, and Jupiter Award from the Instructors of Science Fiction in Higher Education, both 1974, both for

Rendezvous with Rama; Bradford Washburn Award from the Boston Museum of Science, 1977, for his "outstanding contribution to the public's understanding of science"; GALAXY Award, 1979.

Voice across the Sea was selected one of New York Public Library's Books for the Teen Age, 1980, *The Fountains of Paradise,* 1980, and 1981, and *Rendezvous with Rama,* 1982; Special Emmy Award from the National Academy of Television Arts and Sciences, 1981, for his contributions to satellite communications; "Lensman" Award, 1982; Marconi International Fellowship from Polytechnic University, 1982, for his invention of the geosynchronous communications satellite; *Playboy* Award for Best Major Work, 1983, for *2010;* Centennial Medal from the Institute of Electrical and Electronics Engineers, 1984; E. M. Emme Astronautical Literature Award from the American Astronautical Society, 1984; Grand Master Award from the Science Fiction Writers of America, 1986; Vidya Jyothi Medal (Presidential Science Award), 1986; Charles A. Lindbergh Award, 1987; named to Society of Satellite Professionals Hall of Fame, 1987; named to Aerospace Hall of Fame, 1988; D. Litt, University of Bath, 1988; Commander of the British Empire (CBE), 1989; Special Achievement Award from the Space Explorers, 1989.

■ Writings

Nonfiction:

Interplanetary Flight: An Introduction to Astronautics, Temple, 1950, Harper, 1951, 2nd edition, 1960, reissued, Berkley, 1985.

The Exploration of Space, Harper, 1951, revised edition, Pocket Books, 1979.

The Young Traveller in Space (juvenile), Phoenix, 1954, published as *Going into Space,* Harper, 1954, another edition published as *The Scottie Book of Space Travel,* Transworld, 1957, revised edition with Robert Silverberg, published as *Into Space: A Young Person's Guide to Space,* Harper, 1971.

The Exploration of the Moon (illustrated by R. A. Smith), Muller, 1954, Harper, 1955.

The Coast of Coral (illustrated with photographs by Mike Wilson), Harper, 1956.

The Reefs of Taprobane: Underwater Adventures around Ceylon, Harper, 1957.

The Making of a Moon: The Story of the Earth Satellite Program, Harper, 1957, 2nd edition, 1958.

Voice across the Sea, Harper, 1958, revised edition, 1975.

(With Mike Wilson) *Boy beneath the Sea* (juvenile), Harper, 1958.

The Challenge of the Spaceship: Previews of Tomorrow's World (essays), Harper, 1959, reissued, Pocket Books, 1980.

(With M. Wilson) *The First Five Fathoms: A Guide to Underwater Adventure* (juvenile), Harper, 1960.

The Challenge of the Sea (juvenile; ALA Notable Book; illustrated by Alex Schomburg), Holt, 1960.

(With M. Wilson) *Indian Ocean Adventure* (juvenile), Harper, 1961.

Profiles of the Future: An Inquiry into the Limits of the Possible, Harper, 1962, revised edition, Holt, 1984.

(With M. Wilson) *The Treasure of the Great Reef*, Harper, 1964, revised edition, Ballantine, 1974.

(With M. Wilson) *Indian Ocean Treasure* (juvenile), Harper, 1964.

(With the editors of *Life*) *Man and Space*, Time-Life, 1964.

Voices from the Sky: Previews of the Coming Space Age, Harper, 1965, reissued, Pocket Books, 1980.

(Editor) *Time Probe: Sciences in Science Fiction*, Delacorte, 1966.

(Editor) *The Coming of the Space Age: Famous Accounts of Man's Probing of the Universe*, Meredith, 1967.

The Promise of Space, Harper, 1968, reissued, Berkley, 1985.

(With Neil Armstrong, Michael Collins, Edwin E. Aldrin, Jr., Gene Farmer, and Dora Jane Hamblin) *First on the Moon*, Little, Brown, 1970.

(With Chesley Bonestell) *Beyond Jupiter: The Worlds of Tomorrow*, Little, Brown, 1972.

Report on Planet Three and Other Speculations (essay collection), Harper, 1972.

(Contributor) *Mars and the Mind of Man*, Harper, 1973.

(With others) *Technology and the Frontiers of Knowledge* (lectures), Doubleday, 1975.

The View from Serendip (autobiography), Random House, 1977.

(With Simon Welfare and John Fairley) *Arthur C. Clarke's Mysterious World* (based on television series), A. & W. Publishers, 1980.

Ascent to Orbit, a Scientific Autobiography: The Technical Writings of Arthur C. Clarke, Wiley, 1984.

1984: Spring—A Choice of Futures, Ballantine, 1984.

(With S. Welfare and J. Fairley) *Arthur C. Clarke's World of Strange Powers* (based on television series), Putnam, 1985.

(With Peter Hyams) *The Odyssey File*, Ballantine, 1985.

Arthur C. Clarke's July 20, 2019: Life in the Twenty-first Century, Macmillan, 1986.

Arthur C. Clarke's Chronicles of the Strange and Mysterious, edited by S. Welfare and J. Fairley, Collins, 1987.

Astonding Days (science-fictional autobiography), Bantam, 1989.

Fiction:

Prelude to Space, World Editions, 1951, new edition published as *Master of Space*, Lancer, 1961, another edition published as *The Space Dreamers*, Lancer, 1969.

The Sands of Mars, Sidgwick & Jackson, 1951, Gnome Press, 1952.

Islands in the Sky (juvenile), Winston, 1952, reissued, New American Library, 1987.

Childhood's End, Ballantine, 1953, reissued, Del Rey, 1981.

Against the Fall of Night, Gnome Press, 1953, reissued, Berkley, 1983, revised edition published as *The City and the Stars*, Harcourt, 1956, reissued, New American Library, 1987.

Expedition to Earth (short stories), Ballantine, 1953.

Earthlight, Ballantine, 1955.

Reach for Tomorrow (short stories), Ballantine, 1956.

The Deep Range, Harcourt, 1957, reissued, New American Library, 1987.

Tales from the White Hart (story collection), Ballantine, 1957, reissued, 1981.

The Other Side of the Sky: Stories of the Future (story collection), Harcourt, 1958, reissued, New American Library, 1987.

Across the Sea of Stars (story collection; includes *Childhood's End* and *Earthlight*), Harcourt, 1959.

A Fall of Moondust, Harcourt, 1961.

From the Oceans, from the Stars (story collection; includes *The Deep Range* and *The City and the Stars*), Harcourt, 1962.

Tales of Ten Worlds (story collection), Harcourt, 1962, reissued, New American Library, 1987.

Dolphin Island: A Story of the People of the Sea (juvenile), Holt, 1963, reissued, Penguin Books, 1986.

Glide Path, Harcourt, 1963, reissued, New American Library, 1987.

An Arthur C. Clarke Omnibus (contains *Childhood's End, Prelude to Space,* and *Expedition to Earth*), Sidgwick & Jackson, 1965.

Prelude to Mars (story collection; includes *Prelude to Space* and *The Sands of Mars*), Harcourt, 1965.

The Nine Billion Names of God: The Best Short Stories of Arthur C. Clarke, Harcourt, 1967.

2001: A Space Odyssey (novel; ALA Notable Book), New American Library, 1968, new edition, 1982.

A Second Arthur C. Clarke Omnibus (contains *A Fall of Moondust, Earthlight,* and *The Sands of Mars*), Sidgwick & Jackson, 1968.

The Lion of Comarre, and Against the Fall of the Night, Harcourt, 1968, reissued, 1986.

(Author of foreword) *Three for Tomorrow*, Meredith, 1969.

Of Time and Stars: The Worlds of Arthur C. Clarke (short stories), Gollancz, 1972.

The Lost Worlds of 2001, New American Library, 1972.

The Wind from the Sun: Stories of the Space Age, Harcourt, 1972.

Angus Wells, editor, *The Best of Arthur C. Clarke 1937-1971*, Sidgwick & Jackson, 1973, published as two volumes, Volume 1: *1937-1955,*, Volume 2: *1956-1972*, 1977.

Rendezvous with Rama, Harcourt, 1973, large print edition, G. K. Hall, 1980, reissued, Ballantine, 1988.

Imperial Earth: A Fantasy of Love and Discord, Gollancz, 1975, expanded version published as *Imperial Earth*, Harcourt, 1976, large print edition, G. K. Hall, 1980.

Four Great Science Fictin Novels (contains *The City and the Stars, The Deep Range, A Fall of Moondust,* and *Rendezvous with Rama*), Gollancz, 1978.

The Fountains of Paradise, Harcourt, 1979, large print edition, G. K. Hall, 1980.

2010: Odyssey Two, Ballantine, 1982.

(Editor with George Proctor) *The Science Fiction Hall of Fame* Volume 3: *The Nebula Winners 1965-1969*, Avon, 1982.

The Sentinel: Masterworks of Science Fiction and Fantasy (short stories), Berkley, 1983.

Selected Works, Heinemann, 1985.

The Songs of Distant Earth, Del Rey, 1986.

(Author of afterword) Paul Preuss, *Breaking Strain*, Avon, 1987.

2061: Odyssey Three, Del Rey, 1988.

A Meeting with Medusa (bound with *Green Mars* by Kim Stanley Robinson), Tor Books, 1988.

(With Gentry Lee) *Cradle*, Warner, 1988.

(Author of afterword) P. Preuss, *Maelstrom*, Avon, 1988.

(With G. Lee) *Rama II*, Bantam, 1989.

(With G. Lee) *The Garden of Rama*, Bantam, 1990.

Opus 700, Gollancz, 1990.

Screenplays:

(With Stanley Kubrick) "2001: A Space Odyssey," Metro-Goldwyn-Meyer, 1968.

Also author of television screenplay "All the Time in the World."

Commentator:

"The Communications Revolution Series" (film or videocassette), MTI Film & Video.

Other:

Also author and host of television series "Arthur C. Clarke's Mysterious World," ITV (England), 1980, "The World of Strange Powers," ITV, 1984, PBS-TV, February 6, 1988, and "The Future with Arthur C. Clarke," 1990, and a movie treatment based on *Cradle*.

Clarke's books have been translated into more than thirty languages, including Polish, Russian, French, German, Spanish, Serbo-Croatian, Greek, Hebrew, and Dutch. Contributor of more than six hundred articles and short stories, occasionally under pseudonyms E. G. O'Brien and Charles Willis, to numerous magazines, including *Harper's, UNESCO Courier, Modern Science Fiction, Playboy, New York Times Magazine, Vogue, Holiday,* and *Horizon.*

■ Adaptations

"2001: A Space Odyssey" (record or cassette), Caedmon, 1975.

"A Fall of Moondust" (record), Harcourt, 1976.

"Transit of Earth, The Nine Billion Names of God, The Star" (record or cassette; based on short stories), Caedmon, 1977.

"Rescue Party" (film; based on short story), BFA Educational Media, 1978.

"Childhood's End" (cassette or record), Caedmon, 1978.

"Fountains of Paradise" (cassette or record), Caedmon, 1978.

"2010: Odyssey Two" (cassette), Caedmon, 1982, (motion picture), Metro-Goldwyn-Mayer/United Artists, 1984.

Keir Dullea as he appeared in the 1968 M-G-M film "2001: A Space Odyssey."

"The Star" (based on short story), episode for "The New Twilight Zone," CBS-TV, 1985.
"Reading Science Fiction" (filmstrip with cassette), Random House, 1986.

■ Work In Progress

Credo for Doubleday; introduction to *Project Solar Sail* for New American Library; afterword to *Venus Prime IV: The Medusa Encounter* and to *Venus Prime V: The Diamond Moon*, both for Avon; *Tales from Planet Earth* for Bantam; *First Contact* for New American Library; *Astounding Days* for Bantam; *Beyond the Fall of Night* for Putnam; foreword for *Space Commerce* (working title) by McLucas; *Rama Revealed* with G. Lee for Bantam; *The Ghost from the Grand Banks* for Gollancz; *Venus Prime VI* for Avon/Preiss; *Arthur C. Clarke's Century of Mysteries* with John Fairley and Simon Welfare, for Collins; "The Future with Arthur C. Clarke" for television; "A Fall of Moondust" (a television miniseries) for Paramount; "The Deplorable Inventions of Arthur C. Clarke," for television.

Several of Clarke's books have been optioned for films: "The Songs of Distant Earth," "The Fountains of Paradise," "Cradle," and "Childhood's End."

■ Sidelights

Arthur C. Clarke is author of over fifty books, six hundred articles and short stories, several television series, a number of screenplays, and has even acted in movies and commercials. Clarke, in his seventies, is an avid scuba diver who has spent most of his life living in remote Sri Lanka, and is in constant communication with the world through the satellite technology he is credited with inventing.

As a T.V. commentator with Walter Cronkite, Clarke covered the Apollo missions and has come to count many astronauts, scientists and authors among his friends. He is recipient of numerous prizes for science and science-fiction writing, and shared an Oscar nomination with Stanley Kubrick for the screenplay of *2001: A Space Odyssey*.

A vocal advocate for world peace, Clarke has spoken at various conventions, before the U.S. Senate, N.A.S.A., the United Nations, and UNESCO. He is Chancellor of the University of Moratuwa near Colombo, Sri Lanka, where he supports, and is supported by, a large household of animals and friends.

Clarke was born in Minehead, a coastal town in Somerset, England. "The fact that I was born half a mile from the sea—or at least from an arm of the Bristol Channel, which to a child seemed positively oceanic—has certainly affected all my life.

"Much of my youth was spent on the Minehead beach, exploring rock pools and building wave-defying-battlements. Even now I feel completely relaxed only by the edge of the sea—or, better still, hovering weightless in the sea, over the populous and polychromatic landscape of my favorite reef. So in an earlier age I would probably have written stories about the sea. However, I was born at the time when men were first thinking seriously of escaping from their planetary cradle, and so my imagination was deflected into space.

"Yet first I made a curious detour, which is obviously of great importance to me because it involves virtually the only memory I have of my father—a shadowy figure who has left no other mark, even though I was over thirteen when he died. The date would have been around 1925. We were riding together in a small pony cart near the Somerset farm into which he had sunk what was left of his World War I army gratuity, after an earlier and still more disastrous adventure as a gentleman farmer. As he opened a pack of cigarettes, he handed me the card inside; it was one of a series illustrating prehistoric animals. From that moment, I became hooked on dinosaurs, collected all the cards on the subject I could and used them in class to illustrate little adventure stories I told the other children in the village school. These must have been my first ventures into fiction.

"There is a certain irony in the fact that tobacco peddling (one of the few activities for which I consider a mandatory death penalty justified) had such a decisive and beneficial impact on my career. To this day I retain my fascination with dinosaurs and eagerly look forward to the time when the genetic engineers will recreate the tyrannosaur.

"For a couple of years I collected fossils and at one time even acquired a mammoth's tooth, until the main focus of my interest shifted rather abruptly from the past to the future. Once again, I can recall exactly how this happened, though almost all the other events of my childhood seem irretrievably lost. There were three separate crucial incidents, all of equal importance, and I can even date them with some precision. The earliest was in 1929, when at the age of twelve I saw my first science-fiction magazine, the November, 1928 *Amazing Stories.*...It really *is* amazing, for a reason that neither the editor, Hugo Gernsback, nor the artist, Frank Paul, could ever have guessed. A spaceship looking like a farm silo with picture windows is disgorging its exuberant passengers onto a tropical beach, above which floats the orange ball of Jupiter, filling half the sky. The foreground is, alas, improbable because the temperature of the Jovian satellites is around minus 150 degrees centigrade. But the giant planet is painted with what has proved to be such stunning accuracy that one could

use this cover to make a very good case for precognition. Frank Paul has shown turbulent cloud formations, cyclonic patterns and enigmatic white structures like earth-sized amoebas that were not revealed until the Voyager missions over fifty years later. *How did he know?*

"Young readers of today, born into a world in which science-fiction magazines, books and movies are part of everyday life, cannot possibly imagine the impact of such garish pulps as that old *Amazing* and its colleagues *Astounding and Wonder.* Of course, the literary standards were usually abysmal—but the stories brimmed with ideas and amply evoked that sense of wonder that is, or should be, one of the goals of the best fiction. No less a critic than C. S. Lewis has described the ravenous addiction that these magazines inspired in him; the same phenomenon has led me to call science fiction the only genuine consciousness-expanding drug."[1]

When Clarke's father died, the family moved to a small farm in Taunton, where he built a telescope out of cardboard tubes and old lenses and proceeded to map the moon. In later years he made an audio transmitter by modulating the light beam from a recycled bicycle lamp.

1927-1936. Clarke attended Huish's Grammar School in Taunton, Somerset. "During my lunch hour away from school I used to haunt the local Woolworths in search of my fix, which cost threepence a shot, roughly a quarter today. Much of the hard-earned money my widowed mother had saved for my food went on these magazines, and I set myself the goal of acquiring complete runs. By 1940 I had almost succeeded—but, alas, all my beloved pulps disappeared during the war years. That collection would now be worth thousands of dollars.

"In 1930 I came under the spell of a considerably more literate influence when I discovered in the Minehead Public Library W. Olaf Stapledon's just published *Last and First Men.* No book before or since has had such an impact on my imagination; the Stapledonian vistas of millions and hundreds of millions of years, the rise and fall of civilizations and entire races of men, changed my whole outlook on the universe and has influenced much of my writing ever since.

"By the time I encountered Stapledon I had begun my secondary education in the nearby town of Taunton, making the 10-mile round trip by bicycle ever day *after* sorting the local mail in the small hours of the morning and then delivering it. It was

Clarke's 1986 work about a fallen paradise.

at Huish's Grammar School—now Richard Huish College—that I began to write sketches and short stories for the school magazine.

"I can still recall those editorial sessions fifty years ago. About once a week, after class, our English master, Capt. E. B. Mitford (who was a fiery Welshman) would gather his schoolboy staff together, and we would all sit around a table on which there was a large bag of assorted toffees. Bright ideas were rewarded instantly; Mitty invented positive reinforcement years before B. F. Skinner. He also employed a heavy ruler for *negative* reinforcement, but this was used only in class—never, so far as I recall, at editorial conferences.

"My very first printed words thus appeared in the *Huish Magazine*, and from the beginning my science-fiction tendencies were obvious. The following Christmas, 1933 message purports to come from 'Ex-Sixth Former,' stationed at a torrid and high-altitude Outpost of Empire (Vrying Pan, British Malaria).

"'The precautions we have to take to preserve our lives are extraordinary. Our houses are built on the principle of the Dewar vacuum flask, to keep out the heat, and the outsides are silvered to reflect the sunlight....We have to take great care to avoid cutting ourselves in any way, for if this happens our blood soon boils and evaporates.'

"Such attention to technical detail shows that even at sixteen I was already a hard-core science-fiction (as opposed to fantasy) writer. Credit for this must go to the book that had almost as great an impact on me as Stapledon's epic and that illustrates rather well the fundamental distinction between art and science. No one else could ever have created *Last and First Men*, but, if the American author David Lasser had not written *The Conquest of Space*, in 1931, someone else would certainly have done it soon. The time was ripe.

"Although there was already considerable German and Russian literature on the subject, *The Conquest of Space* was the very first book in the English language to discuss the possibility of flight to the moon and planets and to describe the experiments

Michael Whalen's jacket painting for the 1987 hardcover.

and dreams (mostly the latter) of the early rocket pioneers. Only a few hundred copies of the British edition were sold, but chance brought one of them to a bookstore a few yards from my birthplace. I saw it in the window, knew instinctively that I *had* to read it and persuaded my good-natured Aunt Nellie, who was looking after me while Mother struggled to run the farm and raise my three siblings, to buy it on the spot. And so I learned, for the first time, that space travel was not merely fiction. *One day it could really happen.* Soon afterward I discovered the existence of the British Interplanetary Society, and my fate was sealed."[1]

1936-1941. Unable to complete his education because of the expense, Clarke went to London to work as an auditor of teachers' pensions for His Majesty's Exchequer and Audit Department. During this time he wrote reviews, articles and stories for fan magazines and science-fiction magazines and became very active in the British Interplanetary Society (B.I.S.) which met at local pubs.

1941-1946. During World War II, Clarke served as a flight lieutenant in the Royal Air Force. Because of his poor eyesight he could not become a pilot, so he was assigned to work as a radar instructor and technical officer. "I specialised in radar and was eventually in charge of the first Ground Controlled Approach (G.C.A.) unit during its experiment trials, taking it over for the R.A.F. from its American inventors. During this period I published a number of papers on electronics and also sold my first science-fiction stories."[2]

In October, 1945, he published an article in *Wireless World* entitled "Extraterrestrial Relays: Can Rocket Stations Give Worldwide Radio Coverage?" in which he suggested communications satellites in stationary orbits. This concept of geosynchronous communications evolved into "Early Bird" twenty years later, and the orbital pathways now used by multiple communications satellites has been named "The Clarke Belt." This area is 22,300 miles above the earth, and satellites placed within the belt remain almost motionless due to the synchronous rotation of the earth. Clarke calls this "The most important idea of my life....This was the first proposal for the use of satellites for radio and television communication. Had I realized how quickly the idea would materialize I would have attempted to patent it—though it is some slight consolation to know that an application would probably have failed in 1945."[3]

1946-1948. Clarke studied at Kings College, Cambridge, receiving his B.A. of Science in physics and math with first class honors.

1949-1951. He began graduate school, but his dean suggested he take a job working as the assistant editor of *Science Abstracts*, published by the Institute of Electrical Engineers. "It was certainly a fascinating job. Every science journal in the world arrived on my desk in all languages. It was a job which suited me perfectly, but in two years my first books and articles had started to sell. My part-time income was higher than my full-time. I just resigned and that was it. A year later, in 1952, my book *The Exploration of Space* was taken up by the Book-of-the-Month Club and, of course, I was sitting pretty."[4]

During this period he was president of the British Interplanetary Society, whose oldest member, recruited by Clarke, was George Bernard Shaw, then in his nineties. Members of B.I.S. were considered eccentrics, if not lunatics, because "it would not be a big-headed exaggeration to say that we carried the torch for space flight. There was still a bit of a tendency in the corresponding American Rocket Society to regard space flight as a bit far out. They tended to concentrate on more immediate applications like guided missiles."[1]

Clarke also took up scuba diving. "Sea and space—to me these are two sides of the same coin. Looking back upon the last three decades, I now realize that it was my interest in astronautics that led me to the ocean. The process seems so inevitable that I grow more than a little impatient with those people who ask: 'What *are* you doing underwater when you've written so many books about exploring space?'

"Well, both involve exploration—but that's not the only reason. When the first skin-diving equipment started to appear in the late 1940s, I suddenly realized that here was a cheap and simple way of imitating one of the most magical aspects of spaceflight—'weightlessness.' In those days, many physiologists were firmly convinced that the apparent absence of gravity would be fatal to the human organism: the blood would rush to the head, vertigo would be incapacitating, the heart would race out of control, etc., etc. We 'space cadets,' on the other hand, were equally certain that weightlessness would be a delightful experience—as, on the whole, it has turned out to be.

"I can remember when I had learned to use the basic flipper-and-face-mask gear, how I used to dive to the bottom of the local swimming pool, close my eyes and spin around in the water until I

Arthur C. Clarke, the great visionary of his time. (Photo by Dilip Mehta/Contact.)

had deliberately disoriented myself. Then I used to imagine that I was a spaceman and ask myself the question, 'Which way is up?' I never dreamed that, twenty years later, I would be taking *real* space-men underwater.

"In due course I graduated to scuba gear and to the open sea. (Well, to the English Channel, which in those days was not carpeted—top and bottom—with oil-tankers.)"[5]

"Despite these influences, I was well over thirty before my writing changed from a pleasant and occasionally profitable hobby to a profession. The Civil Service, the Royal Air Force, and editorship of a scientific journal provided my bread and butter until 1950. By that time I had published numerous stories and articles and a slim technical book, *Interplanetary Flight*. The modest success of this volume led me to seek a wider public with *The Exploration of Space*, which the Book-of-the-Month Club, in a moment of wild abandon in 1952, made a dual selection. To allay the alarm of its anxious readership, Clifton Fadiman explained in the club's newsletter that *The Exploration of Space* was no mad fantasy but a serious and level-headed work because 'Mr. Clarke does not appear to be a very imaginative man.' I've never quite forgiven him; and my agent, Scott Meredith, has never forgotten my plaintive query: 'What *is* the Book-of-the-Month Club?'

"This stroke of luck in being chosen by the club—repeated exactly thirty years later with *2010: Odyssey Two*, so I can claim it wasn't a fluke—encouraged me to give up my editorial job and become a full-time writer. It was not a very daring or heroic decision. If all else failed, I could always go back to the farm."[1]

June, 1953. Clarke married Marilyn Mayfield of Jacksonville, Florida, but the marriage soon soured. "In a remarkably short time, with consider-able initial impetus from a disintegrating marriage, I was on my way to the mecca of all undersea explorers, the Australian Great Barrier Reef.

"I can recommend the sea voyage from London to Sydney for anyone who wants both to read *The Lord of the Rings* and to write a novel of his/her own—though I cannot claim to have produced the whole of *The City and the Stars* aboard the P & O's venerable *Himalaya*. A good deal of my time was spent at the bottom of the swimming pool, hoping to improve the capacity of my lungs, since there was no guarantee that underwater breathing equipment would be available in the remoter regions of the Reef. (It wasn't.) Eventually I was able to stay submerged for almost four minutes, but then gave up out of consideration for the other passengers, who viewed my activities with increasing alarm.

"It was, indeed, a foolish exercise, and I am perhaps lucky to have survived. Many divers have killed themselves by this trick of 'hyperventilation'—flushing out the CO2 in the lungs by taking deep, rapid breaths, thus inhibiting the normal breathing reflex and destroying, for several minutes, any further desire for oxygen. Hyperventilation can also produce permanent brain damage. My God, do you suppose...?

"Anyway, in mid-December 1954 I arrived safely in Colombo, the largest city and main port of Ceylon. The *Himalaya* would be there for half a day, which allowed time for a fair amount of local sightseeing."[6]

"There was just time for a visit to the world-famous zoo when I met the assistant director, Rodney Jonklaas—a trained zoologist and the only expert skin diver I know who *never* used a snorkel (I think he can breathe through the back of his neck). He convinced me that if I survived the perils of the Great Barrier Reef, I should look at the seas of Ceylon. In 1956 I followed his advice, never imagining that I would get hooked and would make the island my home. For...years I have left it only with great reluctance, and only for unavoidable reasons.

"But Ceylon, although it is much better off than India, Pakistan, and newly formed Bangladesh, is no earthly paradise; it has serious social and economic problems. Like New York, it is a fascinating place to visit, but anyone considering permanent residency should think twice. He must be prepared to face acute shortages of consumer goods—film, razor blades, suntan lotion, carbon paper, records—all the little necessities of life we take for granted in the West. Too, unless he has a fondness for ferocious curries, he may find the food rather monotonous. And, of course, it is very hot for much of the year, though the presence of the sea—never more than sixty miles away—has a moderating influence, and the hundred-plus extremes found in India are very rare. I have never been as uncomfortable in Ceylon as I have been in, say Washington, D.C.

"Because the island is so close to the equator, the length of the day hardly varies throughout the year; it is always dark by 7 P.M., and there is not much to do after sunset. A few cinemas and modest nightclubs provide the available entertainment—and there is, as yet, no television. You're on your own as soon as the sun commits its spectacular nightly suicide.

"I long ago accepted these disadvantages, such as they are; indeed, to a writer, many of them are positive boons. Over the years I have built up a large library, and, if all else fails, the Great Books could keep me busy....For other stimuli I have a small computer, a beloved German shepherd named Sputnik, a battery of cameras and a fully equipped darkroom, a Questar telescope and a thousand miles of coastline to explore."[5]

1956. Clarke moved to Sri Lanka, formerly known as Ceylon or Serendip, where he lived with his partner and former *Life* photographer, Mike Wilson, and his wife. But because of the high taxes on foreigners, he had to leave from time to time. "During my years of tax-imposed exile from Sri Lanka, when I was compelled to absent myself from the country for at least six months out of every twelve, I filled in some of the time very profitably and pleasantly by lecturing. Much has been written about the horrors of the American lecture circuit, but I was lucky. I had the best agent in the business (Bill Colston Leigh), and when I gave him the dates between which I was available, I could confidently leave all the details to him and his efficient staff. I would arrive in New York, be handed an itinerary and a wad of tickets—and thereafter merely followed instructions, like a well-programmed computer. Never once did I have to send the Leigh Bureau the equivalent of G. K. Chesterton's fabled telegram, which in my case might have read: AM IN GOPHER CROSSING SOUTH DAKOTA STOP. WHERE SHOULD I BE? And only once did I miss an engagement—when a metre of snow descended on my Greyhoud bus *and* the lecture venue towards which I was heading, thus neatly cancelling out the audience as well."[6]

However, Clarke was sure he had found his true home. "Not until I came to Ceylon did I fall in love with an exquisite arc of beach on the island's south coast and decide to establish a home there.

"It takes a long time to see the obvious, and in this case perhaps there was some excuse. After all, there was little apparent similarity between dull gray English sea and turquoise Indian Ocean; between boardinghouses, Butlin camp, railway station—and an unbroken wall of closely packed coconut palms.

"One day, after a lecture somewhere in the American Midwest, a young lady asked me just *why* I liked Ceylon. I was about to switch on the sound track I had played a hundred times before, when suddenly I saw those two beaches, both so far away. Do not ask me why it happened then; but in that moment of double vision, I knew the truth.

"The drab, chill northern beach on which I had so often shivered through an English summer was merely the pale reflection of an ultimate and long-unsuspected beauty. Like the three princes of Serendip, I had found far more than I was seeking—in Serendip itself.

"Ten thousand kilometres from the place where I was born, I had come home.

"Towards the end of 1957, my love affair with Ceylon and its seas was interrupted by a persistent beeping at 20.005 megahertz.

"There are some traumatic experiences that remain frozen in time, so that every man remembers to the end of his life exactly where he was when he heard, for example, of the assassination of John F. Kennedy or the attack on Pearl Harbor. In my case, I can add the dropping of the first A-bomb and the orbiting of the first Sputnik.

"In the small hours of 5 October, on the opening day of the Eighth International Astronautical Congress, I was awakened in my Barcelona hotel room by a phone call from London; the *Daily Express* wanted my comments on the new Russian satellite. Being as surprised as everyone else, I was hardly in a position to make any informed statement; after the initial exhilaration, I realised that I would have to hurry back to the typewriter. The

Roy Scheider and John Lithgow starred in the 1984 United Artists release "2010."

previous month I had published *The Making of a Moon: The Story of the Earth Satellite Program,* and it was now obvious that the United States Navy's Vanguard—to which my book had been largely devoted—was not going to be first into space."[6]

"The first steps on the rather long road to '2001: A Space Odyssey' were taken in March 1964, when Stanley Kubrick wrote to me in Ceylon, saying that he wanted to do the proverbial 'really good' science-fiction movie. His main interests, he explained, lay in these broad areas: '(1) The reasons for believing in the existence of intelligent extra-terrestrial life. (2) The impact (and perhaps even lack of impact in some quarters) such discovery would have on Earth in the near future.'

"As this subject had been my main preoccupation (apart from time out for World War II and the Great Barrier Reef) for the previous thirty years, this letter naturally aroused my interest. The only movie of Kubrick's I had then seen was 'Lolita,' which I had greatly enjoyed, but rumors of 'Dr. Strangelove' had been reaching me in increasing numbers. Here, obviously, was a director of unusual quality, who wasn't afraid of tackling far-out subjects. It would certainly be worthwhile having a talk with him; however, I refused to let myself get too excited, knowing from earlier experience that the mortality rate of movie projects is about ninety-nine percent.

"Meanwhile, I examined my published fiction for film-worthy ideas and very quickly settled on a short story called 'The Sentinel,' written over the 1948 Christmas holiday for a BBC contest. (It didn't place.) This story developed a concept that has since been taken quite seriously by the scientists concerned with the problem of extraterrestrials, or ETs for short.

"During the last decade, there has been a quiet revolution in scientific thinking about ETs; the view now is that planets are at least as common as stars—of which there are some 100 billion in our local Milky Way galaxy alone. Moreover, it is believed that life will arise automatically and inevitably where conditions are favorable; so there may be civilizations all around us which achieved space travel before the human race existed, and then passed on to heights which we cannot remotely comprehend.

"But if so, why haven't they visited us? In 'The Sentinel,' I proposed one answer (which I now more than half believe myself). We may indeed have had visitors in the past—perhaps millions of years ago, when the great reptiles ruled the Earth.

As they surveyed the terrestrial scene, the strangers would guess that one day intelligence could arise on this planet; so they might leave behind them a robot monitor, to watch and to report. But they would not leave their sentinel on Earth itself, where in a few thousand years it would be destroyed or buried. They would place it on the almost unchanging Moon.

"And they would have a second reason for doing this. To quote from the original story:

"'They would be interested in our civilization only if we proved our fitness to survive—by crossing space and so escaping from the Earth, our cradle. That is the challenge that all intelligent races must meet, sooner or later. It is a double challenge, for it depends in turn upon the conquest of atomic energy, and the last choice between life and death.

"'Once we had passed that crisis, it was only a matter of time before we found the beacon and forced it open. . . .Now we have broken the glass of the fire-alarm, and have nothing to do but to wait.'

"This, then, was the idea which I suggested in my reply to Stanley Kubrick as the take-off point for a movie. The finding—and triggering—of an intelligence detector, buried on the Moon aeons ago, would give all the excuse we needed for the exploration of the Universe."[7]

Kubrick and Clarke were suited to work together. "On our first day together, we talked for eight solid hours about science fiction, 'Dr. Strangelove,' flying saucers, politics, the space program, Senator Goldwater—and, of course, the projected next movie.

"For the next month, we met and talked on an average of five hours a day—at Stanley's apartment, in restaurants and automats, movie houses and art galleries.

"Eventually, the shape of the movie began to emerge from the fog of words. It would be based on 'The Sentinel' and five of my other short stories of space exploration; our private title for the project was 'How the Solar System Was Won.' What we had in mind was a kind of semi-documentary about the first pioneering days of the new frontier; though we soon left that concept far behind, it still seems quite a good idea. Later, I had the quaint experience of buying back—at a nominal fee—my unused stories from Stanley.

"Stanley calculated that the whole project, from starting the script to the release of the movie, would take about two years, and I reluctantly

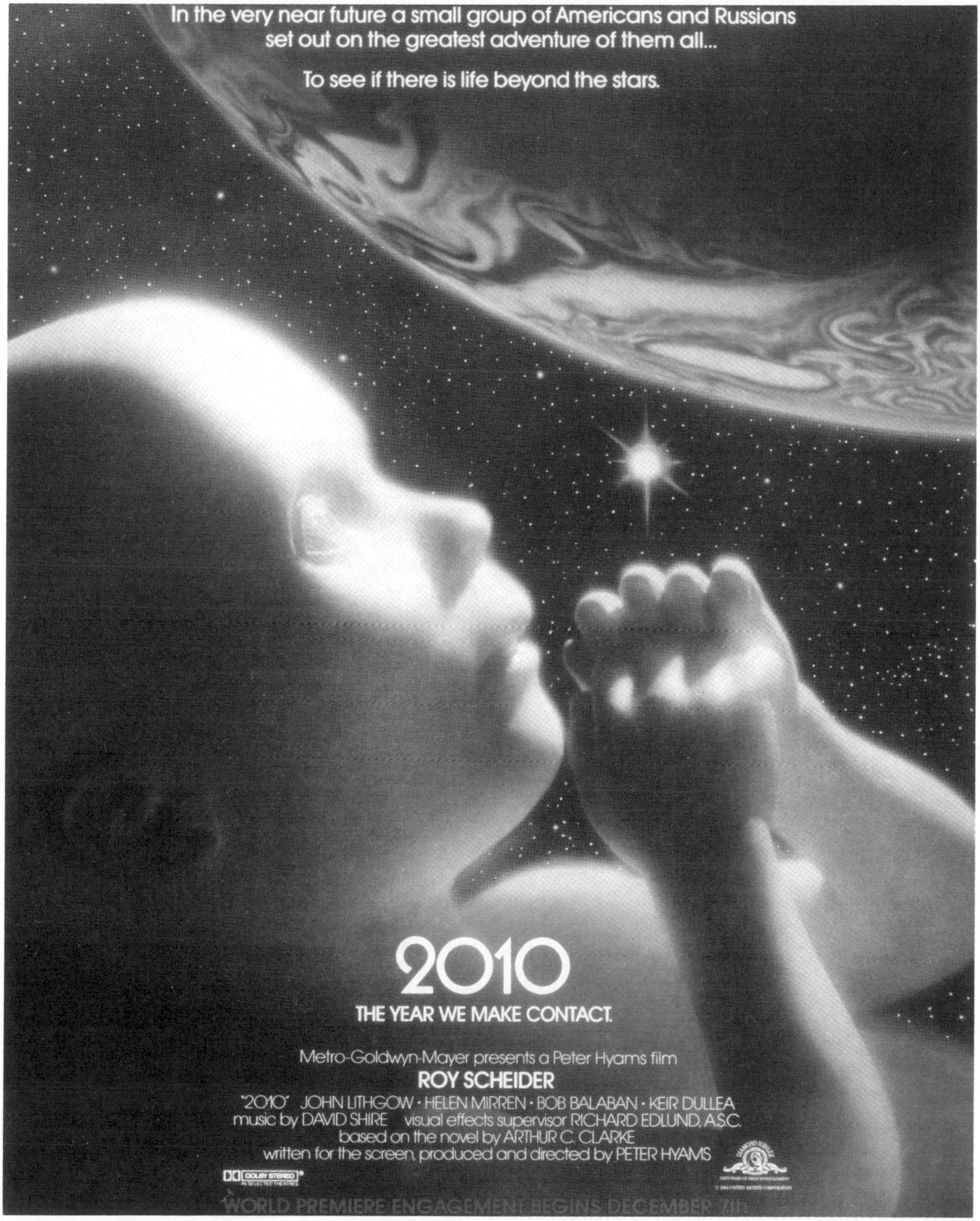

Poster for the movie adaptation of Clarke's 1982 novel.

postponed my return to Ceylon—at least until a treatment had been worked out."[7]

"As I was engaged in writing the novel and screenplay in the United States—specifically, in Room 1008 of the famous Hotel Chelsea on New York's Twenty-third Street—it was necessary for me to become a United States resident, and to go through all the formalities of obtaining a Resident Alien card. This document always made me feel like a certified extraterrestrial, which seemed highly appropriate under the circumstances.

"However, it did complicate my image and make it hard to define my status; it was easy to sympathise with the bafflement of journalists when I explained that I was a British citizen, an American resident, and a Ceylon householder. In fact, I was to be exiled from Ceylon for well over a year, and it is not surprising that during the almost three years of scripting and shooting (at the M.G.M. Elstree Studios, just north of London) I had no time for any writing that did not directly concern '2001.'"[6]

1968. The movie *2001: A Space Odyssey* was released. Both he and Kubrick wrote the screenplay and each won an Oscar nomination for it. Clarke describes the collaborative process. "Once the contracts had been signed, the actual writing took place in a manner which must be unusual, and may be unprecedented. Stanley hates movie scripts; like D. W. Griffith, I think he would prefer to work without one, if it were possible. But he had to have *something* to show MGM what they were buying; so he proposed that we sit down and first write the story as a complete novel. Though I had never collaborated with anyone before in this way, the idea suited me fine.

"Stanley installed me, with electric typewriter, in his Central Park West office, but after one day I retreated to my natural environment in the Hotel Chelsea.

"Every other day Stanley and I would get together and compare notes; during this period we went down endless blind alleys and threw away tens of thousands of words. The scope of the story steadily expanded, both in time and space.

"During this period, the project had various changes of title: it was first announced as 'Journey beyond the Stars'—which I always disliked because there have been so many movie Voyages and Journeys that confusion would be inevitable. Indeed, 'Fantastic Voyage' was coming up shortly, and Salvador Dali had been disporting himself in a Fifth Avenue window to promote it. When I

mentioned this to Stanley, he said, 'Don't worry—we've already booked a window for you.' Perhaps luckily, I never took him up on this.

"The merging of our streams of thought was so effective that, after this lapse of time, I am no longer sure who originated what ideas; we finally agreed that Stanley should have prime billing for the screenplay, while only my name would appear on the novel. Only the germ of the 'Sentinel' concept is now left; the story as it exists today is entirely new—in fact, Stanley was still making major changes at a very late stage in the actual shooting.

"Our brainstorming sessions usually took place in the Kubrick Eastside penthouse off Lexington, presided over by Stanley's charming artist wife Christiane, whom he met while making 'Paths of Glory.' (She appears in its moving final scene—the only woman in the entire film.) Underfoot much of the time were the three—it often seemed more—Kubrick daughters, whom Stanley is in the process of spoiling. Very much of a family man, he has little social life and begrudges all time not devoted to his home or his work."[7]

The initial reviews were poor. "At the beginning, it was a flop. I can well remember, at the premiere, an MGM executive's saying, 'Well, that's the end of Stanley Kubrick.' And the day of the premiere was right after President Johnson announced he wouldn't run again. I remember one of the MGM people saying, 'Well, today, we lost two presidents,' meaning also the president of MGM. The reviews were disastrous, too—the *New York Times'* Renata Adler panned it. I later called her 'the critic who came in from the cold,' because she went back and saw it again and wrote something to the effect that, hmmmm, maybe this isn't so bad, after all."[8]

The novel was published in July, 1968, after the movie's release.

When "man" walked on the moon, Clarke joined Walter Cronkite as a T.V. commentator. "I wasn't a very good prophet. I never really thought a moon landing would occur in my lifetime. But, you know, even the space enthusiasts of my youth didn't believe it would be in this century. When I wrote my book *Prelude to Space* in 1948, I put the landing thirty years in the future, in 1978. I remember thinking when I wrote it, This is hopelessly optimistic.

"When you go to a launch, it is an emotional experience. Television doesn't give any idea of it, really. Walter wiped away a tear or two, as well—

as did Eric Sevareid. The last time I'd cried was when my grandmother died, twenty years before it."[8]

In 1975, when Sri Lanka hosted the Satellite Instructional Television Experiment of India, a satellite ground station was installed on Clarke's roof. He owned the only functioning television in Sri Lanka and encouraged local visitors. As many as fifty people a day sat on his veranda watching programs on family planning, hygiene, and agriculture. Even the president of Sri Lanka, a neighbor, came. "The language problem did not stop viewers sitting for hours, hypnotised by the miracle of images falling down from the sky after a journey of more than seventy thousand kilometres. As I was anxious for as many people as possible to see the programs, I (somewhat rashly) issued an open invitation. So at any moment, a bus was liable to arrive from some remote corner of the island and disgorge a load of virginal viewers."[6] Unfortunately, the experiment ended after a year, and Clarke's television went dead.

1977. Now that he was permanently settled in Sri Lanka, Clarke brought his mother, Nora, to live with him. At the age of eighty-six she wrote a book entitled *My Four Feet on the Ground*, in which she describes the world in which Clarke grew up. "With the appearance of this book, we now have three authors in the family, since my brother Fred's *Small Pipe Central Heating* is a standard reference in its own field."[5]

Clarke's household includes his two secretaries, his partner, Hector Ekanayake, who runs his diving business, Hector's family, and various household servants. Clarke estimates that he supports at least thirty people. The house was formerly owned by the Anglican bishop. His office houses a variety of shortwave radio equipment, computers, VCR's, movie projectors, word processors and many photos of heads of state, astronauts, engineers and celebrities, many of whom have visited Clarke in Sri Lanka and have gone on his underwater safaris.

"I work thirteen to fourteen hours a day, back home. I'm at my desk at seven in the morning. Luckily, my office is three paces from my bedroom. And I find that using a computer is a tremendous time-saver. When I was working on the screenplay of '2010' with Peter Hyams, the director, we communicated by computer link. The transcript of our dialogue is being published in book form: *The Odyssey File.* Also, of course, it helps me that I have a staff. I push a button, I get a cup of tea. Push a button, clean laundry. Which consists of a sarong and a shirt."[9]

1986. Clarke began work on a book with *Omni* magazine called *Arthur C. Clarke's July 20, 2019: A Day in the Life of the 21st Century.* His work was interrupted by the civil war in Sri Lanka between Hindu Tamils and Buddhist Sinhalese. Clarke was writing a chapter on futuristic weapons when a Tamil Tiger bomb exploded in his neighborhood, killing several residents. "Before commenting on the chapter on war. I have to declare my interest— or lack of it. The whole subject disgusts me.

"In the long run—no, the very short run—we have to become intelligent mammals, not turn ourselves back into armored dinosaurs."[10]

Clarke recently published a book for Warner Bros. with Gentry Lee of NASA called *Cradle.* Bantam reportedly paid a four million dollar advance for *Rama II* and the next two collaborative "Rama" novels with Gentry Lee. As a writer, Clarke feels he has been "...Lucky. Unlike most of the writers I know, I had very few setbacks or disappointments, and my rare rejection slips were doubtless justified. And, because every author is unique, the only advice I have ever been able to pass on to would-be writers is incorporated in a few lines on the notorious form letter that Archie, my word processor, spits out for all hopeful correspondents: 'Read at least one book a day, and write as much as you can. Study the memoirs of authors who interest you. (Somerset Maugham's *A Writer's Notebook* is a good example.) Correspondence courses, writer's schools, etc., are probably useful but all the authors I know were self-taught. There is no substitute for living; as Hemingway wisely remarked, 'Writing is not a full-time occupation.'''

"Nor is reading, though it would have to be if I tried to keep up with the avalanche of science fiction now being published. I estimate that almost as much is printed each *day* as appeared every year when I was a boy.

"Today's readers of science fiction are indeed fortunate; this really is the genre's Golden Age. There are dozens of authors at work who can match all but the giants of the past. Yet I do not really envy the young men and women who first encounter science fiction [now], for we old-timers were able to accomplish something unique. We were the last generation able to read *everything.* No one will ever do that again.''[1]

Footnote Sources:

[1] Arthur C. Clarke, "In the Beginning was Jupiter," *New York Times Book Review*, March 6, 1983.

[2] Stanley J. Kunitz, editor, "Arthur Charles Clarke," *Twentieth Century Authors*, H. W. Wilson, 1959.

[3] "Dolphin Island: A Story of the People of the Sea," *Junior Literary Guild*, February, 1963.

[4] Godfrey Smith, "Astounding Story! About a Science Fiction Writer!," *New York Times Magazine*, March 6, 1966.

[5] A. C. Clarke, *1984: Spring: A Choice of Futures*, Del Rey, 1984.

[6] A. C. Clarke, *The View from Serendip*, Del Rey, 1977.

[7] A. C. Clarke, "Son of Doctor Strangelove, or, How I Learned to Stop Worrying and Love Stanley Kubrick," *Turning Points: Essays on the Art of Science Fiction*, edited by Damon Knight, Harper, 1977.

[8] Ken Kelly, "Playboy Interview: Arthur C. Clarke," *Playboy*, July, 1978. Amended by Arthur C. Clarke.

[9] Roger Ebert, "Exploring the Cosmos with Arthur C. Clarke," *Chicago Sun-Times*, December 2, 1984.

[10] Dick Teresi, "Brave New Tales of 2019," *Omni*, September, 1986.

■ For More Information See

Periodicals:

New Worlds, summer, 1950.
Analog, November, 1951.
Book-of-the-Month Club News, June, 1952.
New York Herald Tribune, August 10, 1952, June 25, 1965.
Galaxy, October, 1952.
Space Science Fiction, February, 1953.
Magazine of Fantasy and Science Fiction, October, 1953, November, 1968, November, 1969, September, 1979.
Worlds of If, January, 1954.
New York Times Book Review, March 14, 1954, April 14, 1963, December 3, 1967, August 25, 1968, September 23, 1973, January 18, 1976, October 30, 1977, March 18, 1979, January 23, 1983, May 11, 1986, December 20, 1987.
Venture Science Fiction, July, 1957.
Newsweek, October 30, 1961, September 12, 1966.
Wilson Library Bulletin, March, 1963 (p. 598).
New Yorker, August 9, 1964, May 27, 1967, July 27, 1968, September 21, 1968, August 9, 1969, December 13, 1982 (p. 38ff).
Manchester Guardian, January 20, 1966.
Spectator, April 22, 1966.
Esquire, May, 1966 (p. 114ff).
Horn Book, December, 1966.
Best Sellers, April 15, 1967.
Senior Scholastic, May 9, 1968.
New York Times, May 29, 1968, July 5, 1968, August 22, 1973, December 2, 1984 (section 2, p. 1), February 26, 1985.
Films and Filming, July, 1968 (p. 24ff).
Time, July 19, 1968, September 24, 1973, November 15, 1982, January 11, 1988.

Science, August 30, 1968.
Book World, September 1, 1968, December 19, 1971.
Punch, January 1, 1969.
Economist, January 4, 1969.
Reader's Digest, April, 1969.
Erb-dom, July, 1970 (p. 8ff).
English Journal, December, 1970.
Sky and Telescope, March, 1972.
Publishers Weekly, September 10, 1973, June 14, 1976 (p. 47), August 8, 1977.
American Artist, October, 1973.
Algol, November, 1974 (p. 6ff).
Observer, December 8, 1974.
Prairie Schooner, fall, 1976.
Millimeter, March, 1977 (p. 40ff).
Library Journal, October 1, 1977.
Science Digest, February, 1978 (p. 8ff), March, 1982 (p. 56ff).
Men Only, April, 1978.
Future, May, 1978 (p. 20ff).
Writer's Digest, January, 1979 (p. 24ff).
Omni, March, 1979, December, 1984 (p. 76ff).
Chicago Tribune, April 22, 1982 (p. 12).
Starlog, December, 1982 (p. 30ff).
New York Times Magazine, December 9, 1982 (p. 32ff).
People Weekly, December 20, 1982 (p. 89ff).
Geo, July, 1983 (p. 10ff).
Profiles, October, 1984 (p. 26ff).
Los Angeles, December, 1984 (p. 250ff).
Analog Science Fiction/Science Fact, December, 1983 (p. 6ff), December 17, 1987.
Playboy, July, 1986, January, 1989 (p. 133ff).

Books:

Stanley J. Kunitz, editor, *Twentieth Century Authors, First Supplement* H. W. Wilson, 1955.
Sam Moskowitz, *Seekers of Tomorrow: Masters of Modern Science Fiction,* World, 1966.
Current Biography 1966, H. W. Wilson, 1967.
Jerome Agel, editor, *The Making of Kubrick's 2001,* New American Library, 1970.
Martha E. Ward and Dorothy A. Marquardt, *Authors of Books for Young People,* 2nd edition, Scarecrow, 1971.
Carolyn Geduld, *Filmguide to 2001: A Space Odyssey,* Indiana University Press, 1973.
Contemporary Literary Criticism, Gale, Volume 1, 1973, Volume 4, 1975, Volume 13, 1980, Volume 16, 1981, Volume 18, 1981, Volume 35, 1985.
Donald H. Tuck, compiler, *The Encyclopedia of Science Fiction and Fantasy through 1968,* Advent, 1974.
Thomas D. Clareson, editor, *Voices for the Future: Essays on Major Science Fiction Writers,* Bowling Green University, 1976.
Joseph D. Olander and Martin H. Greenberg, editors, *Arthur C. Clarke,* Taplinger, 1977.
George E. Slusser, *The Space Odysseys of Arthur C. Clarke,* Borgo Press, 1978.
Doris de Montreville and Elizabeth D. Crawford, *Fourth Book of Junior Authors and Illustrators,* H. W. Wilson, 1978.
Dick Riley, editor, *Critical Encounters: Writers and Themes in Science Fiction,* Ungar, 1978.

Experiencing Science, Basic Books, 1978.

Eric S. Rabkin, *Arthur C. Clarke,* Starmont House, 1979, revised edition, 1980.

A. C. Clarke, "Einstein and Science Fiction," *Einstein: The First Hundred Years,* edited by Maurice Goldsmith, Alan Mackay and James Woudhuysen, Pergamon Press, 1980.

Rex Malik, editor, *Future Imperfect: Science Fact and Science Fiction,* Frances Pinter, 1980.

Isaac Asimov, *Asimov on Science Fiction,* Doubleday, 1981.

David N. Samuelson, *Arthur C. Clarke: A Primary and Secondary Bibliography,* G. K. Hall, 1981.

E. F. Bleiler, editor, *Science Fiction Writers,* Scribner, 1982.

Charles Platt, *Dream Makers,* Volume 2, Berkley, 1983.

John Hollow, *Against the Night, the Stars: The Science Fiction of Arthur C. Clarke,* Harcourt, 1983, expanded edition, Ohio University Press, 1987.

Curtis C. Smith, editor, *Twentieth-Century Science-Fiction Writers,* 2nd edition, St. James Press, 1986.

Collections:

Kerlan Collection at the University of Minnesota.
Mugar Memorial Library at Boston University.

Paula Danziger

Born August 18, 1944, in Washington, D.C.; daughter of Samuel (worked in garment district) and Carolyn (a nurse; maiden name, Seigel) Danziger. *Education:* Montclair State College, B.A., 1967, M.A. *Residence:* New York City and Bearsville, N.Y. *Agent:* Donald C. Farber, 99 Park Ave., New York, N.Y. 10016.

■ Career

Substitute teacher, Edison, N.J., 1967; Title I teacher, Highland Park, N.J., 1967-1968; junior-high school English teacher, Edison, N.J., 1968-1970; Lincoln Junior High School, West Orange, N.J., English teacher, 1977-1978; full-time writer, 1978—. Worked for the Educational Opportunity Program, Montclair State College, until 1977.

■ Awards, Honors

New Jersey Institute of Technology Award, and Young Reader Medal Nomination from the California Reading Association, both 1976, Massachusetts Children's Book Award, first runner-up, 1977, winner, 1979, and Nene Award from the Hawaii Association of School Librarians and the Hawaii Library Association, 1980, all for *The Cat Ate My Gymsuit*; one of Child Study Association of America's Children's Books of the Year, 1978, Massachusetts Children's Book Award from the Education Department of Salem State College, 1979, Nene Award, 1980, California Young Reader Medal Nomination, 1981, and Arizona Young Reader Award, 1983, all for *The Pistachio Prescription*; Children's Choice from the International Reading Association and the Children's Book Council, 1979, for *The Pistachio Prescription*, 1980, for *The Cat Ate My Gymsuit*, and *Can You Sue Your Parents for Malpractice?*, 1981, for *There's a Bat in Bunk Five*, and 1983, for *The Divorce Express*.

New Jersey Institute of Technology Award, and selected one of New York Public Library's Books for the Teen Age, both 1980, and Land of Enchantment Book Award from the New Mexico Library Association, 1982, all for *Can You Sue Your Parents for Malpractice?*; Read-a-Thon Author of the Year Award from the Multiple Sclerosis Society, and Parents' Choice Award for Literature from the Parents' Choice Foundation, both 1982, Woodward Park School Annual Book Award, 1983, and South Carolina Young Adult Book Award from the South Carolina Association of School Librarians, 1985, all for *The Divorce Express*; CRABbery Award from Prince George's County Memorial Library System (Md.), 1982, and Young Readers Medal, 1984, both for *There's a Bat in Bunk Five*; Parents' Choice Award for Literature from the Parents' Choice Foundation, exhibited at the Bologna International Children's Book Fair, and selected one of Child Study Association of America's

Children's Books of the Year, all 1985, all for *It's an Aardvark-Eat-Turtle World*.

■ Writings

Young Adult Novels:

The Cat Ate My Gymsuit (Junior Literary Guild selection), Delacorte, 1974.
The Pistachio Prescription, Delacorte, 1978.
Can You Sue Your Parents for Malpractice?, Delacorte, 1979.
There's a Bat in Bunk Five, Delacorte, 1980.
The Divorce Express, Delacorte, 1982, large print edition, G. K. Hall, 1988.
It's an Aardvark-Eat-Turtle World, Delacorte, 1985.
This Place Has No Atmosphere, Delacorte, 1986, large print edition, ABC-CLIO, 1989.
Remember Me to Harold Square, Delacorte, 1987.
Everyone Else's Parents Said Yes, Delacorte, 1989.

■ Adaptations

"The Cat Ate My Gymsuit" (cassette), Listening Library, 1985, (filmstrip with cassette), Cheshire, 1985.
"The Pistachio Prescription" (cassette), Listening Library, 1985.
"There's a Bat in Bunk Five" (cassette), Listening Library, 1985.
"Can You Sue Your Parents for Malpractice?" (cassette; teacher's guide available), Listening Library, 1986.
"The Divorce Express" (cassette; teacher's guide available), Listening Library, 1986.

■ Work In Progress

Sequel to *Everyone Else's Parents Said Yes*, tentatively titled *Mischief Is My Middle Name*. "I've written a third-person narrative. All my previous books are first-person. My protagonist, an eleven-year-old boy, is also a departure because most of my main characters have been girls. Writing third person was fun, a new experience. It allowed me to be more descriptive and to have a larger perspective.

"There's a book I've been wanting to do for a number of years called *Pardon My Two Left Wheels*. Its protagonist, a girl, is confined to a wheelchair. I know it will be difficult for me, as I've spent a lot of time with braces, casts, and crutches myself. But I want this to be a funny book,

because laughing helps us survive adversity. The main theme I'll be exploring is the ways in which people relate and identify with abilities and disabilities. An ex-editor gave me some great advice regarding this protagonist: 'Make sure she has pimples.' And he's right, everyone who's thirteen has pimples, why shouldn't she? Because she's in a wheelchair?"[1]

■ Sidelights

Paula Danziger is one of the best-selling authors for young adults currently working in the United States, perhaps most widely known for *The Cat Ate My Gymsuit*. Her characters tend to be good-hearted 'outlaws' rebelling against rigid and confused parents, dictatorial school systems and unhappy social situations.

"My life as an author began as a small child when I realized that was what I wanted to do and started mentally recording a lot of information and observations. That's also when I started to develop the sense of humor and the sense of perspective that allows me to write the way I do.

"Technically, I suppose that many people would say that I began my career as an author when I signed the contract for my first book in 1973 for *The Cat Ate My Gymsuit*.

"For years I had nightmares about the small Pennsylvania town in which I spent a substantial part of my childhood. We rented a farmhouse, unlikely as that sounds, because my mother was afraid of everything on the farm. I seem to remember that my brother and I were not allowed to touch anything, and were not encouraged to spend a lot of time outside—weird for kids living on a farm. I felt very isolated and buried myself in books. For the first time I realized that my family was hardly 'The Brady Bunch,' that, in fact, my parents were very unhappy and that our family functioned with difficulty.

"On some level I knew I'd grow up to be a writer, especially when my father yelled at me, I'd think, 'That's fine, I'll use this in a book someday.' My favorite game was something I called the Dot Kingdom. By connecting dots, I created all the people, dogs and houses in the kingdom. If I got angry with a character, I'd erase him. Quite a power trip—creating a whole world over which I had absolute control.

"Thank goodness for the local librarian. She gave me lots of wonderful books to read and generally let me know she cared. I devoured one book after another—*Nancy Drew, Sue Barton, Cherry Ames, The Hardy Boys,* all the landmark books.

"My family moved back to New Jersey. I'd been raised to believe that I was not particularly bright, not college material. My father's refrain was, 'Paula can be a secretary.' I certainly have nothing against secretaries, except that I never wanted to be one. Family dynamics were such that I fell into fulfilling their low expectations. 'I'm not supposed to be smarter than my father, so why try,' was my thought. I wrote off-beat features for the school newspaper and a column in the town newspaper. Someone was noticing that I wasn't a total idiot.

"I think I read *Catcher in the Rye* every day for the three years I was in high school. It set me free. It told me that I wasn't alone. Other books important to me were *Pride and Prejudice, Wuthering Heights, A Tree Grows in Brooklyn, Marjorie Morningstar.*

"I desperately wanted to go to college—maybe a state teachers college. Years later I discovered that I was accepted into a special program for kids who didn't work up to their potential.

"Not surprisingly, the town librarian was important to me. One of my college projects was to find an 'average' child and do a study on him or her. The librarian put me in touch with poet John Ciardi's son, who in fact was quite brilliant. My study led to babysitting jobs with the family and attending Breadloaf Writers Conferences with them for several summers. This was no typical *au pair* situation—the kids were not supposed to bother me if I wanted to go to a lecture or a party. I used to spend Christmas with the family. The Ciardis were very special to me.

"John Ciardi taught me more than anyone else about poetry and writing. Their house was full of books, and I borrowed liberally from the shelves. I tried to read e.e. cummings' *anyone lived in a pretty how town* with no success at all. Ciardi taught its meaning to me. It was the best lesson I've ever had in my life. He read the poems and explained them, giving me a sense of language structure.

"During my third summer with the family, I came home from a party one night and Ciardi and I talked for a long, long time. Finally I got up the courage to ask him if he thought I'd ever become a writer someday. 'No, your ego's not strong enough,' was his response. Years later we laughed over the conversation."[1]

Jacket for the 1978 Delacorte edition.

Danziger's first book, *The Cat Ate My Gymsuit,* dedicated to John Ciardi, was published in 1974. "I wrote this book in therapy, bringing newly-drafted pages to many appointments. I'd been in a very serious car accident and writing *Cat* was part of my coming back. The accident—actually there were two—was very freaky. In the first, I was hit from behind by a policeman and knocked into an intersection. The whiplash was immediate, but the damage took a couple of days to appear. As the pain became more severe, my mother drove me to a doctor's appointment. En route, we were hit head-on by another car and I was thrown into the windshield, cut my face and sustained some temporary brain damage. I lost the ability to read. Eventually I entered a master's program in reading. I could write backwards—a perfect mirror image of normal writing. I had recurring nightmares about the accidents and functioned with a great deal of difficulty. My feelings of helplessness and terror dredged up a lot of material from my childhood. It was time for therapy.

"*The Cat Ate My Gymsuit* is in some ways my angriest and most autobiographical book. Like

Marcy, I was a fat kid who hated her father and was frustrated with her mother. My editor would say, 'Paula, the father is too one-dimensional. No father would say that to a daughter.' I'd reply, 'Wanna bet?' I don't think the father is a complete monster. Toward the end of the sequel, *There's a Bat in Bunk Five*, particularly after his heart attack, he became more sympathetic and Marcy has to confront her fear of losing him.

"I handed a set of galleys of *Cat* to my father and said, 'Daddy, I love you.' I hardly ever called him Daddy since growing up, always Sam. His reading the book made an enormous difference in our relationship.

"An important letter I've received from a reader was in response to *The Cat Ate My Gymsuit*. When I was a child, I used to ask my parents if I was adopted. And my mother, understanding the implications of my question, would respond with 'No, I love you and your father loves you.' I used those lines in *Cat*. Well, one of my readers, who had adopted children, let me know that out of context, the lines were quite devastating in a way I had not intended. From all subsequent editions of the book, I had those lines deleted. I wrote back to her, and she answered that she was the one who was upset, not her children. Through a misunderstanding, I had caused hurt, and I didn't like that. I felt good about the revision."[1]

The Cat Ate My Gymsuit garnered its fair share of favorable reviews, and Danziger likes to point out that fifteen years after its original publication it's still going strong. But the approbation—as with all her books—has not been unanimous. "I once wrote an article, 'Why I Will Never Win the Newbery.'"[1]

Perry Nodelman, writing in *Children's Literature in Education*, finds fault with what he discerned as the willful 'typicality' of the book. "In *The Cat Ate My Gymsuit*, readers find out many things about Marcy Lewis, her family, her appearance, and her attitudes. But interestingly enough, not one of these details is unusual or surprising; none of them separates Marcy from the vast sea of theoretically typical teenage girls we all assume exists somewhere outside our immediate acquaintance in towns we have never visited.

"In carefully avoiding distinguishing details, *The Cat Ate My Gymsuit* prevents our consciousness of otherness. In fact, we cannot possibly understand the story unless we fill in its exceedingly vague outlines with knowledge from our own experience. Marcy Lewis has no life unless we give it to her;

her town and her school have no physical substance unless we provide it. The book demands, not distance, but involvement."[2]

"I basically don't listen to critics very much. I listen to my editor and to friends whose opinions I trust. If I were to define myself according to what reviewers said about my work, I'd be in deep trouble. I am aware that certain critics have said my books are 'light.' I know that certain critics have been discomforted by my sense of humor and the attention I pay to controversial matters: the Holocaust, the homeless, divorce, bi-racial kids, and so on. Sometimes I really wonder; a number of reviewers don't seem to like kids or books. Why do they do what they do?

"I don't like reviewers who don't seem to have a clear idea of the kids who will be reading the books, or I don't like reviewers who are more concerned about what they write, rather than what they read. There have been reviews that I think are good, not necessarily because they say that my books are great (although I do like those a lot), but those who offer constructive criticism, where I can learn something about becoming a better writer. I also like reviews that are written by someone that I know is a good writer. Anne Tyler once reviewed one of my books. I was so excited because I love her books and because she wrote a good review.

"I was autographing books at the American Library Association Convention and people were *actually* lining up for my signature. A librarian called out, 'I'm not going to stand in line, but I'll tell you one thing, regardless of what I may think of your books, the kids would kill me if I don't order them.' And that is what matters to me that the kids like my books, and that my books touch their lives and make them feel less alone. They are the best gauge."[1]

"If when we start to write we say, 'I'm going to teach them this,' rather than tell the story we care about, we're in trouble. But when we're telling [the story], again it comes back, for me, to survival—when we're talking about what I do, survival with a sense of humor and a sense of compassion. In [*Remember Me to Harold Square*] there's a chapter on the Holocaust. The book is set in New York City, and the kids are very affected by what they see at the Jewish Museum. I cried a lot [while I wrote] that; I cry a lot when I deal with, when I feel anything about the Holocaust. And when the kids started to talk about all the injustices that go on in the world today...I felt that very strongly. So personally, I feel that...it's important for that to be

Dust jacket for the 1985 Delacorte edition.

Jacket for the 1982 Delacorte edition.

in books, for us to be witnesses. I go back to that feeling of being witnesses in a way and also, again, saying that we are survivors. So if that's bibliotherapy, I do care about it."[3]

"I get so tired of the question, 'So when are you going to do your adult book?' As though I've just been practicing all these years to become 'good enough' to write for grown-ups. One of my ex-teachers even said, 'Still writing kiddie-lit?' Children are unarguably the most important members of society—they are the future. And they can be very tough critics, particularly as they are often forced to deal with problems of their parents' making. Kids of divorces go through hell with feelings that are raw and often confused as their lives are turned upside down. Children of divorce often say they feel alone in the midst of chaos. For anyone who has ever felt alone—and who hasn't, in truth—a book can make a very good friend. Like a good friend, a book can help you see things a little more clearly, help you blow off steam, get you laughing, let you cry.

"There is a widespread misconception that it is easier to write for young people than for adults. It is not. Ask any children's or young adult writer. All writers write from deep experience. For me, that is childhood. From it flow feelings of vulnerability, compassion, and strength. Perhaps it would be better to say that I write 'of' young people rather than 'for' or 'to' them. Writers tell the best stories we possibly can, hopefully in ways that others will like. And how many books intended for a so-called specific audience are read by many age groups, generation after generation? But I must say, kids are very picky readers. They know what they like, and won't be 'conned.' They know what's authentic and what is not. If a book doesn't work for them, they chuck it no matter what the reviewers might have to say. And it is the responsibility of librarians, teachers and parents to respond to the needs of kids, not to critics. The 'dialogue,' if we may call it that, is between the writer and the reader. Reading is, after all, a deep and intimate experience.

"Young adult books are in no way marginal in terms of the commercial arena. In fact, YA books comprise the lion's share of publishers' backlists. That is to say, our sales not only justify promotion efforts on our behalf, but foot the bills for other, less marketable genres—a source of pride for those of us who write young adult books.

"It's much more enjoyable—and fruitful—to talk about writing. Our society suffers keenly from a media glut, and as an author I must say it is distressing that reviews so often become a focal point in conversations about books. Reviews are usually written within a few days, or a few hours. A book can take years. That sort of long-term, rather solitary, concerted effort deserves to be more highly valued than it currently is in our society.

"Some of the most important things I've learned about writing come from an acting course I once took. Also, Dr. Jerry Weiss once suggested I read Uta Hagen's *Respect for Acting*, which for me is still a 'Bible' for writing. Hagen lays out an acting system based on sense memory which allows an actor to know almost everything about the character. By following these sense memory exercises, the actor comes to know far more about the character than appears even between the lines of the play. I do sense memory work as a preparation for writing. I imagine what a character's closet

Jacket for Danziger's seventh novel.

might look like. For me stories begin with character rather than plot, so for a book to hang together, the characters must be fully imagined.

"Being a teacher was absolutely an influence on my writing life. In the early books, some of the incidents came from real situations that happened in my classes. Some of my characters did the same things that my students did (like crazy-gluing down desks, saying things like 'I cried all the way through the movie "Gone with the Wind," and someone stole my popcorn.') I also spent a lot of time listening to my students and their concerns about appearance, parents splitting up, fighting in the family, dating, school pressures, and tried to include a lot of that in my writing.

"I still spend a lot of time in classrooms. Sometimes I go to a school and speak for the day. As much as I like doing that, it doesn't give me the chance for real dialogues with the kids. So there are some places where I spend more time: a week in Columbus, Georgia, a week in Providence, Rhode Island, a couple of days in Los Angeles, a week at the American International School in Budapest, Hungary.

"Every once in a while, I think about going back to teach full time for a year. I miss working with the kids, but I don't miss the faculty meetings, taking attendance, and grading papers. I'm also not great about getting papers back on time. My strength as a teacher was that I really cared about kids, books and creativity. I enjoy working with teachers who work with kids, showing an easy technique I use to teach in creative writing.

"Ideas for books come to me all the time. But before I can sit down and start writing, I have to have lived with the idea for quite a while."[1]

Danziger's book carry dedications and grateful acknowledgements to a host of people. "I have a circle of several extraordinarily insightful friends to whom I read draft pages over the phone. They give me their reactions, comments and suggestions. I also read books in progress to kids, who tend to be excellent critics. Rewrites and revisions are an integral part of my process on every book. So is hysteria.

"But writing is terrific in some ways. I get a lot of sensual enjoyment from the act of writing. The feel of felt-tip pens against the paper, the movement of my hand making the letters, the look of all those marks across the page—even the way the keyboard feels.

"I do notice that my work has changed over the years. In the beginning there was a lot of anger, and the humor was more biting. The books have softened somewhat, which does not displease me. On the contrary. Writing has taught me that one can work through painful feelings and happenings, then let go of them. I think my characters have gradually become less neurotic and self-centered, and more sensual. My favorite character is Rosie from *The Divorce Express*. She dresses and thinks the way I do and sees things others often don't. This is not to say we're identical—Rosie, the product of a mixed marriage, is black, white, Protestant and Jewish while I am only white and Jewish. But Rosie has a certain light and fire that I think represents the best part of me. Phoebe, who becomes Rosie's stepsister, gave me a lot of trouble. She is so angry throughout the book that she can hardly see or speak the truth. I know about that kind of anger from experience. Originally

while writing, I found myself not liking Phoebe, which of course made the work even harder. Once I changed the narrator to Rosie, it was easier to write about Phoebe.

"I favor characters who are 'outlaws,' who want to find their own voices and their own way of looking at things. Mindy and Phoebe's father are two characters of whom I'm particularly fond. They go their own ways, able to operate without imposed structures, and have made difficult choices in order to do so. They're the gentlest of outlaws and nurture gentleness and sensitivity in their kids.

"My least favorite characters are Phoebe's mother and Marcy's father, both of whom are overly concerned with playing by the rules, not making waves, and creating a good impression. They exert a stifling influence, each in their own way.

| Cover for the 1979 Dell paperback edition. | Cover for the 1987 Dell edition. |

"I've also dealt more and more with place. In *The Divorce Express*, for example, Woodstock, New York is rendered in great detail. I loved how the sights, sounds, scents, not to mention mores of the place had permeated my consciousness, and were there for me in the writing. And in *Remember Me to Harold Square*, New York City is as much a character as any of the people in the story. The city, is filled with history, culture, ethnic and culinary variety, as well as plain old *fun.*

"A question frequently asked female authors is, 'Do you like to be referred to as a woman writer?' I'm a writer first, I have to say that. But I am a woman, and the two go together. It disturbs me to think of a hard-and-fast division between men who write and women who write. My mother's friend once said to me, 'I don't read girl writers.' I would hope that men and women would read men and women. I do consider myself a feminist and take a very strong stand on women's rights. But I also take a strong stand on the rights of girls, boys and men. There are so many struggles, so many fights to be fought: world peace, the environment, basic freedoms, education, opportunity and health care for everyone. We must stand together."[1]

Danziger is still a voracious reader. "It's gratifying that there are so many excellent writers at work today. I hesitate to begin a list of my favorites, for I'm certain I won't remember them all. Jane Austen is terrific. What a great sense of humor. I love Anne Tyler. Her characters are spun all around you. *A Mother and Two Daughters*, by Gail Godwin, is a most powerful book. Toni Morrison is a writer whose work I revere, particularly *The Bluest Eye*. Among those who write for children and young adults, I admire Judy Blume for her gutsiness and spunk. E. L. Konigsberg's books are intelligent, elegant and diverse. Francine Pascal's novels and Lois Lowry's are also favorites.

"Writing is a lot more fun now that living is, because I know I'm going to survive. I have survived. I've got the equipment. I'm not fragile.

"I've been thinking a lot about comedy lately. In order to be really funny, I think one has to have a certain way of looking at things. It's about turning pain and anger into constructive laughter. I don't like the kind of humor that makes fun of other people, the kind that is mean spirited. (Although in my books, I do have things that aren't kind, the sort of things that brothers and sisters say to each other. It wouldn't be realistic not to include that.)

"At a Breadloaf Writer's Conference, John Ciardi taught a poem called 'Love Poem' by John Frederick Nims. Ciardi said that if you took the funny lines and underlined them in red and the serious lines and underlined them in blue, by the end of the poem, the lines would be purple. I've never forgotten that. I think there is so much in life that is hard and sad and difficult and that there is so much in life that is fun and joyous and funny. There's also a lot of in between those two extremes. As a writer, I try to take all of those things and put them together. That way people can say 'I know that feeling' and identify with it. My major ability as a writer, hopefully, is to tell a good honest story and let people laugh when it is appropriate.

"Of course my other ambition is to be a stand-up comic. But I have trick knees and can't stay up too late."[1]

Footnote Sources:

[1] Based on an interview by Marguerite Feitlowitz for *Authors and Artists for Young Adults.*
[2] Perry Nodelman, "How Typical Children Read Typical Books," *Children's Literature in Education,* winter, 1981.
[3] Paula Danziger, "Writing for Children," *PEN Newsletter,* September, 1988.

■ **For More Information See**

New York Times Book Review, March 18, 1979, June 17, 1979, November 16, 1980, December 23, 1980.
New Yorker, December 3, 1979.
Los Angeles Times Book Review, July 25, 1982.
Contemporary Literary Criticism, Volume 21, Gale, 1982.
Washington Post Book World, May 12, 1985.
Alleen Pace Nilsen and Kenneth L. Donelson, *Literature for Today's Young Adults*, 2nd edition, Scott, Foresman, 1985.
Guardian, August 12, 1987.
School Library Journal, March, 1989 (p. 120ff).

Collections:

Kerlan Collection at the University of Minnesota.

Lois Duncan

Born Lois Duncan Steinmetz, April 28, 1934, in Philadelphia, Pa.; daughter of Joseph Janney (a magazine photographer) and Lois (a magazine photographer; maiden name, Foley) Steinmetz; married second husband, Donald Wayne Arquette (an electrical engineer), July 15, 1965; children: (first marriage) Robin, Kerry, Brett; (second marriage) Donald Jr., Kaitlyn (deceased). *Education:* Attended Duke University, 1952-53; University of New Mexico, B.A. (cum laude), 1977. *Home and office:* 1112 Dakota N.E., Albuquerque, N.M. 87110. *Agent:* Claire Smith, Harold Ober Associates, 40 East 49th St., New York, N.Y. 10017.

■ Career

Writer of youth books, adult novels, magazine articles and short stories; magazine photographer; University of New Mexico, instructor in department of journalism, 1971-82. Lecturer at writers' conferences. *Member:* New Mexico Press Women, National League of American Pen Women, Phi Beta Kappa.

■ Awards, Honors

Three-time winner during high school years of *Seventeen* magazine's annual short story contest; Seventeenth Summer Literary Award from Dodd, Mead & Co., 1957, for *Debutante Hill*; Best Novel Award from the National Press Women, 1966, for *Point of Violence*; Edgar Allan Poe Award Runner-up from the Mystery Writers of America, 1967, for *Ransom*, and 1969, for *They Never Came Home*; Zia Award from the New Mexico Press Women, 1969, for *Major Andre: Brave Enemy*.

Grand Prize Winner from the Writer's Digest Creative Writing Contest, 1970, for short story; Theta Sigma Phi Headliner Award, 1971; one of American Library Association's Best Books for Young Adults, 1976, Dorothy Canfield Fisher Award from the Vermont Congress of Parents and Teachers, 1978, Young Readers' Medal from the California Reading Association, 1983, Land of Enchantment Award from the New Mexico Library Association, 1984, selected for the Children's Books of the Year Exhibition in England, and Colorado Blue Spruce Young Readers Award nomination, 1986, all for *Summer of Fear*; one of American Library Association's Best Books for Young Adults, 1978, Massachusetts Children's Book Award from the Education Department of Salem State College (Mass.), and California Young Readers Medal Runner-up, both 1982, Alabama Young Readers' Choice Award, 1982-83, and 1986-87, selected for Librarians' Best Book List in England, 1986, and one of New York Times Best Books for Children, 1988, all for *Killing Mr. Griffin*.

Ethical Culture School Book Award, one of American Library Association's Best Books for Young Adults, one of the Library of Congress' Best Books, one of *New York Times* Outstanding Books of the Year, and one of *English Teacher's Journal*'s, and University of Iowa's Best Books of the Year for Young Adults, all 1981, Best Novel Award from the National League of American Pen Women, 1982, Zia Award from the New Mexico Press Women, 1983, South Carolina Young Adult Book Award from the South Carolina Association of School Librarians, Iowa's Young Readers Award nomination, and California Young Readers Medal, all 1984, Arizona Young Readers Award nomination, 1985, Florida Sunshine Authors Young Readers Award, selected one of Twenty Titles on Top Teen Read List in England, and Indiana Young Hoosier Award, all 1986, and Colorado Blue Spruce Young Adult Book Award nomination, 1988, all for *Stranger with My Face*; Notable Children's Trade Book in the Field of Social Studies from the National Council for Social Studies and the Children's Book Council, and one of American Library Association's Best Books for Young Adults, both 1982, both for *Chapters: My Growth as a Writer*; OMAR Indiana Children's Book Award, 1983, for *A Gift of Magic*.

Edgar Allan Poe Award Runner-up, and Children's Books of the Year Exhibition (England), both 1985, Texas Spring Jackrabbit Young Readers' Award nomination, and one of Child Study Association of America's Children's Books of the Year, both 1986, Land of Enchantment Award nomination, Colorado Blue Spruce Young Adult Book Award, Indiana Young Hoosier Award, and West Australian Young Readers Award, all 1987, and Volunteer State Book Award nomination (Tenn.), 1988, all for *The Third Eye*; Children's Book Award from the National League of American Pen Women, 1987, for *Horses of Dreamland*; Children's Choice from the International Reading Association and the Children's Book Council, 1985, Edgar Allan Poe Award Runner-up, Children's Books of the Year Exhibit (England), and one of Child Study Association of America's Children's Books of the Year, all 1986, South Carolina Young Adult Book Award, Indiana Young Hoosier Award nomination, and Nevada Young Readers Award, all 1988, and Colorado Blue Spruce Award nomination, 1989, all for *Locked in Time*; Parents' Choice Honor Book for Literature from the Parents' Choice Foundation, 1987, Edgar Allan Poe Award Runner-up, and Outstanding Book of the Year from the Iowa Books for Young Readers Program, both 1988, Indiana

Young Hoosier Award nomination, 1989, and Oklahoma Sequoya Young Adult Book Award nomination, 1990, all for *The Twisted Window*.

■ Writings

Debutante Hill (young adult), Dodd, 1958.
The Littlest One in the Family (juvenile; illustrated by Suzanne K. Larsen), Dodd, 1960.
The Middle Sister (young adult), Dodd, 1961.
Game of Danger (young adult), Dodd, 1962.
Silly Mother (juvenile; illustrated by S. K. Larsen; Junior Literary Guild selection), Dial, 1962.
Giving Away Suzanne (juvenile; illustrated by Leonard Weisgard), Dodd, 1963.
Season of the Two-Heart (young adult), Dodd, 1964.
Ransom (young adult), Doubleday, 1966, published as *Five Were Missing*, Signet, 1972.
Point of Violence (adult), Doubleday, 1966.
They Never Came Home (young adult; Junior Literary Guild selection), Doubleday, 1969.
Major Andre: Brave Enemy (young adult nonfiction; illustrated by Tran Mawicke), Putnam, 1969.
Peggy (young adult), Little, Brown, 1970.
A Gift of Magic (juvenile; illustrated by Arvis Stewart), Little, Brown, 1971.
Hotel for Dogs (juvenile; illustrated by Leonard Shortall), Houghton, 1971.
I Know What You Did Last Summer (young adult), Little, Brown, 1973.
Down a Dark Hall (young adult), Little, Brown, 1974.
When the Bough Breaks (adult), Doubleday, 1974.
Summer of Fear (young adult; Junior Literary Guild selection), Little, Brown, 1976.
Killing Mr. Griffin (young adult), Little, Brown, 1978.
Daughters of Eve (young adult), Little, Brown, 1979.
How to Write and Sell Your Personal Experiences (nonfiction), Writers Digest, 1979.
Stranger with My Face (young adult), Little, Brown, 1981.
Chapters: My Growth as a Writer (autobiography), Little, Brown, 1982.
From Spring to Spring: Poems and Photographs (juvenile; self-illustrated), Westminster, 1982.
The Terrible Tales of Happy Days School (juvenile poetry; illustrated by Friso Henstra), Little, Brown, 1983.

The Third Eye (young adult; Junior Literary Guild selection), Little, Brown, 1984, published in England as *The Eyes of Karen Connors*, Hamish Hamilton, 1985.

Locked in Time (young adult; Junior Literary Guild selection), Little, Brown, 1985.

Horses of Dreamland (juvenile; illustrated by Donna Diamond), Little, Brown, 1985.

The Twisted Window (juvenile; Junior Literary Guild selection), Delacorte, 1987.

Wonder Kid Meets the Evil Lunch Snatcher (illustrated by Margaret Sanfilippo), Little, Brown, 1988.

The Birthday Moon (illustrated by Susan Davis), Viking, 1989.

Songs from Dreamland (juvenile; illustrated by Kay Chorao), Knopf, 1989.

Don't Look behind You (young adult), Delacorte, 1989.

Young Adult; Under Pseudonym Lois Kerry:

Love Song for Joyce, Funk, 1958.
A Promise for Joyce, Funk, 1959.

Narrator of cassettes:

"Dream Songs from Yesterday," RDA Enterprises, 1987.
"Our Beautiful Day," RDA Enterprises, 1988.
"The Story of Christmas," RDA Enterprises, 1989.

Contributor of over 500 articles and stories to periodicals, including *Good Housekeeping*, *Redbook*, *McCall's*, *Woman's Day*, *The Writer*, *Reader's Digest*, *Ladies' Home Journal*, *Saturday Evening Post*, and *Writer's Digest*. Contributing editor, *Woman's Day*.

■ Adaptations

"Strangers in Our House" (television movie, adapted from *Summer of Fear*), NBC-TV, 1978.

"Down a Dark Hall" (cassette), Listening Library, 1985.

"Killing Mr. Griffin" (cassette), Listening Library, 1986.

"Summer of Fear" (cassette), Listening Library, 1986.

"Stranger with My Face" (cassette), Listening Library, 1986.

"Selling Personal Experiences to Magazines" (cassette), RDA Enterprises, 1987.

■ Sidelights

An author of over thirty-eight novels, and a successful free-lance writer, Lois Duncan has fulfilled aspirations that began early. Her first story was published at age thirteen. "It had not been a good day.

"To begin with, I had botched up my first-period math test. Then, at noon, I had discovered that my lunch ticket had run out, and I had forgotten to take money to buy another. My combination lock had stuck, so I hadn't been able to get my gym clothes out of my locker and had received another demerit in P.E.

"After school I'd gone to the orthodontist to have my braces tightened and had been told that I'd have to wear them for at least another year because my teeth weren't lining up properly....All in all, I was in a rotten mood as I slammed into the house and dropped my books in a heap on the coffee table.

"Mother called from the kitchen, 'There's mail for you on the piano.'

"I wasn't surprised. I got more mail than most teenagers dreamed of getting, all large manila envelopes addressed in my own handwriting.

"But this was something different.

"It was a narrow, white envelope with the name and address of a magazine in the top left corner, and when I opened it two pieces of paper fell out. One was a letter, and the other a check for twenty-five dollars.

"'Mother?' I said weakly. 'Mother?' My voice did not carry to the kitchen. I drew in a deep breath and let it out in an explosive shout. 'Mother! They want it! They've bought it! *Calling All Girls* has bought my story!'

"It was the most incredible moment of my life."[1]

"Those were the days when teenagers babysat for thirty-five cents an hour, and twenty-five dollars seemed like a fortune. How proud I was to have made it into the Big Time at such an early age!

"Over the next fifteen years, however, my definition of the Big Time changed considerably. By then I had been married and divorced and was writing twelve hours a day to support myself and three children, grinding out stories, articles, and verse by the carload and selling most of what I wrote. But the two-figure checks I was receiving (supplemented occasionally by a three-figure windfall) were barely keeping us in macaroni and cheese. Every

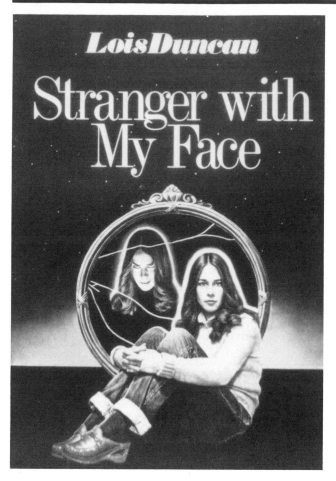

Dust jacket from the 1981 multi-award winning novel.

time I mailed a submission off to one of the large-circulation, national magazines, it came back so quickly it was hard to believe anyone had even glanced at it.

"I gazed wistfully at those high-paying slicks with their glossy paper and full-color ads and asked myself, 'How does anyone ever get published there?' There were some writers whose by-lines appeared there regularly, writers who were paid thousands of dollars. Obviously, I thought, those contributors knew something I didn't. What was the secret? How did those lucky people break in?

"Now, years later, my children are grown, and I am one of those writers I used to envy. My own work now appears regularly in such publications as *Ladies' Home Journal, Redbook, Woman's Day,* and *Good Housekeeping.* Editors even phone me to offer assignments.

"It is just as much of an ego trip as I dreamed it might be, but my present enviable situation was a long time coming. The journey from two-figure checks was an agonizingly slow one."[2]

The journey had begun in Philadelphia in 1934. "A writer 'gets started' the day he is born. The mind he brings into the world with him is the amazing machine his stories will come out of, and the more he feeds into it the richer those stories will be.

"When I was three years old I was dictating stories to my parents, and as soon as I learned to print, I was writing them down myself.

"My first—and only—poetry recitation was given at age five, and it was a disaster. It was kindergarten show-and-tell time, and since I had forgotten to bring anything to show, I volunteered to recite a 'made-up poem.'

"My performance was greeted by a long silence, during which I waited patiently for the deluge of praise I was sure would come.

"Instead my teacher said coldly, 'You didn't make that up.'

"I spent the rest of the day in the corner, and it was years before I trusted a teacher again."[1]

But Duncan continued to write. At age ten she had submitted her first manuscript to the *Ladies' Home Journal.* "I chose it because my mother subscribed to it, and I was able to find the address at the bottom of the 'Table of Contents' page.

"The story was titled 'Fairy in the Woods,' and when the editor returned it, it was with a kind letter saying that he appreciated my effort and that the story was a nice one, considering the age of the author, but that his particular publication was not currently in the market for stories about the supernatural. He also informed me that professional writers always enclosed a stamped, self-addressed envelope for their manuscript's possible return.

"The warmth of the letter cushioned its impact. I swallowed my disappointment and mailed the story off to another magazine, this time enclosing the return envelope. And I wrote another story and sent it to the *Journal.* By the time that one came back, I had another ready to mail off, and so it continued. I now had a hobby: getting rejection slips. It was painful, but exciting. Each day when other, better-adjusted children were skipping rope and playing hopscotch and going over to play at each other's houses, I was rushing home to check the mail and see which stories had come from which magazines."[1]

"My writing attempts became more and more ambitious. Tales of flaming romance, blood-spurting violence, pain and passion, lust and adventure flew back and forth to New York in a steady stream. My parents thought me cute and funny. My teachers thought me horrid and precocious. As for myself, I was proud. I—plump, bespeckled, and unimpressive as I might seem—was plunging ahead to advance my glamorous career.

"Three years passed, and I accumulated so many rejection slips that my mother made me stop saving them."[3]

Then a stinging piece of advice from Pulitzer Prize-winning writer Mackinlay Kantor changed Duncan's approach. "He was a new neighbor who had just moved in down the beach from us.

"'Lois,' my father said after introductions had been made, 'why don't you show Mr. Kantor that story that just came back from the *Saturday Evening Post*?'

"He did not have to ask me twice. What an opportunity! I rushed to get the story and stood expectantly at his elbow as Mr. Kantor scanned the pages.

"'My dear,' he said finally, 'I hate to tell you, but this is trash.'

"'Mack!' my mother exclaimed. 'Lois is only thirteen!'

"'I don't care how old she is,' said Mr. Kantor. 'If she is trying to sell her stories, she's old enough to be told what's wrong with them. What kind of subject matter is this for a kid? Lois has never had a love affair or seen a man get murdered. Good writing comes from the heart, not off the top of the head.'

"I was crushed. I was also challenged. Later that week I did write a story about a fat, shy little girl with braces and glasses who covered her insecurity by writing stories about imaginary adventures. I submitted it to a teen publication called *Calling All Girls*.

"From then on my fate was decided. I wrote what I knew about, and could hardly wait to rush home from school each day to fling myself at the typewriter. The pain and joy of adolescence poured onto page after page. My first kiss, my first heartbreak, both became subjects for stories. When I wasn't invited to Carol Johnson's slumber party, I wiped away my tears and wrote about it. When I lost the lead in the class play to Barbara Werner, I wrote a story in which I *got* the lead."[3]

"I shared a room with my younger brother, and at night I would lie in bed inventing tales to give him nightmares. I would pretend to be the 'Moon Fairy,' come to deliver the message that the moon was falling toward the earth.

"'And what will happen to *me*?' Billy would ask in his quavering little voice.

"'You'll be blown up into the sky,' the Moon Fairy would tell him. 'By the time you come down the world will be gone, so you'll just keep falling forever.'

"Eventually, our parents had the good sense to put us in separate rooms."[1]

"Aside from tormenting Billy, I had few hobbies. A shy little girl, I was a bookworm and a dreamer. My parents, Joseph and Lois Steinmetz, were magazine photographers. They moved us from Philadelphia, Pennsylvania, soon after Billy was born, to settle us in Sarasota, Florida, from which they were in a good position to take photo assignments through the southeast United States and the Caribbean. They planned most of these trips for summer so Billy and I could go with them."[3]

Duncan's 1984 novel that combines adventure, romance and mystery.

"It's interesting to note that in every story I wrote during those early years, the main character was a boy. I had always wanted to be a boy. Boys didn't have to be pretty. An overweight boy was 'husky' while an overweight girl was 'fat.' I dressed like a boy as often as my mother would let me and almost pulled my arm out of the socket trying to kiss my elbow, which I'd heard was the magic formula for changing sex. Needless to say, I was unsuccessful.

"What I couldn't accomplish in real life, I *could* do on paper.

"Then when I was thirteen a miracle occurred: I lost my baby fat. I don't know how it happened; it just fell away. I looked in the mirror, and suddenly there were bones and hollows in all the places where there used to be bulges. The following year the braces which I'd worn since the age of seven came off at last, and I graduated to a nighttime retainer. Soon after that a boy named Roger invited me to go to the movies, and I decided that being a girl wasn't such a bad thing.

"As I matured, so did my writing. As with any other activity, if you keep hacking away at it day after day, you're bound to make some progress."[1]

Spurred on by her early success, Duncan continued to accumulate stories and lessons. "Those first magazine sales went to my head. The local newspaper ran an article about me, and I went floating around, feeling famous, wishing somebody would ask me for my autograph. When nobody did, I went back to the typewriter and wrote another story. I made this one very dramatic. It was about a cheating woman, murdered by her jealous husband. I submitted it to *Senior Prom* and sat back to wait for my check.

"It didn't come.

"Instead, the story came back by return mail with a letter saying, 'We can't use this. It's stilted and unnatural. You're trying too hard.'

"I wrote another story, and this one came back also.

"What had happened? I asked myself frantically. It had all been so wonderful! Could it really be over? Was it possible that I would never have another story published as long as I lived?

"After three more rejections, it certainly started to look that way."[1]

Devotion to writing began to take a toll in other areas. "My English teacher loved me, but nobody else did. I was dipping toward a D in geometry, and—dear Lord, was it really possible?—I was

flunking home economics. I, Miss Superbrain, the published author, was getting an F!

"And now, I guess, is the time to explain that I have never been Miss Superbrain. I'm lopsided. I have always been good with words, but I make up for that by my lack of ability in many other areas. I am poor at math and science. I have a total block against foreign languages. And I am terrible at sports. If somebody tosses a ball to me, my automatic response is to cover my face and duck.

"There is something else wrong as well, something that as a teenager I was so embarrassed about that I couldn't even discuss it with my parents. I have almost no visual memory. I cannot remember what things and people look like. If I meet someone new and analyze his looks, telling myself, 'He has red hair and freckles and a hook nose,' I will remember the description, but I won't be able to bring to mind a picture of the face.

"If two people fit the same description, I'm lost. I can't tell them apart.

"Add to these defects my shyness and the fact that I spent so many years being fat and bucktoothed, and you can see why it was so terribly important to me to be a success at something.

"The fourth rejection from *Senior Prom* came in the form of the usual little printed slip saying, 'Sorry, we can't use this,' but at the bottom the editor had written a personal note.

"'This story and the last few you sent us are too contrived,' it said. 'You've lost the naturalness of your earlier submissions. Reach into your own life. Write about something you yourself have experienced.'

"Contrived? Those spontaneous outpourings about love, lust and murder? I was so upset by the criticism that I threw a towel over the typewriter and vowed never to write again. By the following day, however, I had reread the rejected manuscript and come to realize that the editor was right. I was writing on subjects about which I knew nothing....The most dramatic thing that had happened to me lately was flunking Home Ec.

"The next thing I submitted was a short personal-experience piece called 'Home Economics Report,' and not only did *Senior Prom* buy it, they raised the purchase price to $50."[1]

This publication brought more than monetary rewards. "[My] Home Ec teacher was so overwhelmed by the fact that someone in her class had actually sold her report to a national magazine that she changed my grade to a C. She also made me promise not to refer to her by name in the story.

"[Then] I received my first fan letters. It seemed that half the teenage girls in the United States hated Home Ec as much as I did and were in complete sympathy with me."[1]

Duncan learned an invaluable lesson when *Seventeen* magazine exercised their editorial control over one of her romantic poems. "When the poem came out in *Seventeen,* the boys' names were changed to 'Johnny' and 'Steve' and quick-eyed editors changed 'I know damned well' to 'I know so well.' I was in favor of the first alteration, but I was very upset by the second. I felt that the ending of the poems needed that extra punch.

"When I wrote the editor about this, I was stunned to discover that I didn't have any say-so.

"'It is not our policy to publish profanity,' she told me. 'Our advertisers wouldn't approve.' She also pointed out that, since her magazine had purchased my poem, it now belonged to them, and they could do anything with it they chose. I had created a product and sold it, and it was no longer mine.

"'What can I do?' I asked Mother. 'I don't want my work to be hacked up by strangers.'

"'Then don't offer it for sale,' she said reasonably.

"'But I want it published!'

"'It's your choice,' Mother said. 'Either you're a professional or you're not. Nobody is forcing you to submit to magazines. There are plenty of people who enjoy writing just for the fun of putting thoughts on paper.'

"I was not such a person. I considered writing communication. I wanted my stories to be *read.* The money was unimportant. In truth, I didn't even spend it. I had never gotten much pleasure out of buying things. I had my car and my typewriter, and except for the gas and ribbons necessary to keep them going, there wasn't anything I especially wanted. But I had tasted the power that comes with knowing that you can affect the lives of others, and I wasn't about to give that up by hiding my stories in bureau drawers.

"So, I decided to accept the situation. I decided, also, to find out as much as I could about writing as a profession. I had never realized that advertisers had control over what a magazine printed. I had not thought about such things as 'rights.' Now, suddenly, it came home to me that I didn't know a thing about the business end of the career I had

chosen for myself, and I started reading everything I could find on the subject."[1]

Professionalism paid off for Duncan while she was still in high school. "Out of the chaos of my junior year there came a story that won me first place in *Seventeen*'s annual creative-writing contest."[1]

The Korean conflict provided the inspiration for that story which concerned a soldier's uneasy return home. "This was not the first war for my generation. We had been children during World War II, and most of our fathers had served in the military. My own father had been Chief Training Officer at the Naval School of Photography at Pensacola during the year I wrote 'The Fairy in the Woods,' and the woods I described in the story were on the outskirts of the naval base. But although my classmates and I remembered air-raid drills and food rationing and the glorious excitement of D-Day, for all practical purposes it had been our parents' war, not ours.

"The Korean War belonged to us. It was our generation who would be fighting it. To underline this fact, barracks were thrown up at our local airport and an Air Force training program estab-

Lois Duncan and family, 1974.

lished there. Suddenly our town was filled with young men in uniform, few of them looking much older than high school age. I looked about me at the boys I knew—handsome Don; gentle Roger; Tom, the trumpet player; Fenton, the cartoonist; Bob and Lee and Barry and Sumner—and I tried to imagine them killing people. It was impossible. Still, they were most of them seniors, one short year away from being drafted. And what about my brother? Bill was only an eighth grader, but wars seemed to have a way of hanging on and waiting for people.

"It was the first story in many years that I had written from a male viewpoint.

"I had finally reached a point as a writer where I could step back from my subject and view it through someone else's eyes. That ability to detach and move slightly away from what you are writing is not easily developed, but it is necessary. Sometimes I feel that I am two people in one, with a part of me living each experience and another part observing."[1]

In 1952 Duncan entered Duke University. "Within weeks I was longing desperately for the ocean—the long stretch of empty beach, the whisper of waves and the cry of gulls—and solitude.

"To make things worse, all the girls I met looked alike to me. Back in high school my visual memory problem had not affected my life too greatly because I'd been with the same classmates from seventh grade through twelfth. Since the school was a small one, they had become as familiar to me as members of my family. At Duke I felt I was drowning in a sea of faces that ran together into a churning, gibbering blur.

"The whole thing was a nightmare. It was like playing a word game in which everyone but you has had a look at the answer sheet.

"And I couldn't write! That was the most frustrating thing. Oh, I cranked out term papers at appropriate intervals, but I didn't consider that real writing. It wasn't communication, because no one got to read them except the graduate assistants who graded them. It seemed a waste to me to spend days dredging up information and setting it on paper if nobody was going to publish it.

"When I went home at Christmas, I told my parents that I thought one year of college might turn out to be all I wanted.

"They regarded me blankly, 'But, if you drop out, what will you do?'

"It was a question I could not answer. What *could* I do except move back home again?...This was an era in which eighteen-year-old girls did not have their own apartments. They lived at home until they were married.

"I returned to college, made the honor roll with my first semester grades, and started dating a senior pre-law student. Buzz was attractive, intelligent and charming. He was also very persuasive—and I was at a point in life when I was vulnerable to persuasion. When he proposed, I said, 'Yes.'

"We were married in May [1953], three weeks before his graduation and four days after my nineteenth birthday.

"Was I in love? I certainly thought so.

"I had begun to write again: not stories, but odes to the Prince Charming who would be to me what my father was to my mother—lover, friend, companion, confidant—and would bring me, as all fairy-tale princess brought their princesses, happiness ever after.

"Buzz was a member of the R.O.T.C. unit at Duke, so when he graduated he automatically became a second lieutenant in the Air Force. He went through a short training program in Georgia, during which time I stayed with my family, and he then was sent to upper New York State. I accompanied him there."[1]

She spent the next few years moving around the country, discovering the joys of being an Air Force wife. "We lived in a boardinghouse in a room that was decorated with the huge head of a stuffed elk. It hung there opposite our bed, staring down at us with glazed eyes. I was allowed use of the community kitchen for fifteen minutes each evening, and since I didn't know many fifteen-minute recipes, we ate out a lot.

"Fun, for Buzz, was hiking. And mountain climbing. And hunting. He hunted with a bow, and assumed that I, naturally would do so too. And I did. I carried my own bow and marched along beside him through the forest, looking for things to kill. I never managed to hit anything, but I did learn to pull the arrow back far enough so that it didn't fall directly to the ground. And when Buzz killed a rabbit, I skinned it. And cooked it. And threw up at the table.

"Buzz was transferred to Livermore, California. There we rented a two-room apartment, a guesthouse stuck out behind a private residence, and I became a housewife. My day began at six in the morning when I got up and fixed breakfast. Then Buzz took the car and left for work, and I cleaned up the apartment. Cleaning two rooms does not take long. It was done by seven-thirty. Which left nine and half hours to fill—with nothing.

"With *nothing*? Why wasn't I *writing*? I, who had despaired of college because the pressures were so intense that I could not be creative—now I had all the time in the world, and I couldn't write a word. It was as though, suddenly, there was nothing feeding *in*. The days were long and empty. There was no one to talk to, not even a dorm mother. Buzz had to take the car, so there was no place I could go. If I'd had the car, I don't know if I would have used it—where *would* I go, in this strange place where I had no friends?

"We did not stay long in Livermore. Buzz was transferred to a base in Everett, Washington, where we rented a small house. Now there was more housework with which to fill the empty hours, but for a Home Economics flunker, cleaning was not too fulfilling. I suggested looking for a job, but Buzz preferred that I didn't, since he worked erratic hours and liked me to be at home when he was. Besides, he reminded me, there was little chance anyone would hire me since I had no training in anything and had dropped out of college.

"Why wasn't I happier? I was holding the pot of gold at the end of the rainbow. I had a handsome husband, a cute little house to fuss around in, all the trappings that went with the role of an adult woman. Why did I feel so empty and disatisfied?

"I settled upon the same answer as millions of other young women."[1]

Robin, her first daughter, was born. "Suddenly the days were filled with activity. There were bottles

Paperback edition of Duncan's occult gothic tale.

Duncan's suspenseful account of a sinister seduction.

to sterilize and formula to mix; there were the bath and the feedings to administer, the diapers to wash and fold; there was the daily airing when I wheeled my miracle child in her carriage, relishing the admiring comments from passersby.

"And I was writing again! Strangely enough, now that my free time was limited, I was writing richly and happily. When Robin went down for her naps, I flew to the typewriter and worked steadily until she woke up.

"Buzz was the proud father during the early weeks, but became less enthusiastic when the realities of parenthood came home to him. No longer were there quiet, candlelight dinners. Evening was Robin's time to exercise her lungs. No longer was I free to go hiking and hunting and target shooting at a moment's notice, nor could we go casually to a movie or dancing at the Officers' Club. Robin was not a healthy baby. She was born with a kidney problem, and I spent many nights walking the floor with her and bathing her to bring down fevers. It is not particularly romantic to sleep with a woman who is constantly jumping out of bed to see to a howling infant, and Buzz became increasingly more resentful.

"One evening when he came home from work and I suggested he go in and see the baby, freshly bathed and dressed, waiting in her crib, he regarded me coldly.

"'I saw the kid yesterday,' he said. 'Has she changed any since then?'

"I laughed as though he were joking. He *had* to be joking, didn't he? All Daddies adored their children!"[1]

In 1955, "when Buzz received his discharge from the service, he entered law school in St. Petersburg, Florida, and there our second daughter, Kerry, was born.

"Back in school in a class composed of mostly single young men, Buzz swung quickly into a single way of living. If he wasn't in the library studying, he was out playing tennis, or water-skiing, or chatting in bars, or attending parties. Since we couldn't afford a babysitter, I usually stayed home.

"To fill the lonely hours, I began work on a novel. Since I was still so close to my own teen years, it seemed natural that this—my first long project— would be a teenage love story. Its title was *Debutante Hill,* and it was sweet and sticky and pap, but in the 1950s that's the kind of book teenagers read."[3]

"The idea for this book came to me when I read a notice on the society page of my hometown newspaper listing a schedule of events for 'this season's debutantes.' I was incredulous. The one high school had such a small student body that when I had attended there had been no dividing line between students from well-to-do families and those from poorer ones. We had all gone around together, and popularity was based upon personality rather than social background.

"What a sad season, I thought, for a girl whose friends were chosen to be 'debs,' but who herself was excluded from all the dances and parties. How might such a girl be affected by this experience? How would she be changed as a person?"[1]

"When it was finished, I dedicated the novel to my mother and entered the manuscript in the 'Seventeenth Summer Literary Contest,' sponsored by Dodd, Mead and Company. It was returned for revisions because in it a young man of twenty drank a beer.

"'We can't judge this,' the editor told me. 'You can't mention liquor in a book for young people. Clean it up and resubmit it, and then we'll read it.'

"I changed the beer to a Coke and resubmitted the manuscript."[3]

"To my amazement, my book won the contest.

"Along with my prize money and the contract to publish, I received a hand-written note from one of the judges. 'Hooray for you!' she wrote. 'The minute I saw your name on that manuscript, I knew this was one submission I was going to read immediately.'

"Nine years before, this editor, now working for a major publishing company, had been the intern who had 'discovered' me at *Calling All Girls.*"[2]

"'I am an *author*!' I told myself incredulously. 'I am—*Lois Duncan*!'

"If this were a work of fiction, here is where I would choose to end it. What better climax could there be than myself, clutching the phone receiver, glorying in my moments of triumph and self-discovery!

"But real life does not conveniently freeze at its high points, and new chapters keep unfolding."[1]

"My marriage was rapidly fading into nothing. Buzz graduated from law school, passed the bar, and became a lawyer. From then on, he was so busy that I never saw him. For the next seven years I continued to write books and to raise our children—a little boy, Brett, had now joined the family—and to try to pretend to myself that I was happy."[3]

"Aside from my writing projects, I was totally wrapped up in my [children]. There were several other young mothers living in our neighborhood, and we would discuss colic and toilet training while our husbands talked torts and tax law. I didn't realize how shallow we must have sounded until I overheard Buzz one day commenting to a friend that 'It's nice for women to have babies, because it gives them something to talk about.'

"The words were a shock to me. Was I really all that boring? Was it because I was a woman, with women's interests, or because I was *me*?"[1]

"When I was twenty-seven, the inevitable happened—Buzz fell in love with somebody else. We were divorced, and I was devastated. Those were days when marriages were expected to last forever. I had never known a divorced person. In a desperate effort to start my life over, I took the children and moved to Albuquerque, New Mexico, where my brother (now called 'Bill,' not 'Billy') was living.

"I had a half-dozen books in print by this time, but they were far from best sellers. If I remember right, they were earning me about $2,000 a year. I knew I couldn't support myself and the children on my tiny royalty check, so for the first time in my life I went out to find a 'real' job."[3]

Duncan supported herself by answering phones for an ad agency. After winning a contest in *True Story*, she began to write for confession magazines. "Soon the kids and I were living better than we had since the divorce. I gave up our awful apartment and bought a house. The little girls took dancing lessons and piano lessons and ice skating lessons, while Brett went to a private kindergarten. We ate steak at least once a week and sometimes more often. I got very good and very fast. I could start a confession Monday and have the final draft completed and in the mail by Wednesday. Among the titles of the stories of mine that were published (anonymously, thank God!) during those busy years were 'We Killed Our Baby,' 'I Made My Son a Daughter,' and 'Twenty-nine and Mother of Two, I Wanted an Affair with a Teenage Boy.' I won't elaborate upon their contents.

"After two years on this schedule, however, I began to run out of sins to write about. Glued to my typewriter, I had had no time for doing research. One day Bill, who worked for the government, took pity on me.

"'Get a babysitter,' he told me, 'and I'll take you out to the base and introduce you to some of the bachelor types who work in missile design: They'll tell you about sins you never dreamed of.'

"That evening I met Don Arquette, the man to whom I'm now married.

"Don and I knew each other two years before he proposed. Each time he was ready to pop the question, another confession story would come out and he would panic. The week he did ask me to marry him, *Personal Romance* published 'I Carry That Dreadful Disease,' and he almost reneged. On our wedding day, out came 'Can He Bear to Touch Me on Our Wedding Night?' which made him think twice. But he did go through with the

The 1985 thriller about a young woman's effort to escape her mesmerizing stepmother.

ceremony and adopted the children, and another stage of life began for us all.''[3]

Duncan no longer bore the responsibility for supporting the family, which enabled her to concentrate on writing. ''But sweet romances now bored me. I had grown used to marathon writing, and I'm a creature of habit; I automatically jumped up in the morning and sat down to confess. Story followed story, until one day I wrote 'One of My Babies Must Die,' about the operation to separate our Siamese twins. This story brought in mail from all over the country from readers who wanted information about the operation and the doctor who had performed it. It was evident, even to me, that I had gone too far.

''' 'Don't you think it's time to move on a little?' Don said. 'Why don't you stop this confession writing and start writing articles for nice wholesome magazines like *Good Housekeeping* and *Ladies' Home Journal*?'

''To please him, I wrote a two-page featurette called 'The Year I Won the Contest' and mailed it off to *Good Housekeeping.* Back came a check for three times the amount I was used to receiving for a sixteen-page confession story. I was incredulous. Somehow, during those years of sitting down every day and forcing out words, I had learned the professional way of telling a story, and those storytelling techniques could evidently be transferred over into other forms of writing. From then on, I continued to write regularly for the national women's magazines, and to this day I have never written another confession story.

''Now that the financial pressure was off, I also felt free to turn back to my non-lucrative, but immeasurably enjoyable, hobby of writing teenage novels. I immediately discovered that something had happened in the time that I had been away. The world had changed, and so had the books that were considered acceptable reading for young people. No longer did any writer have to worry about getting a manuscript back because someone in it drank a beer. When I browsed the young adult section of our local library, I found books on alcoholism, drug use, social and racial problems, premarital sex, parental divorce, mental illness, and homosexuality.

''Thus began a whole new period of my writing career. The first novel I wrote under the new set of ground rules was *Ransom*, an adventure story about teenagers kidnapped by their school bus driver. Dodd, Mead wouldn't publish that book ('It's not your style of writing,' the editor told me), but it was accepted by Doubleday, who published it in 1966.

''*Ransom* was more successful than anyone expected, and the Dodd, Mead editor was very unhappy. It was runner-up for the Edgar Allan Poe Award which is presented by the Mystery Writers of America for each year's best mysteries. Suddenly librarians, who hadn't known before that I existed, began to notice me.''[3]

''*Suddenly*? That is how it may have seemed to others. In truth, there was nothing sudden about it. This was simply another 'corner' of that long road I had been traveling since early childhood.''[1]

''When my next book, *They Never Came Home*, appeared. . .[librarians] stocked it. That book, too, was runner-up for the Edgar. It also was taken by the Junior Literary Guild.

''Meanwhile, at home, both good and bad things were happening. On the good side, my marriage to Don was a happy one, and within the next several years I gave birth to two children, Don Jr. and Kate. On the bad side, I lost my mother, who was my dearest friend, and for a long time I was so numbed by grief that I couldn't function.

''Finally I came to the realization that I had to force myself to get back to work. If I didn't break this block, I might never write again. The book I had been working on when Mother died had been a murder mystery. I took that manuscript now, and threw it in the trash can. There was no way that I could write about death, so I decided to do the opposite. I would write something light and humorous, aimed at a younger age group, and I would accept in advance the fact that it would not be publishable. It would simply serve as an exercise to get me moving.

''The book was called *Hotel for Dogs*, and to my surprise, Houghton Mifflin published it in 1971. It did quite well, and is still in print in paperback. For the next thirteen years, this book served as my token attempt at humor. Then, in 1984, I wrote *The Terrible Tales of Happy Days School* which was published by Little, Brown. Each of these books was reviewed as having been written by a 'new author, not to be confused with the Lois Duncan who writes teenage suspense novels.' Because I was not known as a writer of humor, nobody realized that the two Lois Duncans were the same person.

''Something else important happened in 1971. I was invited to teach a class in magazine writing at the University of New Mexico. The idea of doing this scared me to death. I wasn't a teacher, in fact, I wasn't even educated. I'd had only one year of college, and that had been long ago."[3]

With encouragement from her husband, Duncan returned to school. "I became a lecturer for the journalism department, a position I held for eleven years. I also became a student. I had always regretted my decision to drop out of college, and being back on a university campus was exciting. I began by taking just one or two classes—a literature course here—a psychology class there.

"Going back to school in middle age was a strange experience. In some of my classes, my own students were my fellow classmates. I would be lecturing them one hour as 'Professor Duncan,' and the next they would be nudging me and saying, 'Lois, can I borrow your notes?' In 1977, I finally graduated, cum laude, with a B.A. degree in English, and we celebrated the event with a family party.

"On the day of my graduation I was too excited to think about anything else, so I spent the morning at my desk, writing about it. The result was an article, 'A Graduate in the Family,' which subsequently sold to *Good Housekeeping.* The check they sent me covered the cost of my whole tuition."[3]

"For my own part, I continue to write books, most of them for teenagers.

"Where do the ideas come from now that my own teen years lie behind me? In part, from my children. The character of Mark in *Killing Mr. Griffin* is based on Robin's horrible first boyfriend. Kit, in *Down a Dark Hall*, is Kerry, and the mischievous Brendon in *A Gift of Magic* is Brett. Young Don is Neal in *Stranger with My Face*, and Kate is April in *Don't Look behind You.*"[1]

"*A Gift of Magic* was my first book about psychic phenomena, and it was published by Little, Brown in 1971. During my year at Duke, back in 1952, the freshman class had served as subjects for ESP (extrasensory perception) experiments conducted by a Dr. Rhine. I became fascinated by the subject, and from that time on read everything about it that I could find. I decided that it would be fun to write a fiction story for eight-to-twelve-year-olds about a girl who had this gift, but it took me years to find someone willing to publish it. Every publisher I sent it to told me, 'Kids aren't interested in things like that.' I didn't agree with this, I thought young readers would love it. When *A Gift of Magic* did finally make it into print, I was proven right. The

book did well and established me as a forerunner in a genre that has since become hugely popular.

"*Down a Dark Hall* taught me about the newest in taboos for youth novels. With all the freedom we writers now had in choice of subject matter, I had assumed I could write about almost anything I wanted to. *Down a Dark Hall* was a strange sort of Gothic about a girl who went off to boarding school and discovered too late that the head mistress was a medium. Ghosts of long dead artists, writers, and composers came flocking back to invade the minds and bodies of the unfortunate students.

"This book was returned for revisions, not because the plot was so wild, but because the ghosts in the story were male and the victims were female. Like an echo from the past—'Librarians won't touch a book in which a sister and brother share a hotel room,'—I was now told 'Librarians won't touch a book that portrays women as the weaker sex.' When I changed the ghost of a male poet into the ghost of Emily Bronte, the book was accepted."[3]

When her book, *Summer of Fear*, was adapted into an NBC "Movie of the Week" titled "Strangers in Our House," Duncan gained insight into television and its impact on today's readers. "When the movie appeared on television, there wasn't much about it that I recognized. Like most authors, I preferred the book.

"Television has had an enormous effect upon youth books. Not only has it exposed young people to sophisticated subject matter at an early age, it has conditioned its viewers to expect instant entertainment. Few of today's readers are patient enough to wade through slow paced, introductory chapters as I did at their ages to see if a book is eventually going to get interesting. If their interest isn't caught immediately, they want to switch channels.

"Because of this, writers have been forced into utilizing all sorts of TV techniques to hold their readers' attention. In *Killing Mr. Griffin*, I began with the sentence, 'It was a wild, windy southwestern spring when the idea of killing Mr. Griffin occurred to them.' I knew I was not going to have this man die until a third of the way into the book, and I was afraid that if I didn't give my readers an inkling that dramatic action lay ahead, they would not be willing to hang around that long."[3]

"*The Twisted Window* is a suspense novel, and my primary goal in writing it was to produce a fast-paced page-turner that would be exciting enough to lure teenagers away from TV screens. I like to think, though, that the book may be more than that. In adolescence, emotions tend to distort reality, and young people often come to consider their own personal views of life the only ones imaginable. The concept that there might be more than one way to perceive the world is not an easy one to grasp, but that message forms the foundation of *The Twisted Window.*"[4]

"When writing *The Third Eye,* for instance, I originally envisioned the story as being laid in the autumn with high-school football games churning in the background and all the trees leafed out in gold. Then, a quarter of the way through, I realized that I was going to need to have a little girl down in the Rio Grande. Since this is a river that runs fast and deep only in springtime, I would have to switch my autumn-based story to spring.

"Formerly that simple change in season would have meant retyping sixty pages of manuscript. With the word processor, the changes took me ten minutes. All I had to do was go through the manuscript, locate the pages of description, and change gold leaves to green and football to softball. Then I scattered around a few daffodils. I pressed a button on the keyboard, and the printer went into action and ground out a nice, new, perfectly typed springtime manuscript."[3]

Duncan has come to terms with the many years she's spent writing. "I spend so much of my time submerged in the minds of the teenage characters in my novels that it comes as a shock when I look in the mirror and find I have gray in my hair.

"I've enjoyed my life, and I expect to continue enjoying it. I look forward to travel and leisure time with Don after his retirement—to watching my children's adult lives unfold—to spoiling my grandchildren.

"People ask, 'Are you going to keep writing?' They might as well ask if I plan to continue breathing. I expect to do both just as long as I possibly can."[3]

Recently Duncan and her family suffered a serious tragedy when her teenage daughter, Kaitlyn, was murdered. An honor student who planned to become a doctor, Kaitlyn was shot twice in the head while driving home from a girlfriend's house on a Sunday evening. Police have come up with no witnesses, no suspects, and no motives for what appears to have been a random "thrill" killing.

Footnote Sources:

[1] Lois Duncan, *Chapters: My Growth as a Writer,* Little, Brown, 1982. Amended by Lois Duncan.
[2] L. Duncan, "Making the Leap: Small Time to Big Time," *Writer,* October, 1988. Amended by L. Duncan.
[3] L. Duncan, *Something about the Author Autobiographical Series,* Volume 2, Gale, 1986.
[4] L. Duncan, "Lois Duncan on the Twisted Window," *Dell Carousel,* spring/summer, 1987.

■ For More Information See

Writer's Digest, December, 1957, December, 1959, May, 1962, June, 1970.
Christian Science Monitor, February 5, 1959 (p. 11).
New York Times Book Review, January 5, 1966 (p. 42), December 11, 1966, January 8, 1969 (p. 42), November 10, 1974 (p. 8ff), March 6, 1977 (p. 29), April 30, 1978 (p. 54), January 27, 1980 (p. 24), February 22, 1981, November 15, 1981, March 26, 1982, February 6, 1983.
Young Reader's Review, May, 1966.
Writer, March, 1969, December, 1973, February, 1976.
Good Housekeeping, October, 1970, September, 1977.
Martha E. Ward and Dorothy A. Marquardt, *Authors of Books for Young People,* 2nd edition, Scarecrow, 1971.
Redbook, October, 1975.
Seventeen, March, 1980.
Times Literary Supplement, March 27, 1981, March 26, 1982 (p. 343), February 22, 1985, May 9, 1986.
Bulletin of the Center for Children's Books, April, 1982.
Alan Review, spring, 1982.
Chicago Tribune Book World, July 4, 1982.
Career World, October, 1983.
Contemporary Literary Criticism, Volume XXVI, Gale, 1983.
"A Visit with Lois Duncan" (videotape), RDA Enterprises, 1985.
Ladies' Home Journal, January, 1986, January, 1987, August, 1987, June, 1988.
L. Duncan, "Letters I'm Glad I Got and a Few I Could Have Done Without," *Society of Children's Book Writers Bulletin,* September/October, 1988.

Collections:

Kerlan Collection at the University of Minnesota.

Russell Freedman

Born October 11, 1929, in San Francisco, Calif.; son of Louis N. (a publisher's representative) and Irene (an actress; maiden name, Gordon) Freedman. *Education:* Attended San Jose State College (now University), 1947-49; University of California, Berkeley, B.A., 1951. *Home and office:* 280 Riverside Dr., New York, N.Y. 10025.

■ Career

Associated Press, San Francisco, Calif., newsman, 1953-56; J. Walter Thompson Co. (advertising agency), New York City, television publicity writer, 1956-60; Columbia University Press, New York City, associate staff member of *Columbia Encyclopedia*, 1961-63; free-lance writer, particularly for young people, 1961—; New School for Social Research, New York City, writing workshop instructor, 1969-86. *Military service:* U.S. Army, Counter Intelligence Corps, 1951-53. *Member:* Authors Guild, Society of Children's Book Writers.

■ Awards, Honors

How Animals Learn was selected one of Child Study Association of America's Children's Books of the Year, 1969, *Animal Instincts*, 1970, *Animal Architects*, 1971, *Animal Fathers*, 1976, *When Winter Comes*, 1981, and *Cowboys of the Wild West*, and *Sharks*, both 1985; *The Brains of Animals and Man* was selected one of *School Library Journal*'s Best Books of the Year, 1972, *Cowboys of the Wild West*, 1985, *Indian Chiefs* and *Lincoln*, both 1987, and *Buffalo Hunt*, 1988; *Growing Up Wild* was named an Outstanding Science Trade Book by the National Science Teachers Association and the Children's Book Council, 1975, *Animal Fathers* and *Animal Games*, both 1976, *Hanging On* and *How Birds Fly*, both 1977, *Tooth and Claw*, 1980, *Farm Babies* and *Animal Superstars*, both 1981, *Dinosaurs and Their Young*, 1983, and *Rattlesnakes*, 1984; New York Academy of Sciences Children's Science Book Award Honor Book, 1978, for *Hanging On*.

Immigrant Kids was named a Notable Children's Book by the Association for Library Service, 1980, and *Cowboys of the Wild West*, 1985; *Immigrant Kids* was selected a Notable Children's Trade Book in the Field of Social Studies by the National Council for Social Studies and the Children's Book Council, 1980, *Children of the Wild West*, 1983, *Cowboys of the Wild West*, 1985, *Lincoln* and *Indian Chiefs*, both 1987, and *Buffalo Hunt*, 1988; *Children of the Wild West* was selected one of *Booklist*'s Children's Editors' Choices, 1983, *Indian Chiefs* and *Lincoln*, both 1987, and *Buffalo Hunt*, 1988; Western Heritage Award from National Cowboy Hall of Fame, and *Boston Globe-Horn Book* Honor Book for Nonfiction, both 1984, both for *Children of the Wild West.*

Cowboys of the Wild West was selected one of *School Library Journal*'s Best Books of the Year, and one of *Booklist*'s Children's Editors' Choices, both 1985; Golden Kite Award Honor Book from the Society of Children's Book Writers, 1987, and Newbery Medal from the American Library Association, Jefferson Cup Award, and one of American Library Association's Best Books for Young Adults, all 1988, all for *Lincoln*; Jefferson Cup Award Honor Book, 1988, for *Indian Chiefs*; Golden Kite Award Honor Book, 1988, for *Buffalo Hunt*.

■ Writings

Teenagers Who Made History, Holiday House, 1961.

2000 Years of Space Travel, Holiday House, 1963.

Jules Verne: Portrait of a Prophet, Holiday House, 1965.

Thomas Alva Edison, Study-Master, 1966.

Scouting with Baden-Powell, Holiday House, 1967.

(With James E. Morriss) *How Animals Learn*, Holiday House, 1969.

(With J. E. Morriss) *Animal Instincts* (illustrated by John Morris), Holiday House, 1970.

Animal Architects, Holiday House, 1971.

(With J. E. Morriss) *The Brains of Animals and Man* (Junior Literary Guild selection), Holiday House, 1972.

The First Days of Life (illustrated by Joseph Cellini), Holiday House, 1974.

Growing Up Wild: How Young Animals Survive (illustrated by Leslie Morrill), Holiday House, 1975.

Animal Fathers (Junior Literary Guild selection; illustrated by J. Cellini), Holiday House, 1976.

Animal Games (illustrated by St. Tamara), Holiday House, 1976.

How Birds Fly (illustrated by Lorence F. Bjorklund), Holiday House, 1977.

Hanging On: How Animals Carry Their Young (Junior Literary Guild selection), Holiday House, 1977.

Getting Born (Junior Literary Guild selection; illustrated with photographs and with drawings by Corbett Jones), Holiday House, 1978.

How Animals Defend Their Young, Dutton, 1978.

Immigrant Kids (ALA Notable Book), Dutton, 1980.

Tooth and Claw: A Look at Animal Weapons, Holiday House, 1980.

They Lived with the Dinosaurs, Holiday House, 1980.

Farm Babies, Holiday House, 1981.

When Winter Comes (illustrated by Pamela Johnson), Dutton, 1981.

Animal Superstars: Biggest, Strongest, Fastest, Smartest, Prentice-Hall, 1981.

Killer Fish, Holiday House, 1982.

Killer Snakes, Holiday House, 1982.

Can Bears Predict Earthquakes? Unsolved Mysteries of Animal Behavior, Prentice-Hall, 1982.

Dinosaurs and Their Young (illustrated by L. Morrill), Holiday House, 1983.

Children of the Wild West (ALA Notable Book; Junior Literary Guild selection), Clarion Books, 1983.

Rattlesnakes, Holiday House, 1984.

Cowboys of the Wild West (ALA Notable Book; Junior Literary Guild selection), Clarion Books, 1985.

Sharks (self-illustrated), Holiday House, 1985.

Holiday House: The First Fifty Years, Holiday House, 1985.

Lincoln: A Photobiography (ALA Notable Book; Junior Literary Guild selection), Clarion Books, 1987.

Indian Chiefs (ALA Notable Book), Holiday House, 1987.

Buffalo Hunt (ALA Notable Book), Holiday House, 1988.

Contributor to *Columbia Encyclopedia*, 3rd edition, and to the *New Book of Knowledge Annual*, 1981-89. Also contributor to periodicals, including *Cricket*, *Ranger Rick*, *Horn Book*, and *School Library Journal*.

■ Adaptations

"Lincoln: A Photobiography" (filmstrip and video), McGraw-Hill Media, 1989.

■ Work In Progress

Biographies of Franklin Delano Rossevelt, Eleanor Roosevelt and the Wright Brothers.

■ Sidelights

Russell Freedman has a long career of publishing nonfiction children's books in a pioneering format, using compelling photographs to illustrate his work. After painstaking research in photograph

Slave market in Atlanta. (From *Lincoln: A Photobiography* by Russell Freedman.)

archives, he was able to illustrate his informative natural history series and has utilized historical photographs to illustrate his books about cowboys, children, and Indians of the American West. *Lincoln: A Photobiography* won the 1988 Newbery Medal.

Freedman was born on October 11, 1929 in San Francisco, one of two children. "My father was a great storyteller. The problem was, we never knew for sure whether the stories he told were fiction or nonfiction. He was also a dedicated bookman. In fact, my parents met in a bookshop. She was a sales clerk, and he was a sales representative for Macmillan. They held their first conversation over a stack of bestsellers, and before they knew it, they were married. I had the good fortune to grow up in a house filled with books and book talk."[1]

"Two of my favorite books while I was growing up were Robert Louis Stevenson's *Treasure Island* and Ernest Thompson Seton's *Wild Animals I Have Known*. In those innocent days I didn't worry about distinctions like fiction and nonfiction. I don't think I knew the difference. I did know that I was thrilled by both of those books. And I knew that both of them were true. I believe that *Wild Animals I Have Known* was one of the earliest books to popularize natural history to a wide audience of young readers. It's been a long time since I last saw the book, and I have no idea how accurate it is or to what extent, if any, Seton anthropomorphized the wild animals he wrote about. In terms of its lasting influence on me, however, the book's scientific accuracy doesn't seem all that important. What is important is that I read *Wild Animals I Have Known* with as much pleasure and satisfaction as I have any novel or story. And I've remembered the book ever since."[2]

Another favorite was "*The Story of Mankind* by Hendrik Willem Van Loon. I still have my own boyhood copy, a special school edition that I read when I was ten or eleven years old. I remember where I read it—curled up on the maroon chesterfield that dominated our San Francisco living room. I spent several foggy summer days on that sofa, absorbed in *The Story of Mankind*. The title is revealing. It was a history book, to be sure, unmistakably a book of nonfiction, yet I read it that summer not to fulfill an assignment or write a report, but because I wanted to. I read it for pleasure, for the thrill of discovery. I think it was the first book that gave me a sense of history as a living thing, and it kept me turning the pages as though I were reading a gripping novel. It wasn't 'just like a story'—it was a story."[1]

Freedman also remembers the biographies he read as a child. "I grew up during the cherry-tree era of children's biography. Recently I looked again at a Lincoln biography I read as a boy; it contains my favorite example of invented dialogue. Abe is eleven years old in this scene, and his father is bawling him out: 'Books!' said his father. 'Always books! What is all this studying going to do for you? What do you think you are going to be?' 'Why,' said Abe, 'I'm going to be President.'

"I read that book as an elementary school student in San Francisco. Apparently the lessons of Lincoln's virtues were lost on me, for I was always being summoned to the principal's office. From the school corridor I would enter a small waiting room, and from there a door with a frosted glass pane led into Mrs. Koeppe's inner sanctum.

"I would sit on the wooden bench in that waiting room—waiting for the ghostly form of Mrs. Koeppe to appear behind the frosted glass as she rose to open the door and say, 'Come in, Russell.' On the waiting room wall hung a pendulum clock, tick-tick-ticking off the seconds as I waited. And looking down at me from an adjacent wall was the bearded visage of Abraham Lincoln. George Washington may have been the father of our country, but Lincoln was the one who always knew when I was in trouble.

"His picture reminded me that in America a boy could travel from a log cabin to the White House. Or rather, a good boy could. And from what I had read, young Abe was definitely a good boy. He was never late to school, and he always kept his clothes clean. As a young man working in a general store, he was so honest that he walked, or maybe ran, miles through drifting snow to return two cents change to a forgetful customer. Honest Abe— always fair in games and work, always kind to man and beast. That's the Lincoln I grew up with, a first cousin to Goody Two-Shoes. It's worth mentioning that *The History of Goody Two-Shoes* was published by John Newbery in 1765."[1]

The Freedman household often hosted famous writers because of Louis Freedman's work as manager of West Coast sales for Macmillan. Among the dinner guests were John Steinbeck, William Saroyan and John Masefield. "And they all had leg of lamb, since that was the one thing my mother trusted herself to cook. Whenever she came home from the butcher with a leg of lamb, I knew another author was coming for dinner."[3]

Freedman also developed an early interest in animal behavior, and at age nine began to take

Between 1872 and 1874 nearly four million buffalo were killed by white hide hunters armed with powerful long-range rifles. (From *Indian Chiefs* by Russell Freedman.)

notes about animals he observed. His own menagerie consisted of a dog, Spot, and a cat, Sally.

From 1947 to 1949, he attended San Jose State College and graduated in 1951 with a B.A. from the University of California at Berkeley. For the next two years he served with the U.S. Counter Intelligence Corps, part of that time in combat duty in Korea with the 2nd Infantry Division.

After his stint in the Army, Freedman went to work for the Associated Press in San Francisco as a reporter and editor. "That was where I really learned to write."[3]

"As a young man, I worked as a journalist and later a television publicity writer before discovering my true vocation. One day I happened to read a newspaper article about a sixteen-year-old boy who was blind; he had invented a Braille typewriter. That seemed remarkable, but as I read on, I learned something even more amazing: the Braille system itself, as used today all over the world, was invented by another sixteen-year-old boy who was blind, Louis Braille. That newspaper article inspired my first book, a collection of biographies called *Teenagers Who Made History*.

"I hadn't expected to become a writer of nonfiction books for children, but there I was. I had wandered into the field by chance, and I felt right at home. I couldn't wait to get started on my next book. As Sid Fleischman said in his [Newbery] acceptance speech,...'It was as if I had found myself—and I didn't even know I had been lost.'"[1]

"When I first started writing about science and natural history during the 1960s, I had what might be called a definitiveness complex. For example, James E. Morriss and I co-authored a series of books called *How Animals Learn*, *Animal Instincts*, and *The Brains of Animals and Man*. They were solid, substantial books, comprehensive and up-to-date, and they were well received. By the time they came out, however, I had become dissatisfied with writing that kind of definitive, comprehensive volume. I wondered, does anyone really sit down and read a book like this from beginning to end? Or do they just dip into it and use it to write reports?

"That thought was a depressing one, so I began to experiment with different formats and approaches. After a period of trial and error, I discovered that for me the most satisfying way to approach natural history was to narrow my scope—to focus sharply, for instance, on particular kinds of animals or on particular kinds of animal behavior and to illuminate my subjects by using striking and revealing photographs. I began to think in visual terms as soon as I had the idea for a book. Sometimes a particular photograph I had chanced upon suggested the idea in the first place"[2]

"One day I was browsing through a book on bats, and I came upon a close-up photograph of a mother bat flying past the camera. Clutching her furry chest was a scrawny, helpless baby. Its eyes were closed, and it was hanging on with its teeth and claws as its mother flew about, hunting for insects. She was a bat, to be sure, but the photo presented a timeless and powerful image of a mother and her infant. The photograph was an enormously affecting one and fascinating because the infant's very life depended on its ability to hang on to its mother.

"Hanging on, I thought. That's a terrific title for a book. So I made up a list of baby animals that hitch rides with their parents and began searching for photographs. The hardest photo to find, believe it or not, was the mandatory one of a plain ordinary house cat carrying a kitten. I had collected rare and unusual photographs of baby-toting pangolins, anteaters, scorpions, beavers, and marmosets—but a house cat? My editor, Margery Cuyler, came up with a solution. She knew a photographer whose pet cat had just given birth to some kittens. We got in touch with him, and he agreed to stand by with his camera ready, waiting to catch his cat in the act of carrying a kitten.

"The cat wouldn't cooperate. What she did behind the photographer's back is anyone's guess, but she refused to pick up a kitten while he was watching. After her kittens had grown too big to be picked up by their mom, we finally found the cat-and-kitten picture we needed at a commercial photo agency."[2] *Hanging On* was published in 1977.

"My next book was suggested by a scene I had witnessed as a child—a scene that also involved a house cat. I can remember sitting cross-legged on the kitchen floor beside my mother, my father, and my sister as our pet cat, Sally, gave birth to her first litter. It was late at night. My parents, finding Sally in labor, had awakened my sister and me so we could watch the kittens being born.

"For days I had been pressing my hand against Sally's belly, where I could feel the kittens moving inside her. And now she was actually giving birth before our eyes. I can still see the cheerful expression on her black-and-white face as the first wet, squirming kitten emerged. What impressed me more than anything else was Sally's easy self-confidence as she bit the umbilical cord, licked the kitten clean, and nuzzled it against her belly. 'How does she know what to do?' I asked. 'It's instinct,' my father replied. 'She just follows her instincts.'

"That night my attitude toward Sally changed. She was a wonderful pet, mischievous and cuddly, and I had always loved her. But now I had to respect her. She had delivered four kittens with dignity and skill, and though it was her first experience as a mother, she knew exactly how to clean them, feed them, and protect them. Sally, I realized, was a lot more complicated than I had suspected. I could never look at her in quite the same way again. And it was Sally who inspired my book *Getting Born.*

"Since then, I've done many other books about animals and animal behavior that combine photographs and text. The photos, of course, are more than just a come-on. They're an essential part of the story I want to tell, the information I want to convey. Ideally, the photographs should reveal something that words alone can't express. And the text, in turn, should say something that isn't evident in the photographs. In my recent book *Rattlesnakes*, for instance, there is a wonderful photograph of a rattlesnake yawning, taken especially for the book by Jessie Cohen, the photographer at the National Zoo in Washington, D.C. Few people have ever seen a rattlesnake yawn. If you want to find out why the snake is yawning, you have to read the text. But no words could possibly capture the priceless expression on the face of that yawning rattler—only photographs can do that."[2]

In 1980, Freedman became interested in doing another type of photographic book, this time about people. "A few years ago I went to see an exhibit of old photographs at the New York Historical Society. The exhibit, 'New York Street Kids,' commemorated the 125th anniversary of the Children's Aid Society. Many of the photographs in the show dated back to the nineteenth century and showed children, primarily poor children, playing, working, and just hanging out on the teeming New York City streets of that era. What impressed me most of all was the way that those old photographs seemed to defy the passage of time. They were certainly of their own time, for they depicted, in their vivid details, a particular era from the past. And yet

Dr. Konrad Lorenz was the first thing goslings saw moving as they struggled out of their shells. From then on, [they] tried to follow the scientist wherever he went. He called this "imprinting." (From *How Animals Learn* by Russell Freedman and James E. Morriss.)

those same photographs were also timeless. They captured scenes from life that are as familiar and recognizable today as they were then, scenes that have been frozen and preserved for future generations to see.

"There was a photograph of a newsboy and a newsgirl standing on a New York City street corner. The picture had been taken a century ago, or more. The boy and girl had grown up and grown old. As I stood there in the New York Historical Society looking at them, I knew they were dead and gone. But in the photograph they were still children, grinning at me from out of the past. Their clothing, the horses and wagons passing by on the street, the architecture of the building around them all showed that these children were time-bound—locked in their own era. But the expressions on their faces were timeless and made me wonder at what is timeless in all of us.

"I also had a personal interest in those photographs. My grandparents had arrived in New York City as immigrants at the turn of the century, and my father had spent his earliest years playing on the New York City streets that the photographs depicted. I actually began looking for the child that was my father among the photographs. I didn't find him, of course, but the photographs made me feel closer to him, to his past, and to my own past. I asked my editor, Ann Troy, to visit the exhibit with me, and the outcome was my book *Immigrant Kids*. It was followed by *Children of the Wild West* and by a companion book, *Cowboys of the Wild West*. Other books using historical photographs are in the works for the future, and meanwhile, I've continued to write natural history books."[2]

In order to research books on the West, Freedman visited historical societies and libraries through the western states, as well as the National Archives and the Smithsonian Institution in Washington, D.C. *Children of the Wild West* won the Western Heritage Award from the National Cowboy Hall of Fame in 1984, and was followed by a sequel, *Cowboys of the Wild West. Publishers Weekly* wrote: "Cowboys, readers discover, were really boys. Many were teenagers, a few 'old hands' were in their early 20s; and they were responsible for driving great herds across the plains in the 1800s. Freedman describes the buckaroos' clothes and equipment, how they passed the days on the ranch and on the trail, during the big round-ups, etc. There were black and Indian cowboys as well as whites, all working hard together. Although these storied riders of the purple sage are different from the gun-totin', steely-eyed movie types, they are as

exciting and interesting to meet and learn about here. One feels wistful when the book ends with a lament from a man who remembers: 'I would know an old cowboy in hell with his hide burnt off.' He says the fellows punching cows today couldn't match their predecessors, independent and proud, who sang as they earned a tough dollar, 'I've roamed the Texas prairies,/ I've followed the cattle trail;/ I've rid a pitchin' pony/Till the hair come off his tail.'"[4]

Freedman decided to follow up these two books with a study of Indians, entitled *Indian Chiefs* and another called *Buffalo Hunt.*

Lincoln: A Photobiography won him the prestigious Newbery Award. "A passing remark in a piece by Mary McCarthy ignited my interest in Lincoln. Mary McCarthy, hardly a sentimentalist, said that she was fascinated by Lincoln's intellect and melancholy. Melancholy? That was my first inkling that a complex and paradoxical man—a believable human being—was concealed behind the layers of historical make-up. After that, Lincoln intrigued me, and when Clarion Books suggested that I write a presidential biography, Lincoln was my first and immediate choice.

"One of the great joys of writing nonfiction for youngsters is the opportunity to explore almost any subject that excites your interest. I picked Lincoln as a subject because I felt I could offer a fresh perspective for today's generation of young readers, but mostly I picked him because I wanted to satisfy my own itch to know.

"Approaching a biography of Lincoln is daunting. There have been more books written about him than any other American—thousands of titles covering every imaginable aspect of his life and career. Luckily, a friend told me about the Abraham Lincoln Bookshop in Chicago, so I made a beeline to that shop. I introduced myself to Daniel Weinberg, the proprietor, and told him what I was planning to do. Dan Weinberg saved me. He helped me chart my course through the Lincoln literature and decide which books to focus on. If it weren't for him, I'd probably still be researching Lincoln. My book wouldn't be finished today.

"Along with my reading, I had a chance to enjoy the pleasures of eyewitness research. I visited Lincoln's log-cabin birthplace in Kentucky, his boyhood home in Indiana, and the reconstructed village of New Salem, Illinois, where he lived as a young man. I went to Springfield, with its wealth of Lincoln historical sites, and to Washington, D.C., for a firsthand look at Ford's Theatre and the

Children's rooftop playground at Ellis Island. (From *Immigrant Kids* by Russell Freedman. Illustrated by Augustus F. Sherman.)

rooming house across the street where the assassinated president died.

"There's something magic about being able to lay your eyes on the real thing—something you can't get from your reading alone. As I sat at my desk in New York City and described Lincoln's arrival in New Salem at the age of twenty-two, I could picture the scene in my mind's eye, because I had walked down those same dusty lanes, where cattle still gaze behind split-rail fences and geese flap about underfoot. When I wrote about Lincoln's morning walk from his house to his law office in downtown Springfield, I knew the route because I had walked it myself.

"I'll never forget my visit to the Illinois State Historical Library in Springfield. One afternoon while I was working there, Tom Schwartz, the curator of the Lincoln Collection, came over and asked, 'How would you like to see the vault?' I followed him through narrow aisles past crammed library shelves to an impressive bank vault. He twirled the big combination lock, swung open the heavy door, and invited me to step inside. It was cool and still in there, with temperature and humidity precisely regulated. Tom began to show me original documents written in Lincoln's own hand—a letter to his wife, a draft of a speech, scraps of paper with doodles and notes scrawled during long-ago trials in country courthouses. Each document had been treated with a special preservative that removed all traces of acid from the paper. Tom Schwartz pointed to one of Lincoln's courtroom notes and told me, 'This will last a thousand years.'

"I didn't actually learn anything new in that vault or see anything that wasn't available in facsimile. And yet looking at those original documents, I could feel Lincoln's presence as never before, almost as though he had reached out to shake hands.

"The more I learned about him, the more I came to appreciate his subtleties and complexities. The man himself turned out to be vastly more interesting than the myth. Of course, I was never able to understand him completely. I doubt if it's possible to understand anyone fully, and Lincoln was harder to figure out than most people, 'the most secretive—reticent—shutmouthed man that ever lived,' according to his law partner, William Herndon, who knew him as well as anyone. That's something I wanted to get across to my readers—a sense of the mysteries of personality, the fascinating inconsistencies of character.

"I was never tempted to write an idealized, hero-worshiping account. A knowledge of Lincoln's weaknesses throws his strengths, and his greatness, into sharper relief. And it certainly wasn't necessary to embellish the events of his life with imaginary scenes and dialogue. Lincoln didn't need a speech writer in his own time, and he doesn't need one now.

"One of the beauties of his speeches was their eloquent brevity. He agonized over his speeches, revising and cutting and polishing until the moment he mounted the podium. He couldn't stand folks who were long-winded. Referring to one such person, Lincoln said, 'That...[man] can compress the most words in the fewest ideas of anyone I ever knew.'

"He loved to tell the story about the lazy preacher who was notorious for his long-winded sermons. When asked how so lazy a man could write such long sermons, one of his deacons replied, 'Oh! he gets to writing and is too lazy to stop.'

"I've been asked, 'How long did it take to write your Lincoln biography?' Well, *Lincoln* was my thirty-fourth book, so let's say it took thirty-three books to write it. And it took the help and support of a great many people."[1]

In his Newbery acceptance speech Freedman noted: "When I learned of their decision, I was thrilled. And I was astonished, as, I am sure, were many others who didn't expect a nonfiction book to win a Newbery Medal. The last time it happened was in 1956—thirty-two years ago. Of the sixty-seven Newbery winners to date, only six, including my own book, have been nonfiction.

"Strangely, the book that launched these awards in 1922 was a work of nonfiction."[1] That book was his old favorite, *The Story of Mankind.*

"Since *The Story of Mankind,* every nonfiction winner of the Newbery Medal has been a biography—the story of a life.

"Along with the medal winners, there have been a number of nonfiction honor books through the years, including two previous biographies of Lincoln.

"And yet the fact remains that until recently, nonfiction books received a disproportionately small and meager share of the awards and prizes designed to honor the best literary work for children. While nonfiction has never been completely ignored, for a long time it was brushed off and pushed aside, as though factual books were socially inferior to the upper-crust stuff we call literature. Upstairs, imaginative fiction dwelled grandly in the House of Literature. Downstairs, hard-working, utilitarian nonfiction lived prosaically in the servants' quarters. If a nonfiction book were talented and ambitious enough, it could rise above its station, but for the most part, children's nonfiction was kept in its place."[1]

Now, Freedman's Newbery Medal has assured the place of nonfiction children's books in the awards arena, and there is no doubt that Freedman will continue to be a leading contender. "Whenever I'm starting a new book, I often think of a story that my father liked to tell about himself. He was still a small child when his family moved from New York to a rockbound farm near Windsor, Connecticut. One afternoon, as my father would tell it, he ran across a field to meet *his* father, who would soon be coming down the road with his horse and wagon. As my father waited and dawdled, he noticed a big stone on the other side of the field. He ran over, picked up the stone, which was almost too big for him to hold, and started carrying it back toward the road, stopping here and there to put the stone down and catch his breath, then picking it up again and carrying it a bit farther. When he reached the side of the road, he carefully put the stone down for good.

"When his father came rolling down that dirt road and climbed out of his wagon, my father said, 'Do you see that big stone? I picked it up and carried it all the way across the field.'

"'Why did you do that?' his father asked.

"And my father replied, 'God put the stone down over there, and *I* moved it over here!'

"My father loved to tell that story because to him it signified that he had the power to effect change—and that everyone big and small has that power. Today when I begin a book, I'm hoping to move a stone or two myself. I'm hoping to change the landscape of the reader's mind, if just a little—to leave the reader with a thought, a perception, an insight, perhaps, that she or he did not have before. If I write about rattlesnakes, I want the reader to come away from the book with a greater appreciation of these remarkable living creatures and their place in nature. If I write about immigrant children or frontier children, I want to leave the reader with a deeper understanding of our nation's history and a feeling of kinship with youngsters from another time. But most of all, I want to write a book that will be read willingly, read from beginning to end with a sense of discovery and, yes, with a feeling of genuine pleasure."[1]

Footnote Sources:

[1] Russell Freedman, "Newbery Medal Acceptance," *Horn Book,* July/August, 1988.
[2] R. Freedman, "Persuing the Pleasure Principle," *Horn Book,* January/February, 1986.
[3] Frank J. Dempsey, "Russell Freedman," *Horn Book,* July/August, 1988.
[4] "Children's Books," *Publishers Weekly,* November 15, 1985.

■ For More Information See

Horn Book, December, 1963, March/April, 1985 (p. 222).
Dorothy A. Marquardt and Martha E. Ward, *Authors of Books for Young People,* 2nd edition, Scarecrow, 1971.
New York Times Book Review, November 13, 1983, February 12, 1989 (p. 23).
School Library Journal, January, 1988 (p. 27).
Journal of Youth Services in Libraries, summer, 1988 (p. 421ff).
New York Times, March 23, 1989 (p. C11).

Carlos Fuentes

Born November 11, 1928, in Panama City, Mexico; son of Rafael (a career diplomat) and Berta (Macias Rivas) Fuentes; married Rita Macedo (an actress), 1959 (divorced, 1969); married Sylvia Lemus (a journalist), 1973; children: (first marriage) Cecilia, (second marriage) Carlos Rafael, Natascha. *Education:* National University of Mexico, LL.B., 1949; graduate study, Institut des Hautes Etudes Internationales, Geneva, Switzerland, 1949-50. *Politics:* Independent leftist.

■ Career

International Labor Organization, Geneva, Switzerland, began as member, became secretary of the Mexican delegation, 1950-52; United Nations Information Center, Mexico City, Mexico, press secretary, 1952-53; Ministry of Foreign Affairs, Mexico City, assistant press secretary, 1954; National University of Mexico, Mexico City, secretary and assistant director of cultural department, 1953-56; Ministry of Foreign Affairs, Mexico City, head of department of cultural relations, 1957-59; writer, 1959—; Mexico's ambassador to France, 1975-77; Harvard University, Cambridge, Mass., Robert F. Kennedy Professor. Collaborator on screenplays. Member of jury, Casa de las Americas Literary Competition (Cuba), 1960, Locarno Film Festival, 1961, Venice Film Festival, 1967, and Cannes Film Festival. Lecturer at University of Mexico, University of California at San Diego, Barnard College, Princeton University, University of Concepcion in Chile, University of Paris, University of Pennsylvania at Philadelphia, Columbia University, Harvard University, and in several Italian cities.

■ Awards, Honors

Centro Mexicano de Escritores Fellowship, 1956-57; Premio Biblioteca Breve from the Seix Barral (publishing house; Barcelona), 1967, for *Cambio de piel;* Fellow, Woodrow Wilson Institute for Scholars, 1974; Xavier Villarrutia Prize, 1975, and Romulo Gallegos Award from the Fundacion Juan March, 1977, both for *Terra Nostra;* honorary degrees from Columbia College, and Chicago State University; Alfonso Reyes Prize (Mexico), 1980, for his body of work; named Literary Lion at the New York Public Library, 1982; Miguel de Cervantes Prize from the Ministerio de Culture (Spain), 1987, for *La Muerte de Artemio Cruz* and *Terra Nostra;* Medal of Honor for Literature from the National Arts Club, 1988; Ruben Dario Award (Nicaragua), 1988.

■ Writings

Novels, Except As Indicated:

Los dias enmascarados (short stories; title means "The Masked Days"), Los Presentes, 1954.

La region mas transparente, Fondo de Cultura Economica, 1958, translation by Sam Hileman published as *Where the Air Is Clear*, Ivan Obolensky, 1960.

Las buenas consciencias, Fondo de Cultura Economica, 1959, translation published as *The Good Conscience*, Ivan Obolensky, 1961.

La muerte de Artemio Cruz, Fondo de Cultura Economica, 1962, translation by S. Hileman published as *The Death of Artemio Cruz*, Farrar, Straus, 1964.

Aura, Ediciones Era, 1962, translation by Lysander Kemp published under same title, Farrar, Straus, 1965.

Cantar de ciegos (short stories; title means "Songs of the Blind"), J. Mortiz, 1964.

Zona sagrada, Siglo Vientiuno Editores, 1967, translation by Suzanne Jill Levine published as *Holy Place*, Dutton, 1972.

Cambio de piel, J. Mortiz, 1967, translation by S. Hileman published as *A Change of Skin*, Farrar, Straus, 1968.

Dos cuentos mexicanos (two short stories previously published in *Cantar de ciegos*), Instituto de Cultura Hispanica de Sao Paulo, Universidade de Sao Paulo, 1969.

Cumpleanos (novella; title means "Birthday"), J. Mortiz, 1969.

Poemas de amor: Cuentos del alma, Imp. E. Cruces (Madrid), 1971.

Cuerpos y ofrendas (anthology), introduction by Octavio Paz, Alianza Editorial, 1972.

Chac Mool y otros cuentos (short stories), Salvat, 1973.

Terra Nostra, Seix Barral, 1975, translation by Margaret Sayers Peden published under same title, Farrar Straus, 1976.

La cabeza de hidra, J. Mortiz, 1978, translation by M. S. Peden published as *The Hydra Head*, Farrar, Straus, 1978.

Aqua Quemada (short stories), Fondo De Cultura Economica, 1981, translated from the Spanish by M. S. Peden, published as *Burnt Water*, Farrar, Straus, 1981.

Una familia lejana, Era, 1980, translation by M. S. Peden published as *Distant Relations*, Farrar, Straus, 1982.

The Old Gringo, translated from Spanish by M. S. Peden, Farrar, Straus, 1985.

Christopher Unborn, translated by Alfred MacAdam, Farrar, Straus, 1989.

Constanica and Other Stories for Virgins (short stories), translated by Thomas Christensen, Farrar, Straus, 1989.

Holy Place [and] Birthday: Two Novellas, translated from Spanish by S. J. Levine and M. S. Peden, Farrar, Straus, in press.

Nonfiction:

The Argument of Latin American Words for North Americans, Radical Education Project, 1963.

(Contributor) *Wither Latin America?* (political articles), Monthly Review Press, 1963.

Paris: La revolucion de mayo (essay; title means "Paris, the May Revolution"), Ediciones Era, 1968.

La nueva novela hispanoamericana (essay; title means "The New Hispanic American Novel"), J. Mortiz, 1969.

El mundo de Jose Luis Cuevas (essay; title means "The World of Jose Luis Cuevas"), Tudor, 1969.

Casa con dos puertas (essays; title means "The House with Two Doors"), J. Mortiz, 1970.

Tiempo mexicano (essays; title means "Mexican Time"), J. Mortiz, 1971.

(Editor and author of prologue) Octavio Paz, *Los signos en rotacion y otros ensayos*, Alianza Editorial (Madrid), 1971.

Cervantes o la critica de la lectura (essay), J. Mortiz, 1976, translation published as *Cervantes; or, The Critique of Reading*, Institute of Latin American Studies, University of Texas at Austin, 1976.

(Author of introduction to Spanish edition) Milan Kundera, *La vida esta en otra parte*, Seix Barral, 1977.

(With others) *Latin American Fiction Today: A Symposium*, Ediciones Hispamerica, 1980.

Myself with Others: Selected Essays, Farrar, Straus, 1986.

Selected Literary Essays, Farrar, Straus, 1986.

Also author of *Lineas para Adami* (essay; title means "Lines for Adami"), 1968.

Plays:

Todos los gatos son pardos (title means "All Cats Are Gray"), Siglo Veintiuno Editores, 1970.

El tuerto es rey (title means "The One-Eyed Man Is King"; first produced [in French], 1970), J. Mortiz, 1970.

Los reinos originarios: Teatro hispanomexicano (title means "The First Kingdoms"; contains "Todos los gatos son pardos" and "El tuerto es rey"), Barral Editores (Barcelona), 1971.

"Orchids in the Moonlight," first produced in Cambridge, Mass. at American Repertory Theater, June 9, 1982.

Collaborator on several film scripts, including "Pedro Paramo," 1966, "Tiempo de morir," 1966, "Los caifanes," 1967, and "Mexico, Mexico," 1968. Fuentes' works have been translated into eighteen languages, including French, Portuguese, Spanish, German, Italian, Russian, Polish, and Japanese. Contributor to numerous periodicals in the United States, Mexico, and France, including *New York Times, Washington Post, Le Monde, Playboy,* and *Los Angeles Times.* Founding editor, *Revista mexicana de literatura,* 1956-58, *El Espectador,* 1959-61, *Siempre,* 1960, and *Politica,* 1960.

■ Adaptations

"The Witch" (motion picture; based on novel *Aura*), Arco Film (Italy), 1969.

"Old Gringo" (motion picture), starring Jane Fonda and Gregory Peck, Columbia Pictures, 1989.

■ Work In Progress

"The Buried Mirror," a television series about Columbus' voyage, commissioned by the Smithsonian Institution.

■ Sidelights

November 11, 1928. Carlos Fuentes was born in Panama City to Berta Macias Rivas and Dr. Rafael Fuentes Boettiger, a diplomat attached to the Mexican legation. "The problem of my baptism then arose. As if the waters of the two neighbouring oceans touching each other with the iron finger tips of the canal were not enough, I had to undergo a double ceremony: my religious baptism took place in Panama, because my mother, a devout Roman Catholic, demanded it; but my national baptism took place a few months later in Mexico City, where my father, an incorrigible Jacobin and priest-hater to the end, insisted that I be registered in the civil rolls established by Benito Juarez [Mexican revolutionary and statesman]. Thus, I appear as a native of Mexico City for all legal purposes, and this anomaly further illustrates a central fact of my life and writing: I am Mexican by will and imagination."[1]

In his early childhood Fuentes lived in Quito, Montevideo and Rio de Janeiro, followed by a stay in Washington, D.C. where his father was counselor of the Mexican Embassy. Fuentes attended the Henry D. Cooke School. "My school—a state public school, [was] non-confessional and co-educational....I believed in the democratic simplicity of my teachers and chums, and above all I believed I was, naturally, in a totally unselfconscious way, a part of this world. It is important, at all ages and in all occupations, to be 'popular' in the United States; I have known no other society where the values of 'regularity' are so highly prized. I was popular, I was 'regular.'"[1]

"I came into contact with an alien society—one which, in a way, became my society. There was a great social and racial variety as well, and that was also extremely important for me. Those were years that were imprinted for ever in my consciousness and my memory because they were the years of the New Deal. And for me the thirties is something that is very living, very present. I think sometimes

Jacket for the 1978 hardcover.

this feeling comes out strongly in my books. I started reading very soon. I was interested in dramatics, in drawing—I was a good cartoonist. I had a very happy childhood in Washington."[2]

Rafael Fuentes Boettiger made sure his son did not neglect his Mexican heritage. "I was a child who never had a vacation from school. I went to public school in the United States from September to July. But then my father would say, 'You will not become a pocho [U.S. citizen of Hispanic descent who speaks an incorrect Spanish], you will not forget Spanish.' So during the summer I went to Mexico City and was put in school. So during the winter I read a lot of Mark Twain and Robert Louis Stevenson and *Winnie the Pooh*, God knows. *The Wizard of Oz*, too. And during the summer, I read a lot of Salgari, and Zevaco and other writers that are essential to the understanding of what makes a child in Latin America and, generally speaking, in the Latin World."[2]

"At home, my father made me read Mexican history, study Mexican geography and understand the names, the dreams and defeats of Mexico: a non-existent country, I then thought, invented by my father to nourish my infant imagination: a land of Oz with a green cactus road, a landscape and a soul so different from those of the United States that they seemed a fantasy.

"A cruel fantasy: the history of Mexico was a history of crushing defeats, whereas I lived in a world, that of my D.C. public school, which celebrated victories, one victory after another.

"To the south, sad songs, sweet nostalgia, impossible desires. To the north, self-confidence, faith in progress, boundless optimism. Mexico, the imaginary country, dreamed of a painful past; the United States, the real country, dreamed of a happy future.

"Many things impressed themselves on me during those years. The United States—would you believe it?—was a country where things worked, where nothing ever broke down: plumbing, roads seemed to function perfectly, at least at the eye level of a young Mexican diplomat's son living in a residential hotel on Washington's Sixteenth Street, facing Meridian Hill Park, where nobody was then mugged and where our superbly furnished seven-room apartment cost us 110 pre-inflation dollars a month. Yes, in spite of all the problems, the livin' seemed easy during those long Tidewater summers when I became perhaps the first and only Mexican to prefer grits to guacamole. I also became the original Mexican Calvinist, and an invisible task-

master called Puritanical Duty still shadows my every footstep: I shall not deserve anything unless I work relentlessly for it, with iron discipline, day after day."[1]

Fuentes came to admire Franklin D. Roosevelt and the New Deal. "The nation that Tocqueville saw was destined to dominate over half the world realized that only a continental state could be a modern state; in the thirties, the USA had to decide what to do with its new power, and Franklin Roosevelt taught us to believe that the United States had to show that it was capable of living up to its ideals. I learned then—my first political lesson—that this commitment to its idealism is the true greatness of the United States, not (the norm in my lifetime) material wealth, not power arrogantly misused against weaker peoples, not ignorant ethnocentrism burning itself out in contempt for others. As a young Mexican, I saw a nation of boundless energy and the will to confront the great social issues of the times without blinking or looking for scapegoats. It was a country identified with its own highest principles: political democracy, economic well-being and faith in its human resources, especially in that most precious of all capital, the renewable wealth of education.

"I saw the United States in the thirties lift itself from the dead dust of Oklahoma and the grey lines of the unemployed in Detroit, and this image of health was reflected in my life, in my reading of Mark Twain, in the movies and newspapers, in the North American capacity for mixing fluffy illusion and hard-bitten truth, self-celebration and self-criticism: the madcap heiresses played by Carol Lombard co-existed with Walker Evans's photographs of hungry migrant mothers, and the nimble tread of the feet of Fred Astaire did not silence the heavy stomp of the boots of Tom Joad."[1]

1938. When Lazaro Cardenas, the president of Mexico, nationalized foreign oil companies, Fuentes' status in school changed. "I suddenly became a pariah in my school. The newspapers of the time were full of blazing headlines denouncing the Communist government of Mexico, threatening President Cardenas and demanding sanctions against Mexico. Some were even demanding the invasion of Mexico in the sacred name of private property. There were epithets in my school; there were even blows. Children know how to be cruel, and the cruelty of elders is basically a residue of that malaise we feel from childhood toward things, other things, strange things that we do not understand. But this political act suddenly revealed to me that my country existed, that it was not a figment of my father's imagination made to entertain me, and that I was part of it. I saw pictures of Cardenas, and he did not belong to the glossy repertoire of American ideals. He was a 'mestizo,' a man of mixed blood, Indian and Spanish, with a grim far-away look in his eyes that made him look as if he were trying to remember a mute and ancient past. I asked myself, 'Is this past mine as well? Is this identity mine as well?' It was a tremendous revelation that my identity was Mexican, an identity that I really did not complete until the second stage of my childhood."[3]

"The United States had made me believe that we live only for the future; Mexico, Cardenas, the events of 1938, made me understand that only in an act of the present can we make present the past as well as the future: to be Mexican was to identify a hunger for being, a desire for dignity rooted in many forgotten centuries and in many centuries yet to come, but rooted here, now, in the instant, in the vigilant time of Mexico that I later learned to understand in the stone serpents of Teotihuacan and in the polychrome angels of Oaxaca.

"In 1939, my father took me to see a film at the old RKO-Keith in Washington. It was called 'Man of Conquest' and it starred Richard Dix as Sam Houston. When Dix/Houston proclaimed the secession of the Republic of Texas from Mexico, I jumped on the theatre seat and proclaimed on my own and from the full height of my nationalist ten years, '*Viva Mexico!* Death to the *gringos!*' My embarrassed father hauled me out of the theatre, but his pride in me could not resist leaking my first rebellious act to the *Washington Star*."[1]

1940. Fuentes' father became charge d'affaires at the Mexican Embassy in Santiago, Chile. Living there became essential to Fuentes' political and literary formation. "When we moved to Chile, [Pedro] Aguirre Cerda was in power and it was an extraordinary period because I saw that democracy and freedom could function in Latin America. Chile, in that moment, was a land of great poets— Pablo Neruda, Gabriela Mistral; they were part of the democratic culture of Chile. The figure of Neruda had a tremendous influence. He was representative of a Latin Americn tradition that said, 'The writer is not separated from the political realities of the country.' At that point I already knew I wanted to write. Actually, I'd known that since I was seven, when I produced my first short stories. But in which language? English? Spanish? What? Being in Chile then in the midst of all that ferment of the Popular Front, I came to realize that the English language didn't need one more writer,

but that the Spanish language did; that there was, indeed, something to be said in Spanish that could not be said otherwise."[4]

"In Chile I came to know the possibilities of our language for giving wing to freedom and poetry. The impression was enduring; it links me forever to that sad and wonderful land. It lives within me, and it transformed me into a man who knows how to dream, love, insult and write only in Spanish. It also left me wide open to an incessant interrogation: what happened to this universal language, Spanish, which after the seventeenth century ceased to be a language of life, creation, dissatisfaction and personal power, and became far too often a language of mourning, sterility, rhetorical applause and abstract power? Where were the threads of my tradition, where could I, writing in mid-twentieth century Latin America, find the direct link to the great living presences I was then starting to read, my lost Cervantes, my old Quevedo, dead because he could not tolerate one more winter, my Gongora, abandoned in a gulf of loneliness?"[1]

First articles and short stories published in the *Boletin del Instituto Nacional de Chile*. Began reading the English novel. "I remember as a young man reading Emily Bronte and Jane Austen. I was

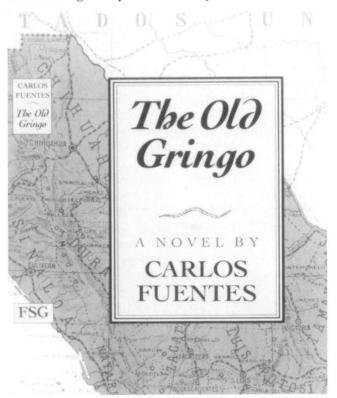

The 1985 novel about Mexico at the time of Pancho Villa.

seduced by both of these ladies. Jane Austen led me down a garden path, and we talked of human frailties and psychologized for a while together. But Emily Bronte taught me that characters are interesting not for themselves but for what they represent. I'm not interested in Heathcliff's psychology but in the energy he generates—the love, lust, anger that emanate from him and that are a part of all men. The same is true of Poe. I'm not interested in Roderick Usher as a character but in what he produces—the reality of passion and fear."[5]

Fuentes was also fond of the Gothic novel and began to collaborate on one with his friends at school. Its plot moved between Marseille and Haiti and involved a black tyrant whose mad French mistress was hidden in the attic. "I started reading all the Gothic novels like hell at that time, yes. I went into everything from Monk Lewis to Bram Stoker, passing through the marvellous *Vathek* of William Beckford. Yes, when I was thirteen, I wrote a Gothic novel about 400 pages long, and every afternoon I read it to David Alfaro Siquiros, the Mexican muralist who was in exile in Chile. And since I was the son of the *Charge d'Affaires*, he had no choice but to listen to my droning on with this terrible Gothic novel, which had Haiti as a setting, as I remember. There was a great mansion on the top of a hill and lots of voodoo. I think we should try to write Gothic novels and police stories and chivalric novels. These are being written all the time, and Hammett wrote them, of course. So did Chandler. They still wrote novels of chivalry. I think that Phillip Marlow is the last knight-errant. I never read either one as examples of pulp or thrillers. I would compare Hammett with Hemingway and say, 'well obviously there's no comparison possible.' Hammett is a thousand leagues above Hemingway. Chandler reaches the end of the American expansion, where you have the precipice, the Pacific, the sea, and you can go no further. The same feeling appears in Nathanael West's *The Day of the Locust*, too. But Chandler is the quintessential Los Angeles writer. Without California, I don't think he can be understood. But strangely, he is still an Englishman, a gentle one. If you read the poems he wrote when he was a young man, it's incredible—that he should be the author of such hard, brilliant novels, those he wrote in California."[2]

1944. Spent six months in Buenos Aires, Argentina. "They were, in spite of their brevity, so important in this reading and writing of myself. Buenos Aires was then, as always, the most beautiful, sophisticat-

ed and civilized city in Latin America, but in the summer of 1944, as street pavements melted in the heat and the city smelled of cheap wartime gasoline, rawhide from the port and chocolate eclairs from the *confiterias*, Argentina had experienced a succession of military *coups*.

"A stultifying hack novelist who went by the pen name Hugo Wast was assigned to the Ministry of Education under his real name, Martinez Zuviria, and brought all his anti-Semitic, undemocratic, pro-fascist phobias to the Buenos Aires high school system, which I had suddenly been plunked into. Coming from the America of the New Deal, the ideals of revolutionary Mexico, and the politics of the Popular Front in Chile, I could not stomach this, rebelled and was granted a full summer of wandering around Buenos Aires, free for the first time in my life."[1]

"I went everywhere—the bars, the tango dance halls, the cinemas—morning, noon, and night. It's the first city where I got drunk, the first city where I made love to a woman. It was many, many things for me."[2]

"I started reading Argentine literature, from the gaucho poems to Sarmiento's *Memories of Provincial Life* to Cane's *Juvenilia* to *Don Segundo Sombra* to...to...to—and this was as good as discovering that Joan of Arc was also sexy—to Borges. Borges belongs to that summer in Buenos Aires. He belongs to my personal discovery of Latin American literature."[1]

As World War II was still raging, Fuentes' father, in the capacity of Mexico's charge d'affaires, tried to convince the Argentine regime to break relations with the Axis countries. To protect his family from possible reprisals, he sent them home to Mexico. "And there, for the first time, my mother had a say, and she said, 'The best schools in Mexico are the Catholic schools.' And for the first time I was put into school with priests. And that was terrible, especially when I was sixteen and when I had the furious life experience of Buenos Aires. Suddenly, I came face to face with the most horrible aspects of the Catholic religion as practiced in Latin America—prohibitions, guilt, sin— all that, and constantly pounded into you by terrible hypocrites who did exactly the reverse of what they preached and what they punished you for."[2]

"The brothers who ruled this institution were preoccupied with something that had never entered my head: sin. At the start of the school year, one of the brothers would come before the class

Gregory Peck, Jane Fonda and Jimmy Smits starred in the movie "Old Gringo." A Fonda Films Production, 1989.

with a white lily in his hand and say: 'This is a Catholic youth before kissing a girl.' Then he would throw the flower on the floor, dance a little jig on it, pick up the bedraggled object and confirm our worst suspicions: 'This is a Catholic boy after.'

"Well, all this filled life with temptation. Retrospectively, I would agree with Luis Bunuel that sex without sin is like an egg without salt. The priests at the Colegio Frances made sex irresistible for us; they also made leftists of us by their constant denunciation of Mexican liberalism and especially of Benito Juarez. The sexual and political temptations became very great in a city where provincial mores and sharp social distinctions made it very difficult to have normal sexual relationships with young or even older women.

"All this led, as I say, to a posture of rebellion that for me crystallized in the decision to be a writer."[1]

"I think the writing process really started in earnest for me when I was sixteen and went to live in Mexico. My relationships to Mexico had been unusual. Because my father was a diplomat, I'd lived much of my childhood abroad. Traveling with my family, I had been forced to invent a Mexico for myself, an imagined Mexico. That imagined country contrasted enormously with the one I discovered when I moved back to the real place. I saw things, perhaps because I'd been abroad, that other writers of my generation could not see. For instance, that the ancient gods were living in the basements of Mexico City and trying to get out through the stairs and elevator shafts. I could *see* that. Also, Mexico, by the late 1940s, was an incredibly dramatic place, and I saw that extremely clearly, and with great fascination. The country had a rising middle class, a powerful bourgeoisie that was benefiting enormously from the fruits of the Mexican Revolution. The Mexico of my childhood had been almost feudal. The Mexico I returned to in 1944 was industrializing. There were great expectations and problems: the problem of saturating the rising middle class with consumer products while the rest of the country was left outside the money economy. With all this going on, I knew that there were great stories to tell of this ascendant, developing Mexico—tremendous stories."[4]

1946. Graduated from high school in Mexico City. Wrote the first short story he felt happy with. "I wrote when I was eighteen, 'A Garden in Flanders.' It has to do with a young man who takes a house in Mexico that has a beautiful garden. Soon he discovers that outside the house there is the climate of Mexico—the sun, the smog, and all the rest. But inside the garden it is raining and cold. Then he sees this ghostly figure of an old woman who wanders into the garden, and she happens to be the Empress Carlotta. When I finished this story of two times and two places together, and found I had discovered something that expressed me, I got so happy. I remember I started slapping the light bulb in my room around. I got so excited that I just banged it and slapped it so that the shadows would elongate and engulf me and come back. I was sort of in an incredible vertigo. And I said, 'I'm going to write fiction. This is what I'm definitely going to do. The rest is second best.'"[6]

Fuentes' parents, however, convinced that no writer could live off his writing in Mexico, insisted that their son become a lawyer. The Mexican writer Alfonso Reyes, whom Fuentes had known and admired since childhood, explained that he must become a lawyer in order to do as he pleased. "So I entered the School of Law at the National University, where, as I feared, learning tended to be by rote and where cynical teachers spent the whole hour of class taking attendance on the two hundred students of civil law, from Aguilar to Zapata. But there were exceptions: the true teachers—mainly exiles from defeated Republican Spain who enormously enriched Mexican universities, publishing houses, the arts and the sciences—understood that the law is inseparable from the concerns of culture, morality and justice. Don Manuel Pedroso, former dean of the University of Seville, made the study-of-law compatible with my literary inclinations. When I would bitterly complain about the dryness and boredom of learning the penal or mercantile codes by heart, he would counter: 'Forget the codes. Read Dostoevsky, read Balzac. There's all you have to know about criminal or commercial law.' He also made me see that Stendhal was right: that the best model for a well-structured novel is the Napoleonic Code of Civil Law. Anyway, I found that culture consists of connections, not of separations: to specialize is to isolate."[1]

"I had fantastic energy. I went to law school from eight in the morning until eleven, then I worked in the foreign ministry from eleven to three, then I went home and at four I was writing my novel. At seven I went out to cocktail parties, to see girls, to dance the mambo, all the things you did at the time. The next day I was up at six o'clock and ready to go again."[7]

Published short stories in the reviews *Manana* and *Ideas de Mexico* and his first critical essay in *Revista de la Universidad*. "...I've been writing criticism since I was very young, since I was twenty or twenty-one. I was driven more than anything...by the desire to inform in my own culture, in my own country. There has always been such a lack of information in Latin America in general, and in Mexico in particular, about what happens outside our countries. When I was a very young man, Mexico was riding a wave of literary nationalism, an extreme wave of chauvinism, in which a very applauded literary critic would say from the supreme cultural podium of the nation, the Palacio de Bellas Artes, 'to read Proust is to *Proustitute* yourself.' Don't do that, he would say; it is against the national spirit. Stupidities of this sort. So, what I did with my friends was to try to inform.

"I remember the first critical essay I ever wrote in my life. It was about George Orwell in the *Revista de la Universidad*. I tried to redress injustices, as Don Quijote tried to make people realize who Alfonso Reyes was, since he was not read by young people, was despised in fact by young people and attacked as an un-Mexican writer."[8]

1949. Earned law degree from the Universidad Nacional Autonoma de Mexico.

1950. Graduate studies in international law at the Institut des Hautes Etudes in Geneva, Switzerland. "In Geneva, I rented a garret overlooking the beautiful old square of the Bourg-du-Four, established by Julius Caesar as the Forum Boarium two millennia ago. The square was filled with coffeehouses and old bookstores. The girls came from all over the world; they were beautiful, and they were independent. When they were kissed, one did not become a sullied lily. We had salt on our lips. We loved each other, and I also loved going to the little island where the lake meets the river to spend long hours reading. Since it was called Jean-Jacques Rousseau Island, I took along my volume of the *Confessions*. Many things came together then. A novel was the transformation of experience into history. The modern epic had been the epic of the first-person singular, of the I, from St. Augustine to Abelard to Dante to Rousseau to Stendhal to Proust. When Odysseus says that he is non-existent, we know and he knows that he is disguised; when Beckett's characters proclaim their non-be-

HOW TV STOLE ROCK'S SOUL • MEXICO'S NEW REVOLUTION

NOVEMBER 1988
$2.50
£1.50/UK

MOTHER JONES

The
Dangerous
Mind of
Carlos
Fuentes
Is Coming to a
Theater Near You

The Making
of a Presidential Guy

Beyond
Day-Care Guilt

Tobacco Row:
Reynolds Heir
Fights Back

Cover courtesy of *Mother Jones* magazine.

ing, we know that 'the fact is notorious': they are no longer disguised.

"I did not yet know this as I spent many reading hours on the little island of Rousseau at the intersection of Lake Geneva and the Rhone River back in 1951. But I vaguely felt that there was something beyond the exploration of the self."[1]

1954. Published his first book, the short story collection *Los dias enmascarados* ("The Masked Days"). His first novel was published four years later—*La region mas transparente* (*Where the Air Is Clear*). "I didn't want to offer identifications, served up on a Lazy Susan. When Octavio Paz first read the book he said it would not be successful at all because it was so private, so idiosyncratic, so solipsistic, and he was right. It is a very very personal view of Mexican life. People say it was not written by a Mexican, it was probably written by a foreigner, which in a way I was, of course. Then I could see certain things that Mexicans did not see. But the thing is that it became a huge bestseller, as it still is today. So there must have been an identification, but it was sort of a negative identification. This is what we don't want to be, or perhaps we are this, but it's awful. I just don't know."[2]

"The characters in *Where the Air Is Clear* are really an image, a sort of forecast of the destiny of Mexico City. Because it has become the most stupid city in the world. I hate it for its stupidity, for what it has done to itself....You drown in excrement and horror and become breathless with smog and with carbon monoxide and tinge its waters with refuse and aghh...throw these garbage-can cancers around it. It's terrifying. So what am I to think...what am I to feel then but this love and this hate? This love for what? For the great city I always felt so much in me and the cancerous cadaver I am seeing before me."[6]

"I think my weakest novel is certainly *Las buenas conciencia*, [*The Good Conscience*] but it is the novel that sells best in Mexico because of the identification factor. There isn't a young person in Mexico who doesn't read *Las buenas conciencia*. It is the novel which they must read in order to identify themselves, so it sells enormously. But I think that's probably a weak novel."[8]

"I mean that so many kids of seventeen buy the book and identify with Jaime Ceballos and with that provincial world of the family and the bourgeoisie, and the act of breaking from it. It's a notorious theme, it's so facile, and you identify so easily. You see, there is a great residue of naturalism, of slice-of-life in Latin America and all over

the world, for that matter. The innovation of our generation and the people immediately before us lies in the fact that we're trying to offer, not a slice-of-life, but a slice-of-imagination. And the audiences still never look for the imagination, they want the slice-of-life."[2]

1962. The State Department declined to issue Fuentes a visa to enter the United States for an NBC television debate with Richard Goodwin, President Kennedy's special advisor on Latin American affairs. "...I'm in excellent company.

"Can you imagine? There's me, Dario Fo, Garcia Marquez, Graham Greene, Mrs. Salvador Allende. But it's hard to imagine that the institutions of this great republic, its democratic edifice, its vast economic and military power, can be in any way endangered by us.

"If my books get in, our plays get in—why shouldn't we get in? What am I going to do? Blow up the Post Office? It couldn't make the mail worse, anyway. The whole thing is applied capriciously."[6]

The text Fuentes had prepared for the debate triggered no interest among American mass-circulation magazines and was published by *Monthly Review Press*. "South of your border, my North American friends, lies a continent in revolutionary ferment—a continent that possesses immense wealth and nevertheless lives in a misery and a desolation you have never known and barely imagine. Two hundred million persons live in Latin America. One hundred and forty million of them work virtually as serfs. Seventy million are outside the monetary economy. One hundred million are illiterate. One hundred million suffer from endemic disease. One hundred and forty million are poorly fed.

"Today, these miserable masses have decided to put an end to this situation. Latin America, for centuries nothing more than an object of historical exploitation, has decided to change—into a subject of historical action.

"You will ask yourselves: what has caused this Latin American backwardness? Why, if we won political independence more or less at the same time, are North Americans prosperous, free, democratic—and Latin Americans poor, subjugated, unable to govern themselves? You will sigh with relief: now, everything is going to change, thanks to American generosity. The Alliance for Progress will solve all the problems afflicting Latin America. Thanks to those $20 billion, Latin Americans will forget the spectre of revolution so stained with blood and destructive of democracy and human rights, will manage to develop peacefully and, in a short time, will set up democratic societies, twins of the United States.

"You are much given to good wishes, to what you call 'wishful thinking.' You have always believed that what is valid for you is valid for all men in all nations and at all times. You forget the existence of specific historical factors. You fail to realize that in reality there are two worlds, one of rich countries and one of poor countries. You fail to recognize that, of necessity, the poor countries require solutions different from yours. You have had four centuries of uninterrupted development within the capitalistic structure. We have had four centuries of underdevelopment within a feudal structure.

"Understand this: Latin America is not going to be your back yard any more. We are going to enter the world. What kind of world?

"Apparently, a world characterized by the political polarization of two power centers: the United States and the Soviet Union, facing one another from unchangeable positions—but both limited by the knowledge that a 'hot war' will end not with victor and vanquished but with the total destruction of the human race.

"But behind this obvious factor there is now another one: the upsurge of the underdeveloped countries and the possibility that they may dissolve this polarization, diversify and rationalize the international political positions, and confront the world with the primary job of peace—to cooperate in the economic and social development of those underdeveloped countries. The Soviet Union, as much as it can, is already doing so. And you? The first measure of cooperation is to know how to respect the revolutionary change that is taking place in those countries.

"And there is a third factor, of truly universal perspective: over and above the visible conflicts of our world, there is emerging the development of modern science and the opportunity it offers to all men, without any distinction of political ideology, religious belief, sex, or race, to achieve a truly human life, free from illness, ignorance, and hunger and full of promise for personal and collective creation. Please, try to see beyond the intellectual provincialism of the cold war. Try to see where we want to arrive, we men of the underdeveloped world, hungry, revolutionary. We do not want the destruction of the American people, which we love for the expressions of its great people, its great

First edition of the 1981 book.

political names—Lincoln, Franklin Roosevelt—and artistic names—Poe, Melville, Faulkner, Marian Anderson, O'Neill, Miller. We do not want atomic hatred, or a permanent cold war, but a world of peace in which we may grow without anachronistic deformations, without irrational exploitations. We want a world in which everyone coexists, not in mutual tolerance but in mutual respect and friendship."[9]

"I wrote [The Death of] *Artemio Cruz* many, many years after seeing 'Citizen Kane,' a film I saw at the age of eleven in New York City. It was pretty heady stuff at the time. I was certainly overpowered with the impression of finally seeing what power, ambition, greed, frustration, politics, and history were all about. Orson Welles had achieved a sort of magnificent synthesis of multiple aspects of life. So, yes, many years later, it became a model."[4]

"I've always maintained that without the poets who preceded us, there would have been no Latin American novels. The instruments of expression we have were fashioned by the poets—Pablo Neruda, Reuben Dario—because Latin America didn't have an interesting novel till the 1930s....The great novels of Latin American begin, I think, with Luis Borges and Miguel Angel Ansurias—two mythifiers, two men with the oldest imaginations of the Americas. I've always felt I was telling the Mexican part of what was really a Latin American story: the movement of our part of the hemisphere into this modern world."[6]

With a waiver arranged by senator William Fulbright, Fuentes was able to enter the United States in 1969.

1975. Published *Terra Nostra*, inspired by his first visit to Spain in 1967. The novel received Mexico's Xavier Villarrutia Prize and Venezuela's Romulo Gallegos Award. "What I wanted to do was to create a narrative that is told simultaneously by several different characters. This should produce a collective voice. It has already been done by certain Southern writers in the United States—by Faulkner and Carson McCullers especially. Defeated people seem to be able to produce a literature of this sort. It doesn't exist in the North. Success is I. Failure is we."[5]

"After *Terra Nostra*, I...did nothing for two years. It gave me a respite. I always take a respite between books."[10]

In the late seventies and early eighties Fuentes taught at various universities, among them the Colegio Nacional in Mexico City, University of California at San Diego, University of Concepcion in Chile, University of Paris, University of Pennsylvania at Philadelphia, Columbia University, Cambridge, Princeton, Harvard, and universities in several Italian cities.

In 1979 he received Mexico's Alfonso Reyes Prize for the body of his work. "[The reader] is a co-creator of the novel. There would be no novel without the reader which is also bringing the novel to its crisis. You are not a spectator; the novel is not a screen; you are not going to the theatre when you read a novel. You are helping us to break through this crisis; you are helping us to create it at the same time that the writer and the characters, if they can be called characters, and the narrator write the novel.

"I'm sure that the structure of the novel depends completely on the mind of the reader: the degree of his participation in the novel. That is why the novel *prima facie* does not have such an evident structure—it's a very loose novel, I think. Some-

times it's mushy, it's jello, like a sponge. But I'm sure that the reader will give it a structure, or *deny* it a structure if he is not interested in the novel."[11]

"I believe that there's a constant reflection on the genre, a criticism of creation within the created work, that destroys any illusion, either naturalist or realist, that the reader might have. And for that reason, the reader is disturbed, disturbed because he formerly could rely on the novelist's assuring him that what he was reading was real, that the novel was reality, and that the characters actually existed—that in fact the novel was true. The soap opera tells us these things, flaunting its reality to the viewer, assuring him of its truth, while the authentic novelist of today is saying to his readers that what they believe is reality is not so. He's saying that there's something more than that reality. The novelist is then attacking the reader's conformity, his acceptance of what is presented, and forces him to participate as a co-creator of the novel. The author imposes upon his reader a responsibility identical to his own....The poem creates the author, and it also creates its reader. I believe that this is a must for today's new novel, and Latin American novelists realize it."[12]

June 9, 1982. First production of the play "Orchids in the Moonlight" at American Repertory Theater in Cambridge, Massachusetts, directed by Joann Green. "My play is about the myth of culture and the culture of myths. But even more it is a play about memory. The movies I saw years ago in Mexico. The interesting thing about modern archetypes is that they are embedded in fashion, they go in and out of style. Our icons are ephemeral, our gods disposable. We throw them away. Our civilization is based on amnesia. So writing this play was a journey into the past and an evocation of two beautiful Mexican women who were important to me in my youth. Growing up, I used to say that I descended from Montezuma, Hernando Cortes, Maria Felix, and Dolores Del Rio. They were my ancestors.

"I loved those two actresses because they were strong and independent. They shattered all the macho myths. They were not what Latin women were supposed to be. They were not little dolls men could cuddle. Maria Felix was a Pancho Villa in skirts.

"My work is probably becoming less and less 'Mexican.' I've been living outside my country for a long time. Maybe I've paid my nationalistic dues by now. Nonetheless, even in 'Orchids' there is an element of identification with Mexico. But it never entered my head that I should write a Mexican play. I was writing a play about two women who need each other desperately. It's a play about loneliness, and loneliness is universal. Anyone who has been in love will understand my play.

"I wrote the play in English and Spanish at the same time. It's very curious. I had the two Mexican actresses in mind so I started in Spanish. But the third character, the fan, was American, and this character ran away from me. He started doing a series of puns on 'Citizen Kane' that simply wouldn't work in Spanish. They had to be put in English. There were some jokes I could not say in Spanish. I had to fall back on English, which had this tremendous, protean capacity for word play that we don't have in Spanish. The demands and opportunities of Spanish are very great and very exciting, but they are other. The particular kind of humor I wanted I could get only in English."[13]

1985. Published the novel *El Gringo viejo* ("The Old Gringo"). "It's a novel about Latin America and the United States. It deals with the destiny of the American writer Ambrose Bierce, who in 1914 was facing a very bad personal and professional situation. His family had fallen apart; he felt that his life was over and that his work was done. But he did not dare commit suicide. Instead, he disappeared into the Mexican frontier, and his parting words to a friend were, 'To be a gringo in Mexico, that is suicide.'"[4]

"[He] is looking for a frontier, and he feels the end of the frontier, and feels this is the most dramatic situation. The North American continent has been conquered. The frontier is over. And that's when Americans start thinking of other frontiers. You start wandering into other people's territory, and then you discover that you're a foreigner. But the Americans when they travel have a tendency to treat everyone who lives there as foreigners. This is what happens to the female character, Harriet Winslow. It is also the story of how she comes to realize that *she* is the foreigner. It is the story of how she sheds her Manichaeanism, the American aptitude for defining right and wrong, good and evil. We see this Manichaeanism even in our contemporary life. For instance, 'The Sandinistas are bad. The Contras are good.'"[6]

The novel became a best-seller, and Columbia Pictures released a movie version starring Jane Fonda and Gregory Peck.

In 1987 Fuentes received the Cervantes prize from the King of Spain; in 1988 the Medal of Honor for Literature from the National Arts Club in New York, and in Managua, Nicaragua's highest cultural award, named after Ruben Dario, the nineteenth-century poet and national hero.

Footnote Sources:

1 Carlos Fuentes, "The Discovery of Mexico," *Granta 22*, autumn, 1987.
2 Alfred MacAdam and Alexander Coleman, "An Interview with Carlos Fuentes," *Book Forum*, Volume IV, number 4, 1979.
3 "Carlos Fuentes at UCLA," *Mester*, Volume 9, number 1, 1982.
4 Claudia Dreifus, "Silence Is Death," *Mother Jones*, January, 1986.
5 Frank MacShane, "A Talk with Carlos Fuentes," *New York Times Book Review*, November 7, 1976.
6 C. Dreifus, "When Eternity Moves. . .," *Film Comment*, May-June, 1986.
7 Harriet Shapiro, "Carlos Fuentes Conquers the Land of the Gringos with a Haunting Tale from South of the Border," *People Weekly*, March 3, 1986.
8 Jonathan Tittler, "Interview: Carlos Fuentes," *Diacritics*, September, 1980.
9 C. Fuentes, "The Argument of Latin America: Words for the North Americans," *Whither Latin America?*, Monthly Review Press, 1963.
10 Regina Janes, "'No More Interviews': A Conversation with Carlos Fuentes," *Salmagundi*, winter, 1979.
11 Herman P. Doezema, "An Interview with Carlos Fuentes," *Modern Fiction Studies*, winter, 1972-73.
12 John P. Dwyer, "Conversation with a Blue Novelist," *Review*, fall, 1974.
13 Arthur Holmberg, "Carlos Fuentes Turns to Theater," *New York Times*, June 6, 1982.

■ For More Information See

Books:

John S. Brushwood, *Mexico in Its Novel: A Nation's Search for Identity*, University of Texas Press, 1966.
Luis Harss and Barbara Dohman, *Into the Mainstream: Conversations with Latin-American Writers*, Harper, 1966.
Jean Franco, *The Modern Culture of Latin America: Society and the Artist*, Praeger, 1967.
Octavio Paz, *Corriente alterna*, 2nd edition, Siglo Veintiuno Editores (Mexico City), 1968.
Selden Rodman, *South America of the Poets*, Hawthorn, 1970.
Walter M. Langford, *The Mexican Novel Comes of Age*, University of Notre Dame Press, 1971.
Kessel Schwartz, *A History of Spanish American Fiction*, University of Miami Press, 1971.
Helmy F. Giacoman, editor, *Homenaje a Carlos Fuentes*, Las Americas, 1971.
Luis Leal, *Historia del cuento hispanoamericano*, 2nd edition, Ediciones de Andres (Mexico City), 1971.
Daniel de Guzman, *Carlos Fuentes*, Twayne, 1972.

Jose Donoso, *Historia personal del "boom,"* Editorial Anagrama (Barcelona), 1972, translation by Gregory Kolovakos published as *The Boom in Spanish American Literature: A Personal History,* Columbia University Press, 1977.

Contemporary Literary Criticism, Gale, Volume III, 1975, Volume VIII, 1978, Volume X, 1979, Volume XIII, 1980, Volume XXII, 1982.

Authors in the News, Volume II, Gale, 1976.

Gloria Duran, *The Archetypes of Carlos Fuentes: From Witch to Androgyne,* Shoe String, 1980.

Salvador Bacarisse, editor, *Contemporary Latin American Fiction,* Scottish Academic Press (Edinburgh), 1980.

Robert Brody and Charles Rossman, editors, *Carlos Fuentes: A Critical View,* University of Texas Press, 1982.

Wendy B. Faris, *Carlos Fuentes,* Ungar, 1983.

Periodicals:

Saturday Review, November 19, 1960, December 16, 1961, January 27, 1968, October 30, 1976, September, 1980.

Commonweal, February 10, 1961, October 23, 1981.

New Yorker, March 4, 1961, January 26, 1981.

Lee Baxandall, "An Intreview with Carlos Fuentes," *Studies on the Left,* Volume 3, number 1, 1962.

Nation, June 1, 1964, January 3, 1966, December 25, 1976, January, 16, 1982.

New York Review of Books, June 11, 1964, January 20, 1977, October 22, 1981.

New Statesman, August 7, 1964, February 6, 1981.

Books Abroad, autumn, 1964, summer, 1966 (p. 261ff), spring, 1971.

Hispania, May, 1966, March, 1973, March, 1976, May, 1976, May, 1978, December, 1978.

New York Times, February 4, 1968, January 2, 1979, December 3, 1980, August 15, 1989.

Times Literary Supplement, November 13, 1970, July 15, 1977, December 14, 1979, June 6, 1982 (p. 1ff), July 9, 1982.

Leslie Cross, "Carlos Fuentes, Our Latin Writing Neighbor," *Milwaukee Journal,* October 12, 1975.

Washington Post Book World, October 26, 1976, January 14, 1979, November 26, 1980, March 14, 1982.

Review, winter, 1976.

Newsweek, November 1, 1976.

New Republic, April 9, 1977, December 23, 1978, December 30, 1978.

Symposium, summer, 1977.

Romance Notes, fall, 1977.

Revista de estudios hispanicos, January, 1978.

World Literature Today, winter, 1978.

American Hispanist, February, 1978 (p. 7).

New York Times Book Review, January 7, 1979, October 19, 1980, March 21, 1982, August 4, 1984 (p. 29ff), December 2, 1984 (p. 42).

Los Angeles Times Book Review, January 7, 1979, January 4, 1981.

Hispania, May, 1980 (p. 415).

Atlantic Monthly, November, 1980.

Chicago Tribune Book World, November 16, 1980, March 21, 1982.

Village Voice, January 28, 1981.

National Review, April 3, 1981.

Paris Review, winter, 1981 (p. 167ff).

Los Angeles Times, May 13, 1982.

New York Times Magazine, March 13, 1983 (p. 28ff).

Vance Bourjaily, "The Revenge Symposium," *Esquire,* May, 1983.

World Literature Today, autumn, 1983.

Harper's, June, 1984 (p. 35ff).

Gloria Duran, "Carlos Fuentes as Philosopher of Tragedy," *Modern Language Review,* April, 1986.

Novel: A Forum on Fiction, fall, 1986 (p. 62ff).

Publication of the Modern Language Association of America, October, 1986 (p. 778ff).

Mother Jones, November, 1988 (p. 20ff).

Rosa Guy

S urname rhymes with "me"; born September 1, 1925 (some sources say 1928), in Diego Martin, Trinidad, West Indies; came to the United States in 1932; daughter of Henry and Audrey (Gonzales) Cuthbert; married Warner Guy (deceased); children: Warner. *Education:* Attended New York University; studied with the American Negro Theater. *Residence:* New York. *Agent:* Ellen Levine Literary Agency, Inc., 432 Park Ave. S., Suite 1205, New York, N.Y. 10016.

■ Career

Writer, 1950—. Lecturer. *Member:* Harlem Writer's Guild (co-founder; president, 1967-78).

■ Awards, Honors

The Friends was selected one of American Library Association's Best Book for Young Adults, 1973, *Ruby,* 1976, *Edith Jackson,* 1978, *The Disappearance,* 1979, and *Mirror of Her Own,* 1981; *The Friends* was selected one of Child Study Association of America's Children's Books of the Year, 1973, and *Paris, Pee Wee, and Big Dog,* 1986; *The Friends* was selected one of *New York Times* Outstanding Books of the Year, 1973, and *The*

Disappearance, 1979; *The Friends* was selected one of *School Library Journal's* Best of the Best Books, 1979; *The Disappearance* was selected one of New York Public Library's Books for the Teen Age, 1980, and *Edith Jackson,* 1980, 1981, and 1982; Coretta Scott King Award, 1982, for *Mother Crocodile;* Parents' Choice Award for Literature from the Parents' Choice Foundation, 1983, for *New Guys around the Block;* Other Award (England), 1987, for *My Love, My Love; or, The Peasant Girl.*

■ Writings

Novels, Except As Indicated:

Bird at My Window, Lippincott, 1966.
(Editor) *Children of Longing* (anthology), Holt, 1971.
The Friends, Holt, 1973.
Ruby: A Novel, Viking, 1976.
Edith Jackson, Viking, 1978.
The Disappearance, Delacorte, 1979.
Mirror of Her Own, Delacorte, 1981.
(Translator and adapter) Birago Diop, *Mother Crocodile: An Uncle Amadou Tale from Senegal* (ALA Notable Book; illustrated by John Steptoe), Delacorte, 1981.
A Measure of Time, Holt, 1983.
New Guys around the Block, Delacorte, 1983.
Paris, Pee Wee, and Big Dog (illustrated by Caroline Binch), Gollancz, 1984, Delacorte, 1985.
My Love, My Love; or, The Peasant Girl, Holt, 1985.
And I Heard a Bird Sing, Delacorte, 1986.

The Ups and Downs of Carl Davis III,
Delacorte, 1989.

Plays:

"Venetian Blinds" (one-act), first produced at
Topical Theatre, New York, 1954.

Contributor:

Julian Mayfield, editor, *Ten Times Black,*
Bantam, 1972.
Donald R. Gallo, editor, *Sixteen: Short Stories
by Outstanding Writers for Young Adults,*
Delacorte, 1984.

Guy's novels have been translated into many
languages including, Japanese, German, Danish,
French, and Italian. Contributor to periodicals,
including *Cosmopolitan, New York Times Magazine,
Redbook,* and *Freedomways.*

■ **Adaptations**

"Documentary of *The Friends,*" Thames
Television, 1984.

■ **Work In Progress**

Alexander Hamilton: The Enigma; Benidine, a novel
dealing with a Trinidadian family in New York;
Sun, Sea, a Touch of the Wind; Dorine Davis, a
biography of a step-mother; research in African
languages.

■ **Sidelights**

Rosa Guy's novels have brought her acclaim and
international recognition as one of today's most
perceptive authors writing on the lives of black
Americans. Best known for her award-winning
young adult novels, her humble beginnings in
Harlem were a motivating factor in attaining
success as a writer. "Whether. . .to act or write or
do something! It was a driving force in me. It was a
driving force in that orphan, out there on the
streets. . .who needed something through which to
express herself, through which to become a full-
bodied person."[1]

Specifics about Guy's early years are limited. Two
dates of birth, September 1, 1925 and September
1, 1928 appear in standard biographical sources,
but she declines to verify either one. She was born
in Trinidad, West Indies, the second of two daughters of Henry and Audrey Cuthbert. "I was born in
Trinidad, a British colony at that time. How proud
we were to be a part of that great empire on which
the sun never set. We learned from British books

and rejected as nonsense our folklore—clinging
rather to the books that made for great dreams,
accepting everyone's myth as our reality.

"But my peasant feet were too large ever to fit into
Cinderella's glass slippers. And, where was the
princess to kiss my brother and change him back
into a prince and restore his meaning. . .our kingdom? And, which dashing prince would ever kiss
and awaken me to my full potential after years of
sleep?"[2]

Small wonder that Guy grew into a powerful
storyteller; the oral tradition in Trinidad is strong.
"My life in the West Indies, of course, had a
profound influence on me. It made me into the
type of person I imagine that I am today. The
calypso, the carnival, the religion that permeated
our life—the Catholic religion—superstitions,
voodoo, the zombies, the djuins, all of these
frightening aspects of life that combine the lack of
reality with the myth coming over from Africa, had
a genuine effect on me. But it was an effect that I
knew nothing about, didn't realize played an
important part in my life until much later when I
was writing. But they made for an interesting
background. . .something that I could call back on,
something that I could hold onto as I went into a
new life, a new environment. Something that gave
me a stake, I suppose one would say. So that when
I say I am West Indian, I have all of these little
things—all of that broad background—that makes
up the thinking, the searching of a person when art
becomes relevant."[1]

Guy's parents emigrated to the United States and,
when she was about eight year old, Rosa and her
older sister, Ameze, joined them in Harlem. Shortly after their arrival, their mother became ill.
Because of her illness, the two girls were sent to
live with cousins who were followers of the charis-
matic Garvey. Years later, Guy attributed her
activism in human rights and her love for language
to those Garveyite influences. "That's where I did
my first little poem at the Garvey meeting and
stood up at the corner and listened to the Black
Garveyites. I had an awareness of Africa that other
people didn't have. I had an awareness of language
because my cousin spoke so many different languages."[1]

Her mother's death led to the two girls' return to
their father in Harlem, but he also died a few years
later. Guy and her sister were left orphans. "Being
an orphan at a young age, had to affect my
personality, the way I see things, the way I absorb
things.

"The whole [experience] of always being on the outside looking in, in a way formed me."[1]

This early experience had a profound effect on her writing. "...I was confronted with the worst aspects of the society, without all of the sham. People take off on Black women who are writing about ideas and issues that are pertinent. But, if we really were to write about the things that happen to us the way they really happen—things that are done to us by our people just because of a lack of understanding of where we come from—then we would really run into a lot of trouble, because nobody wants to hear it!"[3]

As orphans, the two girls grew up quickly. At the age of fourteen, Guy quit school to work in a brassiere factory in New York City's garment district in order to take care of her older sister who had become ill. "Tiptoeing my way through the casualties of poverty in the ghettos—an orphan in New York, ostracized for those traits which being West Indian and Catholic had etched into my personality—wasn't easy. I shall never forget the day I walked, cringing, the length of a snowbound street and not one snowball was hurled at my head. I knew I was grown up: I believed myself immune from those influences molding the lives of the Americans among whom I lived.

"Rubbish, of course. I realized that when I looked through the galleys of my soon-to-be published first book....I had internalized all their pain, their resentment—to the snowballs hurled relentlessly at my head, and firecrackers at my feet—as I ducked and dodged my way through adolescence. But I never looked back in hate—but with a kind of sadness, a regret that there had been no books yet written, no guidelines from caring adults who might have made a difference, guiding us over the deep but narrow ravines dividing us."[4]

After her marriage and after the birth of son, Warner, Jr., Guy became involved in the American Negro Theatre. "I sort of went out of my way to meet them."[1]

At the end of the war, Guy divided her time between night school, the study of drama, her marriage, and her job in the clothes factory. She was part of a support group of writers and actors who had formed the committee for the Negro in the Arts. "What we wanted to do was to have a group that really projected the life, the style, the dialogue, the type of writing, [the] expression that could only come from the black experience in the United States, and in my situation, of course, the U.S. and the West Indies. So together with these people we formed a workshop—a workshop called the Harlem Writers Guild."[1]

Formed in 1951, the group supported themselves, both critically and emotionally, in their common need to write. "All of us were workers, doing some other type of work. I was working in a brassiere factory making brassieres. And every evening I had to come home to write. Mornings, I had a son to get dressed and get off to school, and then I'd go to work. I did this for a period of years because at the time publishers were not necessarily interested in black writings, nor in our concept of what writing should be."[1]

During the early years with the Harlem Writers Guild, Guy tried writing short stories, but it wasn't until 1966 that her first book was published. Besides writing, the group was involved in the politics of the 1960s. "The 1960s, for all its traumas, was one of the most beautiful periods in

Guy's 1973 novel about friendship.

American history. Only yesterday? So it seems to those of us who lived through it. Television sets were in the homes but had not yet taken over the responsibility of parents. Drugs on the streets had not yet changed youth gangs, fighting over turf, into addicts, robbing everybody's turf.

"Young people, strong in their beliefs, came out in numbers to follow Martin Luther King, Jr. They marched, sang, professed unity, a dedication to justice and human dignity for all. Black and white students, understanding the dehumanizing effect of poverty, shouted slogans, 'Black Power,' 'Black is Beautiful,' into Black communities to arouse the youth to their potential.

"What an outpouring of literature—about Blacks, about Spanish, about Indians, Chinese. Americans suddenly wanted to know the kind of world they were a part of. They were eager to do something for the good of that world, help cure its ills."[4]

Besides political ideology, the sixties was also a period of violence, and Guy was not immune to the events of the period. When her former husband, Warner, was murdered in 1962, Guy left the United States for Haiti. There, "The trauma of [my] husband's death and an earlier moment of violence in the life of a childhood friend. . ."[1] provided the reasons to start work on her first novel.

Another event during this period—the assassination of Malcolm X in 1965—compelled her to work on her novel. She recalled being in a hospital near the scene at the time of his murder. "The hospital was right across the street from the Audubon Ballroom and I could look out of the window and see this crowd while I'm listening to the radio and hearing about his being shot down. I saw when they brought him across and I was just about out of my mind, up on the sixth floor someplace and knowing that he was downstairs, and not knowing if he was dead.

"I'd probably never be in the hospital again for the longest time in life—and there I was right on the scene at that particular moment. And I always felt very strange about it. There I am, the person looking in; I'm always there."[1]

In 1966, after years of learning her craft, *Bird at My Window* was published. "All these years I have been wondering—and grumbling—about the reasons I had chosen, and stuck to, so low-paying, so rigidly disciplined, so devastatingly lonely a profession. . . .Looking forward from my first book, *Bird at My Window*—which I dedicated to Malcolm X—to those still to be published, the one constant I lay claim to is *caring*."[4]

In his review of the book, Thomas L. Vince called it, "the most significant novel about the Harlem Negro since James Baldwin's *Go Tell It on the Mountain*.

"This is Rosa Guy's first novel, but considering the intensity and power it evokes, we can expect more from such promising talent. Her demonstrative skills in character portrayal and in the etching of crucial incidents are certain to keep the reader absorbed. Some of the language and a few of the scenes may upset the prudish, but there is none of the garish prurience or repetitious vulgarity so common in modern fiction. *Bird at My Window* may even become a commercial success; but whatever its fate, it deserves critical attention."[5]

Another assassination of an American hero led Guy to investigate what young people were thinking throughout America. When Martin Luther King, Jr. was murdered in 1968, Guy went south. "I was so affected by the death of these two leaders; I could say three, because Lumumba's death certainly had affected me. And just the fact that no sooner than you start building up heroes—they get knocked down like that.

"I felt that when Dr. King died I just had to go. So I went to my editor at that time [Greg Armstrong at Bantam], and I said 'I want to find out what the young people are thinking.'"[1]

The result of her travels was a non-fiction book, *Children of Longing*. "I especially wanted to know how these painful events had affected their lives and their ambitions. I traveled throughout the United States from coast to coast, going into Black high schools and colleges in urban and rural areas, into writers' workshops, the cotton fields and the ghettos, seeking answers from young Black people between the ages of thirteen and twenty-three.

"I have not edited their responses for spelling, grammar, or sentence structure, except when the meaning was too unclear. Their writing skills vary according to their different (and sometimes nonexistent) educations, ages, and life experiences. Yet each possesses and clearly communicates the one quality that is the undercurrent of this book—an intense desire to overcome the obstacles of a slave past that remains in the conditions of their present lives.

"In Chicago I visited the home of one girl whose mother works as a servant for a white family. The mother was upset by my request that her daughter

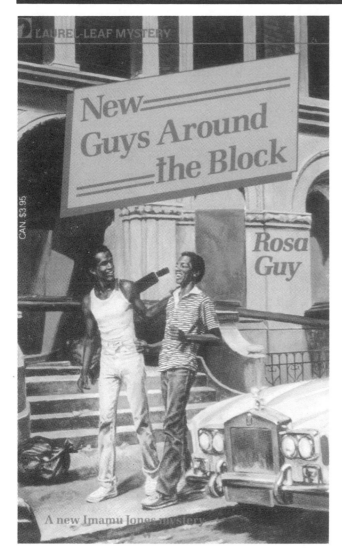

The 1983 Dell paperback edition.

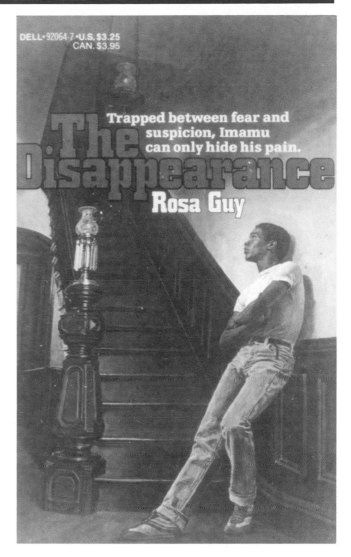

An ALA Best Book for Young Adults.

write an essay on what she wanted to be. 'Don't put no ideas in that girl's head,' she said to me. 'She got enough crazy ideas already. Black like she is, she got big ideas. I tell her she better get some sense and study something where she gets decent pay, never mind all them high-sounding ideas.' Sitting smugly in her expensively furnished, slum, walk-up flat (she let me know her couch cost six hundred dollars), she had no idea she was part of the quickly dying past. Young people are saying, 'Black is beautiful.' They believe it.

"I visited a mother in Harlem, New York, living in a broken-down apartment building where I had to climb over dozing winos to gain entrance. The poor woman greeted me as though all her energy had been spent by the three robust children shouting and chasing each other over old, tortured furniture. She became just a bit more energetic when I asked the whereabouts of her son. 'I don't

know where that damn fool is. Out there getting in some kind of trouble. Talking about he want to go to college. He ain't even finish high school.' I insisted on knowing why she thought he was getting into trouble. I had come to interview him because I had been told he was active in the strike at Queens College, aimed at getting more students from the ghetto areas. 'All that ain't nothing but some damn foolishness. Waste of time. They ain't never gonna let Black people do nothing nohow. If he knew what's good for him, he would be going downtown to get hisself a job.'

"But today's Black students are not going to be pinned down by negative parents, by white prejudice, by liberal put-offs, or the power structure. They intend to go beyond these obstacles, and to go beyond themselves. The intensity of their desire is clearly evident in the essays of 'Inner Cities.' One girl asserts, 'I want to be somebody.' A young boy wants Black people to stop hurting each other and unite for BLACK POWER. Another girl 'stands for good education.' Two young mothers, who started out in the dead-end street to which slum living leads, write about the ancient mistakes they made that have so often devastated the lives of the young—but they also fought back to a greater definition of themselves when opportunity presented itself. Hardest of all is the problem of the young addict who is trying to pull himself up from the very bottom of ghetto life."[6]

In the early 1970s, after publishing *Bird at My Window* and *Children of Longing*, Guy began traveling in the Caribbean. Her second novel, *The Friends*, was the result. It was her first novel for young adults, and the first in a trilogy about the Cathy and Jackson families. Named by the American Library Association as "one of the Best of the Best Books," it was also adopted as part of the English curriculum for high schools in Great Britain.

In a 1973 *New York Times* review, Alice Walker, described the book as a "heart-slammer. [In] *The Friends*, I relive those wretched, hungry-for-heroines years and am helped to verify the existence and previous condition of myself.

"[The] struggle that is the heart of this very important book [is] the fight to gain perception of one's own real character; the grim struggle for self-knowledge and the almost killing internal upheaval that brings the necessary growth of compassion and humility *and courage*, so that friendship (of any kind, but especially between those of notable economic and social differences) can exist.

"This book is called a 'juvenile.' So be a juvenile while you read it. Rosa Guy will give you back a large part of the memory of those years that you've been missing."[7]

The second novel in the Jackson-Cathy trilogy was begun while Guy was in Haiti. *Ruby* was reviewed by *Horn Book* as "a teenage novel: rich, full-bodied, and true in its portrayal of the world of the Black teenager. . . .Ruby, deeply sensitive and lonely, finds love in a secret homosexual relationship with Daphne, a beautiful, arrogant Black classmate. Their experience fills a desperate need at a crucial time in the lives of both girls, affording them an early insight into the depths and complexities of human relations and emotions. The author writes gracefully in the West Indian idiom as she analyzes perceptively the problems of young Blacks facing up to the emotional, political, social, and educational responsibilities of their own lives."[8]

Her final book in the trilogy about three young black women, *Edith Jackson*, was completed in 1978. "I took the two characters Phylissia and Edith—and I left Sylvia, who's a very interesting character—and made *The Friends*. And then *Ruby*—who was very special to me—and then the other side of Phylissia, of course, was *Edith Jackson*."[1]

The trilogy makes a powerful statement about the failure of adults to meet the complex needs of young people. "I do believe that I'm trying to say that we live in one world and it's a damn small world and we have to care for each other. We have to be concerned about that world. The survival of one of us depends upon all of us."[1]

Young people, too, however, have responsibilities to assume. "I believe that life is before any teenager. I try to leave all my characters with the hope that they can change their future—that they have the right to change their future; that they have the right to question parents; that they have the right to make decisions based on moral values."[9]

Critic Zena Sutherland, in her 1979 review of *Edith Jackson*, said: "The characterization is excellent, the writing style smooth, and the depiction of an adolescent torn between her need for independence and achievement and her feeling of responsibility (which has pushed her into protecting the sisters who don't want protection) strong and perceptive."[10]

The Disappearance, Guy's fourth young adult novel is a suspenseful story about a streetwise Harlem teenager Imamu Jones. The mystery led to sequels. "Believing as I do that world survival rests with the young, I like to think that my contribution as a writer to their understanding of the world lies in exposing a segment of society often overlooked, ignored, or treated with contempt. It's a segment that cannot be wished away, and in the final analysis, our approach to its problems can determine the kind of people we shall ultimately be. As spokesman for that segment, I give to my readers Imamu Jones—the detective.

"'Issue oriented' books or 'required reading' can most times be a bore. But the world loves a good mystery. So do I. A good mystery can force the mind to reach just a bit further than it believes it's capable of reaching. And because I have great respect for the capabilities of the young, the possibility that I might provide stimulation, forcing minds to stretch just a bit beyond, is a great challenge. I like to imagine that in attempting to unravel a tightly woven work old prejudices and fixed ideas may be examined and rethought. And I live in hope that with rethinking comes joy.

"In *The Disappearance* and also its sequel, *New Guys around the Block*, the challenge to the reader is two-fold: solving a mind-boggling whodunit on the one hand, and on the other, attempting to unlock secret passages of minds that have been closed to us—minds developed in the so-called underbelly of our society, where wits are sharpened by the constant struggle for survival—from criminal elements and from daily confrontation with the law.

"Thus Imamu Jones—poor, orphaned by the death of his father and chronic alcoholism of his mother—rises above the ugliness of his environment to shoulder the burden of *my* imposed responsibility. A shrewd observer of people, sensitive, with a natural intelligence, a boy who accepts as normal

Guy's re-working of a Hans Christian Andersen fable.

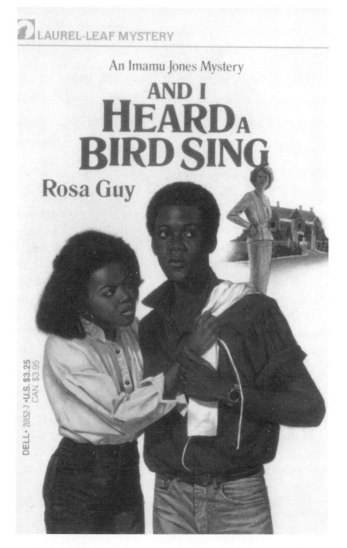

Guy's third in the series of "Imamu Jones" novels.

the fragility of his friends' morals, a high school dropout, Imamu with his street wisdom can solve crimes that baffle the police.

In *New Guys around the Block*, the second of the Imamu series, Imamu is joined in his detective pursuits by Olivette, an exceedingly brilliant youth who because of his great intelligence and broad experiences—he has lived in every inner city in the country—is able to bring a new approach to Imamu, a new insight, as they join forces in their attempt to solve the series of crimes plaguing the city.

"What a joy it is to construct a mystery! How challenging to scatter carefully thought-out clues that must fit into the novel through characters, their motives, patterns of thought, and environmental framework. Every piece must matter. Each detail must be studied. What excitement for me, the author, to imagine the alert reader attempting to unravel those events I so painstakingly knitted. Can anyone solve the crimes that took so much hard work and time to render insoluble? How nerve-splitting it is to contemplate: readers crossing ideas like swords, with the uneducated, though highly intelligent, Imamu Jones.

"My characters are drawn from life. In *The Disappearance*, Imamu Jones, Mama, and the Aimsleys are to be found within black communities. In *New Guys around the Block*, the intriguing Olivette, a rare sort, is always a phenomenon wherever he's encountered. But the Olivettes are mesmerizing, especially when found in their natural habitat of the inner cities.

"What happens to individuals like Imamu Jones and Olivette when there are no outlets to channel their active minds or to absorb their energies? Here is the double challenge confronting the reader. The question must occur to many while reading the books and searching for clues. Surely the answers to that question are as important as those leading to the solution of the crimes. But the question confounds even the experts."

About her writing Guy commented: "The arduous task of writing novels implies that one person—an author—believes that he, or she, has a conception of time, place, and events that is unique. A gift: to observe the overlapping patterns, the delicate details of relationships obscured to the sensibilities of the average, in the rush to judgment. I do not judge. I reveal—fragments of the obscure, weaving them into what is already obvious, in order to attach a total portrait to the consciousness of those reared in an ethic of religiosity.

"Fiction is history—if you will. It is the history of emotional events, given substance in time and place. It is as true today as in the *Iliad* and the *Odyssey*, as in Dostoevski's or Flaubert's time, and has validity whether the place is China, Russia, Africa, or the United States.

"I write for people—all people, young and old, black, white, or any others whom my book might fall into the hands of. I write about ordinary people who do ordinary things, who want the ordinary— love, warmth, understanding, happiness. These things are universal. But no life is ordinary. No life is simple. Characteristics such as goodness, selfishness, kindness, wickedness, bravery, cowardice, are all cliches. They are given uniqueness when the universal becomes particular.

"Even in drug-oriented societies, events only seem to fit into the abstract. Beneath the grotesque distortion of the drug culture lies the truth of America—the capitalistic, individualistic, democratic society. My characters are products of that society. They are people continually striving for the promised, but illusory, power to shape their destinies. They are black people and they are oppressed.

"An unequal burden, a distortion, quivers beneath the abstraction of those terms: Equality. Democracy. An American dilemma: Even though much takes place in Harlem in my stories, the lives of my characters reflect all over the country. This reflection is one that all Americans need to be cognizant of. It is our history, the emotional history of our times."

"This is the consciousness through which I write:

"I reject the notion of the innocence of youth. The television sets in our living rooms projecting the global disasters caused by wars have robbed us of innocence;

"I reject a world where the young are sheltered in innocence while the youth of other nations are condemned to perpetual misery by the greed, or wrath, of their fathers;

"I reject the innocence of children whose fathers are more interested in building jails for minority youth of this nation instead of schools;

"I reject the pampering of babies as their parents vote for bombs instead of for books;

"I reject the ignorance of the heirs of Superman and Wonderwoman, who believe themselves inherently stronger and thus immune from catastrophies created by their forefathers, their fathers;

"I reject the young of each succeeding generation who dare to say: 'I don't understand *you* people....' 'I can't stand *those people....*' or 'Do you see the way *they* act...?' They are us! Created by us for a society which suits our ignorance.

"I insist that Everychild understand this. I insist that Everychild go out into the world with this knowledge: there are no good guys. There are no bad guys. We are all good guys. We are all bad guys. And we are all responsible for each other."[2]

Guy continues to write with the conviction that art can change life. "I'm a storyteller. I write about people. I want my readers to know people, to laugh with people, to be angry with people, to despair of people, and to have hope. More than that, I want my readers to know just a little bit more, to care just a little bit more, when they put down a book of mine."[9]

"In this world growing ever smaller and more vulnerable to the holocaust that might mean its end, it is of the utmost importance that young adults break with prejudice—that value system which creates the socio-economic pressures that mangle the minds of minorities and create the dangers of world annihilation. A more profound understanding, a broader vision of those with whom we must share space between shore and sea can only make a coming together easier for the battle in which we all must engage if the world as we know it is to survive. This, I suggest, is the theme of most of my novels for young adults."[11]

Footnote Sources:

[1] Jerrie Norris, *Presenting Rosa Guy*, Twayne, 1988.
[2] Rosa Guy, "Innocence, Betrayal, and History," *School Library Journal*, November, 1985.
[3] Judith Wilson, "Face to Face—Rosa Guy: Writing with Bold Vision," *Essence*, October, 1979.
[4] R. Guy, "All about Caring," *Top of the News*, winter, 1983.
[5] Thomas L. Vince, "Bird at My Window," *Best Sellers*, January 15, 1966.
[6] R. Guy, "Preface," *Children of Longing*, Holt, 1970.
[7] Alice Walker, "The Friends," *New York Times Book Review*, November 4, 1973.
[8] "*Ruby: A Novel*," *Horn Book*, December, 1976.
[9] R. Guy, audiotape of speech, "Children's Writing Today for Tomorrow's Adults," *Boston Globe* Book Festival, November 4, 1984.
[10] Zena Sutherland, "*Edith Jackson*," *Bulletin of the Center for Children's Books*, University of Chicago Press, March, 1979.
[11] Alleen Pace Nilsen and Kenneth Donelson, *Literature for Today's Young Adults*, second edition, Scott, Foresman, 1985.

■ For More Information See

Washington Post, January 9, 1966, November 11, 1979 (p. 21), December 17, 1985 (p. B3).
Negro Digest, March 1, 1966 (p. 33ff).
Redbook, December, 1970 (p. 81).
New York Times Magazine, April 16, 1972 (p. 30ff).

Times Literary Supplement, September 20, 1974 (p. 1006), December 14, 1979, July 18, 1980 (p. 807), August 3, 1984.
Theressa Gunnels Rush and others, *Black American Writers Past and Present: A Biographical and Bibliographical Dictionary*, Scarecrow, 1975.
Freedomways, Volume 16, number 2, 1976 (p. 118ff).
James Page, *Selected Black American Authors: An Illustrated Bio-bibliography*, G. K. Hall, 1977.
New York Times Book Review, July 2, 1978, December 2, 1979 (p. 40), October 4, 1981 (p. 38), August 28, 1983 (p. 22), October 9, 1983, November 10, 1985 (p. 36), December 1, 1985 (p. 24).
D. L. Kirkpatrick, editor, *Twentieth-Century Children's Writers*, St. Martin's, 1978, new edition, 1983.
Washington Post Book World, November 11, 1979, November 10, 1985 (p. 17ff).
Mary Helen Washington, editor, *Midnight Birds: Stories of Contemporary Black Women Writers*, Anchor Books, 1980.
Times Educational Supplement, June 6, 1980 (p. 27), June 5, 1987.
Michael Jaye and Ann Watts, editors, *Literature and the Urban Experience*, Rutgers University Press, 1981.
Los Angeles Times, August 24, 1983.
Contemporary Literary Criticism, Volume XXVI, Gale, 1983.
Claudia Tate, editor, *Black Women Writers at Work*, Continuum, 1983.
Gloria Wade-Gayles, *No Crystal Stair: Visions of Race and Sex in Black Women's Fiction*, Pilgrim Press, 1984.
Dictionary of Literary Biography, Volume XXXIII: *Afro-American Fiction Writers after 1955*, Gale, 1984.
Books for Keeps, January, 1985 (p. 12ff).
Horn Book, March-April, 1985 (p. 220ff).
Sally Holmes Holtze, *Fifth Book of Junior Authors and Illustrators*, H. W. Wilson, 1985.
Geta LeSeur, "One Mother, Two Daughters: The Afro-American and the Afro-Caribbean Female Bildungsroman," *Black Scholar*, March-April, 1986.

Lynn Hall

Born November 9, 1937, in Lombard, Ill.; daughter of Raymond Edwin (a city official) and Alice (a high school teacher; maiden name, Seeds) Hall; married Dean W. Green, May 1, 1960 (divorced, September, 1961). *Education:* Attended schools in Iowa. *Religion:* Protestant. *Home:* Touchwood, Route 2, Elkader, Iowa 52043.

■ Career

Writer, 1968—. Secretary in Fort Worth, Tex., 1955-57; secretary and veterinarian's assistant in Des Moines, Iowa, 1957-66; affiliated with Ambro Advertising Agency, Des Moines, Iowa, 1966-68. *Member:* Society of Children's Book Writers, Dubuque Kennel Club, Bedlington Terrier Club of America.

■ Awards, Honors

Ride a Wild Dream was chosen one of Child Study Association of America's Children's Books of the Year, 1969, *Too Near the Sun* and *Gently Touch the Milkweed,* 1970, *To Catch a Tartar* and *Barry, the Bravest Saint Bernard,* 1973, *New Day for Dragon,* 1975, *Just One Friend,* 1985, and *Mrs. Portree's Pony,* 1987; Charles W. Follett Award, 1972, for *A*

Horse Called Dragon; Sticks and Stones was selected one of American Library Association's Best Young Adult Books, 1972, *The Leaving,* 1980, and *Uphill All the Way,* 1984; Silver Quill Award (Netherlands), 1976 for *Sticks and Stones;* Edgar Allan Poe Award runner up from the Mystery Writers of America, 1980, for *The Whispered Horse; Boston Globe-Horn Book* Award for Fiction, 1981 for *The Leaving;* Tennessee Children's Choice Award from the Tennessee Library Association, 1981, for *Shadows; The Leaving* was selected one of New York Public Library's Books for the Teen Age, 1981, and 1982, and *The Horse Trader,* 1982; *Tazo and Me* was selected an Outstanding Science Trade Book for Children by the National Science Teachers Association and the Children's Book Council, 1985; Golden Kite Award Honor Book for Fiction from the Society of Children's Book Writers, 1986, for *The Solitary;* Children's Literature Award from the Society of Midland Authors, 1987, for *Mrs. Portree's Pony;* Johnson Brigham Award from the Iowa State Historical Society, 1989, for *The Secret Life of Dagmar Schultz.*

■ Writings

The Shy Ones (illustrated by Greta Elgaard), Follett, 1967.
The Secret of Stonehouse (illustrated by Joseph Cellini), Follett, 1968.
Ride a Wild Dream (illustrated by George Roth), Follett, 1969.

Too Near the Sun (illustrated by Stefan Martin; Junior Literary Guild selection), Follett, 1970.

Gently Touch the Milkweed (illustrated by Rod Ruth; Junior Literary Guild selection), Follett, 1970.

A Horse Called Dragon (illustrated by J. Cellini; Junior Literary Guild selection), Follett, 1971, published as *Wild Mustang*, Scholastic, 1976.

The Famous Battle of Bravery Creek, Garrard, 1972.

The Siege of Silent Henry, Follett, 1972.

Sticks and Stones, Follett, 1972.

Lynn Hall's Dog Stories, Follett, 1972.

Flash, Dog of Old Egypt, Garrard, 1973.

Barry, the Bravest St. Bernard (illustrated by Richard Amundsen), Garrard, 1973.

Riff, Remember, Follett, 1973.

To Catch a Tartar (illustrated by J. Cellini), Follett, 1973.

The Stray (illustrated by J. Cellini), Follett, 1974.

Bob, Watchdog of the River (illustrated by Taylor Oughton), Garrard, 1974.

Troublemaker (illustrated by J. Cellini), Follett, 1974.

Kids and Dog Shows, Follett, 1975.

New Day for Dragon (illustrated by J. Cellini), Follett, 1975.

Captain: Canada's Flying Pony (illustrated by Tran Mawicke), Garrard, 1976.

Flowers of Anger (illustrated by J. Cellini), Follett, 1976.

Owney, the Traveling Dog, Garrard, 1977.

Dragon Defiant (illustrated by J. Cellini), Follett, 1977.

Shadows (illustrated by J. Cellini), Follett, 1977.

Careers for Dog Lovers, Follett, 1978.

The Mystery of Pony Hollow (illustrated by Ruth Sanderson), Garrard, 1978.

The Mystery of the Lost and Found Hound (illustrated by Alan Daniel), Garrard, 1979.

The Whispered Horse, Follett, 1979.

The Mystery of the Schoolhouse Dog (illustrated by William Hutchinson), Garrard, 1979.

Dog of Bondi Castle, Follett, 1979.

The Leaving, Scribner, 1980.

Dragon's Delight, Follett, 1980.

The Mystery of the Stubborn Old Man (illustrated by Herman Vestal), Garrard, 1980.

The Mystery of Plum Park Pony (illustrated by A. Daniel), Garrard, 1980.

The Haunting of the Green Bird, Follett, 1980.

The Disappearing Grandad, Follett, 1980.

The Mysterious Moortown Bridge (illustrated by R. Sanderson), Follett, 1980.

The Ghost of the Great River Inn (illustrated by Allen Davis), Follett, 1981.

The Horse Trader, Scribner, 1981.

The Mystery of the Caramel Cat (illustrated by R. Sanderson), Garrard, 1981.

Danza!, Scribner, 1981.

Half the Battle, Scribner, 1982.

Tin Can Tucker, Scribner, 1982.

The Mystery of Pony Hollow Panda (illustrated by W. Hutchinson), Garrard, 1983.

Megan's Mare, Scribner, 1983.

Denison's Daughter, Scribner, 1983.

Uphill All the Way, Scribner, 1984.

Nobody's Dog, Scholastic, 1984.

The Boy in the Off-White Hat, Scribner, 1984.

The Something Special Horse (illustrated by Sandy Rabinowitz), Scribner, 1985.

The Giver, Scribner, 1985.

Just One Friend, Scribner, 1985.

Tazo and Me (illustrated with photographs by Jan Hall), Scribner, 1985.

The Solitary, Scribner, 1986.

Danger Dog, Scribner, 1986.

If Winter Comes, Scribner, 1986.

Mrs. Portree's Pony, Scribner, 1986.

Ride a Dark Horse, Morrow, 1987.

Flyaway, Scribner, 1987.

In Trouble Again, Zelda Hammersmith? (illustrated by Ray Cruz), Harcourt, 1987.

Letting Go, Scribner, 1987.

A Killing Freeze, Morrow, 1988.

Murder at the Spaniel Show, Scribner, 1988.

Zelda Strikes Again!, Harcourt, 1988.

The Secret Life of Dagmar Schultz, Scribner, 1988.

Dagmar Schultz and the Powers of Darkness, Scribner, 1988.

Here Comes Zelda Claus, Harcourt, 1989.

Murder in a Pig's Eye, Harcourt, 1989.

Dagmar Schultz and the Angel Edna, Scribner, 1989.

Where Have All the Tigers Gone?, Scribner, 1989.

Halsey's Pride, Scribner, 1990.

The Tormentors, Harcourt, 1990.

■ Sidelights

Lynn Hall has always loved animals—dogs and horses, in particular—and has kept them around her as much as possible. As a child she was limited to dogs, friends' horses, and the animals found in the horse and dog books at the local library. From her earliest memories she recalled that her big dream was to "live in a little house in the country, preferably all by myself, and to own lots of dogs and a wonderful horse.

"There were years full of false starts and mislaid directions along the way to that goal."

The path Hall traveled to reach her goal began on November 9, 1937 in Lombard, Illinois, a suburb of Chicago. When she was still a child, her family moved to a suburb of Des Moines, Iowa. "I am the middle one of three daughters. My mother was an English and later a Spanish teacher. My father worked for Standard Oil—he owned a bulk plant and then a gas station.

"Of the people in my family, I was by far the one most interested in animals. I don't know where this came from. Perhaps being the middle sibling had something to do with it. Truthfully, I think it's something you're born with. I owned as many pets as I could. For a while, I had a stray dog who followed me home from school."[1]

In her search for a life surrounded by animals, Hall once tried to offer herself for adoption to a farm family. When she was seven, she ran away from home hoping to join a pony-ride concession. "My strongest childhood memories are of trying to escape, not so much *from* something, since ours was a happy family, but *to* something—to the country, to dogs, to horses. I was always going off to be by myself in the country, to visit a horse or other animals I knew. I preferred doing things on my own, which I think worried my mother. She always pushed me toward other children—afraid, I guess, that I'd grow up to be a misfit. She wanted me to go to the movies as part of a group; I wanted to go alone, so I could really get into the story. My nature was to be a loner, and I did manage to have a lot of time to myself. I wrote plays, went to the little local library, read continually, primarily horse and dog stories—wish fulfillment books. They became the center of my life. I wasn't trying to expand my mind, but merely to get a horse or a dog any way I could."[1]

It never occurred to Hall that she would one day write stories for animal-loving kids like herself. "I thought about drawing the pictures, about being an illustrator. But my conception of someone who wrote books was way beyond anything I ever imagined I could be. Writers, I thought, sat at the right hand of God. Henry Gregor Felsen, a children's author, lived in our small town in Iowa. I used to follow him around, not realizing, I'm sure, that on some subliminal level I too wanted to write. We met years later, when I was in my mid-twenties and had written my first book.

"Childhood can be a dreadful time. I wouldn't go back there for anything. There are so many things to be afraid of when you're a kid. For an adult, a visit to the dentist, for example, may summon fears, but to a child any uncertain situation calls up my feelings of *terror*. Every child, I believe, is afraid of something, afraid of not being all that he wants to be, perhaps. There's an essential aloneness during the process of growing up. Everyone has to fight his own devils—a frightening process."[1]

Her childhood was a little less frightening because she spent so much time with the animals she so dearly loved. During her pre-teen and teenage years Hall cleaned stalls at a local riding stable in hopes of earning a spare ride. "And when I was fourteen, as soon as I was able to earn money to pay for it, I got my first horse. Before that, I could

Gail Owens' illustration for the 1983 hardcover.

ride only in stolen moments. Now I could—and you better believe I did—ride every day.

"I left home the day after my high school graduation. I was at the age where I couldn't stand my parents, and was filled with a fierce desire for independence. But being a dutiful child, I wrote home every week while I was out seeing the world and seeking my fortune. I lived and worked for several years in Colorado, Texas, Indiana, Kentucky and Wisconsin. The jobs I held ranged from assistant dog trainer to assistant to a veterinarian, from clerk in a blue jeans factory to secretary in a juvenile parole office, from radio station copywriter to ad agency writer. It was a very difficult time for me. It was full of false starts and mislaid directions. I was searching, almost desperately, for a career. My mother kept hoping that I would try to write a book because I wrote such 'cute letters.' But no one takes her mother seriously when she says such things."[1]

Hall returned to Des Moines and "began to have serious expectations of marriage. It was time. All my friends were married. My jobs were boring, routine office jobs that used only a small fraction of my mind. I felt ready to settle down now, and join the rest of the world.

"So I picked out a husband and married him. He was a mild, pleasant man, a pharmacist in a small town in southern Iowa. He was stability personified, and I had already outgrown him even before the wedding. But, having made and broken several engagements by that time, I felt that I must see this one through. Marriage, after all, was a girl's only hope of real happiness. Everyone told me so.

"With a crushing sadness I put aside my dreams of living alone among the hills and woods, with a family of dogs and horses, and belonging to myself. That wasn't the way women were supposed to live.

"The marriage was predictably short. In less than two years I was on the road again, with all my belongings packed in the back of my '57 Chevy, and a blooming sense of freedom inside me. I felt that I had paid my dues to society, now the rest of my life was going to be my way.

"I worked in a show kennel in Kentucky, and a professional dog handler's kennel in Wisconsin. I raised chinchillas and I painted pet portraits. I was searching seriously now for the trail that would lead to my dream life."[2]

A procession of unsatisfying jobs followed, but gradually Hall began to sift through her options until she stopped at the one marked "writing." "In passing a bookstore window one day, I noticed a display for a new horse book by a local author. I went in to investigate. The book was poorly written in my opinion, and showed a laughable lack of knowledge of horses. This was just what I needed. By this time I had enough technical knowledge about horses and dogs to write about them convincingly. I had the answer I'd been looking for during all those frustrating years. I had my dream.

"I sold my chinchilla herd to finance six months of freedom from my secretarial job during which I hoped to write a saleable children's book. I was so frightened at first that I sat at the typewriter each morning as nauseated as an expectant mother. But six months of labor pains brought forth not one but two books.

"But, of course, far above the small glories was the *big* dream—the life of an author, a lady country gentleman. There was a delay of four more years of working days and writing nights before the books were bringing in even a marginal income. They were exciting years, however, because the dream was growing closer all the time. And the day finally came when I turned in my time card, packed the station wagon, and headed into my new life, more than half expecting that anything so greatly longed for must certainly be a disappointment in reality. It wasn't."[1]

There still remained, however, a few snags, both professional and personal, that had to be overcome. "The first obstacle proved to be Denny. We were in love, or at least I liked to think we were, and he monopolized so much of my free time that I couldn't begin working toward my huge new dream. Denny was a bright, handsome young man, farming a huge showplace of a farm near the city in partnership with his father. He loved the farm but felt, as I did, trapped in a life that used little of his mental ability and therefore earned him insufficient respect. He was frequently moody and demanding, and would stand for no equality on my part. It threatened him.

"When I announced my new goal, to write children's books, he jeered. He began chipping away at my tentative new self-confidence. Finally, sensing the danger, I said we would have to quit seeing each other. Then, in anger, he flung at me the marriage proposal I'd hoped a year for.

"But I was seeing him clearly for the first time. I could see how little growth he would allow me. If I did succeed as an author of children's books, my instincts told me, the marriage would not survive.

"To his proposal I replied with great dignity, 'No, thank you. I'd rather be an author.'"[2]

Hall's first book, *Holly of Silver Hill,* was rejected. Undaunted, she began work on a second book. While Book Two made the publishers' rounds, she went to work on Book Three, Four, and Five. Her tenacity paid off after six months when Follett published *The Shy Ones.* "I couldn't imagine that life would hold a higher moment than my first realization that I was a published author. I was instantly vindicated in the eyes of parents who thought I was a hopeless drifter.

The Shy Ones was a fictionalized treatment of the experience I had with a dog given to me because she was too timid to be a show dog. She had been born and raised in a kennel and had never received any individual attention. I would take her downtown with me every day and make her sit with me in the square to get used to people passing by. It took the entire summer, but she lost her fear of strangers. When I wrote the book, I fictionalized the girl character, making her as timid as her pet. After finding a dog who was hit by a car, she was

Jacket illustration from *The Solitary,* Hall's novel about a seventeen-year-old's struggle for self-sufficiency.

forced to take a job in a vet's office in order to pay the animal's medical expenses. The girl does things of which she never before believed herself capable."[1]

Other books followed in rapid succession. One of them, *A Horse Called Dragon,* won the 1972 Charles W. Follett Award. Hall got the idea for the novel when she first saw the breed called Ponies of the Americas. "I was wandering through the horse barns at the Iowa State Fair. Suddenly the loudspeaker announced the POA stallions class, and the corridor filled with the most beautiful little horses I had ever seen. In size they were somewhere between horses and ponies, but for sheer beauty I had never seen their equal. I discovered that the POA was a new breed which had been developed in Iowa but had swiftly spread throughout the country and into several other countries as well. The POAs were intended to be the ideal children's mount, and they appeared to have attained this goal admirably.

UPHILL ALL THE WAY
Lynn Hall

Jacket illustration by Troy Howell for the 1984 novel.

"A few days later I found a book on ponies which contained a chapter on the POA breed. With mounting excitement I read of a small Mexican mustang stallion, Dragon, who was credited with being one of the most important of the POA foundation sires. He had been a wild stallion, living in the Mexican mountains until a plague of poison weeds forced him and his mare to raid the fields of outlying ranches. The government had put a bounty on him and he was captured. Just before he was to have been butchered for dog food he was seen by an American who was looking for foundation stock for the POA breed. After continuing a virtually wild existence on a Texas ranch and being used only for breeding, he was sold to an Iowa family whose son ignored the warnings that Dragon was dangerous and promptly made a pet of him. By the following year, the sixteen-year-old boy and the sixteen-year-old stallion had won an international performance championship in grueling show competition. The story of Dragon needed little writing. I merely put down on paper the storybook life of an amazing little horse."[3]

The sequel to *A Horse Called Dragon*, entitled *New Day for Dragon*, tells the story of sixteen-year-old Dragon who has been shipped from Texas to an Iowa farm. In a 1975 review of the book, *Bulletin of the Center of Children's Books*, said: "The book has elements of achievement, wishes granted, and kindness to animals to strengthen the appeal to lovers of horse stories."

If her books are not specifically centered around animals, often the stories will use animals as major characters. The child protagonist in Hall's book often turns to animals for affection. "Animals are so very important—not only as receivers of affection, but as unqualified givers of love. This is particularly true of dogs. You don't have to be good and you don't have to clean your room or put away your bike in order to be loved by your dog. And it isn't that animals are kinder than people, but that there is no dishonesty among animals. Animals and people are both self-serving by nature, but people dress it up as something else. They fool you. My dogs worship and adore me, but I know they would worship and adore anyone who gave them the same kind of attention I do. I can enjoy them for what they are and not expect anything beyond what they can give. Something that shocked me when I got my first horse was to see how distant horses essentially are when compared to dogs. I was totally unprepared for this, having grown up reading unrealistic horse stories. You know, the stallion comes galloping across the pasture to throw its front hooves around your neck. In my horse stories, I try to portray these animals as they really are—wonderful, as long as you don't expect them to act like a dog or a person.

"*Lynn Hall's Dog Stories* is a kind of autobiographical work. Each of the stories is about a particular dog I owned at one time. The first story is about a dog I'd begged from a neighbor of ours. He grew up to become a car chaser—he'd run into traffic, bark, and make a big fuss. I was nine or ten at the time and have never quite forgiven my father for giving greater consideration to neighbors who were upset with my dog than to my need for a pet. One day when I'd gone shopping in Des Moines with my mother, he took my dog out into the country and dumped him. The dog was later found dead along the road. It took me many, many years to get over this. My father didn't respect me enough to discuss the problem with me and perhaps suggest that we find another home. This seemed to me proof that I was unloved. Years later, I wrote the story exactly as it had happened. My parents were infuriated.

"*The Stray* is also an incident from my life. As I said, when I was young I had a very strong urge to live in the country, to be among animals and farmers. I thought maybe I would offer myself to a farmer—he would adopt me and I could work in the fields and tend the animals. I figured that since my parents had two other daughters, they'd never miss me. I never actually got to the point of approaching a farmer, but I daydreamed about it a lot. I also wanted to deal with the theme of loving and letting go and learning that there are some people and animals that simply cannot be owned. A very hard lesson to learn. All of the relationships my characters have with animals are real relationships, experiences that make the character learn and grow.

"*The Horse Trader* is a fictionalized account about my experience of buying my first horse. It tells about the relationship between the girl and the horse dealer who sells her a load of manure along with the horse. The girl must get to the difficult point of trusting her perception about this man's dishonesty and tell him to buzz off."[1]

Besides writing animal stories, Hall also writes about young people growing up, sometimes in disturbing situations. In *Just One Friend*, for instance, Hall writes about a young girl whose alcoholic mother sits in a nearly catatonic state all day while the younger children are left unattended. In a 1986 *Wilson Library Bulletin* review, Patty

Jacket for the 1982 Scribner's edition.

Campbell called it a "beautiful book. To write from the perspective of a simple-minded person without writing a simple-minded book is a neat literary trick, and in *Just One Friend* Lynn Hall has pulled it off rather well. In this touching little story of Dori, who is 'simple' in the spiritual as well as the clinical sense, we feel her frustration and resentment at her own slowness, at her need to read a school assignment three times to begin to understand, when others can grasp it in a moment. Yet, we also see with the freshness of her innocence the complex beauty of the wild grasses in a bale of hay, the delicate colors of a slice of cantaloupe, the sweetness of a dog trying to perform a difficult trick."

In another story about a teenager in turmoil, *The Solitary,* Hall wrote about Jane, a seventeen-year-old who chooses to go off to live in the woods Thoreau-like to escape a bitter family situation. Her mother has been sent to the state penitentiary for killing her father. In *The Giver* fifteen-year-old Mary falls in love with her teacher, middle-aged

Mr. Flicker. A review in the *Bulletin of the Center for Children's Books* described the story as: "poignant and potent, a story of love that is wise and altruistic. Mary is not interested in the boys she knows, finding them callow; she is convinced that her feeling for her teacher, middle-aged Mr. Flicker, is more than a crush. He, too, feels affection but is aware that it would ruin Mary's life and might well end his career. He does love her, and he treats her love with respect and dignity, gently telling her that she must find someone her age. In a brief epilogue after Mary is married years later, she sees Mr. Flicker at a homecoming dance and thanks him. Other facets of Mary's life (particularly her familial relationships) give balance to a story written with insight and craft."

Hall, who has been writing books since 1968, describes her writing process as a form of self analysis. "I like to write stories from more than one point of view to get inside the heads of several characters. That's the best part of writing—going deep into those feelings, memories, and fantasies.

"I usually spend about six weeks writing my books, writing two or three books a year because that's all my publishers can absorb. Winter is my main writing time. This may sound like a very short work year, but before I actually sit down to write a book, I've spent months thinking about it, working it out

Jacket from Hall's 1981 novel.

in my mind. During the early stages, I busy myself with activities that don't take much brain power—housework, lawn work, gardening, long highway drives.

"In the. . .years that I've been writing, things have changed in the field of children's books. Language has loosened up considerably. I don't cringe at putting in a *damn* or a *hell* if it's called for in the dialogue. Writing *heck* or *darn* would seem artificial and call attention to itself. And more and more, we're encouraged to write books with strong female protagonists. I don't think there's any subject one can't write about these days. I. . .wrote a book about a little boy who was sexually molested. I'd wanted to write this for a long time because I had suffered a few such incidents in my childhood—nothing serious, but they are still clear memories. There is a lot of guilt attached for the child, which is the most damaging part. It felt good to finally be able to write about this and have my publisher accept *The Boy in the Off-White Hat* without any qualms."[1]

When she's not writing, Hall rides horses, takes long walks, plays the piano, and in winter skis cross-country. She also continues to breed English cockers and to enter them in obedience trial competitions. "I do quite a bit with the local 4-H club—training classes to get the kids started showing their own animals, that sort of thing. I don't do readings, but I visit schools, which I very much enjoy. Usually, I'm invited to the upper elementary grades. Those kids are super question askers—they want to know how much money I make and how old I am and how come I don't have a husband. They get right down to the things everybody wants to know but only kids will ask.

"I have always treasured my solitude. This helps me as a writer because I can focus on my story. I don't have to 'surface' in order to take care of other people or listen to their problems or feed them supper.

"I love writing, and just sitting among my unfinished projects, enjoying the breeze, the silence, and the view of the valley. I'm savoring life in the slow lane."[1]

Hall's view of the valley is from a cozy stone cottage set on a hilltop in Northeast Iowa. Named "Touchwood," the house is the result of years of building and planning. It overlooks the Volga River Valley. "From the first time I climbed the hill and looked around me, I knew that this was my place. This was where I wanted to spend the rest of my life, where I wanted to die.

"It was a pasture then, a rolling, sandy-soil hilltop pasture ringed by dark woods of oak and cedar and aspen. The open meadow sloped toward the south and the east, with long views of Grant Wood scenery, folds upon folds of rounded hills. Timber roads and deer trails threaded through the woods and connected small jewels of clearings. There was enough room to get lost on my own land! And all around me, the serenity and solitude I had needed all my life.

"I owned the land for a year before the building began. I visited it, hugged trees, sat in the grass and stared down the valley. Should the house face this way, or that way? Would they be able to build a road I could use in the winter? Would the well cost so much I wouldn't be able to afford the house? All of my parents' dire predictions bounced against me and fell aside. I didn't care. This was my place in the world.

"Finally it was time to begin. There was a little bit in the till, and a buyer ready to give me a comfortable profit on the old house. I found a part-time carpenter named Sox who farmed across the valley, and told him my situation.

"I had more time than money, I told him. And this was going to be my dream house. Would he be willing to let me work with him on the building of it, to save money and for the satisfaction of being involved in every stage of the house. 'Sure,' he said. 'No problem.' I told him I had no blueprints, only pencil sketches. 'Fine,' he said. 'No problem. Blueprints are a pain in the neck.'

"I wanted the house to be small but with big rooms; solid and sturdy and genuine, but cheap. Old Englishy but not fake in any way. 'Sure,' he said. 'No problem.' And he was right.

"Everyone warned me that building a new house would be a nightmare of unexpected problems and expenses. It wasn't a nightmare, it was a dream. I had to stand by and watch other people build the road and dig the house-hole and pour the concrete for the three walls that were to be below-grade. But then the good part began.

"Sox and I, with occasional help from his friend Pete, a biblical-looking man with a white beard, went to work on the framing in, and in just a few weeks, the house was enclosed. My part consisted mainly of unskilled jobs like nailing down sheets of subflooring, and shingling the roof. But it was a magic time for me.

"One afternoon when Pete and I were astride the steep-pitched roof working on gutter flashing, a storm blew in with dark, yellowed clouds, the kind of clouds that can produce tornadoes. For an instant I pictured my dream house being blown asunder before it was even born. But then I knew. I knew it wouldn't happen. I knew this was a special house, where nothing very bad could ever touch me.

"When Sox and Pete packed their tools and left, the house was a one-room shell. The inside walls were bare concrete, the one exposed outside wall was black fiberboard. There were no ceilings, just a grid of joists through which I could see the underside of the peaked roof. The floor was concrete; the plumbing only roughed in. I loved it.

"The dogs and I moved in that weekend, with friends taking over the moving chores above my protests. Onto the insufficiently cured cement floor they joyfully wheeled the piano, while I sucked in my breath and waited for the floor to crack. It didn't.

"Those first months at Touchwood were intensely joyful. The dogs and I camped in the concrete box of a building. I bathed under the garden hose and cooked in the fireplace until the stove was installed. I worked harder and more happily than I had ever worked before, stapling itchy batts of fiberglass insulation to ceiling joists, building stairs to the second floor, laying acres of squares of slate on the concrete floor. I built walls and shelves and doors, blithely ignoring my ignorance in the fine points of carpentry. When Sox came to check on my progress, he politely asked that I initial the door frame at the top of the stairs, so that no one would think it was his handiwork.

"The following year I built the stone exterior on the south wall, from fieldstones gathered in my old station wagon. A local farmer heard that some crazy lady was building a house out of 'niggerheads,' and brought me three truckloads of the beautiful gray, pink, and blue stones, gathered from his bean fields. Another summer's project was to build a wall of those stones, around the front lawn.

"By my second year at Touchwood I could no longer stand my horselessness. I bought a black Arab-Morgan mare named Star, who looked very much like the dream horse that my bicycle had been, thirty years before. But the bicycle had had better manners.

"I was writing for two publishers now, Follett and Garrard, and the fear of financial disaster was becoming a little dimmer. The house progressed,

one area at a time, and I added a small barn, built entirely alone except for the help of a woman friend for the raising of the roof beam. Each year there was more horse-proof fencing, more of the amenities, like water piped to the barn. It was time to look for the perfect horse.

"There were more false starts and disappointments ahead, but eventually that ideal horse came along, as had the home, the profession, and the dog breed.

"He is a beautiful golden buckskin Paso Fino named Tazo, a small, elegant, proud horse, smooth gaited and kind and responsive. He came to Touchwood as a three-year-old, fresh from the Florida show circuits. For the last six years, many of my most intensely happy moments have been on Tazo, sailing down a country road in his floating Paso gait, or cantering through the woods playing I Spy with the deer.

"Adjoining my land is a long strip of woods following a small river. A timber road and several smaller trails are there for our enjoyment, shared only by an occasional mushroom hunter in May,

THE
LEAVING
Lynn Hall

Hall's 1980 multi-award winning novel.

and deer hunters in December. The farmland adjoining Touchwood to the south is a series of small woods-encircled hay fields perfect for riding through, most seasons.

"Although I'd owned show dogs for years, it wasn't until about the time that Touchwood was being built that I finally settled on the one breed that suited me in every way, as the Paso Fino breed did in horses.

"After years of working with dogs of all kinds, and eliminating breeds left and right, I found myself in love once again, this time with a freckled, floppy-eared dog so full of love that no exchange of affection was ever quite enough; so full of joy that it was impossible to be around one, and not feel that joy. I discovered the English Cocker, a somewhat obscure breed in this country, though extremely popular in the rest of the world.

"My first English Cocker was a trouble-finding puppy, that first summer when we camped in the concrete shell of the house. She's gone now, but the sturdy old gramma-dog, who dreams on my foot as I write, is her daughter. The other three who make up the family, at this point in time, are her great-great-grandaughters.

"Through the years my relationship with the world of dog shows had been a love-hate one, vacillating between two poles. Sometimes I loved everything about the shows and was immersed in my dogs almost to the exclusion of everything else. At other times, the less sporting aspects of the fancy depressed me and made me feel that in some way this was beneath me. There were moral compromises to be made, or to be accepted in others.

"At times I'd decide, 'This is my world, warts and all.' Then I'd buy a camping trailer, expand my kennel to several dogs, and spend a year's worth of weekends at dog shows. At other times I'd think, 'I can live without this,' and for a year or two I'd relax, spend my weekends riding or hiking, and aim my breeding program at producing dogs that were true to the breed standard, rather than heavy-coated, hyperactive show-ring winners. Oddly enough, I was equally happy at either end of the pendulum swing. Probably I will go on backing and forthing, never making the progress with my bloodline that the more consistently dedicated breeder-exhibitors do. I'll win a few, lose a lot, and mostly just enjoy the beauty and affection of my doggy family.

"These, then, are the components of my life here at Touchwood. The writing, of course, is at the center of it all. The books are my winter love. I dig in, around November, and write and write and write, getting lost in my stories and going with unflagging enthusiasm from one to the next. On winter days, after the writing stint is done, I go outdoors and ride or ski or just walk through the woods.

"By spring I will have completed two or three books, and it will be time for a change. Speaking trips highlight the spring months, and in between trips I paint fences, plant potatoes, mother the strawberries and raspberries and asparagus along, and ride, ride, ride.

"In the summer there are writing chores, revisions and galley proofs, and ideas to play with, for next winter's writing season. Summer afternoons are for floating in the pool on an inner tube and watching the blue jays and swallows and dragonflies. Early morning is riding time then.

"In the fall the tempo picks up a little; finish off the garden, complete all the fix-it projects I ignored during the hot months, put the pool to bed, go to dog shows, and ride through the crunchy woods.

"Evenings, year round, have become piano time. The haunting melodies of Rachmaninoff, Chopin, Tchaikovsky, go floating out over the valley, not played well enough for human audiences, but fine for the dogs and me. And Tazo, in his pasture that circles the house, doesn't seem to mind the sour notes.

"Sometimes I think about those childish dreams of mine, and I realize that there would probably be more truly happy people in the world if more attention were paid to childhood dreams. They probably hold the keys to our real needs.

"For me, those needs were country and solitude, hills and woods and a family of horses and dogs; work that was a continual joy and a continual challenge; a sense of belonging to myself.

"It worked."[2]

"I find the same magic in horse and dog stories that I did years ago. This will sound like a cliche, and I'm sure every children's author has said it, but I don't write for children, I write for the child within me."[1]

Footnote Sources:

[1] Anne Commire, editor, *Something about the Author*, Volume 47, Gale, 1987.

[2] Adele Sarkissian, editor, *Something about the Author Autobiography Series*, Volume 4, Gale, 1987.

[3] "A Horse Called Dragon," *Junior Literary Guild*, September, 1971.

Nat Hentoff

Born June 10, 1925, in Boston, Mass.; son of Simon (a haberdasher and salesman) and Lena (a housewife; maiden name, Katzenberg) Hentoff; married Margot Goodman (a writer), August 15, 1959; children: (previous marriage) Jessica, Miranda; (present marriage) Nicholas, Thomas. *Education:* Northeastern University, B.A. (with highest honors), 1946; graduate study at Harvard University, 1946, and Sorbonne, 1950. *Home:* 25 Fifth Ave., New York, N.Y. 10003.

■ Career

WMEX (radio station), Boston, Mass., writer, producer, and announcer, 1944-53; *Down Beat,* New York City, associate editor, 1953-57; free-lance writer, 1958—; reviewer, *New York Herald Tribune Book Week, Peace News* (London), *The Reporter,* and *Hi Fi Stereo Review; Village Voice,* New York City, columnist, 1958—; *New Yorker,* New York City, staff writer, 1960—; *Washington Post,* columnist, 1984—. Adjunct associate professor, New York University. Lecturer at schools and colleges. Member: Authors League of America, American Civil Liberties Union, American Federation of Television and Radio Artists, New York Civil Liberties Union, Reporters Committee for

Freedom of the Press (member of steering committee), Freedom to Write Committee of P.E.N.

■ Awards, Honors

Nancy Bloch Memorial Award and *New York Herald Tribune* Spring Book Festival Award, both 1965, and Woodward Park School Annual Book Award, 1966, all for *Jazz Country;* Golden Archer Award, 1980, for *This School Is Driving Me Crazy;* Silver Gavel Award from the American Bar Association for Outstanding Public Service, 1980; Hugh M. Hefner First Amendment Award, 1981, for *The First Freedom: The Tumultuous History of Free Speech in America; Does This School Have Capital Punishment?* was selected one of American Library Association's Best Books for Young Adults, 1981, *The Day They Came to Arrest the Book,* 1982, and *American Heroes,* 1988; The Day They Came to Arrest the Book was included on the CRABerry Award List of the Acton Public Library, 1983; John Phillip Immroth Memorial Award for Intellectual Freedom from the American Library Association, 1983.

■ Writings

(Editor with Nat Shapiro) *Hear Me Talkin' to Ya: The Story of Jazz by the Men Who Made It,* Rinehart, 1955.

(Editor with N. Shapiro) *The Jazz Makers,* Rinehart, 1957, reissued, Greenwood, 1975.

(Editor with Albert McCarthy) *Jazz: New Perspectives on the History of Jazz by Twelve of the World's Foremost Jazz Critics and Scholars*, Rinehart, 1959, reissued, Da Capo Press, 1975.

Jazz Street (illustrated with photographs by Dennis Stouk), Deutsch (London), 1960.

The Jazz Life, Dial, 1961, reissued, Da Capo Press, 1978.

Peace Agitator: The Story of A. J. Muste, Macmillan, 1963.

The New Equality, Viking, 1964.

Our Children Are Dying, Viking, 1966.

(Editor) *The Essays of A. J. Muste*, Bobbs-Merrill, 1967.

A Doctor among the Addicts, Rand McNally, 1967.

(Contributor) Edward E. Davis, editor, *The Beatles Book*, Cowles, 1968.

Journey into Jazz: For Narrator, Jazz Ensemble, and Small Orchestra (illustrated by David S. Martin), Coward, 1968.

A Political Life: The Education of John V. Lindsay, Knopf, 1969.

(Author of introduction) *The London Novels of Colin MacInnes*, Farrar, Straus, 1969.

(Author of introduction) *Black Anti-Semitism and Jewish Racism*, Schocken, 1970.

(With Paul Cowan and Nick Egleson) *State Secrets: Police Surveillance in America*, Holt, 1973.

Jazz Is, Random House, 1976.

Does Anybody Give a Damn?: Nat Hentoff on Education, Knopf, 1977.

The First Freedom: The Tumultuous History of Free Speech in America, Delacorte, 1980.

Boston Boy (memoir), Knopf, 1986.

American Heroes: In and Out of School, Delacorte, 1987.

John Cardinal O'Connor: At the Storm Center of a Changing American Catholic Church, Scribner, 1988.

Novels:

Jazz Country, Harper, 1965.

Call the Keeper, Viking, 1966.

Onwards!, Simon & Schuster, 1967.

I'm Really Dragged but Nothing Gets Me Down, Simon & Schuster, 1967.

In the Country of Ourselves, Simon & Schuster, 1971.

This School Is Driving Me Crazy, Delacorte, 1975.

Does This School Have Capital Punishment?, Delacorte, 1981.

The Day They Came to Arrest the Book (ALA Notable Book), Delacorte, 1982.

Blues for Charlie Darwin, Morrow, 1982.

The Man from Internal Affairs, Mysterious Press, 1985.

Contributor to periodicals, including *Progressive, Inquiry, Cosmopolitan, School Library Journal, Civil Liberties Review, Student Press Law Center Report,* and *Wall Street Journal.* Former associate editor, *Liberation.*

■ Adaptations

"The Day They Came To Arrest the Book," CBS Schoolbreak Special, 1988.

■ Work In Progress

A profile of the Supreme Court. "I'm working on a book concerning this country's uninformed rush to euthanasia and its ramifications for the society."

■ Sidelights

On June 10, 1925, Nat Hentoff was born in Boston, Massachusetts to Russian Jewish immigrants. "I grew up in Roxbury, then a ghetto of Boston. It was in the 1930s and early 1940s, a time of righteous anti-Semitism around the country, but nowhere more fierce than in Boston. Indeed, one journalist, John Roy Carlson, having explored most of the major cities in the nation, concluded in a book that Boston was the capital of American anti-Semitism.

"There were pamphlets, broadsides, newspapers that spread the inciteful word that Jews were simultaneously in the highest ranks of international communism while also being capitalist bloodsuckers who were draining the very life out of working people.

"The printed assaults were scary in view of what the radio and the press told us of what was happening in Germany. But far more frightening were the raids—the squadrons of young hooligans descending on our neighborhood and acting as if they were imitating the newsreels: pushing Jews of whatever age into the gutters and punching out kids. Me included.

"So, being Jewish under these circumstances had a considerable impact. I knew I was an outsider; I thought like an outsider; and therefore I learned to be continually skeptical of what insiders with power said they believed (like, 'America the beautiful land of pluralism') by contrast with what they did. As I grew older, I wasn't in the least surprised that the most prestigious Yankee clubs—supposedly heirs in spirit to the goals of Emerson and Thoreau—had no places for Jews. And, of course, during those years, many colleges had Jewish quotas—a cutoff point on the number of Jewish applicants accepted, no matter how qualified they were."[1]

At age ten, after passing the entrance examinations, Hentoff entered the prestigious Boston Latin School, the oldest public school in America. "I would not have been at Latin School had it not been for Miss Fitzgerald, my sixth-grade teacher at the William Lloyd Garrison School, where nearly all the students were Jewish and nearly all the teachers were Irish.

"[I] knew quite well, even at ten, this was the way to penetrate the great mystery of my life. I would be going to *their* school, in *their* part of town, and so I would be not only learning Latin and Greek but learning about *them.*

"Under the purple-and-white flag of Boston Latin School, we were all united—the Irish, the Italians, the Jews, the Greeks, the Scots, the Armenians, the relatively few Yankees who still went there (the others no longer applied because all the rest of us were there), and the far fewer blacks.

"Whatever part of the city we came from, each of us, because we were going to Boston Latin School, was a special kid on his own street. The other kids, going to ordinary high schools, might well growl that we were snooty beyond words, but they knew we had already gone a few laps around the success track while they hadn't finished one. So to be thrown out of Latin School would mean being put back into the common pool of common students—much to the delight of the common pool, and to the everlasting shame and humiliation of our parents, let alone us.

"Accordingly, the survivors, so long as they did survive, felt they had much, perilously, in common. It mattered more that we were long-distance runners under our purple-and-white colors than that we were Jews or Christians. (In school, anyway.) For the six years I was there, my closest friends were a Greek and an Irish lad. It took me a long time to believe that was possible.

"The masters, moreover, paid no attention to where we came from, to whether our parents worked in grocery stores or were State Street bankers. The only thing that counted was whether we were willing to do the work, the incessant work, it took to stay in this place. If you stuck it out

at Latin School, where, after all, eight signers of the Declaration of Independence had gone, you knew there was really nothing you couldn't accomplish from then on—if you really put your mind to it.

"After I left Boston Latin, I would occasionally complain about how uncaring most of the masters had been about our sensibilities, our souls. Finally, however, it occurred to me that they gave us something a good deal more important—respect. Whatever our backgrounds, we were in the school because we had shown we could do the work. The masters, therefore, expected at least that much of us, and that was why we came to expect even more from ourselves.

"There were some fierce and suspicious Jews in my neighborhood who disapproved of Jewish boys discovering their potential in such a distant place. Distant not so much geographically, though Avenue Louis Pasteur was a far piece from Roxbury. But distant from Judaism. The whole point of this elite Latin School, these Jews said, was to produce

Cover from Hentoff's first juvenile novel.

one-hundred and fifty-percent-American boys. 'So, if you send a Jewish boy there, he will forget what it is to be Jewish.'

"They might have been right if Boston Latin School had been all the world we knew. But on the trolley cars coming home, some of the parochial school boys growlingly reminded us we were Jewish, and back in Roxbury, at night, it was still foolish to go out in the dark alone. Back home, it still made a big difference where, in the old country, your parents were from.

"After the seven hours at Latin School every weekday, there were two more hours in Hebrew school, plus three more hours on Sunday mornings. Both schools, of course, were generous in home-work assignments. On Saturday evenings, more-over, I traveled a long way by trolley car for an hour's clarinet lessons."[2]

"As I grew older, the knowledge of what it feels like to be an outcast led me to learn empathy with others of the excluded—blacks, women, homosex-uals, and in time, Arab-Americans, Hispanics, Catholics (anti-Catholicism being 'the anti-Semi-

tism of liberals'). I lived on the margins of the mainstream, and over the years, I have written primarily about people on the margins.

"Being Jewish shaped me in another way. From my father, from other elders in the ghetto—however much they disagreed among themselves political-ly—I constantly heard that to be just is to be Jewish, and to be unjust is to be un-Jewish. Where I lived, this came not so much out of a religious imperative but from the social and political ethos of the Englightenment—when Jews in Europe freed themselves from the ghettos and the shetls in their minds as well as the geographic ones in which they lived. The sunlight turned many of these Jews into idealists. They believed in the perfectibility of man and therefore of society. Accordingly, they believed justice—economic, personal, national, Zionist—was a realistic possibility, let alone neces-sity, in any new world worth making. Justice not only for Jews."[1]

Hentoff feels that he has always possessed a streak of defiance. "My mother used to say when I was in the crib, if somebody brought me a doll, I'd look at it and throw it across the room. I guess I was a bad seed from the beginning."[3]

Always the rebel, Hentoff performed his first public act of rebellion by eating a huge salami sandwich on a high holy day. "Warren Street is the main route to our shul, our synagogue, a block away. It is Yom Kippur, the Day of Atonement, the day of fasting, the day on which God marks down the fate of every Jew for the year ahead. Some of the Jews who look up at the slovenly, munching boy on the porch shake their heads in disgust. I stare at them, taking another bite. One old man, with a white beard almost as long as our rabbi's, shakes his fist at me. Another old man spits.

"This despicable twelve-year-old atheist is waiting to be stoned. Hoping to be stoned. But not hit. I am, you see, protesting a stoning, or so I will say later that day when my father has discovered how his only son has spent the morning of the holiest day of the year disgracing himself and his father. By then, I am sick. Because of the sandwich. Because of the look on my father's face. But I will not say so. My father also does not speak, for if he did, he would disown me. My mother? I do not remember my mother having been there, but, of course, she was. She was never anywhere else.

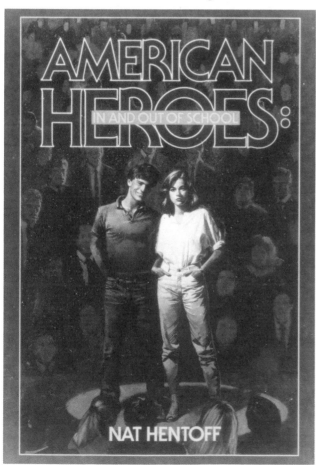

Hardcover edition of Hentoff's 1987 novel.

"I mainly wanted to know if I could do it, if I could stay on that porch until I finished that awful sandwich. I wanted to know how it felt to be an outcast. Except for my father's reaction and for getting sick, it turned out to be quite enjoyable.''[2]

Later that afternoon, he went to synagogue. ''Though quaking, I ached to be publicly denounced. My defiance would have been incomplete otherwise. It would have been silly, frivolous, without an echo. Like a tree falling without a sound in the forest.''[2] At thirteen, he had his bar-mitzvah, but was the last time he stepped into a synagogue for religious purposes. He no longer believed in God.

A voracious reader since early childhood, Hentoff was addicted to books. ''Both the reading of them and the physical possession of them. On the way home from Boston Latin School, I would sometimes stop at an astonishing building that had nothing but used books, four floors of them. . . .And every time my father took me for a ride to the railroad station to make the last mail connection to New York, it was understood that I would not return home without at least one new book. Soon the books burst out of my bedroom and took over nearly all the wall space in the front hall of our apartment as well as the living room.

''Still, for all my lust to own books, all week long I made and remade lists of the books I would take out of the public library on Saturday morning.''[2]

''I looked forward to my Saturday library visits almost as much as I did to the Saturday afternoon picture show, the nearly four-hour long cornucopia every week—a double feature, strings of shorts, and previews, and the literally cliff-hanging serials. The library too was a cornucopia, and I never ceased marveling at the continual surprises that came with my first library card. And unlike-school, the library was—and still is—a place where one can find and keep on finding one's own surprises.''[4]

It was the book *Alice in Wonderland* ''. . .that first made me want to pick up words, shake them, turn them over, and try to see how they're *really* being used. Later, George Orwell and, I must admit it, S. I. Hayakawa's *Language in Action* greatly sharpened my awareness of the shell games that are played with language. But my roots as an avocational, sometimes polemical, semanticist are in *Alice.*''[5]

He had another passion. Ten-year-old Hentoff, walking past a music store playing jazz from a speaker hung over it's door, was suddenly stopped ''by a fierce wailing of brass and reeds, a surging, pulsing cry of yearning that made me cry out too. I'd never before yelled in public; it was not

Jacket from the 1982 Delacorte edition.

something a Boston boy, especially a Boston Jewish boy wandering outside the ghetto, could ever satisfactorily explain to one of *them*. But I didn't care. All I cared about were those sounds.

''I rushed into Krey's to find out what was playing. Artie Shaw's 'Nightmare.' The guy behind the counter at Krey's, Bill Ingalls, had a jazz radio show. He told me when it was on, and from 'Nightmare' I went on to much more astonishing pleasures—Duke Ellington's 'The Sergeant Was Shy,' Louis Armstrong's 'West End Blues,' Billie Holiday's 'Miss Brown to You.' Not only could I hear in this jazz the soul-shaking power of the chassan [spiritual singer in the synagogue] and the spiraling risks of his improvising, but here there were also such inviting sensuousness, the sharing of hip wit, and the colors—my God, there were more different colors in this music than in all of the Boston Museum of Fine Arts.

''And the way the music moved! I'd be walking down the street and suddenly Fats Waller would leap into my head, from a record I'd heard that morning, and I'd be walking differently down that street.

"When I got a record player, on time, I discovered that in and around Scollay Square, there were secondhand book stores that also sold cut-out records. My jazz universe kept expanding: Bessie Smith, Peetie Wheatstraw ('The Devil's Son-in-Law'), Jack Teagarden, Sidney Bechet. But it wasn't enough. I had to *see* the music; I had to see the musicians.

"Acting as if I had no reason to ask what the minimum age was, and already needing a shave practically every day, I went to Sunday jam sessions in downtown Boston at the Ken Club. A dark, sleazy joint, but on those afternoons it was utterly transformed into a glorious battlefield, a tournament of giants, horn-playing giants.

"It was not until I was fifteen or so that I found the courage to actually speak to jazzmen, and some of them—unknown to my father—eventually became my itinerant foster fathers. Rex Stewart, Ben Webster, Frankie Newton. I admired them and carefully considered their advice on how to grow up, because they had so much life in them by contrast with practically all the other adults I knew. And whenever I heard their music, I still wanted to shout aloud—for the surprise and joy of it."[2]

Upon graduation from Boston Latin School, Hentoff entered Northeastern University. "I had not intended by any means to go to Northeastern, which was regarded at the time as a place for children of the working class. Non-Jewish children of the working class. Jewish students of whatever class were expected, if they were college material, to attend Harvard or Yale or Tufts or, if they had slept through high school, Boston University. But not cheerless, sooty Northeastern, which didn't even have a tree, let alone a campus.

"[It] turned out to be a more serious place of learning than I had thought. That is, I learned a lot more from the other students than I had at Boston Latin School. Not only were they of the working class, but many actually had grown-up jobs.

"Nearly all of us were the first members of our families to go to college. There was no way we could have allowed ourselves to drop out, because that would have meant our whole families would be dropping out.

"At Latin School, although I'd had friends, I was essentially an outsider. Most of the boys were in such fierce, constant competition with each other for grades and for the very best places in the world to come that they weren't interested in talking about anything else. At Northeastern, however, while everyone studied hard, we also read the papers, including the funnies; jawed about James Michael Curley [mayor of Boston] and FDR; were curious—at least in the liberal arts division—about Marxism; and sang Gilbert and Sullivan, backwards as well as forwards, in the common room. The course loads were heavy; all of us commuted; and yet there seemed to be a lot of time for fun. A strange word for a Jewish boy to associate with school.

"It was clear that the most fun was in the offices of the *Northeastern News*. As a freshman passing by those offices, yearning to join the rebels, I gathered the courage to apply for a tryout. I worked very hard on my first piece, a straight news story, and proudly presented it, neatly written, to the managing editor. He looked at the manuscript, guffawed in a most demeaning way, showed it to several other braying staff members, and pointed to a typewriter. That day, I learned how to type."[2]

By his third year, Hentoff was editor-in-chief of the paper and became involved with issues concerning the First Amendment. "The staff was composed largely of muckrakers or, to use the more refined term, investigative reporters. We reported, without fear or favor, on what was wrong with the university—too much money going to the athletic department; too many elementary-school kinds of rules imposed by the autocratic president throughout the university; and, of course, cafeteria food that would have violated the Eighth Admendment, if we had known what that was.

"But we didn't stay on campus. The *Northeastern News*—more thoroughly than any of the dailies in the city—covered anti-Semitism in Boston. Who provided the money for the hate sheets? Which 'respectable' organizations were the cover for the ravening bigots?

"The Administration became nervous as our paper grew more and more unpredictable. The tipping point occurred when we decided to do a series on the Board of Trustees. Who were these people? Did they know anything about education, or were they on the board only because they gave large contributions to the university?

"As soon as the president of the university heard of our alarming project, a ukase came down. We were to pledge either to confine all newsgathering to uncontroversial matters on the campus, and only on campus, or we would be dismissed from the paper. All but one of us (who was to be become the

Anne Meara starred as an embattled librarian in the 1988 "CBS Schoolbreak Special: The Day They Came to Arrest the Book."

instant new editor) resigned forthwith, in sorrow and anger.

"At that point, I became passionately interested in freedom of the press, and indeed years later, the page of acknowledgements in my book on the First Amendment, *The First Freedom: The Tumultuous History of Free Speech in America,* began:

"'For my abiding concern with the First Amendment, I am particularly indebted to those officials at Northeastern University in Boston who tried to censor the writings of the staff when I was editor of the *Northeastern News* in the early 1940s.'...I never lost my sense of rage at those who would suppress speech, especially mine. Those administrators truly helped inspire this book."[1]

Throughout his college years, Hentoff continued to feed his passion for jazz. "Not far from Northeastern's then extremely modest campus on Hunting-

Paperback for the 1981 ALA Notable Book.

ton Avenue was another institution of learning, the Savoy Cafe. The Savoy was at the beginning of black Boston. Except for cops, the whites who crossed over the line and into the Savoy were the jazz crazed, of almost all ages, from Boston and its environs.

"I was one of the regulars, and no membership in any organization since has meant as much to me. Nor have I ever been part of as motley a membership.

"Those of us who came out onto Massachusetts Avenue from the Savoy Cafe to find our various ways home occasionally walked in jazz time. But it was hard to sustain that pulse and good feeling in the heavy air of Boston, with its tribal hatreds, the anti-Catholics sometimes being almost as venomous as the anti-Semites, and all mocking the Negroes—which is why they loved listening to Amos and Andy on the radio.

"But behind the closed doors of the Savoy, I felt more at home than anywhere else I had ever been, including home. I could not get enough of the music, the deep warmth and the surprise of it. And I could not get enough of the musicians. They were so unlike all the other adults I had known—my father and my uncles; the masters at Boston Latin School; Samuel Caploe, the mighty engine of Sunday's Candies [where he worked as a young teenager]; my professors at Northeastern. I had hardly known those adults. Including my father. I knew him better than the others, of course, but we had never talked about loneliness, failure, women, death, and such things.

"The jazzmen, many of them, talked to me with remarkable openness. Remarkable in my life up to then, and since."[2]

In 1944, having failed his induction physical, Hentoff continued at Northeastern and got a job at WMEX, a local radio station where he worked as announcer, writer, and producer for nine years. "I wasn't going anywhere at WMEX, as my father, sighing, kept reminding me; but on the other hand it seemed to me there were worse things I could have been doing. Advertising, investment banking, white slavery, working for the State Department, corporate law. The list of appalling alternatives was enormous. And at the radio station at least I had my jazz programs, both in the studio and at nightclubs; I was often in the intriguing presence of James Michael Curley; and I had achieved a boyhood dream by getting the best seats in the house at certain sports events. For I was the station's assistant sportscaster.

"Although the jazz programs attracted a steady, if not a large audience, and although I was a pretty good utility infielder (sports, news, politics), WMEX's portly chief executive officer, William Pote, did not like me. Indeed, he greatly disliked me.

"For one thing, Mr. Pote was convinced I was a Communist. Most of the guests on my programs were black. I never wore a tie, and day in, day out, I wore a black leather jacket. That told him something. Also, he saw me shamelessly reading something called *Partisan Review*, and I had interviewed Pete Seeger on the air without denouncing his un-Americanism. What more proof did he need?

"He particularly disliked me because I had helped convince the other announcers to join AFRA (American Federation of Radio Artists—a 'T' [for television] has since been added. Pote had never dreamed he would live to see his announcers organized, as if they were coal miners. No more split shifts—working four hours in the morning and another four at night. The end of a salary scale that made it very hazardous for any announcer to marry unless his wife worked. And the creation of a cruel

break in the extended family at the station now that this alien presence, the union, had been brought in. And who had brought in this dark presence? Comrade Hentoff."[2]

In 1946 Hentoff received his B.A. from Northeastern, with highest honors while continuing to work at the radio station.

"I parlayed my jazz series into work as a stringer for *Down Beat*, the nation's leading jazz magazine. I was sufficiently controversial in the articles I wrote to be invited in 1953 to become the New York editor of *Down Beat*. For several years, until I was fired, I was utterly immersed in the jazz world—reviewing musicians in the clubs every night, writing during the day and all through the weekends.

"For someone as jazz-struck as I was, and still am, it was a glorious period. The giants of jazz were still jousting and surprising their audiences and themselves. I heard and talked with Thelonious Monk, Charles Mingus, Miles Davis, Cecil Taylor, and many more. When I was a boy, I romanticized jazz creators. By the time I was working for *Down Beat*, I knew their flaws as well as their strengths,

Hentoff in his office at the *Village Voice* (New York City).

but I continued to admire the honesty and courage of their art.

"I was fired from *Down Beat* because I had been agitating for some time for someone black to be hired in the New York office. Here we were writing about and profiting from an essentially black American music, but no blacks were on staff. One day, a dark young woman applied for a job, and I insisted that headquarters in Chicago hire her. Weary of my hectoring, headquarters in Chicago hired her and told me to clear out my desk. The young woman stayed. She wasn't black, as it turned out. She was a dark Arab-American.

"Trying to survive...I quickly discovered that I was stereotyped. Editors knew me as a writer on jazz and they promised assignments whenever something of jazz interest to them came up. Maybe once or twice a year.

"What saved me from penury or almost as bad, work in advertising or promotion, was a job that for a long time paid nothing. In 1956, a very small weekly had started in Greenwich Village, the *Village Voice.* Two years later, I was offered a column. The paper was so financially precarious that only a couple of staff people and the editor received a meager salary. For the rest of the writers, there was only psychic income.

"I worked out a deal. In return for no money, I would never be asked to write a word about jazz. As time went on, I wrote in that column about civil liberties, education, politics, police Red Squads, school segregation in New York, corporal punishment in schools everywhere, and the Supreme Court. Not a word about jazz.

"As the paper's circulation began to rise, I was able to escape from the stereotype of being capable of writing only about jazz."[1]

Hentoff freelanced for a number of other magazines, wrote liner-notes for jazz albums, co-edited books on the subject, and, in 1961, came out with his own book, *The Jazz Life,* a collection of previously published essays.

He diversified his literary work and wrote books on a broad range of subjects: a biography of the influencial radical pacifist A. J. Muste, *Peace Agitator*; *A Doctor among Addicts,* an indictment on this nation's attitude toward drug addiction; *The New Equality,* a civil-rights polemic calling for an alliance of the poor of all colors to bring about social structural change, among others.

In 1965, Hentoff published his first juvenile novel, *Jazz Country,* a book he considers to be his most "durable." "While there was a certain amount of didacticism in my motivation for writing *Jazz Country,* the primary reason was wanting to find out if I could write fiction. And my approach to fiction is one of surprise—self-surprise. Therefore, I did not begin with a list of precepts that had, at all costs, to be imbedded in the text. I did not even have a plot.

"I point this out even though I am convinced that readers can tell the difference between a book deliberately shaped to instruct or influence and a book with some of the spontaneity of, let us say, a jazz solo.

"Young readers tend to resist the former kind of book—one that was written to perform a community service, however virtuous. The young, after all, are preached at incessantly and I hardly think they would voluntarily pick up a book in order to be preached at yet once more.

"So, as is also true with jazz musicians in their approach to music, I wrote *Jazz Country* to please myself first of all. And while I could provide a considerable ex post facto list of observations about blacks and white in this country that I could pretend to have *intended* from the start, it did not work that way. Whatever did emerge in this area resulted from the interplay of the characters as I came to know them.

"But, as I said, I did begin with a rather vaguely didactic purpose. For one thing, jazz is an unknown country to most Americans, adults as well as the young. With very few exceptions, the music—its techniques, its history, its sociology—is not taught in our schools, elementary or advanced.

"I hoped that young black readers would find it of interest that the white protagonist in *Jazz Country* desperately wanted acceptance into the black world of jazz, and it wasn't easy. That, furthermore, there were distinctive values in that black world of jazz. And I hoped young white readers would find those black values of interest and would realize there was more to being black than they had learned from their schoolbooks and their parents.

"Books alone cannot end the barriers between the two countries. Only basic political and economic change can do that, but books can stimulate some of the young to consider taking part in that basic change. Of course, only relatively few readers will become activists, black and white, but books can also help prepare the nonactivists to understand what is happening now and what is going to happen while we still have two countries here."[6]

"The moral minefields in that world outside the school are very much in my mind when I write for young readers. As is my recognition that nearly all of them have watched a great amount of television and thereby know, or think they know, much more about nearly everything than youngsters of my generation thought we did. These kids do not have to be 'protected' from worldly knowledge and its attendant dilemmas. What they are in need of is encouragement to sort out some kind of meaning, some kind of purposeful pattern for themselves out of all that 'information' they're getting from everywhere. The images, the sounds, the skewed polyrhythms of actual and vicarious experiences.

"Although my intention is to help stimulate just that kind of seeking, I must also say that I am occasionally jolted when a young reader writes to say that something I've written actually has affected his life. There's a lot of responsibility involved in that kind of turn, and I begin to worry about some of these distant lives."[7]

While Hentoff's journalistic writing at the *Voice*, *New Yorker*, and the *Washington Post*, covered a wide variety of issues, his abiding concern is the education of our young, an area he has covered extensively, both in books and periodicals. He lectures extensively at schools throughout the country, keeping in touch with their issues and concerns.

"One of my main regrets so far is that although I have occasionally taught college classes for an academic year, I have never spent more than two or three days in a junior high or high school. I'd much rather teach students of that age because, by and large, they have yet to be constricted in their minds and imaginations by careerism.

"What I do try to teach, in classrooms and in lectures, is the necessity of surprising yourself, of discovering that even your most cherished absolutes—including even freedom of expression—are not as one-sidedly unambivalent as you fondly believe.

"...Of the more lasting satisfactions I get from my work, one is the fact that high-school kids still read my book on the First Amendment, *The First Freedom*. I take very seriously what Abraham Lincoln said:

"'All the armies of Europe and Asia...could not by force take a drink from the Ohio River....As a

Cover for the 1976 paperback edition.

nation of free men, we will live forever or die by suicide.'

"If kids do not get a strong sense that the Constitution, very much including the Bill of Rights, actually belongs to each of them, they will grow up indifferent to their own—and others'—liberties and rights. And if enough of the citizenry are careless in these matters, those liberties and rights will be suicidally lost.

"Of all my obsessions, this is the strongest, and that's why in just about all the writing I do, fiction and nonfiction, freedom—how to get it, how to lose it—is a fundamental theme.

"Nonetheless, I also like to tell stories because otherwise, my work would consist of tracts, and they're so boring they're not even remaindered."[1]

In 1982, in a motel room in Tewksbury, Massachusetts, three rabbis excommunicated Hentoff, among others, from the Jewish faith. "[The rabbis] had blown mightily on a ram's horn and had then snuffed the candles, thereby extinguishing the spiritual lives of those once and former Jews on their list. The rabbis used as their text—the *Washington Post* reported—'the 1757 excommunication of a Jewish heretical group called the Satanic Sabbatian Frankists in Brode, Poland.'

"My link with the Satanic Sabbatian Frankists was my having signed a June 20 advertisement in the *New York Times* that year protesting Israel's invasion of Lebanon. I had thereby been charged by the rabbinical triumvirate of 'collaboration with the enemy and committing a traitorous act.'

"Not for the first time, and not only by rabbis.

"I only wished the three rabbis really had the authority to hold that court, that Bet Din. But rabbis these days have no power except over their own congregations, and that power can be removed, along with the rabbi, at the will of the congregation."[2]

Boston Boy, a memoir of his youth was published in 1986. "I had agreed to do this ten years ago, and then the usual thing happened and an editor went somewhere else. It wound up at Knopf, which was fine with me....I had not done much within that time because I had been reluctant to try a memoir. All my life I've been writing about other people, or in novels creating my own world, and I wasn't quite sure I could function comfortably or persuasively in the real first person. But I tried it and I seemed to get the tone fairly quickly. Once I got the tone, the rhythm, the whole perspective, then it was fun."[3]

Hentoff has four children and lives in New York City, with his third wife, writer Margot Goodman. "No one I've ever met is quicker to discern and scornfully reject cant, newspeak, and lies (however unwitting) than my wife Margot. We disagree on a good many things (she is pro-choice, for instance, and I'm pro-life), but she is the most valuable editor I have. She seldom goes over copy as such, but as I talk out ideas for books and articles, I've learned to pay attention to her resounding signals when she hears the slightest trace of buncombe or just plain infirm grammar."[1]

Hentoff still maintains a strict writing schedule, working Monday to Friday from nine a.m. to one p.m., all day Saturday, and half-day Sunday. "I keep thinking I will not do any more nonfiction books because I so enjoy writing fiction, but something always comes up....And I know I will

eventually have to write the sequel to my memoir, *Boston Boy*. It'll be about my years in New York and such tumultuous people I came to know well as Malcolm X, Dr. Kenneth Clark, Charles Mingus, Lenny Bruce, and Mario Cuomo.

"And some day, I would like to do a book for very, very young children, like *Goodnight Moon*. But that takes very special skills, particularly the ability to remember all the way back.

"Meanwhile, from time to time, I receive signals from out there that one way or another, I'm reaching somebody. One afternoon, in the summer of 1987, a teacher from Mowat Middle School in Bay County, Florida, called to tell me that the principal had just banned a number of books. One of them was mine: *The Day They Came to Arrest the Book*."[1]

Footnote Sources:

[1] Adele Sarkissian, editor, *Contemporary Authors Autobiography Series*, Volume 6, Gale, 1988.
[2] Nat Hentoff, *Boston Boy*, Knopf, 1986.
[3] Kenneth C. Davis, "Books and the First Amendment," *Publishers Weekly*, April 11, 1986.
[4] N. Hentoff, "The Saturday Library Matinee," *American Libraries*, April, 1976.
[5] N. Hentoff, "Looking Backwards—and Ahead—with 'Alice,'" *Wilson Library Bulletin*, October, 1970.
[6] N. Hentoff, "Getting Inside Jazz Country," *Horn Book*, October, 1966.
[7] N. Hentoff, "Hearing from the Teen-age Reader," *Wilson Library Bulletin*, September, 1972.

■ For More Information See

Newsweek, December 21, 1964, September 5, 1966, September 15, 1969.
Negro Digest, June, 1965, March, 1967.
Times Literary Supplement, May 19, 1966 (p. 442).
Observer, August 7, 1966.
Time, August 12, 1966, October 11, 1968 (p. 109).
New Yorker, September 17, 1966.
Harper's, November, 1966, April, 1969 (p. 81ff).
America, November 12, 1966.
Nation, November 14, 1966.
Village Voice, November 24, 1966, July 18, 1968, May 23, 1977.
Punch, March 29, 1967.
Instructor, April, 1967, May, 1976.
Spectator, April 7, 1967.
New York Times, May 23, 1968, September 11, 1969, March 21, 1980.
New Leader, August 5, 1968.
Science Books, September, 1968.
Publishers Weekly, September 2, 1968 (p. 21ff), September 10, 1982 (p. 76).
Wilson Library Bulletin, November, 1968 (p. 261ff), May, 1974 (p. 742ff).
Parents' Magazine, May 1969 (p. 46ff), January, 1972 (p. 41ff), January, 1976 (p. 42ff).

Saturday Review, September 19, 1970 (p. 74ff), May 22, 1971 (p. 60ff), July 21, 1979 (p. 22ff).

Negro History Bulletin, March, 1971.

May Hill Arbuthnot and Zena Sutherland, *Children and Books*, 4th edition, Scott, Foresman, 1972.

Doris de Montreville and Donna Hill, editors, *Third Book of Junior Authors*, H. W. Wilson, 1972.

Horn Book, December, 1972 (p. 578), August, 1981 (p. 432ff).

New York Times Sunday Magazine, January 28, 1973 (p. 35), February 18, 1973 (p. 32).

Ms., 1974 (p. 16ff).

Children's Literature Review, Volume I, Gale, 1976.

National Observer, February 28, 1976.

American Libraries, April, 1976.

Progressive, December, 1976, July, 1977.

Times Educational Supplement, January 20, 1978.

Twentieth-Century Children's Authors, St. Martin's Press, 1978.

Los Angeles Times, April 13, 1980.

Boston, December, 1985 (p. 22).

Anne Commire, editor, *Something about the Author*, Volume 42, Gale, 1986.

New York Times Book Review, April 27, 1986 (p. 34).

Christianity Today, November 21, 1986 (p. 30ff).

N. Hentoff, "Finding Malcolm X," *Yale Review*, winter, 1987.

Charles Mority, editor, *Current Biography Yearbook 1986*, H. W. Wilson, 1987.

School Library Journal, March, 1988 (p. 114ff).

Bel Kaufman

B orn in Berlin, Germany; came to the United States at age of twelve; daughter of Michael J. (a physician) and Lyalya (a writer; maiden name Rabinowitz) Kaufman; divorced; children: Jonathan Goldstine, Thea Goldstine. *Education:* Hunter College (now Hunter College of the City University of New York), B.A. (magna cum laude); Columbia University, M.A. (with highest honors). *Religion:* Jewish. *Home:* 1020 Park Ave., New York, N.Y. 10028. *Agent:* Attorney Maurice Greenbaum, 575 Madison Ave., New York, N.Y. 10022.

■ Career

Taught in New York City high schools for over thirty years; New School for Social Research, New York City, instructor in English, 1964; Borough of Manhattan Community College (now Borough of Manhattan Community College of the City University of New York), New York City, assistant professor of English, adjunct professor of English, 1964—. Taught creative writing workshops and seminars at the University of Rochester and the University of Florida. Lecturer; member, Advisory Commission of Performing Arts, Advisory Council Town Hall Foundation. *Member:* Authors League,

Writer's Guild, P.E.N., Dramatists Guild, Commission on Performing Arts, Sholom Aleichem Foundation (board member), Phi Beta Kappa, English Graduate Union (Columbia), Phi Delta Kappan (editorial board).

■ Awards, Honors

Plaque from the Anti-Defamation League, and from the United Jewish Appeal; Doctor of Letters, Nasson College, 1965; Paperback of the Year Award for Fiction from the National Bestsellers Institute, 1966, for *Up the Down Staircase;* named to the Hall of Fame, Hunter College of the City University of New York, 1973; National Human Resource Award from the American Bicentennial Research Institute, 1974, for "professional and civic attainments"; Award for Best Articles on Education from the Educational Association of America, 1976, and 1979; named "Woman of the Year" by the Organization for Rehabilitation through Training, 1980, and Brandeis University, 1980, 1981; National Education Association/P.E.N. Short Story Contest Winner, 1983, for "Sunday in the Park"; selected one of the prominent Americans to meet with Gorbachev at the Soviet Embassy, 1987.

■ Writings

Novels:

Up the Down Staircase, Prentice-Hall, 1964, new edition, 1988.
Love, Etc., Prentice-Hall, 1979.

Author of lyrics for musical "Peabody and the Mermaid," and of an episode of the television series, "Room 222." Translator of Russian poetry. Contributor to periodicals, including *Esquire, Saturday Review, Today's Education, Ladies' Home Journal, English Journal, McCall's,* and *New York Times.*

■ Adaptations

"Up the Down Staircase" (motion picture; starring Sandy Dennis, Warner Bros., 1967, (play) produced in Russia, June, 1977.

■ Work In Progress

Lyrics for a musical; a theatre piece about her grandfather, the Yiddish humorist Sholom Aleichem.

■ Sidelights

"I was born in Berlin, where my father was studying medicine. Russia, however, is the country of my childhood and Russian is my native language."[1]

"I remember...the Russian Revolution in Odessa, where we lived: winter famine, chaos on the streets, terror indoors. I remember standing with my mother in a long line...for our family ration of green bread; green because in the absence of flour, it was made from the dried shells of peas. I remember carefully stepping over a dead body, shot in front of our house and frozen into a grotesque posture. I remember being sent to the Camp for the Children of the Proletariat in order to be eligible for the square inch of meat we were given once a week, and I remember how the children used to separate that meat into its threads to make it last. As for presents, my father brought me a precious gift on visiting day; half of an orange, which I hid under my pillow, to discover later that it was gone, stolen by another child."[2]

Another of Kaufman's childhood memories is of walking with her cousin Tamara and "our grandfather someplace in Switzerland, at a summer resort, each holding on to his hand. 'You see that forest?' He points to the distant woods. 'I've just given it to Tamarochka! You see that lake? I just gave it to Belochka!' We skip with pleasure at his largesse, as delighted as we are with the funny rhymes he thinks up for us, and the secret languages he invents for us, and the little stories he makes up just for us, his grandchildren, that the rest of the

25TH ANNIVERSARY EDITION

Bel Kaufman

UP THE DOWN STAIR CASE

WITH A NEW PREFACE BY THE AUTHOR

The novel that has had forty-seven printings, sold more than six million copies and spent sixty-four weeks on the best-seller lists.

world, which knows him as Sholom Aleichem, the famous writer, does not receive from him.

"I did not realize until later, after he had died, how much I had been given."[3]

"I was only three when he died, but there is one particular scene that has remained in my mind. We were at a zoo in Copenhagen. 'Papa Sholom Aleichem,' as we called him, rolled up a piece of paper into the shape of a cup, filled it with water from a nearby fountain and offered a drink to a monkey. The monkey refused. Papa Sholom Aleichem bent down and said to me in Russian: '*Ona isporchenaya*' ('she is spoiled'), then he refilled the cup and drank thirstily from it. I learned only much later that he was already suffering from one of his illnesses: diabetes insipidus. One of its symptoms is inordinate thirst. But he made a joke even of that. He wrote to my parents: 'Now I know I will never die of hunger. I'll die of thirst.'

"He loved laughter and was himself a superb mimic and raconteur. When we—his grandchildren—were little, he would invent funny stories to amuse us. He left a legacy of laughter in his will: He asked to be remembered on the anniversary of his death by having family and friends gather together to read his humorous stories aloud. This has been an inviolable tradition in the family: Each year, his funniest stories are read aloud, people laugh, drink tea, and go home."[4]

Kaufman's mother, Lyalya, was also a writer, having published some 2,000 stories in Yiddish. "My mother wrote her stories on one foot—so quickly. She had the light touch while I would sweat away at my writing. I remember she said to me in Russian, 'Belochka, why do you take so long? Don't you have any talent?'"[5]

For that matter, the entire family wrote. "My father, although he was a physician, was a poet and translator....I published my first piece, a four-line poem, 'To Spring,' when I was seven, in a Russian children's magazine.

"I just wrote. In our home, you inhaled, you exhaled, you had breakfast, lunch, dinner, and you wrote. When I was eleven, I wrote a drama, also in Russian, with one of those stubby pencils which, when you wet it, writes purple. I had about sixty pages of dramatis personae.

"I describe maybe thirty or forty characters in great detail, and by then I had said everything I wanted to say, so I quit and never got to Act I, Scene I."[6]

"After a childhood spent in Russia, I arrived in New York at the age of twelve, knowing not a word of English.

"The late Sam Levenson used to say that all through life he felt as if he had begun school one day late and had never caught up. I had begun six years late.

"I was taken to the neighborhood public school by my mother, who knew no more English than I did and who acted as my interpreter in my brief interview with the principal. To determine if I could read, he handed my mother a primer that she in turn gave me. I had been brought up on Russian classics, had just finished *War and Peace* (though I had skipped all the war chapters and read only the love story), but I could make nothing out of the words before me. Failed the reading test! The principal then wrote on a card: 2 + 4 and handed that to my mother, who passed it to me. I wrote 6 on the card—and I was enrolled.

"There were no special classes for foreigners then, no English as a second language. I was thrust into first grade, with children half my age, in the hope that somehow, through necessity and osmosis, I would learn English. I would have given anything to be like the other children, the American children in the room. I was tall and skinny with long corkscrew curls bobbing unstylishly down my back. I wore a maroon velvet dress with a lace collar. I was terrified.

"I squeezed my legs under the tiny, immovable desk welded to the floor, eyes front, hands tightly clasped before me as in prayer. I fixed my attention on the teacher and began my education.

"On a chart over the blackboard was printed the English alphabet, each letter a different color. Even today *E* is forever orange to me, and *A* is always green.

"The first English I spoke that first day was 'Moo-woo-oom.' In order to go to the bathroom, I gathered, one had to raise an arm and make this sound, whereupon one was entitled to pick up the square wooden pass that hung by a rope near the door and, wearing it like a reproachful albatross around the neck, leave the room. This was a privilege granted to those who were unsuccessful in fulfilling what was required of them at a specified hour, in the cummunal march to pee.

"I raised a tentative hand and—on the edge of disaster—whispered a frantic 'Moo-woo-oom!' The teacher, Miss Murphy, understood. She put her arm around me and ignoring the wooden pass, led me out of the room, pointed in the direction of the toilet, and waited at the classroom door until I returned. Before we reentered the room, she hugged me, smiled, and said something. I didn't understand the words, but I understood the warm voice. It said I was accepted; it said I was special to her; it said all would be well. I was silent. Even had I known English, what words were there...to tell her I would remember her to this day?

"I soon learned that the password was 'May I leave the room?' and I grasped enough English to begin skipping and catching up with my age group.

"But that first day had already decided my future. It was my unforgettable Miss Murphy, who had put her arm around me and hugged me, who made me want to be a teacher, too."[7]

As a youngster, Kaufman "was allowed to read everything—Dostoyevsky, Tolstoy...whatever I read was filtered through my own inno-cence....When I came to this country and learned

Bel Kaufman talks with then-mayor John Lindsay during the filming of "Up the Down Staircase."

English, a whole new wonderful world of literature opened up for me: *The Bobbsey Twins in School, The Bobbsey Twins in Camp, Anne of Green Gables.* I never knew such books existed."[8]

Kaufman was a regular at the library. "Guided by no reading lists, informed by no book reviews, I had no use for the card catalogue, since I worked each shelf alphabetically, burrowing my way from one end of the stacks to the other, relentless as a mole. I read by trial and error, through trash and treasure; like a true addict, I was interested not so much in quality as in getting the stuff.

"Sometimes I would stumble upon a book that was special; a book unrequired, unrecommended, unspoiled by teacher-imposed chores—'Name 3....Answer the following...'—a book to be read for sheer pleasure.

"Where else was it allowed, even encouraged, to thumb through a book, to linger on a page without being shooed away from handling the merchandise? This was merchandise to be handled. I was

not fooled by the stiff, impassive maroon and dark-green library bindings; I nosed out the good ones. If the pages were worn and dog-eared, if the card tucked into its paper pocket inside the cover was stamped with lots of dates, I knew I had a winner.

"Those dates linked me to the anonymous fellowship of other readers whose hands had turned the pages I was turning, who sometimes left penciled clues in the margins: a philosophic 'How True!'—a succinct 'Stinks.'

"Here, within walls built book by solid book, we sat in silent kinship, the only sounds shuffling of feet, scraping of chairs, an occasional loud whisper, and the librarian's stern 'Shhh!'"[9]

"In my teens, I read contemporary authors, short stories with ironic endings (de Maupassant, O. Henry) and, to clear the air, my old favorite, Chekhov.

"*Cyrano de Bergerac* floored me at fifteen, but not when I was older. So did *The World's Illusion* and

Look Homeward, Angel. Other books survived adolescence....They remained relevant."[8]

Graduating magna cum laude from Hunter College, Kaufman began her teaching career which spanned two decades. "I've taught in every kind of school in New York City, from one where, in the middle of my Lady Macbeth, a handcuff-bearing cop materialized and said, 'Lady, that kid I gotta have,' to one where my classes discussed the meaning of wit in Pope's *Essay on Criticism.* No matter what kinds of students I've had, from those who read nothing but the balloons coming out of the heads of comic book characters to those who read Spinoza and Spengler, every one of them in his own way has been crying, 'Pay attention! Here I am! Listen to me! Care about me!'

"Through paying attention, listening, and caring, teachers get their rewards—immeasureable rewards. One of the characters in my book is a little Puerto Rican boy who has no identity. He signs himself 'Me' and wishes himself 'Happy Birthday' in a note he puts in the suggestion box.

Kaufman on grandfather Sholom Aleichem's knee.

"His teacher...with one of those strokes of inspiration that we teachers sometimes have, assigns him the role of judge in a class courtroom playlet. The following day he appears dressed for the part in graduation gown and mortar board, a big hammer for a gavel, vested in such dignity that no one dares to laugh. When he's challenged about court procedure he says, 'I ought to know. I *been.*'

"Later the teacher gets her reward when he writes, 'You made me feel I'm real.'

"The rewards of the teacher are many: when a child who has been silent all term raises a faltering hand; when a boy takes out a library card for the first time; when a student says, 'You're my favorite subject'; and the most exciting moment of all—when a pupil says, 'Oh, I get it!'

"If I were asked to mention the attributes that are most important to any teacher I'd say, a sense of humor (the ability to see absurdities and to puncture pomposities); physical, emotional, and intellectual stamina; and, above all, what one of my students once described as 'a touch of teacherly love.'"[10]

"We teachers seldom know whom we have influenced, or how, or even why. I once had a student who was bent on quitting school. He was a sullen, friendless boy, an indifferent scholar, with a mild interest in one subject, science. The last day of school before summer vacation I invited him to my home a few blocks away to give him a book I thought might interest him—a collection of biographies of eminent scientists. He shuffled uneasily in my foyer, refused to sit down, turned down a Coke, and fled as soon as I handed him the book, which I had inscribed simply: 'To Joe, With Confidence.' In the fall, I was pleased to see him back in school.

"'I see you decided not to drop out,' I said.

"'Yeah,' he admitted, sheepishly. 'I'll never forget that book you gave me.'

"'It inspired you?'

"'Naw, I never read it,' he said. 'It's just...You gave it to me. You asked me over your house, and you gave me your own hardcover book!'

"Learning is not a product but a process, which goes on as long as we live. We admire its presence in the old—the grandmother who gets a high school diploma, the octogenarian who masters a new hobby. It is this kind of interest outside of ourselves, this lively curiosity, that keeps us youthful. 'The man who is too old to learn was probably always too old to learn.' (I came across this random nugget, a quote by Henry Haskins, quite by chance, while idly browsing through a reference book.)"[11]

"The turning point of my writing career was the publication of my book, *Up the Down Staircase*. Before that, I had found it difficult to be the granddaughter of a great writer. The success of my book made me feel I had permission to be a writer too."

Kaufman's thirty years' experience as a teacher in New York City schools became the basis for her famous book, about the trials of a beginning teacher in the bureaucracy of the public schools. "My book became a plea for the dignity of our profession, and through this, for the dignity of the kids. . . .It evidently had an enormous impact on the lay public, most of whom were unaware of the conditions I described. 'Does this really go on?' they asked. The teachers knew all along, and now the public knows.

"The book is fiction, but drawn on a lifetime of experience. It is neither a case study nor propaganda nor expose, but it's about something very close to me—the teaching profession. . . .I wrote about a large city school, but I touched a common nerve ending everywhere, from the smallest community to the largest city.

"Once my book came out in paperback, the kids started writing me. And their letters have been so touching. Many write 'Dear Miss Barrett' (the book's leading character). They want to know what happened to the students in the book. The book had reached them too, and this was most moving."[12]

About her craft, Kaufman wrote: "I do not LIKE writing; in truth, I HATE writing, and would rather do anything else. But the joy comes when, almost in spite of myself, I come close to what I want to say. A sentence or an insight leaps from the page. I need to write alone, without guidance or suggestions from anyone, until the work is almost done.

"It is only in rewriting that—for me—the pleasures of my craft lie. But first I must get it all down on paper, no matter how careless it may be. Only then can I mold it, like so much clay.

"I write at home, at my desk, in my study, with my back to the view of the Manhattan skyline. But sheer physical comfort is not the answer. In the past, I have written on one knee, in a tiny bedroom. I suppose any place that is quiet will do (I have a low tolerance for noise or disturbance of any kind).

"It is difficult to say *when* I write, for I lack the discipline that I try to instill in my students. Most of the time I try to avoid writing by doing all kinds of things that are the equivalent to sharpening pencils. I write letters, answer the phone, clean out my closets—anything to avoid that confrontation with the typewriter. But when the writing is going well, I have been known to start early in the morning, and when I look up, the windows are dark! That is the kind of concentration that is devoutly to be wished for.

"I suppose when I say I don't like to write, I am referring to prose, for I love writing light verse, lyrics for musicals, skits and playlets. I have done lyrics for shows that were sheer joy to work on. One day I shall go back to my love—the theater."

Up the Down Staircase was a national best-seller for sixty-four weeks and number one in the nation for over five months, selling more than six million copies and translated into sixteen languages. In paperback it is in its forty-seventh printing. *Time* called it "easily the most popular novel about U.S. public schools in history."

In 1967 the book was adapted into a motion picture. "I was hired as technical consultant on the film, which was produced by Alan Pakula and directed by Robert Mulligan, who had prepared themselves by sitting in various classes to absorb the atmosphere of a New York school. Sandy Dennis gave the part of the young school teacher a certain vulnerable quality, but the stars, as far as I was concerned, were the non-professional kids, selected from schools and settlement houses, kids who had never acted before, and who played themselves most touchingly. One Black boy had dropped out of school when he was cast in the film and had his moment of glory on the screen. A shy Puerto Rican boy played one of the main student roles; his mother said to me: 'Please, Miss Kaufman, write another book soon so my boy could be in it!' When they finished shooting on location—a Manhattan high school closed for the summer— Warner Bros. gave a farewell party for everyone connected with the film. When they played the school theme song, I sang along with the kids, and felt tears in my eyes. 'Idiot!' I said to myself. 'Why are you crying? You made up the song, you made up the school. . . .'"

In June, 1977, the play "Up the Down Staircase," an adaptation of Kaufman's book, was performed for her on one of her visits to the Soviet Union. "I find myself as moved as is the rest of the audience by the young, miniskirted teacher and her boister-

Kaufman with cast members on the set of the movie "Up the Down Staircase."

ous pupils, one with face sooted to portray a black student, one with face painted brown to denote a Puerto Rican; for in spite of certain excesses and distortions, what shines through is the glowing feeling of affection, of deep caring.

"'Happy families are all alike,' so opens Tolstoi's *Anna Karenina*: 'every unhappy family is unhappy in its own way.' Good teachers, I think, whatever their country or language, are all alike in their dedication to their profession and commitment to the young. I speak not as an expert or as a political or social commentator; my impressions are limited to my personal observations on two separate visits to the Soviet Union....Because I speak fluent Russian, when I visited schools and camps I was able to talk with teachers, school administrators, librarians—above all, with the children.

"A teacher in whose home in Moscow I dined told me of her first semester in school when, in the middle of a class in which her pupils were diligently writing compositions, the director of the school entered, looked around, approached her desk, and

leaned down to whisper in her ear, 'Irina Mikhailovna, you will never be a teacher!'

"Shocked, she went to see him after class: 'What was wrong? My children were writing quietly.'

"'Ah, yes,' the director replied, 'but when children write, the teacher does not look out of the window; she looks at her children—with affection.'

"This may seem as farfetched to us Americans as the scene I myself witnessed: the teacher arrived in her classroom on that particular morning resplendent in a velvet dress, her hair carefully coiffed. 'Children,' she said to the astonished class, her voice trembling with emotion, 'today we begin to read our great Russian poet Pushkin.'

"I doubt that any American teacher would dress in a cocktail gown to introduce the poetry of Robert Frost to her class, but it's the *feeling* of this teacher we recognize; it's the *feeling* of the director we understand.

"The affection of Russians for their children is evident everyplace, in private homes and public places as well as in schools, where attention is lavished upon them from early infancy in public nurseries throughout the rest of their schooling. Children are treasured—especially after the devastation of war, the scars of which have been passed down unto the third generation. At a matinee performance of the ballet *Spartacus* in Leningrad, during the battle scene of Romans killing slaves, I heard a little girl sitting in front of me in a pink starched dress with a matching ribbon bow in her hair ask her mother in a frightened whisper, 'Are they Germans?'

"The Soviet people are personally involved with children—their own and those of others. One day on the street in Kiev I saw several people berating a mother who was dragging her crying child by the hand. 'Why are they interfering?' I asked my companion.

"'It's not interfering,' she replied, 'it's *caring.*'

"Even authors of children's books make personal contact with their readers; it is customary for them to travel periodically from city to city, often covering vast distances, to address their small readers, answer their questions, and hear their suggestions. Children's books are beautifully illustrated and cost mere kopeks. Russians are avid readers; new books are sold out immediately and are then passed, like precious heirlooms, from hand to hand.

"It starts early, this love of books, from the first grade, when the seven year olds officially begin their education with seriousness, high expectations, and flowers for the teacher."[13]

Years after her successful novel, *McCall's* asked Kaufman to write an article about current schools—a postscript to *Up the Down Staircase.* "The situation has become much worse. I spent four months in some of the toughest high schools in New York. At times, I feared for my life. Even our faculty conferences were different: we used to discuss whether or not to teach Macbeth in the fifth or sixth term; today we are confronted by the problem of a fifteen-year-old girl who is pregnant, a boy who is a junkie. What I had described in my book seemed a utopia compared to what I experienced in my later visits in our schools. I wrote that article and titled it 'Going Back Up the Down Staircase.'"

These problems begin long before a child enters school, according to Kaufman. "They begin with poverty, anger, prejudice. By the time a child enters school, it is often too late. In order to have better schools, we must have a better world. These are societal problems, not educational ones. Still, despite all this, inside each class there is that 'one child,' even if he is one in forty. He can be found, guided, salvaged. That is what the teaching profession is about."

Kaufman describes herself as first a teacher, then a writer. Education, according to Kaufman, "begins with the teacher. Plato didn't even have a room. Often teachers are the only ones who can instill a sense of worth in a child. We all remember the great teachers we had."

"I was a late bloomer. I was fifty-plus when I gathered the courage to scramble out of a deteriorated marriage and found myself for the first time entirely on my own. I was fifty-plus when I wrote my first novel....I was fifty-plus when I discovered a new career of public speaking. And I was fifty-plus when I formed a totally satisfying relationship with a man.

"Not that I spent my earlier years lolling on a chaise lounge, munching chocolates. I taught school, brought up two children, published an occasional story or light verse, but balancing for many years on the tightrope of a perilous marriage did not lend itself to creativity. Nor to independence. Nor to a sense of identity. I knew how to be a daughter, a wife, a mother; I did not know how to be *me.*

"Now I do. I have learned a simple, powerful lesson: I learned to say NO. What a heady, liberating sound that can be! I do not have to be loved by everyone; I can risk disapproval. I can trust my opinions. I have profited from my mistakes—and they were lulus! With each small success my confidence grew. And with my children's independence came my own. I no longer do what I *have* to do; I now do what I *want* to do.

"I am one of the lucky ones: I have options."[14]

Although Kaufman has always avoided politics, she accepted an invitation from the Soviet Embassy for December 7, 1987 as one of the "prominent Americans" to join Gorbachev and his wife, Raisa, for cultural exchanges. And during that same year she participated in the Moscow International Forum for a Nuclear Free World at the invitation of the Soviet Union. Among those participating with Kaufman were Graham Greene, Daniel Ellsberg, Yoko Ono, Marina Vladi and Gregory Peck. "The Forum was a platform for promoting peace unprec-

RULES FOR ENGLISH
NO SHOUTING
NO SWEARING
FIGHTING

Sandy Dennis starred in the film version of Kaufman's novel, *Up the Down Staircase.* **(Released by Warner Brothers, 1967.)**

edented in its diversity and scope. Nearly 1,000 eminent personalities from more than eighty countries came at the invitation of various Soviet organizations: doctors and writers, scholars and businessmen, politicians and physicists, theater and film people, representatives of six major religions, and some members of the newly formed international organization Retired Generals for Peace and Disarmament.

"All these people met on the weekend of February 14-16, at several places simultaneously. The Forum was divided into various panels; I spoke at one called 'The Role of Culture in Protecting Civilization and Universal Human Values.' The emphasis here was on peace for the children of the world: *Mir detyam mira.* The Russian word *mir* happens to mean both 'peace' and 'the world.'

"Love for children and fear of war go hand in hand. Both are of deepest concern to the Soviet people. There is hardly a family in the Soviet Union untouched by the last war, in which twenty million

had perished. A line by the poet Anna Akhmatova, engraved on the marble wall of the Moscow Writers Union, reads: 'No one is forgotten, nothing is forgotten.' Reminders are everywhere, in the maimed and the bereaved, and in the thousands of manless middle-aged women. Even small children worry about war.

"The culmination of the Forum and its highlight was Mikhail Gorbachev's address at the Kremlin. We walked through the splendid palace, which dates back to the time of Ivan the Terrible, into the Chamber of the Supreme Soviet. It was filled with 1,800 people. At our seats were individual dials for simultaneous translation into twelve languages. A few rows behind me sat Andrei Sakharov, the former dissident physicist, newly released from internal exile."[15]

Kaufman continues her trips to the Soviet Union, the latest in the spring of 1989; she continues her visits into inner-city classrooms, and to address teachers all over the country.

Footnote Sources:

[1] Bella Ezersky "From Russia with 'Love, Etc.,'" *Interview*, January, 1980. Amended by Kaufman.

[2] B. Kaufman, "The Kindling of Memories," *McCall's*, December, 1978.

[3] B. Kaufman, "The Most Touching of All Gifts," *50 Plus*, December, 1985.

[4] B. Kaufman, "Storytelling That Inspires Laughter, Tears, Reflection," *Today's Health*, December, 1973.

[5] B. Kaufman, "Teaching in Triplicate," *Saturday Review*, April 10, 1965.

[6] "The Editor Interviews Bel Kaufman," *NEA Journal*, September, 1966.

[7] B. Kaufman, "First Day of School," *Today's Education*, September/October, 1981.

[8] "Three Writers, Recalling Favorites, Urge Wide Choice of Literature," *New York Times Magazine*, May 29, 1977. Amended by Kaufman.

[9] B. Kaufman, "The Liberry," *New York Times*, July 23, 1976.

[10] B. Kaufman, "The Real World of the Beginning Teacher," *NEA Journal*, October, 1965.

[11] B. Kaufman, "Inspire a Love of Learning," *Today's Health*, September, 1974.

[12] B. Kaufman, "Plea for Professional Dignity," *Scholastic Teacher*, October 14, 1966.

[13] B. Kaufman, "Here's to Children," *Today's Education*, February-March, 1978.

[14] B. Kaufman, "The Beauty of Being a Late Bloomer," *50 Plus*, June, 1986.

[15] B. Kaufman, "From Russia with Hope," *50 Plus*, July, 1987.

■ For More Information See

America, February 6, 1965.
Time, February 12, 1965.
Commonweal, May 14, 1965.
New York Times, May 29, 1977.
Chicago Tribune Book World, October 28, 1979.
Washington Post Book World, November 11, 1979.
Arkansas Democrat, November 5, 1982.

Spike Lee

B orn Shelton Jackson Lee March 20, 1957 in Atlanta, Ga.; son of William (a musician and composer) and Jacqueline (a teacher; maiden name, Shelton) Lee. *Education:* Morehouse College, B.A., 1979; graduate study at New York University, 1982. *Residence:* Brooklyn, N.Y. *Office:* Forty Acres and a Mule Filmworks, 124 DeKalb Ave., Brooklyn, N.Y. 11217.

■ Career

Screenwriter, actor, and director of motion pictures and music videos. Founder and director, Forty Acres and a Mule Filmworks, Brooklyn, N.Y., 1986—. *Member:* Screen Actors Guild.

■ Awards, Honors

Student Director's Award from Academy of Motion Picture Arts and Sciences, 1982, for "Joe's Bed-Stuy Barber Shop: We Cut Heads"; Prix de Jeunesse from Cannes Film Festival, and New Generation Award from the Los Angeles Film Critics, both 1986, both for "She's Gotta Have It."

■ Writings

Spike Lee's "Gotta Have It": Inside Guerilla Filmmaking (includes interviews and a journal; illustrated with photographs by brother, David Lee), foreword by Nelson George, Simon & Schuster, 1987.
(With Lisa Jones) *Uplift the Race: The Construction of "School Daze,"* Simon & Schuster, 1988.
(With L. Jones) *"Do the Right Thing": The New Spike Lee Joint,* Fireside Press, 1989.

Screenplays; And Director:

"She's Gotta Have It," Island, 1986.
"School Daze," Columbia, 1988.
(And producer) "Do the Right Thing," Universal Studios, 1989.

Films:

"Variations on the Mo' Better Blues," Forty Acres and a Mule Filmworks, 1990.

Also writer and director of short films, including "The Answer," 1980, "Sarah," 1981, and "Joe's Bed-Stuy Barbershop: We Cut Heads," 1982. Contributor of short films to "Saturday Night Live," and to Music Television (MTV) network.

■ Sidelights

After the release of only three films, Spike Lee has become one of the most provocative young filmmakers to emerge in the late '80s. "I truly believe I was put here to make films, it's as simple as that. I'm doin' what I'm 'posed to be doin'. It's not for me to say whether ['She's Gotta Have It'] is a landmark film (I make 'em, that's all) but I do want people to be inspired by it, in particular, black people. Now there is a present example of how we can produce. We can do the things we want to do, there are no mo' excuses. We're all tired of that alibi, 'White man this, white man that.'....It's on us. So let's all do the work that needs to be done by us *all.* And to y'all who aren't down for the cause, move out of the way, step aside."[1]

Lee was born in Atlanta, Georgia, where he earned his nickname, Spike. "A lot of people think it's made up—one of those stage names. My mother...said I was a very tough baby....I was like three or four months old when I got the nickname."[1]

Lee's father, a jazz musician, Bill Lee, soon moved his family to the jazz mecca, Chicago. "Then there was an exodus of jazz musicians from Chicago to New York....And my father went with that. I think we came to New York in '59, '60. I remember we lived on Union Street in Crown Heights. I remember Eastern Parkway. I remember Hasidic Jews. And then we moved to Cobble Hill. We were the first blacks in that neighborhood. But we didn't have any problems."[1]

Then the family moved to Fort Greene which had a bad reputation. "Undeserved, I think....It still does now. But it's getting better....Everything you read in the papers is negative."[1]

Although his father was one of the jazz greats, Lee chose not to follow in his footsteps. "Being the first born, not becoming a musician was a part of my rebelliousness."[1]

Although Lee always had a good ear for music he preferred to hang around with his friends and play sports. "There was...a whole group of us that lived on the same block. We had enough people to have a team in every sport....We played all the time. Whatever the season was. Touch football, tackle in the park, stickball, softball, basketball, roller hockey. There were no fights, nothing like that. It was cool....I was always the captain of the team, the spark plug. Not the best athlete, though....[I had] leadership qualities."[1]

He also liked movies. "My mother used to take us to movies all the time. But I'm not a classic case where I saw one film and decided right then that I wanted to be a filmmaker."[1]

A jazz purist, Lee's father placed strains on the family by adhering to his artistic principles. "In the early sixties [my father] was the top folk/jazz bassist. If you look on the albums of Peter, Paul and Mary, Bob Dylan, Judy Collins, Odetta, Theodore Bikel, Leon Bibbs and Josh White, you'll see that my father was playing with all of them. He also played with Simon and Garfunkel. He got tired of playing that music, though, and then the electric bass became popular and he refused to play it. To this day he's never played Fender bass.

"With that kind of stance, you don't work. So when he stopped working my mother became the sole breadwinner of our family. She taught at St. Ann's, a school in Brooklyn Heights....For a whole lot of years she was the only one bringing in any money.

"It's kind of hard...when you have a wife and five kids. But...my mother loved him and believed in the music. That's why she dragged herself to work on many days when she didn't want to....It's something that all artists have to deal with.

"I got some of my stubbornness from him, if the word is stubbornness....[It's] nonconformist, to a degree."[1]

Lee attended John Dewey High School where he did enough to get by. "I cared about the subjects that I liked—social studies class. I hated math and science....It was a special high school. You could pick your classes the way you wanted. I graduated there in 1975."[1]

Summers were spent down South. "I think every black kid in the North who had relatives in the South was sent away for the summer. We would spend half the summer with each set of grandparents—half the summer in Atlanta with my mother's parents and half the summer with my father's mother in Snow Hill, Alabama—ninety miles from Montgomery, seventeen miles from Selma."[1]

Lee never found an interest in drugs and, as a young man, didn't even drink beer. "It tasted nasty to me. You have to acquire a taste for beer....Hardly any of the people we played with got high."[1]

Following a long family tradition, Lee enrolled at Morehouse, an all-black college in Atlanta. "My great grandfather was a disciple of Booker T. Washington. He founded Snow Hill Institute in Alabama. I'm a third-generation Morehouse graduate. My father and grandfather went to Morehouse. My mother and grandmother went to Spelman. The Lee family has always been like that.

"I stayed on campus but I went to see my grandmother every day. To eat. Morehouse food is terrible."[1]

From Lee's 1988 movie "School Daze."

Majoring in mass communications, he decided by his sophomore year to become a filmmaker—though he still did a bit of everything else. "I had my own radio show...[on] WCLK, a jazz station. I played jazz and sometimes I played disco on Sunday mornings....I was [also] doing a little writing for the school newspaper."[1] But most importantly, he began making films. Rolanda Watts (now a New York television reporter) was in the first film Lee wrote, "Black College: The Talented Tenth." "I do not like that film at all....It's a corny love story at a black campus. Real corny....I'm glad there's only one copy in existence.

"I [also] did a couple of dance pieces. I did a film called 'Last Hustle in Brooklyn.'...It was the summer of '77. That was like the big summer in

disco and that was also the summer of the blackout....When every night there was a block party and people were hustling and stuff like that....So I incorporated both."[1]

During this time, he began to gather some of the people who would become important in his career, namely Monty Ross, who would later act in, and produce Lee's films.

After graduation from Morehouse, Lee enrolled at the New York University Film School. "There's no way I could have made the films I made if I lived in L.A. 'cause I didn't know anybody. I couldn't have called people for locations. Also you had to have an astronomical score on the GREs to get in. Plus at USC and UCLA, not everybody makes a film. The teachers assign by committee who gets to make a film.''[1]

The filmmaker battled against conformity that first year at NYU. "Most of those people at that school, their works sucks. And the thing about it, their films were the ones that the teachers praised. They were held up as the levels that should be reached.

"Any time a black person is in a white environment and they are not always happy—smiling, eating cheese, then they say he's a militant or he has an attitude. The first year at NYU is probation period for everybody. So they tried to kick me out my first year. They said I didn't know film grammar....Knowing how to put a film together. Knowing technique....[They said that] my films were no good.

"I would put the film I made, 'The Answer,' up against any third film a first-year student did that year."[1]

"The Answer" told the story of a black screenwriter hired to direct a fifty-million dollar remake of D. W. Griffith's "Birth of a Nation," a film-school staple. Lee's film included clips from the original, and pointing out the racism inherent in Griffith's film. "They didn't like that thing at all. How dare I denigrate the father of cinema."[1]

He doesn't remember his grade for that film. "It had to be a good enough mark for me to stay there. Even though I almost got kicked out. I still got a teaching assistantship. So that helped me get through the next year. I didn't have to pay tuition. So I used the money that would have gone to pay for tuition for my films. My grandmother put me through Morehouse and NYU. She has a producing credit on 'Joe's Bed-Stuy Barbershop' also."[1]

Filmed his senior year, "Joe's Bed-Stuy Barbershop" earned Lee a student academy award. Monty Ross starred in the film about a local barber who gets caught up in the numbers racket and organized crime. "That summer before my final year in school I was in Atlanta writing a script. I let Monty read it and he suggested that he act in it. I never thought of Monty...coming up to New York, dropping what he was doing, to act in it. But he did. I think Monty gave a very fine performance. What people don't realize is that Monty—a very unselfish person—was not only acting in the film, he was driving the van, he was crewing, he was doing a lot of other things that no doubt affected his performance. But we got the film made."[1]

Several elements, Lee felt, contributed to his film's success. "The gangster genre and the incorpora-

tion of negritude into that, which is the numbers and the barbershop—the barbershop being right behind the church as the number-one congregation spot for people in the black community, and humor.

"I still think it's a good film. There were a lot of instances where I was too busy worrying about getting the shot off and not worrying about what was happening in front of the camera."[1]

Winning the student academy award didn't really surprise Lee. "Because I know that NYU is one of the best film schools, and I saw a lot of films that came out of the school. I know that this was as good or better than anything that was in USC or UCLA.

"They are like factories now. Everybody wants to be a filmmaker. If you get two or three filmmakers out of forty a year I think that's a good rate. I think, me, [cinematographer] Ernest [Dickerson], Jim Jarmusch and Sara Driver [were] the ones when I went to NYU. I never went to NYU expecting teachers to teach me. I just wanted equipment, so I could make films, and learn filmmaking by making films....That's the only way to learn. People call me now wanting to know what the secret to successful filmmaking is. I get so mad. There *is* no secret formula let's say, for the success of 'She's Gotta Have It.' I'm not gonna tell them anything that will help them. We just killed ourselves to get it made. That's how we did it.

"Ernest and I were in the same class. We came in together. He was from Howard. I was from Morehouse. Ernest is older than me. After he graduated, he had like four or five years experience as a medical illustrator at Howard's med school. Interestingly enough, he had been an architecture major. We were the only blacks at NYU. There were two sections the first year and we were in different sections. The second year he shot my film 'Sarah.'...[A film about] a family in Harlem on Thanksgiving Day. In my senior year he shot 'Joe's [Bed-Stuy Barbershop']."

"[Ernest is also] a very good director. He never brought his films to completion. But he has two films that will be very good when they are finished."[1]

After winning the student academy award, some of the larger talent agencies approached Lee and, although they represented him for a year-and-a-half, nothing much materialized. "I had the first draft of what is now 'School Daze,' but then it was called 'Homecoming.' The script was a lot different but I had the third draft of it. It was an all-black film. They said nah. Forget it. Nothing. Not even an 'Afterschool Special.' And there were a lot of my classmates who didn't even win Academy Awards who did get 'Afterschool Specials.'"[1]

Since then, Lee hasn't had, nor ever intends to have, an agent. "You've got to make your own personal choice. I will not have an agent, though I have a good lawyer and a good accountant. That's all you need. That's all I need. You can only brag so much saying, 'Yes, I'm at William Morris. I'm at ICM.' After that,...you still have to find a job like everybody else."[1]

In 1984, Lee attempted to put together his first feature-length production, "The Messenger." "It was about a family in Brooklyn. The [main] character is a bike messenger. We spent something like forty thousand dollars....With the chance to spend a lot more. But I said, 'Whoa! We have to pull the plug.' There was other money that was supposed to happen. It never happened."[1]

Difficulties with Screen Actor's Guild contributed to the failure. "The actors I wanted to use were Larry Fishburne, Giancarlo Esposito, and some others. And we wanted to get experimental film rates. There's a thing where any film budgeted under a certain amount of money can apply and be granted a waiver. We applied for a waiver and SAG denied it....There are too many black actors out of work for them to nix it. [But] they said no. So I had to recast the entire picture in four days with non-SAG people. And it never came together so we were all devastated.

"I got a list of ten films that had been given a waiver within the last year. All of them were done by white independent filmmakers. All of them worked with a whole lot more money than I had. Yet they said my film was too commercial. I still have a suit against SAG with the Human Resources Administration. But they have a four-year backlog of racial suits here in New York City....But that was a definite case of racism."[1]

The very next year, Lee responded by starting his next project, "She's Gotta Have It." "You begin with an idea and you try to push it all the way through to its completion. The trick is not to go insane, go broke, or lose faith along the way....I recently read my journals assembled for the first time and realized that I had forgotten the actual pure hell we went through to see 'She's Gotta Have It' to fruition. Everybody and his mother has a script or is a filmmaker, but the ones who get their films done are the ones who don't listen when everybody says, 'Forget it, you're wasting time and money.' The ones who believe, have an unwavering faith in their films and ability and are almost, but not quite, willing to kill to get that 'bad boy' made, will prevail—'cuz dat's what it takes."[1]

"She's Gotta Have It," explores black female sexuality through it's main character, Nola Darling, played by Tracy Camilla Johns. "Tracy was great. I think the one reason why there hasn't been a universal clamor that the film is pornographic is because of how well the sex scenes were done, and I have to attribute that to Tracy. She's very comfortable with her sexuality, therefore the actors were comfortable with her, so the audience is comfortable with the scenes."[1]

Nola dates three different men, Jamie Overstreet, Greer Childs, and Mars Blackmon. Each character satisfies a different aspect of her needs. Jamie, played by Tommy [Redmond] Hicks, offers stability. "If you looked closely, she only lit the candles for Jamie. She never lit them for Mars or Greer.

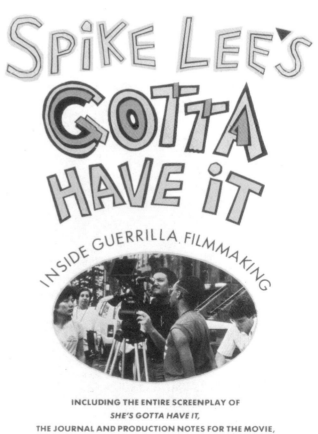

Cover from the journal of Lee's first movie.

"With Greer it's a pure physical thing, pure, pure sex. She's physically attracted to him and that's all it's about, just sex. And Mars makes her laugh.

"Everybody's character was reflected in how they perceived Nola. That's the whole film, how everybody perceives Nola."[1]

Lee played the character Mars. "I decided to cast myself halfway through writing it. I thought all of these actors were a lot like their characters."[1]

Acting in the film, as well as directing, presented special challenges. "There was a problem at the beginning of the shoot when I was in front of the camera. I was divided. I was still playing the role of the director and I was saying, 'Ok, everybody. Sound. Roll sound. Camera. Action.' Then I was acting. And this wasn't working. So the gaffer, Mike Hunold—a good friend of ours who went to NYU—said, 'Let's just try this: Let's leave all that stuff to Ernie.' I said fine, and everything went smoothly after that. When I was in front of the camera all I had to worry about was Mars Blackmon and Ernest was the director."[1]

"I think I was fair to everyone. Especially black males, because there is no hatred in it. If you look at a work like 'For Colored Girls Who Have Considered Suicide' by Ntozake Shange, or possibly 'The Color Purple,' I think you will see hatred of black men. I have no hate for black men or black women and I don't see that in this film.

"We wanted to—and I think we've been successful—make an intelligent film that showed black people loving each other and black people falling out of love. We wanted to show some kind of black sensuality that I know people want to see, but for whatever reason don't—because white people don't know how to handle it, or whatever."[1]

Lee's films draw heavily on jazz; his father has written the musical scores for each. "The sad thing, though, is that we have whole generations of black people who know nothing about jazz. And they look down upon it. I was reading this interview where Wynton Marsalis said black people are ignorant. He gets tired of going to concerts and playing only for white people. Jazz music is black music and that's what we're projecting in my film....I'm just happy that [my films give my father] more recognition than he's probably gotten in years."[1] .

For each film he has made, Spike Lee has also released a companion film journal. The journal to "She's Gotta Have It" chronicled the enormous pressures on a young filmmaker trying to shoot his first film. "I knew the money was out there. It was just a matter of finding it. We juggled the couple of pennies we had and tried to keep the creditors away for just a couple more days. The actors, crew members, the lab were calling for money and rightfully so. People wanted their money and I knew I would get it some way.

"There were tense days, like when...the lab was going to auction my negative. Now I know they would have never done that, but it was a threat. And I couldn't afford to find out. It was just a matter of somebody out there having the foresight and vision to take my film."[1]

The American Film Institute refused to let Lee transfer a $20,000 grant he had received to make "The Messenger" to the production of "She's Gotta Have It." Lee sent this letter in protest. "I feel AFI has done me wrong. To tell me that I can apply next year is no consolation at all. AFI should know more than anybody that nothing is certain. This is the nature of the movie industry. I tried everything I could to make 'Messenger.' There were extraordinary circumstances surrounding the project (Screen Actors Guild) and all of that should have been taken into consideration. When I finally realized that it could not be made, the review was in progress. If there was ever a time to bend the rules this was it.

"I close with the immortal words of the Brooklyn Dodgers faithful: WE WUZ ROBBED."[1]

Most potential investors demonstrated a similar lack of vision. "It was a very spiritual experience getting this whole film made. There were times when I didn't know where the next nickel was coming from, but it would come. Sure enough, the money came whenever we needed it."[1]

The film's eventual critical success (as well as a gross of over $8,000,000) left many investors feeling foolish. "I'm not a vindictive person. It's them that feel embarrassed. I don't even want to bring it up. It's fine. It's history. Yet twelve months later, they are still apologizing when there's really no need for it."[1]

The popularity of "She's Gotta Have It" became evident at the Cannes Film Festival. When the power failed during the film's screening, the audience refused to leave until they saw the end.

This success allowed Lee to form his own production company: Forty Acres and a Mule, named for what every black person in America had been promised at the end of slavery. Lee remained determined to make only the films he wanted to.

Tracy Camilla Johns and Redmond Hicks starred in Spike Lee's first feature film, "She's Gotta Have It."

"You really carry a burden as a black filmmaker. There are so few black films that when you do one it has to represent every black person in the world.

"If you're white, you're not going to protest in front of a theater because the film is about this or that because it is one of two hundred white Hollywood films that might have been released that year. But when we talk about a black film, you're carrying the whole burden of the black race on your shoulders. That's really unfair, though I can see their point because there are so few black films. So, when one comes along, you put so much hope into it. It's the aspirations of a race upon you. When Richard Pryor got his deal with Indigo, he became the messiah with black people, Jesus Christ. Every black actor, actress, director, screenwriter in the world was knocking on his door like he was going to be the salvation for all of us. And it's never going to be like that.

"We're a small company....We'd like to build a strong financial base....I'm determined not to let people turn me into a savior. I'm not trying to right everything that's been wrong as far as film and black people are concerned for the last hundred years."[1]

Yet, Lee still feels an underlying sense of responsibility. "Every filmmaker hopes he has the financial clout to make the films he wants....If I could have the power that Spielberg has but not be Steven Spielberg, nobody would turn that down. I'm not just out there to make it myself. I want to bring as many people along with me as possible. There are a lot of really good black filmmakers out there. If I can get into a position to produce other films, I will."[1]

His next script, "The Homecoming," evolved into the musical film, "School Daze." It draws heavily on Lee's days at Morehouse College. "There's nothing like going to a black school and seeing homecoming. That's why we took the cast and a lot of the potential cast down. We took them to the homecoming game...to see Morehouse play Howard University. You should have seen Vanessa Williams. Her mouth was open the whole time. Said she had never been around that many intelligent, good-looking, beautiful black people in her life. Like Richard Pryor talked about in his concert film of his experience going to Africa, and the wonderful feeling he had being in a place where everybody is black. Black professors, black doctors, it's a great experience in Atlanta. It's not just Morehouse. There's Spelman College, Clark College, Morris Brown College, Atlanta University. All these schools make up the Atlanta University Center and they're all across the street from each other."[1]

"I'm not going to say there are not a lot of ills on black college campuses. We [hoped] to address some of those things in the film 'School Daze.' But I still love Morehouse, regardless. The thing that amazed me about being there was how some guys couldn't get no play from women, but the minute they pledged to a fraternity the women were all over them. It was amazing."[1]

This practical perception of black college life would get Lee into trouble during the filming. "Almost halfway through the shoot, with footage already in the can, the colleges of the Atlanta University Center decided to bar the School Daze Picture Company from filming on their campuses. The reason for the boot? They feared that 'School Daze' would portray a negative (...that word

again) image of Black colleges, and more importantly of Black people as a whole. You have to understand that historically Black colleges have been very conservative. They consider themselves the guardians of the integrity of the race.

"[We'd begun] shooting on the campuses in March without a contract, apart from an agreement signed early on with AU. After three weeks we still didn't have one. Heading towards our fourth week, we received a letter from the AUC's lawyer demanding that we stop shooting until the script was made available. We again refused and were barred from the campuses. Not only that, but the footage we shot previously could not, or so they told us, be used in the movie.

"There were so many rumors circulating around the AUC about the movie. Women at Spelman thought that Kelly Woolfolk—who played Vicky, football player Grady's love interest—had the role of a prostitute. The students were influenced by the propaganda being pushed out by the administrations. When I was at Morehouse the atmosphere was different. The student body was more vocal and certainly more political. We didn't take what the administration told us at face value. I think we would have been really upset if a young Black filmmaker came to our campus to shoot a film and got kicked off by the school. But there wasn't a whimper from any of the students at Morehouse, Spelman, Clark, or Morris Brown. In fact, we never had a chance to shoot anything on Spelman's campus. The acting president was quite adamant about us not being there.

"I'm all for Black colleges. I'm a third-generation Morehouse man, and I hope my sons choose Morehouse. But there are certain things wrong at Black colleges and I address some of them in 'School Daze.' To me, this doesn't mean that I'm putting forth a negative portrayal of these institutions. The AUC presidents were after squeaky clean images of Black colleges. I refuse to be caught in the 'negative image' trap that's set for Black artists. Yes, Black people have been dogged in the media from day one. We're extrasensitive and we have every right to be. But we overreact when we think that every image of us has to be 100 percent angelic—Christ-like even."[2]

Lee had to finish his filming exclusively on the campus of Atlanta University.

"School Daze" probes many sensitive issues for blacks and highlights the friction and prejudice present within his own race; the film deals with issues of skin tone, hair type, and general elitism.

BUSH AND THE SOVIETS
The Politics of Diplomacy

Newsweek

October 2, 1989 : $2.00

The Innovators

25 Americans on the Cutting Edge

■ Science
■ Technology
■ Medicine
■ Business
■ Education
■ Fun & Games
■ Design
■ The Arts

Filmmaker
Spike Lee

Guerilla filmmaker and his choice of weapons.

But with typical nonconformity, Lee turned these subjects into a musical comedy. "This script takes place at a fictitious, predominantly Black college in the south. The student body is divided into two factions: the Haves and the Have-Nots. This division is based upon class and color. The Haves, the affluent students at Mission, are all with light skin, 'good hair,' blue or green eyes, and so forth. While across the tracks are the Have-Nots. They are dark, have kinky nappy hair, and many of them are the first members of their families to ever get a college education; in other words, the black underclass. Each faction has a name for the other. It's the WANNABEES VS. THE JIGS!!! Wanna Be White and Jigaboos. Remember, it's about class and color."[2]

Cinematographer Ernest Dickerson recalled the conception of "School Daze." "In the summer of '86 we began talking about how to approach 'School Daze.' We both agreed about the energy we had to bring to the screen. We wanted to keep the camera moving. The camera was going to whiz all over the place. We felt that this was a way of really capturing the energy. I don't think we did it as much as we wanted to because of time constraints, but that was the initial goal—lots of camera angles and movement.

"We also knew that 'School Daze' would have a huge Black cast, more Black people than have been seen on screen in a long time. We were determined to make a film which would allow Black folks to see themselves up on the screen and really feel proud; proud about who they are and how they look. And since the film is about beauty—how there are different types of beauty, not just the Western standard—we knew that we had to make all the Black folks in the film look good.

"The debate over Black beauty that you see in the film is a political statement unto itself. The Wannabees have straightened hair and they wear blue contact lenses. They are pursuing a Eurocentric form of beauty to the point that they deny all that is Afrocentric. Even though both forms of beauty are valid, the film says don't turn your back on what's really you. You notice that the Gamma Rays (the ultimate Wannabees) look slightly ridiculous with their blue contact lenses and exaggerated hair styles. They're beautiful women, but there's something about them that's just not right. Even more than their eye color, it has to do with their values and aspirations."[2]

Ever the provocateur, Lee emphasized the class friction in his script by segregating his cast. This had a profound effect on the entire crew. Casting director Robi Reed recalled: "The color and class issue that the film explores was a very real thing for the actors, and it started early on with separate hotel arrangements–the Jigs at the modest Ramada Inn and the Gamma Rays and all the male actors at the plush Regency Suites. At the auditions I spoke with various actors about the issue, and they said, 'It's only a movie, we can step away.' But many weren't able to. There were some Jigs who gave Tisha a hard time, just disliked her, refused to see beyond her character. The dark skin/light skin thing had a noticeable effect on them and the Gamma Rays. With the Gamma Rays it was about acting like 'superior beings.'

"Tyra Ferrell (Gamma Ray 'Tasha') is very Black, very culturally aware, very much into being who she is. She was adamantly against Black people changing the color of their eyes with contact lenses. But then we cast her in this role, the darkest Gamma Ray. She made such a personal adjustment. She went and bought a pair of blue contacts even before she got to Atlanta and wore them around town in L.A., just to get used to it. She became this very difficult person. I know Tyra personally and I know she's not who she played in the film. But in Atlanta I couldn't stand her when she was 'Tasha,' which was most of the time. The Jigs felt left out and mistreated the entire shoot. They had qualms about how there was never as much time spent on their hair and makeup as there was with the Gamma Rays. They never understood that was just the nature of the roles. But it really bothered them, so we had to go to the makeup and hair department and ask them to spend a little more time with the Jigs, even if they weren't actually applying any more makeup.

"It's a very sensitive subject, class and color. And I think the majority of the people on the shoot thought they were beyond it. They were forced to examine it, though, and many realized they weren't as far removed from the issue as they thought."[2]

Lee extended this discourtesy even to his sister, whom he had first used in "She Gotta Have It," and then cast as Jigaboo "Lizzie Life" in "School Daze." She recalled: "The first week of rehearsal was horrible actually. I felt really out of place and I wanted to go home. Spike was trying to create this friction and I was resistant to it at first because it didn't seem natural. The first day of rehearsals when we broke for lunch he had everyone separate into their groups. I had wanted to ease into it naturally, stay on the outside and look in, but Spike wouldn't let me. He was kind of growling over my shoulder, pushing me to make myself known."[2]

This tactic achieved it's desired effect. The Jigaboo women developed a sense of community among themselves which eventually made the others envious.

Unlike "She's Gotta Have It," "School Daze," had a six million dollar budget, a large cast, and was much more difficult to shoot. Lee may have had more money, but he had tackled a much more complex project. "There ought to be a study done on how many questions a film director is asked during a shoot. With a film of this size and scale, a director gets faced with thousands of questions a day. It's said that if the brain were receptive to all the stimuli that is out there, a person would have a nervous breakdown. When I'm directing I try to operate with this in mind. I tell people only what they need to know to do the jobs they were hired to do. Otherwise I'd be spending the entire shoot answering questions."[2]

Lee provided much of the comedy in the film through his antics as Half-Pint, a fraternity pledge who is determined to lose his virginity. His final actions inadvertently unite the campus. "In the final scene of the film, we call it 'Wake Up,' I wanted to show that the people at Mission College had come to some kind of realization, some kind of meaning, some kind of truth. (I had the Gamma Rays take out their weaves and their blue contact lenses for this scene.) and when 'Dap' calls everyone out of bed, they come because they've realized something, not just because they're being summoned. That's the way I wrote it. And I hope it comes off that way. It is a metaphor for the sleeping that we as a race have done.

"There's this line in 'Joe's Bed-Stuy Barbershop' when two of the thugs come to the shop to get 'Zachariah Homer' and bring him to see the numbers kingpin, 'Nicholas Lovejoy,' played by Tommy Hicks. 'Zachariah' is asleep in the barber's chair and the two thugs say, 'Wake up, the Black man has been asleep for four hundred years.' That's what the Wake Up scene in 'School Daze' says; it's about who we are, where we've been. And to me that's what this film is about. Our need to come together. Black people are sometimes like crabs in a barrel. In my case, if a Black person tries to do something, I will support it. On the other hand, though, if people are doing things I don't agree with, I will speak out against them. That doesn't mean that I don't support Black people or I'm being that crab in the barrel."[2]

This willingness to dissent has often caused Lee trouble. Although "School Daze" impressed many with it's scope and daring, Lee was criticized personally for exposing differences which many blacks would have preferred to ignore. ". . .I. . .did an interview with Bryant Gumbel on the 'Today' show. Bryant Gumbel jumped all over me, but I kept my composure. He disapproved of 'School Daze' because I aired Black folks' dirty laundry."[3]

Lee regarded all of this bickering unfortunate. "Last fall I went to the world premier of 'Tougher Than Leather,' the Run-D.M.C. film. It was a disappointment. I went wanting to like the film, but, I must admit, expecting the worst. I say expecting the worst because Russell Simmons, president of Def Jam Recordings and Run-D.M.C.'s manager, had given me the script a while back and asked me to direct it. I read it and politely declined. The script was a reworking of the Blaxploitation genre, and tell you the truth, I never went to those films, never liked them. Run, D, and Jam Master Jay spend the entire film running around and shooting people. I certainly didn't want to be responsible for any more Black youth killing each other.

Paperbound cover for the 1989 book.

"The real failure of the project, in my eyes, is that the Black producers chose record producer Rick Rubin, a white man with no film experience, to cowrite and direct. There are too many talented young Black filmmakers out here who need a break to justify handing the project over to a person, of any race, who doesn't have the necessary experience.

"Not just anyone can make a good film. Film is not to be played with. It may be our most powerful medium and should be treated as such. Now, wait a minute, hold up, wait a minute. I'm not suggesting that I'm the only person in the world qualified to make a film. If it were up to me, there would be a hundred Robert Townsends and Spike Lees cranking out films. In fact, the continuity of Black cinema is only assured if it is bigger than the two or three individuals who are getting play now, which brings me to my next point.

"As a few of us have made our way in the cutthroat film industry, something disturbing has happened. I see factions emerging, the Eddie Murphy camp, the Robert Townsend camp, the Keenen Wayans camp, and the Spike Lee camp. I've had actors and production people come to me and say they were turned down for a job because they were considered to be down with me, with the Spike Lee camp.

"There is no need to point fingers or name names, but this kind of backward thinking is gonna hurt us all in the long run. Now more than ever we have to join forces. That's not to say we have to make the same films and agree on everything. Not at all. Each of us has a distinct voice, our own stories to tell."[3]

After the release of "School Daze," Lee progressed from internal prejudice to external when he began work on "Do the Right Thing."

In the journal to this film, he noted: "In this script I want to show the Black working class. Contrary to popular belief, we work. No welfare rolls here, pal, just hardworking people trying to make a decent living. Earlier I wanted to get into the whole gentrification issue, but I'm less enthusiastic about it now."[3]

Occurring on the hottest day of the year, "Do the Right Thing" takes place in Bedford-Stuyvesant. "This block is in a Black neighborhood in Brooklyn. On one corner is a pizza parlor run by an Italian family who have refused to leave the neighborhood. One of the young Black characters [Mookie, played by Lee] will have a job at the pizzeria.

"Although the Black and Puerto Rican block residents seem to get along with the Italian family, there is still an undercurrent of hostility. Of course this tension explodes in the finale."[3]

"If I go ahead in this vein, it might be in conflict with the way I want to tell the story. It can't be just a diatribe, WHITE MAN THIS, WHITE MAN THAT. The treatment of racism will have to be carried in the subtext until the end of the film. Then again, being too avant-garde, too indirect, might trivialize the subject matter. Any approach I take must be done carefully and realistically. I won't be making any apologies. Truth and righteousness is on our side. Black folks are tired of being killed.

"I must be careful to avoid stereotypes in 'Do the Right Thing.' You know, the Italian guy...yelling, Yo, Carmine. Only real characters, no types. Even Radio Raheem should not be a type, even though he carries a box and everybody has seen guys like him.

"Radio Raheem is the misunderstood Black youth. White people cross the street when they see him coming. The Bernie Goetzes of the world want to kill him. It's important that Radio Raheem be a sympathetic character, but he's not an angel, either. He's lost, like a lot of Black youth. Their value systems are all screwed up. They're after more gold teeth, gold chains, and gold brass knuckle rings. They don't understand how worthless that shit is in the long run. They are still BLACK, POOR, and UNEDUCATED. Gold won't change that."[3]

Danny Aiello (Sal), agreed with Lee on the subject of stereotypes. "When I sat down to read the script for the first time, I opened to page one and saw the word *pizzeria*. I nearly put the damn thing down. For me, *pizzeria* immediately brings to mind the worst stereotypes of Italians. It's like sticking a watermelon in a Black man's hand....But I sat back and read on. I ended up loving the script. I saw the possibilities of it being an important film."[3]

Although he had originally offered Robert De Niro the role of Sal, Lee had great respect for Aiello. "Danny Aiello is an opinionated guy, but he's a great actor, and he respects a director. Actors who have worked with me know I'm always open to suggestions. And if I don't think something will work, I give them my no immediately. I said plenty of no's to Danny. And what's wonderful about

Lee with actor Danny Aiello in a scene from "Do the Right Thing."

Danny is his feelings were never hurt. He didn't clam up. He'd say, 'Spike, you're right, that's a bad idea.' I did end up incorporating many of Danny's suggestions and we have a better film because of his insight."[3]

Lee felt that the time was right for a film like "Do the Right Thing." "While I was in the grocery. . .I heard a radio newscast that two Black youths had been beaten up by a gang of white youths in Bensonhurst. The two Black kids were hospitalized. They were collecting bottles and cans when they got jumped. This happened on Christmas night. Just the other day some Black kids fired up a white cab driver in Harlem. New York City is tense with racial hatred. Can you imagine if these incidents had taken place in the summer, on the hottest day of the year? I'd be a fool not to work the subject of racism into 'Do the Right Thing.'"[3]

Trouble, in this comedy, begins when Bugin' Out, a black patron, asks Sal to add some black people to the pizzeria's "Wall of Fame," which consists of only Italian-Americans. Sal refuses, setting a chain of minor events in motion. Bugin' Out first attempts an unsuccessful boycott of the popular pizzeria. He then enlists the aid of Radio Raheem

in a second, more heated, confrontation with Sal and his sons. "It's been my observation that when the temperature rises beyond a certain point, people lose it. Little incidents can spark major conflicts. Bump into someone on the street and you're liable to get shot. A petty argument between husband and wife can launch a divorce proceeding. The heat makes everything explosive, including the racial climate of the city. Racial tensions in the city are high as it is, but when the weather is hot, forget about it. This might be the core of a vicious climax for the film."[3]

The climax occurs when the police wind up choking Radio Raheem to death in front of the whole neighbhorhood. Sal's delivery boy, Mookie, then incites a riot by throwing a garbage can through the pizzeria window. "My most pressured moment as an actor on this film was definitely when I had to throw the garbage can through the pizzeria window. No one thought about this beforehand, but the window glass was almost one-quarter inch thick. Breaking glass that thick is no easy feat. I was throwing hard, but it took four or five takes before I could get the garbage can through the window. On one take it even bounced off like a rubber ball. I was on the spot: We were filming with a special crane that had to be sent back to the rental house the next day, and the sun was coming up. Finally we got the shot.

"This is a hot one. The studios might not want to touch this film. I know I'll come up against some static from the white press. They'll say I'm trying to incite a race riot."[3]

"I flew out to Los Angeles to show the big cheeses at Universal a rough cut of the film. When the lights came up at the end of the screening, the studio brass just sat there in silence, almost stupefied. The silence went on for what seemed like an eternity. Finally I asked Tom Pollock, president of Universal, 'So are we gonna get a release?' Everyone started to laugh, the ice had been broken.

"Universal's main concern, just like Paramount's, was the ending. Was it too open-ended? How would audiences feel leaving the theater? Will Blacks want to go on a rampage? Will whites feel uncomfortable?"[3] Suggestions for alternative endings were tossed around.

"Flying back to Nueva York, I thought about these endings, but none felt right. Smiley's postcard, that photograph of Malxolm X and Martin Luther King shaking hands, kept coming back to me. I had to find a way to tie those two great men into the finale.

"King and Malcolm. Both men died for the love of their people, but had different strategies for realizing freedom. Why not end the film with an appropriate quote from each? In the end, justice will prevail one way or another. There are two paths to that. The way of King, or the way of Malcolm.

"Am I advocating violence? No, but goddamn, the days of twenty-five million Blacks being silent while our fellow brothers and sisters are exploited, oppressed, and murdered, have to come to an end. Racial persecution, not only in the United States, but all over the world, is not gonna go away; it seems it's getting worse (four years of Bush won't help). And if Crazy Eddie Koch gets reelected for a fourth term as mayor of New York, what you see in 'Do the Right Thing' will be light stuff. Yep, we have a choice, Malcolm or King. I know who I'm down with."[3]

In one of the films most memorable sequences, Lee stopped the story to have his characters spout racial-slurs into the camera. "[It] was meant to rouse emotions. It's funny the way people react to it. They laugh at every slur except the one directed at their ethnic group. While we were watching the dailies of Pino's slur of Blacks, a woman in the Kraft Services [catering] department started hissing at John [Turturro]. She couldn't separate John from his character and was less than courteous to him for the rest of the shoot.

"Most wrap days are joyous occasions, unless your film is a real bomb. I felt I had a lot to be thankful for when we wrapped 'Do the Right Thing.' We had a relaxed, practically hassle-free shoot. We had shot an entire film for eight and a half weeks at one location. (What could be easier?) The block residents and the community of Bed-Stuy had given us full cooperation. And the dailies looked good."[3]

The honesty with which Lee treated his subject earned "Do the Right Thing" substantial praise from most critics, and many laughs of self-recognition from audiences, although a few reviewers have criticized Lee's choice to downplay the filth of his ghetto block and his decision to exclude the use of drugs from the story. "I made that choice because any time you hear people say Bed-Stuy, right away they think of the rapes, murders, drugs. There's no need to show garbage piled up high and all that other stuff, because not every single block in Bed-Stuy is like that.

"It would be a fallacy to say that lower-income people always live in burned-out buildings. These are hard-working people, and they take pride in their stuff just like everybody else. So there's no need for the set to look like Charlotte Street in the South Bronx.

"Another thing people ask: 'Where are the drugs?' Drugs is such a massive subject, it just can't be dealt with effectively as a subplot. You have to do an entire film on drugs. This film was not about that. This film was about *racism*."[4]

As for the criticism of his choice to end the film with the quote from Malcolm X saying that violence in self-defense is intelligence, Lee insisted that he is not advocating violence. "...All they have to do is read the last quote of the movie. I'm not advocating violence. Self-defense is not violence. We call it intelligence....Israel could go out and bomb anybody, nobody says nothing. But when Black people go out and protect themselves, then we're militants, or we're advocating violence.

"...These people were intelligent....This is not just a case of *random* violence. People knew *exactly* what they were doing.

"Intelligent people will use violence to their advantage and ignorant people just use violence for violence's sake."[4]

With three successful films in four attempts, Lee has exhibited shrewdness not only as a director, but also as a social commentator, marketer, and businessman. While agreeing to do sneaker ads for Nike, Lee has refused to market such things as Mars Blackmon T-shirts. "I don't want...posters put up, no T-shirts saying, 'Please Baby, Please, Baby Please.' No-T-shirts saying, 'Just Let Me Smell It.'...I want longevity. I don't want to be like Jimmie Walker; all the 'Dy-no-mite' T-shirts. And now he's guest-appearing on 'The Love Boat.'"[1]

Footnote Sources:

[1] Spike Lee, *Spike Lee's "Gotta Have It": Inside Guerilla Filmmaking,* Simon & Schuster, 1987.
[2] S. Lee and Lisa Jones, *Uplift the Face: The Construction of "School Daze,"* Simon & Schuster, 1988.
[3] S. Lee and L. Jones, *"Do the Right Thing": The New Spike Lee Joint,* Fireside Press, 1989.
[4] Marlaine Glicksman, "Bed-Stuy BBQ," *Film Comment,* July/August, 1989.

■ For More Information See

Ebony, September, 1977 (p. 36), January, 1987 (p. 42ff), September, 1987 (p. 36ff).
Rolling Stone, December, 1980 (p. 31ff).
New York Times, March 27, 1983, August 8, 1986, August 10, 1986, September 7, 1986, November 14, 1986, August 9, 1987, February 12, 1988, February 20, 1989 (section IV, p. 7).
New York Times Biographical Service, August, 1986 (p. 1013ff), August, 1987 (p. 782ff).
Chicago Tribune, August 13, 1986, August 20, 1986, October 5, 1986, February 25, 1988, March 3, 1988.
Los Angeles Times, August 21, 1986, February 11, 1988, February 12, 1988.
Washington Post, August 22, 1986, August 24, 1986, August 29, 1986, March 20, 1987, February 19, 1988.
American Film, September, 1986 (p. 48ff), January-February, 1988 (p. 57ff), July/August, 1989 (p. 22ff).
Essence, September, 1986 (p. 29), February, 1988 (p. 50ff), July, 1988.
Newsweek, September 8, 1986, February 15, 1988 (p. 62).
Film Comment, October, 1986 (p. 46ff).
Time, October 6, 1986.
People, October 13, 1986 (p. 67ff), July 10, 1989 (p. 67ff).
Jet, November 10, 1986 (p. 54ff), February 2, 1988 (p. 28ff), May 2, 1988 (p. 9).
Black Enterprise, December, 1986 (p. 56ff), May, 1988 (p. 39).
Film Quarterly, winter, 1986-87.
New York Times Magazine, August 9, 1987 (p. 26ff).
Publishers Weekly, September 18, 1987, January 29, 1988.
New York Times Book Review, December 13, 1987, April 17, 1988.
Booklist, December 15, 1987, February 15, 1988.
Library Journal, January, 1988, March 15, 1988.
Village Voice, February 16, 1988, March 22, 1988.
Life, spring, 1988 (p. 100).
Choice, July, 1988.
Current Biography, March, 1989 (p. 40ff).
Scholastic Update, April 7, 1989 (p. 27).
Variety, July 25, 1989 (p. 11).

Mark Mathabane

First name originally Johannes; name changed, 1976; surname pronounced "Motta-bonny"; born in 1960, in Alexandra, South Africa; son of Jackson (a laborer) and Magdelene (a washerwoman; maiden name, Mabaso) Mathabane; married Gail Ernsberger (a writer), 1987; children: Bianca Ellen. *Education:* Attended Limestone College, 1978, St. Louis University, 1979, Quincy College, 1981, and Columbia University, 1984; Dowling College, B.A., 1983. *Politics:* Humanist. *Religion:* Deist. *Home:* 341 Barrington Park Lane, Kernersville, N.C. 27284. *Agent:* Fifi Oscard Agency, 19 West 44th St., New York, N.Y. 10036. *Lecture Agent:* Gary Muck, Greater Talent Network, 150 Fifth Ave., Suite 1002, New York, N.Y. 10011.

■ Career

Free-lance lecturer and writer, 1985—. *Member:* Authors Guild.

■ Awards, Honors

Christopher Award, 1986, for *Kaffir Boy.*

■ Writings

Kaffir Boy: The True Story of a Black Youth's Coming of Age in Apartheid South Africa, Macmillan, 1986, published as *Kaffir Boy: Growing Out of Apartheid,* Bodley Head, 1987.

Kaffir Boy in America: An Encounter with Apartheid, Scribner, 1989.

■ Adaptations

"Kaffir Boy" (cassette), Dove Books on Tape, 1988.

■ Work In Progress

Oprah Winfrey's Harpo Productions Inc. bought the movie rights to *Kaffir Boy,* tentatively scheduled for fall 1990 release; "Love in Black and White," tentative title, about interracial relationships written with wife, Gail Ernsberger; autobiography of his mother, *The Story of an African Woman*; a second personnal look at the education crisis in America, *Knowledge: A Powerful Weapon of Hope.*

"I am a contributor to the Op-Ed page of the *Los Angeles Times.* I also write book reviews and do a good deal of lecturing, mostly at colleges and universities." About his collaborative effort with wife, Gail, Mathabane wrote: "We are approaching the subject from a human, rather than historical, political, or sociological perspective. So many people are made to sacrifice family relations, job security, and friendships because they have united their lives with someone of another race. Perhaps naively, I supposed that in the United States such unions would not be frowned upon. Luckily, Gail and I have not had to deal with overt hostility, though it is apparent when people are uncomfortable that we are together. My mother, who has suffered brutal white oppression all her life, had absolutely no problem with our relationship and in fact called Gail *skwiza* (Tsonga for 'my son's wife,' said with warmth and fondness) the first time they met, which was before our wedding. What astonished and angered me were the reactions I got from some blacks. I have been interrogated by callers during a number of interviews on black radio stations, who charged that I had no black pride, no solidarity with my race, that I was 'selling out.' I cannot accept this. The arguments I heard sounded similar to the explanations I'd heard all my life for apartheid: racial purity and power. Coming from whites or blacks, it's bigotry. Their logic would seem to dictate a return to hideously anachronistic, tribally-arranged marriages. I firmly believe that one should be free to share love with whomever one wishes. And though some blacks have warned me that I'm 'playing with fire,' I will not hide or disguise my feelings.

"This controversy has stirred up earlier personal pains as well. One of the saddest things I have experienced in this country is the way my own people, which is to say black people, have judged me. Particularly in my early years here, American blacks tended to look down on me, on Africa. They expected me to be ashamed of where I came from and who my parents were. One of the ongoing problems I had in relationships with black women was that they could not reconcile themselves to the fact that my parents are illiterate, that I'd grown up in a shack with no plumbing, that in order to survive we had to eat all manner of vile things like worms and locusts. Yet here I was, a Dean's list scholarship student. I tried to make them see that my appreciation of them went beyond how beautiful they were or how expensively they dressed; but in their judgement of me what seemed to loom largest was my lack of a fancy car and stylish clothes. One of the few people who entered my life, giving me the benefit of the doubt, happened to be Gail, who happened to be white. Here was someone who offered friendship, which developed into intimacy, and respect, which blossomed into the trust that is the basis of our marriage. Before anyone could have guessed my books would be published to acclaim, before anyone could have known that I would be sought after by major

publications and media, Gail looked inside me and was genuine in her treatment of me. Could I really have been expected to turn her away, because she is white?"

■ Sidelights

Kaffir Boy, Mathabane's first book, detailed the brutal hardship of growing up black in South Africa. A driven student and gifted tennis player, Mathabane came to the attention of American tennis pro Stan Smith who helped him secure college scholarships in the U.S. and became his sponsor/surrogate family here. If *Kaffir Boy* won Mathabane instant celebrity, *Kaffir Boy in America* has put Mathabane at the center of heated controversies concerning racism, religion and the English language. Though both books have been translated and published in a number of countries, they are banned in South Africa.

At the entrance to Alexandra, the Bantu township in which Mathabane was raised, there is a sign warning that anyone who enters there without a permit will be prosecuted to the full extent of the law. The sign is directed at whites who under apartheid are not intended to enter, even briefly, the black world.

"Yet the white man of South Africa claims to the rest of the world that he knows what is good for black people and what it takes for a black child to grow up to adulthood. . . .But, in truth, these claims and boasts are hollow.

"The white man of South Africa. . .does not know the conditions under which I was born and had to live for eighteen years. So my story is intended to show him with words a world he would otherwise not see because of a sign and a conscience racked with guilt and to make him feel what I felt when he contemptuously called me a 'Kaffir boy.' [A word of Arabic origin meaning 'infide,' in South Africa it has come to be the equivalent of 'nigger.'].

"When I was growing up in Alexandra it meant hate, bitterness, hunger, pain, terror, violence, fear, dashed hope and dreams. Today it still means the same for millions of black children who are trapped in the ghettos of South Africa, in a lingering nightmare of a racial system that in many respects resembles Nazism. In the ghettos black children fight for survival from the moment they are born. They take to hating and fearing the police, soldiers and authorities as a baby takes to its mother's breast.

"In my childhood these enforcers of white prerogatives and whims represented a sinister force capable of crushing me at will; of making my parents flee in the dead of night to escape arrest under the Pass laws; of marching them naked out of bed because they did not have the permit allowing them to live as husband and wife under the same roof. They turned my father—by repeatedly arresting him and denying him the right to earn a living in a way that gave him dignity—into such a bitter man that, as he fiercely but in vain resisted the emasculation, he hurt those he loved the most.

"The movies, with their lurid descriptions of white violence, reinforced this image of white terror and power. Often the products of abject poverty and broken homes, many black children, for whom education is inferior and not compulsory, have been derailed by movies into the dead-end life of crime and violence. It is no wonder that black ghettos have one of the highest murder rates in the world, and South African prisons are among the most packed. It was purely by accident that I did not end up a *tsotsi* (thug, mugger, gangster)."[1]

From an early age, Mathabane was no stranger to violence. "One late Friday evening when I was nearing the end of my tenth year an event occurred that precipitated the greatest crisis of my childhood: I was an eyewitness to a murder...the dark and dusty streets of Alexandra swarmed with black workers returning home from work, and about to begin celebrating the start of a weekend, a time when many of them would be drowning their pain, sorrow and suffering with all-night orgies and feasting in shebeens [clandestine bars] throughout the township....As I turned the corner...I saw, coming down the street, a group of about six *tsotsis* chasing two men....I fled into a nearby yard...lay flat in the tall grass and watched the scene in the street. The *tsotsis* were rapidly gaining on the two men....Suddenly, one of the men being chased swung into the yard where I was hiding, apparently thinking that he might get help from the inhabitants of several of the shacks in it. He was mistaken, for no sooner had he entered the yard than shutters were closed and doors barricaded.

"What I saw made me gasp with horror. Having drawn gleaming, sharp knives, meat cleavers and tomahawks, the *tsotsis* began carving the man as he howled for mercy....The *tsotsis* paid no heed to his pleas; in fact, they grinned at his cries.

"Through some superhuman effort, it seemed, the man, now bleeding heavily from gaping wounds, managed to break through the cordon of butchers

Cover from the paperbound edition of Mathabane's first novel.

and make a mad dash for the street. The *tsotsis* didn't chase after him immediately, tarrying a while to rummage through the packages he had dropped. The wounded man staggered left and right, clutching his slashed throat, which spewed blood. I was now bathed in perspiration....As the wounded man staggered past me, I detected tube-like things unwinding like a spool of thread through his slashed overalls. His guts were spilling from his belly! Nausea overcame me....The fatally wounded man turned his bleeding head in the direction of the fortified shacks, as if pleading for them to open and let him in. There was a dreadful glint in his eyes, the glint of death creeping in.

"The *tsotsis* caught up with him before he even reached the street. Their gleaming weapons of death remorselessly went about their unfinished, infernal mission.

"The wounded man uttered hideous guttural sounds through his slashed throat. Gradually the sounds grew fewer and fainter. Suddenly his body lurched forward with outstretched arms, and his limbs twitched violently; he pitched forward, uttering one last, ghastly, gurgling sound, as if some beast were lodged within him and were struggling furiously to be set free. He slumped to the bone-dry ground, like a bundle of old newspapers. Before the corpse even hit the ground, the *tsotsis* were already upon it, stripping and searching it, like a bunch of ravenous hyenas wrenching pieces of flesh from a carcass. The *tsotsis* turned the dead body supine, and removed its shoes, its not-worth-anything coat and frisked the back pockets. In a matter of minutes the six shadowy figures had accomplished their dastardly act and were heading for the shadows of the eerie moonlit night, the spoils of their foray ensconced between their murdering paws, their bloodshot eyes gleaming and their teeth grinning like those of cannibals after a kill."[1]

For months after this murder—which had been only one of several in his neighborhood that evening, Mathabane was suicidal. Only his mother was able to give him the strength and love he needed to stay alive.

Not long afterward came another turning point in Mathebane's life. His grandmother, who planted and maintained white people's gardens, began working for the Smith family, who gave her cast-off books to bring home—at first comics, then classics. Eventually Mrs. Smith allowed Mathabane to sometimes accompany his grandmother to work.

One day he spent some time with Clyde Smith, who was about his own age. "My teachers tell us that Kaffirs can't read, speak or write English like white people because they have smaller brains, which are already full of tribal things," Clyde told Mathebane. "My teachers say you're not people like us, because you belong to a jungle civilization. That's why you can't live or go to school with us, but can only be our servants."[1]

The conversation—unkind though it was—actually had a positive effect on Mathebane. "I vowed that, whatever the cost, I would master English, that I would not rest till I could read, write and speak it just like any white man, if not better. Finally, I had something to aspire to.

"My bleak vocabulary did not diminish my enthusiasm for reading. I constantly borrowed [my teacher] Mr. Brown's pocket-sized dictionary to look up the meanings of words, and would memorize them like arithmetic tables and write them in a small notebook. Sometimes I would read the dictionary. My pronunciation was appalling, but I had no way of finding out. I was amazed at the number of words in the English language, at the fact that a word could have different shades of meaning, or that certain words looked and sounded alike and yet differed greatly in meaning.

"My love for reading removed me from the streets and curtailed my involvement with gangs. This infuriated the leaders of my gang, the Thirteenth Avenue Tomahawks. Friends within warned me that there was a plot afoot to teach me a lesson for not showing up at the gang's fights [in which boys routinely were severely maimed, blinded and killed]....Now as an outcast and a marked man, I seldom traveled alone at night."[1]

Adding to Mathebane's problems was his father's depression, which manifested itself in recurrent bouts of drinking and gambling and in fanatical adherence to tribal ways and values. "He couldn't *donder* (whip) me as he used to when I was a child, for I was growing stronger and more stubborn every day. We both knew that we were on a collision course. I was set in my ways, he in his. He disparaged education, I extolled it; he burned my books at every opportunity, I bought more; he abused my mother, I tried to help her; he believed all that the white man said about him, I did not; he lived for the moment, I, for the future, uncertain as it was.

"Years of watching him suffer under the double yoke of apartheid and tribalism convinced me that his was a hopeless case, so long as he persisted in clinging to tribal beliefs and letting the white man define his manhood.

"By pining for the irretrievably gone days of drums, of warriors, of loinskins, of huts and of wife-buying, I knew that he could never travel, in thought and in feeling, the course my life was embarking upon, because everything he whole-heartedly embraced, I rejected with every fibre of my being."[1]

Mathabane's feelings notwithstanding, on his thirteenth birthday his father threatened to take him to a mountain school for the tribal circumcision rites consisting of a week of arduous physical, mental and spiritual tests.

If Mathebane found it impossible to accept his father's tribalism, he found his mother's adoption of Christianity equally offensive. "I frowned upon organized religion for the simple reason that about

Mark Mathabane (flanked on his right by Granny and Mama) on "The Oprah Winfrey Show."

me I saw it being misused: by the government in claiming that God had given whites the divine right to rule over blacks, that our subservience was the most natural and heavenly condition to be in; by some black churches to strip ignorant black peasants of their last possessions in the name of payment for the salvation of their souls; and by the same churches to turn able-bodied men and women into flocks of sheep, making them relinquish responsibility for their lives in the hope that faith in Christ would miraculously make everything turn out right.

"Worst of all, I found among members of some churches a readiness to accept their lot as God's will, a willingness to disparage their own blackness and heritage as inferior to the white man's Christianity, a readiness to give up fighting to make things just in this world, in the hope that God's justice would prevail in the hereafter, that the hungry and the oppressed and the enslaved of His world would feast on cornucopias while singing freedom songs and hosannas in a heaven without

prejudice. In short, organized religion made blacks blind to, or avoid, or seek to escape from, reality."[1]

Another seminal moment in Mathebane's life came in November 1973 when Arthur Ashe, the black American tennis champion, came to South Africa to play in an international tournament. Ironically, the South African government proclaimed Ashe "an honorary white," even though he conducted tennis workshops in the black township of Soweto. While in South Africa, Ashe met with top government officials, pressed for integration and founded the Black Tennis Foundation, which is administered by a multi-racial board.

Mathabane, who had been playing tennis seriously for several years by this time, was galvanized by Ashe. "Though I was some distance away, I could still hear snippets of his speech. His English sounded strange, heavily accented. He was so eloquent that white women giggled in admiration....I marveled at how proudly he walked. I had never seen a black man walk that proudly among whites. He appeared calm, cool and collected, even though he was surrounded by a sea of white faces.

"One thing I found remarkable about Arthur Ashe was that he was not afraid to dismiss questions from white people if he considered them worth ignoring, and say what he considered important. I had never seen a black person do that, unless he or she was mad or something.

"Gradually I became aware that I could never be like [Ashe] for as long as I remained in South Africa. For reasons still unclear, America, the land that had given birth to Ashe and nurtured him, loomed bright as the place to go to realise my fullest potential in tennis, in life. There, it seemed, blacks who had the talent, the will, the resiliency, the ambition, the drive to dream, were turning their dreams into reality."[1]

Mathabane felt increasingly out of place in his school and township. He redoubled his efforts to perfect English, listening to Springbok Radio news broadcasts and literary programming. He was introduced to European classical music through Dvorak's *New World* Symphony. Up until then he had thought the only music was African vibes and American pop. Not only his father, but a number of his classmates, accused him of trying to "become white."

But when the Soweto uprising exploded in June 1976, Mathabane stuck solidly by his fellow black students, exposing himself to the guns and tear gas of the South African military police. In the course of the protest over 600 black students were killed. Mathabane, who had been absent from his job at a white tennis club during the uprising, was presumed dead by many of the members. When he showed up after the protests were over, he was pressed for information about the event, the scope and intensity of which the South African media had deliberately downplayed. Mathabane's extemporaneous talks in the tennis club cafe could almost be said to have been the start of his public speaking career. Before a rivetted audience he explained not only the Soweto uprising and the platform of the ANC (African National Congress), but described details of black ghetto life unknown to most South African whites. Afterward Mathabane was befriended by several whites who not only played tennis with him in public, but went so far as to drive him home to Alexandra, both gestures were crimes.

Mathabane swore to himself that one way or another he would get a tennis scholarship to an American university. With the encouragement of

white friends, Mathabane entered the South African Breweries Open, an international tennis tournament in which a black South African had never before competed. Not only was he threatened with expulsion from black South African tennis—after losing his match, in fact, he was banned—but he received numerous death threats as well. As Stan Smith and Bob Lutz (world doubles champions) were finishing warm-ups, Smith noticed Mathabane and invited him to volley.

"I was ecstatic. There was *the* Stan Smith chasing after balls I had hit and missing some of them! I felt such joy I could have died right at that moment and it wouldn't have mattered. Suddenly all the pain I had endured since entering the tournament seemed not in vain....Some of the pointers he gave me I already knew, but the fact that it was *he* saying them turned them into utterings from an oracle. For about half an hour I played the best tennis of my life, played like a man possessed."[1]

To Mathabane's astonishment, Smith and his wife, Marjorie Gengler, invited him to have lunch in the Players Lounge. "They seemed so eager to know me. I poured out my heart to them....Much of what I said [about life in the ghetto] shocked them....All the time we were talking, Stan and Marjory treated me as an equal, a friend, a human being. Never for a moment did they show signs of condescension....I wondered if white South African celebrities—including those who regarded themselves as liberal—would have deigned to treat me as an equal in a room full of whites."[1]

Upon leaving South Africa, Smith offered to sponsor Mathabane in several important tennis tournaments which had become integrated at Arthur Ashe's insistence in 1974. Smith also offered to help Mathabane in his efforts to gain a tennis scholarship to a university in the United States.

Mathabane received scholarship offers from a number of American universities, including Princeton. He settled on Limestone College in South Carolina, a school with black and white students but no black professors. "[The] students' knowledge of the history of the civil rights movement afforded me a valuable window into the black experience in the South. Up until then I knew little about the history of segregation and slavery in the South. I was shocked at the similarities between apartheid and the old era of Jim Crow....That shock turned to anger and disillusionment at discovering that even today almost every town we visited had roughly two sections, one for blacks and the other for whites.

"I had a strange feeling of *deja vu* whenever I saw the white sections of Southern towns with their beautiful and expensive houses, well-maintained tree-lined streets, large department stores, well-kept parks, swimming pools and golf courses. The sight of the whites who lived in these luxury homes and exuded the same confidence and security and health of whites in South Africa made me wonder how they could champion freedom and equality and democracy around the world without extending the same to their fellow black citizens.

"There were still white churches and black churches. In fact I discovered that 11:00 a.m. Sunday was the most segregated hour in America. Whites attended the First Baptist Church and blacks the Bethel Baptist Church. Again there were no laws forbidding integration during worship, yet the two races seemingly kept apart as if separated by invisible walls.

"Everyone I met at the Bethel Church was eager to know more about South Africa and apartheid, and shared my concern over the well-being of my family. Weekly prayers were said in their behalf in church. Despite having grown up amid terrible poverty and degradation during the years of Jim Crow, many of these blacks, following the gains of the civil rights movement, had quietly gone about getting unionized and better-paying jobs. They were a proud people. They spontaneously took care of each other within their small, closely knit community. Had I confined myself to this relatively comfortable world, the world of the black middle class, I most likely would have been happy and content; my adjustment to America would have had fewer bumps and shocks.

"But my curiosity led me to part of Gaffney and other Southern towns where the majority of blacks, the poorest, lived. These areas were almost like forbidden zones. Even middle-class blacks kept away from them. They formed a crowded world of tiny, run-down tenements and projects, shoddily paved roads, overturned scrapped cars, garbage scattered around, and black men full of despair sitting in clusters along the roadside, drinking and boisterously talking their sorrows away....Just as in Alexandra, where poor blacks had been quarantined without hope and without opportunity, crime and alcoholism were rife in these sections of Southern towns....I saw shacks without running water or indoor plumbing. Adults and children

Gail Ernsberger and Mark Mathabane on their wedding day.

worked all day long in the fields, picking tobacco and other crops, almost like slaves in the antebellum South. Hunger, poverty, neglect, and disease were rampant. Malnourished children ran around barefoot and in rags, their eyes full of pain and confusion and lost innocence and hope. This was not Alexandra. This was not Ethiopia. These children and their parents were American citizens. How could this be in America?''[2]

"In Africa, we looked to American blacks as role models and did our best to emulate them. We wore Afros because we thought it was an American invention. (We had always worn our hair short.) 'Black is Beautiful' is something we had never heard in Africa; the saying galvanized us because it came from the States. In Africa it was common for blacks to bleach their skin, for one's position on the social ladder was a direct reflection of one's skin tone. I was under the impression—the fantasy, really—that in the U.S. educational, professional and social opportunities abounded, no matter the color of one's skin.

"I also assumed that I would be an ignoramus as far as the language went. My vision of America was of a whole population reading and studying, going to libraries. . . .I assumed my fellow students would be light years ahead of me. But they were not, and I couldn't find an explanation for it. Perhaps the greatest shock was discovering that this country is profoundly anti-intellectual. I was ridiculed for devoting so much time to schoolwork, for spending hours and hours in the library reading for pleasure, for trying to keep up with a variety of newspapers and magazines. It is astounding that the American media aims so low in terms of content and sophistication. I found myself feeling really frightened for this so-called American democracy, for if people do not know how to think, do not respect a high quality of thought, then they are doomed to react viscerally. And masses of people acting without thinking is a great danger to democracy.''[3]

Severe culture shock and acute anxiety about the welfare of his family took their toll on Mathabane, adversely affecting his tennis game, studies and social relations. "Though I had an athletic scholarship, I certainly was no 'jock.' I was stigmatized for not being a drinker, a carouser, a 'party boy.' I consciously cultivated the feminine parts of myself as a way to get through these difficult times. You know, in Africa women tend to fare better than men, at least psychically. Women's survival mechanisms—which I would say include greater resourcefulness, dignity and an integrative rather than atomized nature—seem much better devel-

oped. Men become embittered much more easily, become disoriented and lose their sense of reality. I had assumed that in the land of 'liberation,' that my efforts to cultivate sensitivity, gentleness, and cooperativeness would be looked on sympathetically. I couldn't have been more wrong. I was labeled 'effeminate,' to mention the least noxious of the sobriquets I suffered. Most women were as suspicious and hostile to me as men. Hard as it was—and this has been one of the toughest battles for me here—I knew that giving full play to both the male and female in me would enable me to appreciate and experience life more fully and deeply. And as I began to write, I found it crucial. To use just the male side of myself would have been to confine my work to a narrow stream of consciousness.''[3]

Mathabane stayed but one semester at Limestone College and ended up transferring several more times before graduating from Dowling College on Long Island. He lost tennis and/or soccer scholarships because he did not "fit in" with his teamates; he felt alienated from the predominate collegiate culture; and he had difficulty finding faculty members with whom he felt compatible. Through it all, Stan Smith continued his financial support and never once stinted on friendship.

Increasingly Mathabane sought refuge in books. "In the library one afternoon, having completed my homework, I began browsing among the bookshelves. I came upon a paperback copy of *Black Boy*, Richard Wright's searing autobiography. My attention was arrested by the title and by the following defiant words on the back cover of the book: 'The white South said that it knew 'niggers,' and I was what the white South called 'nigger.' Well, the white South had never known me— never knew what I thought, what I felt.'

"I mentally replaced 'white South' with 'white South Africa,' and 'nigger' with 'Kaffir,' and was intrigued by how Richard Wright's feelings mirrored my own. I immediately sat down in a chair by the window and began reading the book. I was overwhelmed; I could not put the book down. I even missed my economics class. . .When the library closed I was three-quarters of the way through the book. Bleary-eyed, I went back to my room and read the rest.

"The next day I went back to the library and asked the head librarian—a good-natured Franciscan priest with white hair and a charming smile—if the library had more books by black authors. He guided me to the treasure. I checked out Richard

Wright's *Native Son*, Eldridge Cleaver's *Soul on Ice*, W. E. B. Du Bois's *Souls of Black Folks*, *The Autobiography of Malcolm X*, Franz Fanon's *The Wretched of the Earth*, Claude Brown's *Manchild in the Promised Land*, James Baldwin's *The Fire Next Time*, and *Notes of a Native Son*, Maya Angelou's *I Know Why the Caged Bird Sings*, James Weldon Johnson's *The Autobiography of an Ex-Colored Man*, and the autobiography and incendiary speeches of Frederick Douglass.

"After this momentous discovery I knew that my life would never be the same. Here were black men and women, rebels in their own right, who had felt, thought and suffered deeply, who had grown up under conditions that had threatened to destroy their very souls; here they were...using words as weapons, plunging into realms of experience I had never before thought reachable, and wrestling with fate itself in an heroic attempt to make the incomprehensible—man's inhumanity to man—comprehensible. Most astonishing was that these men and women had written about what I felt and thought, what I had been through as a black man, what I desired, what I dreamed about, and what I refused to compromise."[2]

Inspired, Mathabane wrote his first essay which garnered praise from his English teacher. At last his efforts to master English, to study and to learn found a focus—he resolved to be a writer, to add his voice to those that had gone before, in service of black freedom, black pride, black equality.

At Dowling College, Mathabane took over editorship of the campus newspaper. At first his editorials against racial, ethnic and sexual discrimination got him hate mail, on the order of "We lynch sassy niggers like you," and "Go back to where you belong, you black ape." But in time Mathabane assembled a likeminded group of editors and reporters and the paper did very well. Mathabane himself had come to the attention of local professional newspapers and upon graduation he had several job offers. But Mathabane had begun writing *Kaffir Boy* and he was determined to finish it before embarking on a career. With Stan Smith's financial support and the friendship and help of several people on Long Island, Mathabane continued living near campus following his graduation, working feverishly in the computer office after hours.

"The easy thing would have been to write a polemic. But I wanted to channel my rage into a human story with which I could make an appeal to people's hearts and minds. Without the rancor and bitterness, I never would have gotten out of South Africa, but I knew now that I had to transcend those feelings if ever I was to write literature."[3]

After a speaking engagement at a local Unitarian church, an audience member approached him, offering to introduce him to a literary agent. Not long afterward his book was sold in an auction between two prestigious publishers.

Meanwhile, he began writing for the *St. Petersburg Times* and *Newsday*. A piece he wrote in *Newsday* on apartheid earned him telephone death threats from white Americans and South Africans. But Mathabane persisted. In 1985, he entered Columbia Journalism School on a full scholarship. In addition to his classwork, he did volunteer work with children in Harlem. He continued to write freelance articles and soon became impatient with being in school. He dropped out, to the astonishment of many, and threw himself into his professional writing assignments.

Mathabane's editors were extremely enthusiastic about the forthcoming *Kaffir Boy*, predicting rave reviews and hefty sales. A disappointment along the way came when Nadine Gordimer, the towering white South African novelist, declined to give the book a blurb or a review, saying that "the book

An ever-present reminder of apartheid.

hardly revealed anything that she didn't already know about black life in South Africa.''[2]

"I was very discouraged by Gordimer's reaction. I hesitate to say too much because her own record is sterling. (I continue to admire her work and still write reviews of her books.) But surely she must know how difficult it is even to daydream about being a writer if you are a black South African. It is a shame that by far most of what the outside world knows about apartheid comes from writers who are white. The world will not fully understand the complexities of South African society until more black writers are heard from.''[3]

Most of the reviews of *Kaffir Boy* were very favorable, and Mathabane suddenly found himself a celebrity. He appeared on television and radio, was quoted in newspapers and magazines and was invited to give speeches. Oprah Winfrey not only signed him for an appearance on her show, but flew his family to New York from South Africa as well. For Mathabane it was the first time he had seen his mother and siblings since he had left, some eight years earlier. During his family's visit, he and Gail Ernsberger were wed and several of his siblings decided to remain in the U.S. with the newlywed couple in order to complete their education.

"What has been fascinating is to contrast the reactions engendered by *Kaffir Boy* with those engendered by *Kaffir Boy in America*. I get the feeling that people felt expiated for liking the first book. Apartheid and all those terrible things were happening far away, 'over there.' But with the second book where I talk about my own hard adjustment to this country and about the many injustices I found here, the reaction has been much less enthusiastic, not only among whites but among blacks as well. And the reactions I get for my journalistic pieces and interviews are often furious.

"Among the more incendiary subjects I've taken up are the importance of speaking proper English and black racism. I believe that black youngsters must learn to master the English language. The reason is that one of the cruel things that white society has been able to do vis a vis blacks is to victimize those who cannot fully express themselves. It is crucial to be able to express yourself, lest others fill in the gaps according to their prejudices. In order to define yourself, you have to speak for yourself. If you cannot, others will define you. And how can you ever get what you want if you can't clearly articulate it? How can you gain empathy if you can't make others understand what you feel? How can you gain respect if you can't let your thoughts be known? One's livelihood in this country depends on knowing English. If you go to a job interview and can't answer a question clearly you're relegated to a low-paying job—if they're willing to hire you at all. This is not to say that I abhor Black English. I do not. But it seems to me redundant to encourage kids to learn it, for they already know it. It's the language of the ghetto streets. As hard as it was for me when I first arrived here, it would have been a thousand times harder had I been unable to negotiate the language.

"In the current reactionary environment, it is more important than ever for blacks to be able to think, speak and act clearly. The powers-that-be apparently are unwilling to give us the benefit of the doubt, and so we must try harder, achieve more *on our own*. This also is a viewpoint that has gotten me into trouble among my fellow blacks. But it seems to me that American whites perceive blacks as always wanting something for nothing. I'm not saying this is in fact the case, but this seems to be their perception. Like it or not, we must change that perception; certainly they aren't going to alter their outlook without some incentive.''[3]

Black racism is another highly-charged topic on which Mathabane has spoken out. "I have been told that it's 'us against them,' that 'all whites are our enemies.' I cannot accept this. Whites helped me out of the ghetto in South Africa, sponsored my attempts to get an education and become a writer. Assigning collective guilt—even for apartheid—is nothing more than prejudice. I know splendid individuals of numerous races. And what about brutal black policemen and soldiers in South Africa? What about black drug dealers here? Things aren't so simple. And racism—black, white, yellow, green, or blue—is ruinous to the human spirit and undermines the very notion of civilization.''[3]

Mathabane has noticed a number of changes not only in the U.S. since his arrival, but in himself as well. "Certainly the Reagan years are taking a heavy toll. There is palpable hostility in the air, and it's coming from all directions. The stronghold of the televangelists—very powerful in North Carolina where I'm living—continues to astonish me. So too does the backlash against women's reproductive rights. Honestly, I never thought I'd see *that* in my lifetime. What worries me is that it seems people want less and less to have a wide range of choices. They want the big decisions to be legislated for them. It is mindboggling to me that great numbers of people apparently wish to give back their rights, to curtail their own civil liberties, not to mention those of others.

"In order for me to make the leap out of Africa I had to disavow much of my tribal heritage. It seemed a trap, a tentacle that would keep me enslaved to ways I considered backward and detrimental to my development. But I have re-evaluated that rejection, and realize that I must be careful about what I discard and what I take on. There is much to be admired in tribal values, particularly in these times when people seem to have gravitated from the soul, which in the end is what really matters. There is a unity of creation, a simplicity in living that I think may best be appreciated by indigenous people. It is rare in tribal villages to see a desecration of the bonds that tie people to one another and humanity to nature. I look around and see that many ancient symbols and ways have been rejected, but little has emerged to take their place.

"I keep coming back to the legacy of African women—my mother, my grandmother, my aunt, who is a tribal healer. The stories that are handed down generation to generation are amazing. A project that I hope is not too far in the future is a volume of my grandmother's tales. Those stories, the integrated faith and vision to which they testify and the ravishing skill with which they are told have nourished and amused my people, inspired and fortified us. They deserve to be better known."[3]

Mathabane has not returned to South Africa since he left in 1978. "I am in the process of becoming a U.S. citizen, which should make it safe for me to travel there. I want very much to go back to Alexandra, to meet with the kids there. Some of them might even remember me. It is crucial for them to know that I was one of them, grew up just like them. With a helping hand, they too can follow their dreams, pursue their ambitions. If I could talk to them, spend time with them, I could make them believe it and help make it happen."[3]

Footnote Sources:

[1] Mark Mathabane, *Kaffir Boy*, Macmillan, 1986.
[2] M. Mathabane, *Kaffir Boy in America*, Scribner, 1989.
[3] Based on an interview by Marguerite Feitlowitz for *Authors and Artists for Young Adults*.

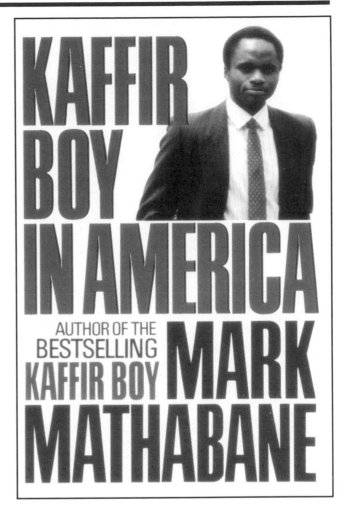

Dust jacket from the 1989 Scribner's edition.

■ For More Information See

Publishers Weekly, February 28, 1986 (p. 111), April 28, 1989 (p. 66).
Los Angeles Times Book Review, March 30, 1986.
Chicago Tribune Book World, April 13, 1986.
Washington Post Book World, April 20, 1986.
New York Times Book Review, April 27, 1986, December 21, 1986 (p. 19), March 29, 1987, August 13, 1989 (p. 19).
World Tennis, May, 1986, June, 1989 (p. 27).
Christian Science Monitor, May 2, 1986.
Mark Mathabane, "Memories of a Native Son; Coming of Age in Apartheid South Africa," *People Weekly*, July 7, 1986.
Black Enterprise, December, 1986 (p. 20).
New York Times, March 2, 1987, September 24, 1987.
San Diego Magazine, June, 1987 (p.72).
Seventeen, August, 1987 (p. 242).
Jet, August 3, 1987 (p. 8).
Times Literary Supplement, August 21, 1987.
Wilson Library Bulletin, December, 1988 (p. 92).

Robin McKinley

Born November 16, 1952, in Warren, Ohio; daughter of William (in U.S. Navy and Merchant Marines) and Jeanne Carolyn (a teacher; maiden name, Turrell) McKinley. *Education:* Attended Dickinson College, 1970-72; Bowdoin College, B.A. (summa cum laude), 1975. *Politics:* "Few affiliations, although I belong to MADD and NOW, and have strong feelings pro-ERA and pro-freedom—and anti-big-business and anti-big-government." *Religion:* "You could call me a lapsed Protestant." *Home and office:* Maine and New York City. *Agent:* Merrilee Heifetz, Writers House, Inc., 21 West 26th St., New York, N.Y. 10010.

■ Career

Ward & Paul (stenographic reporting firm), Washington, D.C., editor and transcriber, 1972-73; Research Associates, Brunswick, Me., research assistant, 1976-77; clerk in bookstore in Maine, 1978; teacher and counselor at private secondary school in Natick, Mass., 1978-79; Little, Brown, Inc., Boston, Mass., editorial assistant, 1979-81; barn manager on horse farm, Holliston, Mass., 1981-82; Books of Wonder, New York, N.Y., clerk, 1983; free-lance reader, copy and line-editor, general all-purpose publishing dogsbody, 1983—.

■ Awards, Honors

Beauty was selected one of New York Public Library's Books for the Teen Age, 1980, 1981, and 1982; *The Blue Sword* was chosen one of the American Library Association's Best Young Adult Books, 1982; Newbery Honor Book from the American Library Association, 1983, for *The Blue Sword; The Hero and the Crown* was chosen a Notable Book by the Association for Library Service to Children of the American Library Association, 1984; Newbery Medal, 1985, for *The Hero and the Crown;* Best Anthology from World Fantasy Awards, 1986, for *Imaginary Lands;* honorary Doctor of Letters, 1986, from Bowdoin College.

■ Writings

Beauty: A Retelling of the Story of Beauty and the Beast (novel; ALA Notable Book; *Horn Book* honor list), Harper, 1978.
The Door in the Hedge (short stories), Greenwillow, 1981.
The Blue Sword (novel; ALA Notable Book), Greenwillow, 1982.
(Contributor) Terri Windling and Mark Arnold, editors, *Elsewhere II*, Ace, 1982.
The Hero and the Crown (novel; ALA Notable Book), Greenwillow, 1984.
(Contributor) T. Windling and M. Arnold, editors, *Elsewhere III*, Ace, 1984.
(Editor) *Imaginary Lands*, Greenwillow, 1985.

(Contributor) T. Windling, editor, *Faery*, Ace, 1985.

(Adapter) Rudyard Kipling, *Tales from the Jungle Book*, Random House, 1985.

(Adapter) Anna Sewell, *Black Beauty* (illustrated by Susan Jeffers), Random House, 1986.

(Editor) George MacDonald, *For the Light Princess* (illustrated by Katie Thamer Treherne), Harcourt, 1988.

The Outlaws of Sherwood (*Horn Book* honor list), Greenwillow, 1988.

■ Adaptations

"The Blue Sword" (listening cassette), Random House, 1984.

"The Hero and the Crown" (listening cassette), Random House, 1986.

■ Work In Progress

A book laid in a different part of *Sword* and *Hero's* world; an adult fantasy; "other miscellaneous bits and pieces."

■ Sidelights

"One of my first memories is of being read aloud to. My mother would prop me in a corner of the sofa and read to me before I was old enough to sit up by myself. But my parents were determined that I *not* learn to read before I went to school; they were afraid I might then start school disliking it and finding it boring. So I went to first grade very eager: I already knew that books were the best things going, and school was going to give them to me. My mother tells the story that I came home from my first day in a rage: 'I haven't learned to read yet!' I think it took about six more weeks.

"My father was in the Navy and came back from his long overseas trips with his suitcases full of books and rolls of film. Wherever we moved, my mother borrowed books by the shelf from the local library, working tirelessly through the fiction racks from A to Z. We moved so often and therefore had to start a new library so often that she sometimes brought the same book home twice. 'Have I read this before?' she'd say, handing me a book across the breakfast table; I was allowed to read at table only at breakfast.

"My earliest childhood was in Arlington, Virginia and Washington, D.C. I attended kindergarten in Long Beach, California, the first place I clearly remember. (I did think kindergarten was pretty boring). First, second, and third grade were spent in upstate New York, and by the end of second grade I was reading sixth grade books. Books were my best friends; people, after all, were pretty insubstantial since we moved so often. I am an only child and a solitary by nature; the world of books was much more satisfactory than the so-called real world. Frances Hodgson Burnett's *A Little Princess*, about a little girl all alone in a strange land who told stories so wonderful that she believed them herself, fascinated me. I never quite lived up to Sara Crewe's standard, but I tried awfully hard.

"After New York we lived in Japan for almost five years. I took my first horseback riding lessons in Japan; I was ten years old. I've been horse-crazy since second grade—I even remember the book that began it all: *Dixie Dobie, a Sable Island Pony*, by two people named Johnson. I first read it sitting cross-legged on the floor of the Watertown Public Library, and I haven't been the same since; I've never grown out of being horse-mad, the way girls are supposed to.

"In Fuchinobe, near Tokyo, where we lived, two Japanese ex-cavalrymen operated a riding school for the American military. My mother took lessons for a little while, but it didn't really appeal to her. My father took to it with almost as much enthusiasm as I did, and we rode faithfully every weekend till we left Japan—in spite of the fact that it was a two-hour drive to the stables each way, and back roads in Japan twenty years ago were seriously harrowing. My mother came along, and cheered us from the bleachers, although I think she closed her eyes when I fell off, and made me always wear my hard hat. Our instructors' method of teaching us riding was to set up jumps higher and higher and make you go over them till the horse refused or you fell off or both. I was not a natural rider—I didn't have that beautiful balance and adaptability you see in natural athletes—and I was scared to death half the time, but anything was worth it to ride.

"We returned to the States, to Rhode Island, in the middle of eighth grade. It was a pretty rough adjustment, in spite of the stable just a few steps from our house where I worked, eagerly if not tirelessly, every day after school and every weekend.

"The States was home, of course. I knew that. I'd known it all the four and a half years we lived overseas; and however much I grew to love Japan and the Japanese countryside, one look at my blond hair and green eyes made me a foreigner, a foreigner inescapably and forever. But when I got back to the States I found that it wasn't home any more—Japan, where I was a foreigner, had become home. The States was strange, the houses were big and sprawly and careless—although the roads were sure a lot better. I had come home too with an abiding love for Oriental art, though it took me a few years to realize this; I hadn't paid that much attention to it while I lived with it. There's an aphorism here, although I'm not quite sure how it goes: you find out what you can't give up when you can't give it up.

"My father retired from the Navy when I was in my mid-teens. We moved to Vinalhaven, Maine, which became a very grim two and a half years. Vinalhaven is a tiny island off the coast with at that time a year-round population of about one thousand, and it was not a good place to be in if you are an introverted teen-ager who doesn't do a whole lot very well except read. My last year of high school was spent at a prep school, Gould Academy, in western Maine. That was the beginning of sorting myself out into the adult I would eventually become. Gould was wonderful. I had two extremely good teachers who believed in me for some reason. They saw within this overweight weird teenager someone who might grow up into an interesting human being. I seem to have outgrown being fat and come into my own as weird, but it can only be prescience that let them see it back then.

"I went to Dickinson College in Carlisle, Pennsylvania, the fall of '70. It had a good reputation as an intellectual school; I thought it was a country club, although whether that was my fault or the school's I'm no longer sure. I dropped out after a year and a half (on my way giving the poor Dean of Women a terribly high-minded little essay on how Dickinson was failing to meet my scholastic needs) and went to Washington, D.C. where I eventually married a boy who had been commuting down to Dickinson to see me on weekends. I became a motorcycle messenger and a transcriber for a stenographic reporting firm—one that covered a lot of Watergate, by the way. My husband and I lived around the corner from the police station that first discovered the break-in, too. We lived across the street from a hospital, had the police station around one corner and a fire station around the other, and the George Washington University hospital emergency room about a block and a half away. It was interesting but it was not peaceful. My husband went into public relations when he got out of the Army. We would walk down the streets together, me in my motorcycle leathers and he in his three-

Dust jacket for McKinley's second book, a collection of four short stories.

piece suit, holding hands. I was nineteen and he was twenty-one and we knew we were hot stuff.

"We decided to go back to school, and I applied to Bowdoin College, in Brunswick, Maine, which my husband had left to join the Army. Bowdoin was very hard to get into in those days and they must have caught my folder when they threw all the transfer applications up in the air and grabbed the first six coming down—my grades from Dickinson were okay but nothing spectacular. I graduated Phi Beta Kappa and summa cum laude, so they didn't choose so badly. I majored in English lit, though, still the kid who didn't do anything too well except read—it was also a good indication of my fine bold disdain for anything so trivial as earning a living. Two years in D.C. should have taught me better.

"After graduation I settled down to write; my husband joined the police department. I worked part time to help keep the rent paid, and in all honesty I spent more time sharpening pencils and reading the *New York Times Book Review* than I did writing. But it was during this period that I finally wrote *Beauty*.

"Writing has always been the other side of reading for me; it never occurred to me not to make up stories. Once I became old enough to realize that authorship existed as a thing one might aspire to, I knew it was for me. But I was also secretly determined to follow in seven-league-boot-sized footsteps like Dickens' and George Eliot's and Hardy's and Conrad's and Kipling's—and J.R.R. Tolkien's. I never will resign myself to the fact that I am not going to write *Tess of the D'Urbervilles* or *Rewards and Fairies*. I don't entirely blame my younger self for spending a lot of time sharpening pencils. I still sharpen a lot of pencils.

"I had been working on the stories that would eventually become the Damarian cycle, which so far is only two books: *The Blue Sword* and *The Hero and the Crown*. I had begun—this would be about '76—to realize that there was more than one story to tell about Damar, that in fact it seemed to be a whole history, volumes and volumes of the stuff, and this terrified me. I had plots and characters multiplying like mice and running in all directions—and I had never even written a short story I was completely happy with.

"Then a friend of mine called me with the news that the Hallmark Hall of Fame was going to present 'Beauty and the Beast' on television, starring George C. Scott. I had seen Scott in 'Jane Eyre' with Susannah York several years before and loved it and was very anxious to see this. My husband kindly borrowed a tiny black-and-white set from his great-aunt (we did not stoop to owning a television; or you could say it was the exigencies of keeping the rent paid) and I sat down on the appointed evening with my heart in my mouth— and hated it. They did everything wrong. About halfway through the show, I was feeling so sour, I started wondering nastily how they were going to turn George C. Scott into a handsome young prince at the end. They didn't, of course. The Beast turns into a middle-aged George C. Scott, with his big nose and bandy legs, although he still had his beautiful voice.

"This was the one thing that hung over me: I had never quite come to terms with how the prince in the fairy tale turns back into this smooth-faced young man at the end after long sad lonely years as the Beast. It didn't fit. So, without a whole lot more in mind than just that, I sat down at my desk that same night to write what I intended to be a short story—and a brief break from Damar, which was driving me nuts—my version of my favorite fairy tale, *Beauty and the Beast*. For five months I sat down at my desk every evening and said, 'Tonight I finish it.'

"To my surprise and uncertain pride I found I had a novel on my hands—but I was at least half embarrassed by it. What a silly thing to have done, to put so much time and energy and heart's blood into retelling a fairy tale. Everybody already knows how it ends; nobody would care, and certainly nobody would publish it. I dithered about this for months and finally sent it to Harper & Row—who, I thought, looking at the science-fiction-and-fantasy section in the town library, seemed to publish the sort of thing I thought I might have written. And they took it.

"I left my husband the spring of '78; *Beauty* came out that fall, and I left Maine shortly thereafter. I first worked at a small prep school in eastern Massachusetts. I was one of those pathetic creatures known as a dorm counselor: it meant you lived there with the kids and at three a.m. dragged yourself out of bed to find out what the row in the hall was about. I hated it: I don't like that kind of authority, and I'm not good at it. I wrote a couple of the short stories that would eventually go into *The Door in the Hedge*, but that's about all; while I know the adolescent years are supposed to be spent testing your boundaries, I felt like a fence that was falling down.

"I was lucky enough to be in the right place at the right time in Boston, and was hired by John Keller to be the new reader for the children's department at Little, Brown. Boston publishing is so small I'm still a little in awe of this stroke of luck. I moved to Boston the spring of '79, and worked two years at Little, Brown; *Door* was published by Greenwillow Books while I was there. I enjoyed the work but it was soon leaving me too little time to write; after I was promoted to editorial assistant, there was simply always too much to do, till *Sword* began to turn into something resembling a permanent migraine headache. I'll always owe John—who has little use for fantasy himself—a debt of gratitude, however, for suggesting I try Susan Hirschman at Greenwillow after I left Harper & Row.

"I met a woman, another writer, owner of a horse farm not far outside Boston, who was looking for someone to live in her farmhouse apartment in return for working part-time in the barn—a very appealing arrangement. As I was casting about for the courage to take such a leap into the unknown, Greenwillow offered me an advance against *Sword* without having seen so much as one word of outline for the book. I lived on tuna fish and hot dogs for a year, worked in the stable, and wrote *Sword*.

"I've said I was never much of a rider. It's hard to explain how serious this was to me when I was a teenager. I was an awkward and self-conscious kid who viewed her body as an essentially alien creation that had, somehow, to be managed. I still feel that way but I've gotten better at the managing. While I was living on the horse farm I started taking dressage lessons. Dressage is something like gymnastics for a human being: the point is to make your horse more supple and balanced, a better athlete. A horse is not necessarily well-coordinated, any more than a person may be; some horses are natural athletes. Most aren't. Once I began to study dressage I realized that lacking a natural gift wasn't a death knell for either you or the horse, if you're willing to put a lot of labor and sweat into learning what is easy for some people. One of my riding teachers turned out to be just what I needed—Kathy is now also one of my closest friends. I can't begin to describe how those two years of dressage lessons justified my pains as a teenager. Some of this is reflected in the way Aerin in *Hero* learns to wield a sword; she had to learn it by rote, too, because she wasn't getting any discernable help from talent.

"Some things you never learn though. Harry's vaulting into the saddle in *Sword* is the same sort of blatant wish-fullfilment as Beauty's being skinny and undersized (although at least I permitted her a few spots) is. One thing I will probably always do badly is mount. The horse staggers off as I drag myself aboard, relocating our balance. The mare I ride most often now is pretty used to me, and I can see her spread her feet when I approach her near side.

"After almost two years at the horse farm, however, I was spending more time in the barn than at my typewriter; and however close a second horses run in my life, the writing still comes first. I left Massachusetts and moved to New York City; friends of mine living on Staten Island had rented half a large house and they, like me, were among the motley crowd of publishing free-lancers, which meant they didn't have much money. I moved into their spare room on Halloween of '82, just in time to help pay the winter heating bills, and started writing *The Hero and the Crown*.

"Damar has never been a trilogy—although fantasies are half expected to be trilogies these days: a

Dust jacket for the 1983 Newbery Honor Book that introduced the Kingdom of Damar.

rather ironic heritage of *Lord of the Rings*, perhaps, which would embarrass Tolkien, who fought against having his story chopped up in three volumes. I've called Damar 'a series of indefinite length' since I began to realize how much of it there is. *Sword* as *Sword* was a late addition—even the name Damar was—to a cacophony of stories rattling around in my brain demanding space and attention. I've said I was taking time out from the tumult to write *Beauty*. But the first disentangled thread of story was Aerin's—or rather the thread of story that led me to the tangle was Aerin's. The first real spark of her story is from my many passionate rereadings of *Lord of the Rings* in junior high, and there's been a lot of brooding, plotting and wondering time between then and now.

"I recognized that there were specific connections between Harry and Aerin, and I deliberately wrote their stories in reverse chronological order, because one of the things I'm fooling around with is the idea of heroes: real heroes as opposed to the legends that are told of them afterwards. Aerin is one of her country's greatest heroes, and by the time Harry comes along, Harry is expected—or Harry thinks she is—to live up to her. When you go back and find out about Aerin in *Hero*, you discover that she wasn't this mighty invincible figure with a cult of acolytes; she had a very hard and solitary time of her early fate.

"As a compulsive reader myself, I believe that you are what you read. I despised myself for being a girl, and ipso facto being someone who stayed at home and was boring, and started trying to tell myself stories about girls who did things and had adventures, to cheer myself up after *The Count of Monte Cristo* and *The Four Feathers*—and 'The Jungle Books' and *Lord of the Rings*. To a great extent I am now merely writing down slighty more coherent versions of the stories I was telling myself twenty and more years ago.

"My books are also about hope—I hope. Much of modern literature has given up hope and deals with anti-heroes and despair. It seems to me that human beings by their very natures need heroes, real heroes, and are happier with them. I see no point in talking about how life is over and it never mattered anyway. I don't believe it. I like getting out of bed in the morning. Or, no—I like having gotten out. The getting is often disagreeable.

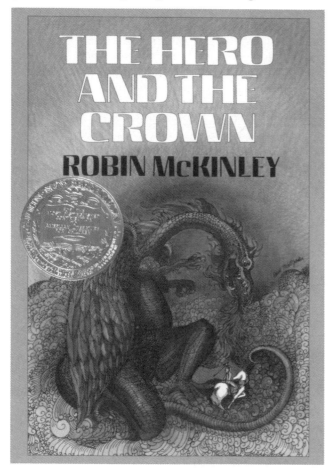

Dust cover for the 1984 Greenwillow edition.

"It is of course significant that Beauty's real name is Honour. Authors—this one anyway—are rarely too bright about what their books 'mean,' but I know that I am preoccupied with honor and duty. I will fight to the death over whether or not my books really 'mean' anything beyond being stories as lively as I can make them (usually about girls who do things), but part of that liveliness comes, I think, from the conflict of honor with inclination, and with fate. It's the way the characters who present themselves to me to be written about behave.

"*Beauty*'s derivation is a fairy tale, however, and I cold-bloodedly named her Honour, and her sisters Grace and Hope. I chose, or was chosen by, the name Anghard for the protagonist in *The Blue Sword* at least partly because I liked calling her 'Harry.' The nickname arrived more or less simultaneously with the name, although it took me a little time to realize they were the same person. But I consciously wanted a name that either was androgynous to begin with or that could be shortened to something confusing. It's all part of my feeling that the gender wars are so bitter because the areas of rightness and propriety for each side are too absolutely defined; anything that muddies the line that society has drawn in the dirt and dared us to step over, is to the good, in fiction or in life. I also think that girls who want to do things are going to have a slightly easier time if they aren't frightened with a silly girly name. Just wanting to do things is enough of a burden. In a story I'm working on now, however, the protagonist's name is Elly. I don't know if she's going to have a harder time than if she were named Jim or Frank or not.

"As an important adjunct to hope and honor, I am obsessed with the idea of freedom, especially because I'm a WASP female of limited imagination. I'm preoccupied with the notion of woman's ability, or inability, to move within her society. I am not so purblind as to think that the only thing seriously wrong with our civilization is that men have more freedom of choice than women, but I strongly believe that that is one important thing wrong, and that it must be changed. Nor will I give up the idea that men and women can cope with each other in some relaxed and affectionate fashion—under this crabby exterior there beats the squashy heart of a romantic. (One of my guiltiest guilty pleasures is rereading Georgette Heyer's frivolous historical novels: I know *Friday's Child* and *These Old Shades* virtually by heart). Some weeks, when the Dewar's ads of successful people all seem to be interesting women and *Ms.* magazine has just arrived, I think

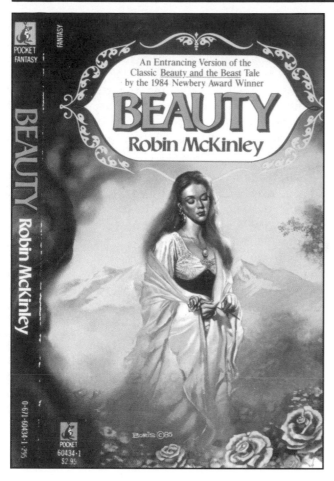

The paperback cover of McKinley's 1978 novel.

at as it rushes by doesn't go down too raggedly on the paper. When people ask me about my style, I mumble a little and change the subject.

"My first draft is in longhand. I try to translate the story in my head into words: It's a process of turning what I see and hear into a story that will look and feel like a story to other people. Since I write by ear, I don't rewrite well. It has to go down more or less right, or at least recognizable, the first time or I have to throw it out. If there's a spot where it's starting to go seriously wrong on me, I stop. I have several half-finished things in drawers waiting to be sorted out; it's often years later that it occurs to me what to do, and then I sometimes have to start over from scratch. This is depressing—I don't like hard work so awfully well that I want to do any more of it than I have to—and I try urgently to avoid it.

"But sometimes during a rough draft I have to be careful that I'm not just stopping at a minor trouble spot; if I stopped every time I knew that I was writing badly I would never get through the first

we're getting somewhere; other weeks, when I've been watching too much MTV and reading too many *New Yorker* stories about passive angst, I think we aren't. But meanwhile there are no princesses who wring their hands and stand around in ivory towers waiting for princes to return from the wars in my stories. Aerin wanted to grow up to be a hero because her mother had died of despair upon learning she had borne a daughter and not a son. The Blue Sword herself is a woman's sword, to be wielded by a woman; as Corlath tells Harry, it will betray any man, come to his full growth, who carries it.

"One of the things I am constantly asked about is my style, which people tell me I have a great deal of. This is pretty amusing, or dismaying, depending on the mood I'm in, because I have almost no control over it. It's the way the stories tell themselves. I write by ear, I hear the rhythm of the story—of the characters talking, of the pace of the plot. While I try my best to get this rhythm down on paper, I don't do much besides hold my heart in my mouth while I listen, and hope that what I catch

Dust jacket for McKinley's much-acclaimed first novel.

chapter. (The humiliating thing is how little difference there is, when I look back, between the bits I think are inspired and the bits I knew were garbage). So I go on, and trust that the story will get itself better put together. In the second draft, which is the first typed draft, the story gets longer, often a lot longer. I start putting in what people who don't know the story as well as I do need to make connections. I also put in the bits that I forgot the first time—getting the story down that first time is the most terrifically hard work I know (worse than posting to the trot without stirrups) and I get sort of glazed over with exhaustion sometimes, and leave out important things.

"In the third and final draft I tinker with the punctuation and try to get the words, both English and Damarian, spelled right, and make sure that character 'A' has the same color hair on page 261 that she did on page twelve. Language, like style, is something I can't say much about. Most of the words come as part of the storytelling. As the story grows, I hear people talking to each other and I hear the names they call each other, the unfamiliar words they use.

"You see, the stories come from somewhere; I don't feel that I make them up. They are certainly very colored by their vehicle—me. But I'm not their place of origin. I say sometimes that there's a crack in my skull, and the stories come through, like sunlight in a cave. It bothers me that I know how much purer the stories were before I started meddling with them. Just the fact that the stories must come through me must change them in some way; and then I am far too opinionated and overbearing to make an ideal medium. One of the things that I'm curious about myself is whether the stories I tell come to me because I am who I am with my set of preoccupations, or if I have become who I am and built up these preoccupations because of the stories that come to me.

"When I'm deeply into a story I begin dreaming it at night, but I very rarely find my way out of any corners I've written myself into while I'm asleep; mostly what I get is a much stronger sense of background, like closing the other eye when you focus through a camera lens. I look for ways out on my long walks. I walk a lot; my daily circle, when I'm home, is about eight miles. It gets the blood flowing again after I've gotten all jammed up at the typewriter—and I get terminally restive and cranky if the weather forces me to stay indoors more than a day or two in a row. I don't begin anywhere so specific as 'I have to get my characters from point A to point B. How am I going to do

it?' I start telling the story to myself—mostly I can control what place in the story I want to think about—and watch and listen, like a movie, maybe, except it feels three-dimensional. Sometimes one of the characters is telling the story—to me or someone; sometimes the story itself happens. I forget sometimes where I am, and stop, or turn my head to listen better, forgetting that's not how I'm listening.

"I know the story very well when I start writing it down. As I said, I write by ear, I can't do a lot of heavy revision. It's getting to be time to try it out on paper when I can begin to organize it—still in my head—into sentences that I can write down, with my this-world hand, on a sheet of this-world paper. I know it's time to start writing when I can see the first sentence of the story, literally, the first sentence, black print on a white page—which won't in fact exist yet till the second draft.

"The writing always has it surprises, however, which is just as well; it's such hard work that if it weren't also astonishing and exhilarating, I could never stick with it. But I do know the characters so well by the time I come to write about them, how they behave and who they are, that when they meet up with something that surprises all of us, I'm right there. We see each other through.

"For example, at the end of *Sword*, Mathin was supposed to die. I kept putting off writing that scene, putting it off and putting it off, because I couldn't bear it. I finally gritted my teeth and sat down to it, and to my amazement, Harry went into this flame-blinded trance and healed him. I was *so glad*.

"I thought I knew how *Hero* was going to end, too; after the battle on the plain in front of the City. And then there was all this business with Tor and Aerin and Maur's head. I went on writing, thinking, well, this is very interesting, what next? And I went on, and on, and then it occurred to me that I'd passed the end of the book I was writing, and was into another book. Whereupon I stopped and went back and tidied off, and that's the first I knew that there would be another book about Aerin.

"One of the reasons I know the Damar stories originate somewhere other than in my mind is because of this kind of lack of 'control' over my 'material.' Another example of what is virtually automatic writing is Aerin's dragon-killing. I've certainly never killed a dragon. When I wrote the first dragon scene in *Hero* I was shocked by how graphic it was. I didn't know, for example, that there was going to be the second dragon, any more than Aerin did. My hand kept moving across the page—my handwritten drafts, by the way, are appalling; they look like they were written while hanging upside-down from the rigging of a small boat in high seas. Occasionally a word or a paragraph will be so bad *I* can't read it—and I was just following along, with my mouth a little open, wishing I could write faster, because I wanted to know how it was going to end. I barely changed a word for the final copy. When I got to the scene where Aerin encounters the huge Black Dragon, Maur, I was dreading it; I knew something of how this was going to go, and I didn't really want to know more. I don't know where it all came from, but they sure know about dragons there. I went around the house for weeks after Aerin kills Maur with my left arm cradled next to my body, and dragging my right foot a little—yes, I do tend to identify with the heroes.

"*The Hero and the Crown* won the 1985 John Newbery Medal. The Newbery award is supposed to be the peak of your career as a writer for children or young adults. I was rather young to receive it; and it is a little disconcerting to feel—okay, you've done it, that's it, you should retire now. And I was informed that I would give a thirty-minute speech of acceptance to maybe 2000 people—a speech by which, by the bye, I am going to be remembered forever. There will be people who know nothing about me except that Newbery speech—it's recorded on tape, and published in several places—which is something I prefer not to think about. Composing that damn speech is the hardest bit of writing I have ever had to do. (The second worst was an essay I was asked to write about Tolkien. Stories are *nothing* in comparison.) I don't like public performances, and I feel that the books are what matter anyway; all us authors are secondary, and, to a very great extent, irrelevent.

"I dislike giving speeches, but I rather like giving informal talks to smaller groups—much smaller groups—at schools and libraries, which give readers an opportunity to meet the author as a human being, a chance to talk back, a chance to ask questions. I also remember very vividly how much it would have meant to me to meet an author—a Real Author—when I was a kid. There's almost always someone like me then in my audiences now: someone who really wants to know about writing, about how it works, about how you live with it.

"I'm almost always asked, too, what my advice is to aspiring writers—young or old; it's not always the kids who ask, and since I get published in paperback as 'adult fantasy' I sometimes draw mixed crowds. My advice is that there's no one right way to do it. But you read as much as you can, and you write as much as you can. You don't have to be organized about it, and you don't have to have a wonderful liberal arts education. I am afraid I take great delight in tweaking teachers who ask me solemnly, 'How has your education helped your career as a writer?' The answer is, 'It hasn't.' I didn't like school; I am so much happier now it is easy to see just how miserable I was for most of my school life. I had a few good teachers, and I owe them a great deal; but I owe them more the debt of inspiration by enthusiasm than anything more formal; as I owe my parents being bitten by the book bug so early.

"Simply read what you like, read what makes you happy, read what makes you enthusiastic. Follow your nose through the library; talk to anyone who will talk to you about what they've read, and learn whose advice to take. And write, and keep writing. Keep a journal; write fragments of stories if you can't write complete stories; but write. Reading feeds your writing, and writing, like anything worthy of being done well, takes practice. When that story you simply must write happens to you,

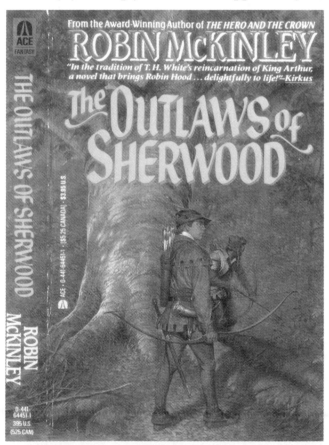

McKinley's 1988 retelling of the Robin Hood legend.

you will be well-exercised in the craft of writing, and ready to take it on. Find out—by practicing— how *you* write. Feel free to plagiarize favorite writers when you're first learning how to put a story together; it will teach you a lot about plot and pacing and development and use of the language. Find out if you're happier writing outlines or not; if you need to go through dozens of revisions or not; if you take notes as you work a story up or if you're better off keeping it in your head till almost the last minute.

"I'm working on several things at once right now, which is something I don't do because I confuse easily; perhaps my muse is trying to teach me something new—or maybe my usual state of disorganization is reaching the terminal. I know that some of this is issue-skirting: after *Sword* was a Newbery Honor Book, I was afraid that the reaction to *Hero*—even though I'd planned to write it next since before I'd written *Sword*—was that I was cashing in on a good thing. Then *Hero* won the Medal itself and now I'm terrified. I have too many tales left to tell about Damar to have any thoughts about giving it up, but the next thing I finish won't be about Damar, and maybe the one after that as well. I'm not entirely sorry for the delay, however (although I'm already getting restive fan mail from readers of *Sword* and *Hero* who demand to know when the next one is coming out). When I wrote *Beauty* I found that the novel, even though it was not the same place in my head where my favorite fairy tale had lived, somehow exorcised the tale from my mind: Beauty and the Beast, which was a place I used to go often, is barred to me now. I've never quite gotten over this; and I couldn't bear it if it happened to me with Damar as well. If I ever find myself running to the end of the Damarian stories, I will stop writing them down, because *I* want to be able to keep on going there."

One of McKinley's latest books, *The Outlaws of Sherwood*, is based on the legendary star of Sherwood Forest, Robin Hood, but gives him a contemporary personality.

Work is always on-going. "But as I began, so I go on. I still read compulsively, and I still travel a lot, although my life is complicated by the possession of several thousand books, about half that many records and tapes, and a baby grand piano, which I play extremely badly. I am very grateful I was born in the era of stereo equipment; I have music going fourteen or sixteen hours a day. (Indeed it's hard to get around in my workroom, with its four doors, two desks, three filing cabinets, a woodstove, a baby xerox machine, stereo gear, and heaps of books, records, and manuscripts-in-process on the floor. No computer—my IBM Selectric isn't a lot younger than I am). I used to sing around the house a lot when I was a kid, but my father—from whom I get my love of opera—couldn't stand it. Without records I might have had to get used to the way I play and sing. A dreadful fate. My latest self-indulgence is a VCR, and I'm busy collecting old 'Star Trek' episodes—speaking of guilty pleasures. I've just about worn out my copy of John Huston's movie of Kipling's story 'The Man Who Would Be King,' the poster from which has hung over my desk—wherever my desk was—for ten years.

"A little over two years ago I bought a little house in a village about two-thirds of the way up the Maine coast—twelve miles from where my parents now live. (For the first time since I left home to go to boarding school I can call my mother any time I like, without worrying about long-distance rates). I had not considered becoming a property owner until I saw my house, which I recognized immediately. Fortunately there was a FOR SALE sign nailed to the maple tree in the front garden.

"Even though I claim to live in Maine now I keep going back to New York City, but sleeping in friends' living rooms gets old quickly—and not every living room has a good place for setting up a typewriter. Being a property owner has proved so compellingly interesting that I recently bought a co-op there—it's so small it makes my tiny house look large—in an attempt to regularize my improbable commute. (I still go for long walks, even in New York City, although it's a little more challenging. I put tapes of my loudest, meanest rock music in my Walkman when I'm there, to get myself in the mood.) I shuttle cheerfully, if slightly manicly, between the two, when I'm not flying to Seattle or London or plotting to get to Australia or back to the Far East. And while my lilac-covered cottage is the light of my life, I still want a castle in Scotland."

■ For More Information See

Kirkus Reviews, December 1, 1978.
Washington Post Book World, December 3, 1978, April 12, 1981 (p. 9).
Newsweek, December 18, 1978.
Horn Book, April, 1979, August, 1981 (p. 433ff), July/August, 1985 (p. 406ff).
Lee Kingman, editor, *Newbery and Caldecott Medal Books: 1976-1985*, Horn Book, 1986.
Children's Literature Review, Volume 10, Gale, 1986.
Dictionary of Literary Biography, Volume 52, Gale, 1986.

Walter Dean Myers

G iven name Walter Milton Myers; born August 12, 1937, in Martinsburg, W.Va.; son of George Ambrose and Mary (Green) Myers; raised from age three by Herbert Julius (a shipping clerk) and Florence (a factory worker) Dean; married second wife, Constance Brendel, June 19, 1973; children: (first marriage) Karen, Michael Dean; (second marriage) Christopher. *Education:* Empire State College, B.A., 1984. *Home:* 2543 Kennedy Blvd., Jersey City, N.J. 07304.

■ Career

New York State Department of Labor, Brooklyn, employment supervisor, 1966-70; Bobbs-Merrill Co., Inc. (publisher), New York City, senior trade books editor, 1970-77; writer, 1977—. Has also taught creative writing and black history on a part-time basis in New York City, 1974-75. *Military service:* U.S. Army, 1954-57. *Member:* P.E.N., Harlem Writers Guild.

■ Awards, Honors

Council on Interracial Books for Children Award, 1968, for the manuscript of *Where Does the Day Go?; The Dancers* was selected one of Child Study Association of America's Children's Books of the Year, 1972, and *Adventure in Granada,* 1987; Woodward Park School Annual Book Award, 1976, for *Fast Sam, Cool Clyde, and Stuff; It Ain't All for Nothin'* was selected one of American Library Association's Best Books for Young Adults, 1978, *The Young Landlords,* 1979, *The Legend of Tarik,* 1981, *Hoops,* 1982, and *Fallen Angels,* and *Scorpions,* both 1988; Coretta Scott King Award, 1980, for *The Young Landlords,* 1985, for *Motown and Didi,* and 1989, for *Fallen Angels;* Notable Children's Trade Book in the Field of Social Studies from the National Council for Social Studies and the Children's Book Council, 1982, for *The Legend of Tarik;* Edgar Allan Poe Award runner-up, 1982, for *Hoops;* Parents' Choice Award for Literature from the Parents' Choice Foundation, 1982, for *Won't Know Till I Get There,* 1984, for *The Outside Shot,* and 1988, for *Fallen Angels;* New Jersey Institute of Technology Authors Award, 1983, for *Tales of a Dead King;* Newbery Honor Book, 1989, for *Scorpions.*

■ Writings

Fiction, Except As Noted:

(Under name Walter M. Myers) *Where Does the Day Go?* (illustrated by Leo Carty), Parents Magazine Press, 1969.
The Dragon Takes a Wife (illustrated by Ann Grifalconi), Bobbs-Merrill, 1972.
The Dancers (illustrated by Anne Rockwell), Parents Magazine Press, 1972.

Fly, Jimmy, Fly! (illustrated by Moneta Barnett), Putnam, 1974.

The World of Work: A Guide to Choosing a Career (nonfiction), Bobbs-Merrill, 1975.

Fast Sam, Cool Clyde, and Stuff (ALA Notable Book), Viking, 1975.

Social Welfare (nonfiction), F. Watts, 1976.

Brainstorm (illustrated with photographs by Chuck Freedman), F. Watts, 1977.

Mojo and the Russians, Viking, 1977.

Victory for Jamie, Scholastic, 1977.

It Ain't All for Nothin' (ALA Notable Book), Viking, 1978.

The Young Landlords (ALA Notable Book), Viking, 1979.

The Black Pearl and the Ghost; or, One Mystery after Another (illustrated by Robert Quackenbush), Viking, 1980.

The Golden Serpent (illustrated by Alice Provensen and Martin Provensen), Viking, 1980.

Hoops, Delacorte, 1981.

The Legend of Tarik, Viking, 1981.

Won't Know Till I Get There, Viking, 1982.

The Nicholas Factor, Viking, 1983.

Tales of a Dead King, Morrow, 1983.

Mr. Monkey and the Gotcha Bird (illustrated by Leslie Morrill), Delacorte, 1984.

Motown and Didi: A Love Story, Viking, 1984.

The Outside Shot, Delacorte, 1984.

Sweet Illusions, Teachers & Writers Collaborative, 1986.

Crystal, Viking, 1987.

Scorpions (ALA Notable Book), Harper, 1988.

Me, Mop, and the Moondance Kid (ALA Notable Book; illustrated by Rodney Pate), Delacorte, 1988.

Fallen Angels, Scholastic, 1988.

"The Arrow" Series:

Adventure in Granada, Viking, 1985.

The Hidden Shrine, Viking, 1985.

Duel in the Desert, Viking, 1986.

Ambush in the Amazon, Viking, 1986.

Contributor To Anthologies:

Orde Coombs, editor, *What We Must See: Young Black Storytellers*, Dodd, 1971.

Sonia Sanchez, editor, *We Be Word Sorcerers: Twenty-five Stories by Black Americans*, Bantam, 1973.

Contributor of articles and fiction to periodicals, including *Black Creation, Black World, Scholastic, McCall's, Espionage, Alfred Hitchock Mystery Magazine, Essence, Ebony, Jr.!,* and *Boy's Life.*

■ Sidelights

Walter Dean Myers is one of modern literature's foremost authors of fiction for black teenagers. His stories are concerned mostly with the tragedies and triumphs of growing up in difficult environments. "I'm drawn to the eternal promise of childhood, and the flair of the young for capturing the essence of life."[1]

Myers was born on August 12, 1937 to George Ambrose and Mary Green Myers. "Where does life begin? I discount the idea that life has a strictly biological beginning. Sometime between the snatching of an unknown African from his native land and this writing, somewhere between the long forgotten past and the confusing present, the person that I perceive as Self came into being.

"I don't remember being born in 1937 in Martinsburg, West Virginia. There are records that indicate that I was and I accept them. I sent for a birth certificate some years ago and I received a neat document which confirmed that I was, indeed, born. It is also noted under 'race' that I am white. That amuses me. In a system that places so much importance on one's race, that error is a small gem of irony.

"My mother died during the birth of my sister Imogene. I have a picture of my mother, borrowed and copied from an older sister. In the picture I see a woman I never knew. I don't remember her ever holding me, or kissing me. She looks kindly, and I am told she was rather tall. I make a lot of this because my father was a short man. I assume, therefore, that physically I take after my mother's people who have been described to me as tall. I am over six feet.

"My father managed to marry a number of quite attractive women. My mother was his second wife. He also managed to father quite a number of children, most of whom are still living. Three of my brothers have been killed—one in Vietnam, one hit by an ambulance, and one during a domestic dispute.

"Hard times are common in West Virginia. When my mother died my father was left to care for Imogene, myself, my brothers Douglas and George, and my sisters Geraldine, Ethel, Viola, and Gertrude. Those old enough to go to school went to the 'Colored' school in Martinsburg. There were few jobs to be had during that Depression era. There were some jobs in nearby mining towns but they hired few Blacks. And they paid mostly in 'Scrip,' which had to be spent at the company store. My father's parents helped as much as they could. My grandfather was a colorful character whom I met years later as a teenager. He was born on a Sunday just before the end of the Civil War. His mother, a slave, managed to keep a newspaper as a record of his birth. My grandfather, of course, didn't remember being a slave. He did remember stories of slavery that his mother related. I remember only that the stories, full of beatings and horrors, frightened me as a child.''[2]

After his mother's death, Myers went to live with foster parents. "Enter the Deans.

"Extended families are common among poor people. If a family is experiencing difficulty it is not out of the ordinary for another family, faring only slightly better, to take in one or more of the first family's children. Herbert and Florence Dean took me to raise.

"Florence Dean had been the daughter of a German mother and American Indian father. Herbert Dean was the son of a small businessman in Baltimore. His grandfather had been a slave in Virginia.

"The Deans settled in Harlem. I am told that I left Martinsburg with them and two of my sisters when I was three, or thereabouts, arriving in New York's Harlem with a snotty nose and wearing a pair of my sister's socks. Harlem became my home and the place where my first impressions of the world were set.

"We weren't poor in any way that I recognized— not that it would have mattered much. Being poor was not as important then as it has become. It had little to do with not having designer jeans, or the latest tapes, or other 'things' that children connect with self-worth today. When I was a child there were two conditions that defined being poor. Were you hungry? Were you cold? With the Deans I was never hungry or cold.

"My foster father was good to me—except for the stories. What he liked to do, especially when Mama was out shopping, was to sit me on his knee and tell endless stories. There were stories of ghosts and of rabbits that came through walls and of strange creatures that rose from the sea (the sea being the Hudson River) in the still of night. I was never quite sure if I wanted Mama to leave me alone with Herbert. I didn't call him Dad because my older sisters didn't. I remember making him stop the stories and tell me that he loved me just before the scary parts came. Sometimes, when the stories were *really* scary, he would act as if he were scared

The 1981 novel about growing up in Harlem.

himself. I remember one Saturday, Mama had gone to Fourteenth Street to shop, and my father told me a story about a huge bunny that escaped from a farm and went around looking for bad children. Apparently, this particular bunny had it in for children who cried when their mamas left them with nothing more tangible then the promise of a charlotte russe. This, of course, meant me. When Dad got to the part about the bunny coming up the fire escape (we lived on the fourth floor) he glanced toward the window, put on his best startled face, and took off running down the hallway of our apartment with me in close and screaming pursuit. We didn't stop until we reached Morningside Park. Years later, when my grandfather came to live with us after the hauling business failed, I discovered that the older man had even scarier stories not about huge bunnies but the very Wrath of God. At least God didn't come jumping through the walls.

"Mama, on the other hand, told very nice stories. Her stories would sometimes include Shirley Temple, Bessie Smith, and an occasional princess whose man had done her wrong. Sometimes the handsome prince who saved them would be German. Clearly, the woman was civilized."[2]

"Thinking back to my boyhood days, I remember the bright sun of Harlem streets, the easy rhythms of black and brown bodies moving along the tar and asphalt pavement, the sounds of hundreds of children streaming in and out of red brick tenements. I remember La Marketa, in East Harlem, where people spoke a multitude of languages and the Penn Central rumbled overhead. I remember playing basketball in Morningside Park until it was too dark to see the basket and then climbing over the fence to go home.

"Harlem was a place of affirmation. The excitement of city living exploded in the teeming streets. If there was a notion that as a black child I was to be denied easy access to other worlds, it mattered little to me if I could have this much life in the place I found myself."

"I lived in an exciting corner of the renowned Black capital and in an exciting era. The people I met there, the things I did, have left a permanent impression on me. My earliest memories are of walking through the streets to Sunday school. The Sunday school teacher would pick up children from the neighborhood, and I would hold hands with my selected partner and sing 'Yes, Jesus Loves Me,' as we walked down St. Nicholas Avenue toward the church. Later, when we had moved to Morningside Avenue and I could go to Sunday school by myself, I would sing the words to the song to myself.

"I went to school in the neighborhood. Most of the teachers were Irish, although a few were Jewish. The Irish had a reputation for not liking Colored children but for being eminently fair. My best friend turned out to be Eric Leonhardt, a German boy I met whose mother befriended my mother. Eric and I became fast friends for three reasons. First, he was as tall as I was and stood in line near me. Second, when I went to his father's bakery I was given chocolate chip cookies, a condition of friendship I still respect. The last reason for his friendship was that he taught me to masturbate. He was truly a wonderful kid.

"When...[he] began going to parties to which I was not invited, I discovered that life was not as simple as had seemed. We had been friends for a long time. We had been noticing girls and he had taught me all I needed to know about the opposite sex. We had even selected girls that we were 'in love' with. He picked a German girl and I picked a Black girl. It was Eric's suggestion that we not tell the girls so that they wouldn't get stuck on themselves, when they discovered their incredible luck.

"But as Eric moved into social situations and I was not invited, it was awkward for both of us. For Eric it meant either becoming a racial crusader or concealing his activities from me. For me it meant either accepting my role as his 'colored' friend or rejection of his friendship altogether. Later in life I could have made other choices; at the time I chose to avoid Eric."[2]

"My education bumped along. I spoke poorly, rushing words out in a bewildering jumble, hating the patience of my teachers as much as the ridicule of my classmates as I tried to express myself...."

"I never understood the source of my speech difficulty. I didn't hear anything unusual when I spoke. I knew what was in my mind but others apparently didn't understand what came out of my mouth. Other children used to laugh at the way I garbled my words. I used to fight children who laughed at me. As a result I found myself suspended from school a great deal. Although I enjoyed school, I found that I didn't always fit in."[2]

"I was frequently in trouble...sitting in the back of the room or in the principal's office. It was during one of these periods, in the fifth grade, that an already annoyed teacher caught me reading a comic book under the desk. Of course, she tore it up, but the next day she came in with a pile of books and announced that, if indeed I was going to spend so much time sitting in the back of the room and reading, I should at least read something good. Suddenly this teacher had given a direction to my reading. I still remember the first book he gave me, *East of the Sun, and West of the Moon*. Reading took on a new dimension for me."

"The teacher, Mrs. Conway, also instituted a new idea that appealed to me. She required that we read in front of the class. That was difficult with my speech problems. I would tense up badly, and my already poor speech would get even worse. Then she suggested that we could write something to read if we so desired. Oh, happy day! There were many words I could not, for the life of me, pronounce. Anything beginning with a *u* or an *r* gave me trouble, as did any word with an *sh* or *ch* sound in the middle. I began writing poems so that I could avoid the words that I could not pronounce.

The electrifying
sequel to *Hoops*

The Outside Shot

Walter Dean Myers

DELL ● 96784 ● $2.9
CAN. $3.9

Softcover edition of the 1984 novel.

"I had been duly classified as a bright child, and had been through an accelerated junior high school program. I assumed I would go to college and eventually take my rightful place in the world of bright, influential people. But as I neared the end of my junior year in high school, I saw that going to college would be financially impossible. I also began to recognize that my 'rightful place' might be defined more by my race than my abilities. I became depressed, disillusioned. What was the use of being bright if that 'brightness' didn't lead me where I wanted to go. I stopped going to school, at least on a regular basis. I began to read even more than the several books a week I had been reading. The books became an escape from a world I felt had rejected me. I was just fifteen.

"But if fifteen was bad sixteen was an absolute disaster. At sixteen I was writing poems about death, despair, and doom. I felt my life was falling apart, that I had no control over my destiny. I had won a minor prize in an essay contest; I also won a set of encyclopedias for a long narrative poem. But my family didn't seem to think it was a big deal. I was from a family of laborers, and the idea of writing stories or essays was far removed from their experience. Writing had no practical value for a Black child. These minor victories did not bolster my ego. Instead, they convinced me that even though I was bright, even though I might have some talent, I was still defined by factors other than my ability.

"I imagine that every adolescent faces a similar problem. We exist in several worlds simultaneously. As young people we hear that there is a world in which all sorts of wonderful things are possible. In that world, we are told that we are limited only by our willingness to work hard. Somewhere in grammar school, I began to suspect that wasn't entirely true. The people in the 'good world' of the movies and the books were all wealthy, attractive, and white. That was not my world. I was poor, considered myself quite homely, and I was Black. I

Walter Dean Myers

FALLEN ANGELS

Jacket from the 1988 Scholastic edition.

remember going downtown, to Fifty-seventh Street, and looking at the people in wonder. Wasn't *this* the real world that people were talking about? But in the books I read there were no Blacks."[2]

"By high school I had a part-time job in the garment district and had purchased, with my father's help, my first typewriter. I wrote short stories and laboriously constructed poems. I enjoyed writing as I had enjoyed reading. Again, it seemed a connection with things and events that I was not part of in 'real' life. More an observer than a doer, I was on my way to becoming a writer. I just didn't know it yet."

"I worked...for a costume jewelry concern on Thirty-fourth Street. There was a girl who worked there named Lavinia, the same name as a girl in T. S. Eliot's *Cocktail Party,* which I read as I packed jewelry into small boxes to be mailed around the country. I fell in love with Eliot's girl. The real girl scared me to death. I fell in lust with her. What I remembered best about that job was imagining how Lavinia would look naked, and being humiliated when I took packages to the post office.

"I ran into the real world at the post office. 'Man, what you got that book in your hands for?' this from a man with a handkerchief tied around his head, sweat dripping from muscular arms, the smell of wine on his breath, 'You ain't nothin' but another nigger, just like me.'

"These were the people I most identified with, that I was forced to identify with, and it depressed me. I have always felt, since that time, that young Black people must have role models with which they can identify.

"I was having doubts about everything in my life, including what had been till then a fairly deep religious conviction. When I discovered *Portrait of the Artist as a Young Man* I knew that I was not alone. If Joyce had these doubts, too, and he was a writer, well—I would also become a writer. I stumbled through *Ulysses,* and carried *Finnegans Wake* around for several weeks before surrendering. I read all the Balzac the George Bruce Branch of the New York Public Library had. I read Zola's *Nana* several times, usually under the covers.

"I 'hung out' with a guy I'll call Tom. He was the son of a famous Black tap dancer. Tom was a good friend, a year older than me but shorter. He had the dubious distinction of being the only one I knew who had actually killed people. He had killed a bus driver in one incident, and two other people

Myers earned an ALA "Best Books for Young Adults" citation for this 1978 novel.

who had insulted his mother in another. Both of these were during periods in which Tom had 'blacked out.' Otherwise he was a pussycat. I used to read poetry to him while he drank beer in the park. Sometimes he would sing to me in what I remember now as a pretty good voice. Tom got involved in being a drug courier for a while and we both were involved in other activities that weren't exactly kosher.

"My parents were quite troubled by my behavior. I had been a fairly good boy till then, but I changed quickly. I was steeped in the mystique of the semihoodlum. I think I imagined myself as Francois Villon, and actually looked forward to going to jail. Thank God I hadn't discovered Genet yet. My mother found out that I was skipping school when someone from the office called her. It was decided that I was 'disturbed.'

"I began to write short stories. A teacher in Stuyvesant, I remember her name as Bonnie Lie-bow, had called me aside and said that I was a gifted writer. Could that really mean something in

MOJO and the RUSSIANS

Walter Dean Myers

Myers' 1977 novel involving espionage and voodoo.

my life? I wrote every day. When I was supposed to be in school I would go instead to Central Park, climb a tree, and write or read until it was time to go home.

"Mrs. Liebow made up a reading list for me. I still remember most of the titles—*Buddenbrooks, Pere Goriot, Penguin Island,* and something by Zola. I fantasized about marrying her.

"I read the poems of Rupert Brooke and suddenly it came to me what I had to do. I would hie myself off to some far-off battlefield and get killed. There, where I fell, would be a little piece of Harlem.

"At seventeen I joined the army. I didn't tell my parents that I had joined until the morning I left.

"My mother cried. My father, at a complete loss to understand my actions, gave me his blessings.

"In the army I went to radio-repair school and learned nothing about radio repair. I spent most of my time in the service playing basketball. I also learned several efficient ways of killing human beings. And, with images from poets like Byron and Brooke and Spender rather loosely in mind, I

was ready to do battle with anyone. Oddly enough, I spent my three years in the army on a strictly vegetarian diet."[2]

"After the service I returned to New York and a series of jobs. By this time I had decided that what I wanted to do most was to write. Writing seemed, and still seems to be, my major involvement with life. I can reach people through my writing, and I can use that writing as a point of reference in my real-life encounters. The sense of isolation I felt as a young person is now relieved by the connecting links of my stories."

"I remembered Harlem as a great place. Full of lively, warm people, most of whom meant you nothing but good....But something...happened in my absence. Drugs had come to Harlem in a big way.

"I moved to the Cort Hotel on Forty-eighth Street in New York City. I shared a room with a lively family of cockroaches. I paid thirteen dollars a week for the room. I assumed the roaches had their own arrangement. That was my starving-artist period. I even went home...and got my copy of Schiller's life to make sure I was doing it well. I read Gide's *Immoralist,* Orwell's *Down and Out in London and Paris,* and others by Corydon, Juan Ramon Jimenez, and Lorca. I wrote bad poems.

"I didn't start writing again in earnest—and by that I mean every day—until I was married and working in the post office, unloading the mail chute. I had married a wonderful, warm, beautiful, religious, caring woman named Joyce. She reminded me somewhat of Dylan Thomas's wife, Caitlin, because she felt my running about in the East Village was symptomatic of an evil neglect rather than an activity she chose not to participate in. It took me years to understand that there actually are people who don't share my passions.

"I was fired from the Post Office. Then I worked for a while as an inter-office messenger and office boy, and later I was a clerk/interviewer in a factory.

"Meanwhile, we had a daughter, Karen, and then a son, Michael Dean. When I had arguments with my wife, I'd take Karen to the bars.

"I was published in Black magazines such as the *Liberator,* and *Negro Digest.* I wrote for men's adventure and girlie magazines. I also drank too much and ran around too much.

"I decided that what I wanted to do with myself was to become a writer and live what I imagined would be the life of the writer, whatever that might be. The marriage suffered and dissolved under the strain of my radically different life style."[2]

Myers eagerly observed the changes taking place in the publishing industry through the 1960s, and was hopeful that they would have lasting impact upon black literature. "When I began writing for young people I was only vaguely aware of the problems with children's books as far as blacks were concerned. My own encounters with black symbols and black characters were no less painful than those of the generations that followed me. There was the first mention of blacks in history. There were 'slaves' being led from ships. Not captives, slaves. In truth, I don't remember *Little Black Sambo*, the large red lips pouting from the page, the wide eyes, the kinky hair going off in all directions, as being particularly bothersome. I'm not sure if it was the awe in which I held the tiger, or if I had just separated myself from this image. But later I do remember suffering through the 'Tom Swift' books, and the demeaning portrait of Eradicate, the major black character in the series.

"The pain was not so much that the images of my people were poor, but that the poor images were being made public. There they were in books for all of my white classmates to see. I had already internalized the negative images, had taken them for truth. No matter that my mother said that I was as good as anyone. She had also told me, in words and in her obvious pride in my reading, that books were important, and yet it was in books that I found Eradicate Sampson and the other blacks who were lazy, dirty and, above all, comical.

"When the images of Dinah, the black maid in the 'Bobbsey Twins,' Friday in *Robinson Crusoe*, Eradicate in 'Tom Swift' and the overwhelming *absence* of blacks in most books were telling the children of my generation that being black was not to be taken seriously, they were delivering the same message to white children. I knew that no homage to racial equality delivered by my teachers could, for me, offset even one snicker when Friday was depicted as a 'savage,' or when Dinah or Eradicate Sampson said something stupid.

"The 1960s promised a new way of seeing black people. First, and by far most important, we were in the public consciousness. Angry black faces stared out from our television sets, commanded the front pages of our tabloids. We were news, and what is news is marketable. To underscore the market the Federal Government was pumping money into schools and libraries under various poverty titles. By the end of the 60s the publishing industry was talking seriously about the need for books for blacks.

"I felt proud to be part of this new beginning. Langston Hughes, the brilliant black poet and novelist, had lived a scant half mile from me in Harlem. He had written for young people and I fancied myself following in his footsteps. I had learned from Hughes that being a black writer meant more than simply having one's characters brown-skinned, or having them live in what publishers insist on describing on book jackets as a 'ghetto.' It meant understanding the nuances of value, of religion, of dreams. It meant capturing the subtle rhythms of language and movement and weaving it all, the sound and the gesture, the sweat and the prayers, into the recognizable fabric of black life. What people like Brenda Wilkerson and Sharon Bell Mathis were doing for fiction, James Haskins was doing for biography, Leo and Diane Dillon were doing for picture books and Eloise Greenfield and others were doing for poetry."[1]

"I understood, and I know the others did too, that it was not only for black children that we wrote. We were writing for the white child and the Asian child too. My books did well, and so did the books of other black writers. Tom Feelings was being published, and so were John Steptoe, Moneta Barnett and Carole Byard. Things were looking up. I believed that my children and their contemporaries would not only escape the demeaning images I had experienced but would have strong, positive, images as well. And, though I was not happy with all the titles being published, the quality of the books written by blacks in the 70s was so outstanding that I actually thought we would revolutionize the industry, bringing to it a quality and dimension that would raise the standard for all children's books. Wrong. Wrong. Wrong.

"No sooner had all the pieces conducive to the publishing of more books on the black experience come together than they started falling apart. The programs financed by the Johnson Administration and his Great Society were being dismantled under President Nixon. By the time President Ford left office the 'Days of Rage' had ended and the temper of the time was lukewarm. Blacks were no longer a hot political issue. The librarians were the major markets for black children's books, and when they began to suffer cutbacks it was books on the black experience that were affected most."[1]

"Where, then, did I fit in as a Black writer? How good a writer was I? If I wrote, 'what I knew best' and reached only a limited market, how could I progress as a writer? There are still no easy answers. Many young Black writers become discouraged and stop writing. I felt like quitting many times when I was younger."[2]

"I remarried, determined not to make the same mistakes I had during my first marital encounter. Joyce knew me as a person in the throes of emotional and artistic growth; Connie had the advantage of knowing me when I was much surer of who I was, both as a person and as a writer.

"I wrote for men's magazines until they gave themselves up to pornography. I also wrote for the *Sunday News Magazine*, *McCall's*, *Alfred Hitchcock*, and other magazines. Like other Black writers before me, I was faced with a dilemma: I had more successful writing for a white audience than writing for a Black audience.

A PUFFIN BOOK

THE YOUNG LAND LORDS

Six kids, one building, and a whole lot of shakin' goin' on.
"It's a neighborhood block party!" —*The New York Times*

WALTER DEAN MYERS

A group of inner city children inhabit this 1979 novel.

"At a party given by my agent, Harriet Wasserman, I met an editor named Linda Zuckerman. I wasn't particularly comfortable at the party—I'm never comfortable with strangers—but she looked as if she wouldn't hurt me, so I talked to her. She had read a story of mine that Harriet had given her and she had liked it very much. Then and there we made plans to publish, *Fast Sam, Cool Clyde, and Stuff*.

"It was my first young adult novel and I wondered where my writing career was headed. I was writing humor in *Fast Sam*. . .something that comes to me fairly easily. I was also writing about the positive side of my Harlem experience, which most of it was."[2]

Set in the 116th Street neighborhood of New York, *Fast Sam, Cool Clyde, and Stuff* takes a group of preteen youths through mistaken arrests, encounters with drugs and violence, and the loss of family members, as they learn and mature together. The novel was critically well-received and Myers' entree into young adult literature proved to be highly successful.

For seven years, from 1970 on, Myers worked as a book editor. "I was hired. . .because the publisher, Bobbs-Merrill, wanted a Black editor. I had no experience editing and more than a little reluctance to take the job. I did take it. . .and found myself in the heart of the publishing world at Fifty-seventh and Fifth Avenue.

"I had this enormous desk, in this enormous office, and a blue-eyed, blonde secretary who kept popping into my office, asking me if I need anything.

"'Would you like coffee?' she asked.

"'No, thank you,' I would respond.

"She was very nice and told me as much as she could about the job. It was an interesting job, especially the lunches. I soon learned to take a writer or an agent to lunch and spend enough money to feed a family of four for an entire week. I also learned the book business from another viewpoint.

"Publishing is a business. It is not a cultural institution. It has no pretensions of 'fairness,' or 'equality.' It is *talked* about as if it were a large cultural organization with several branches. One hears pronouncements like 'Anything worthwhile will eventually be published.' Nonsense, of course. Books are published for many reasons, the chief of which is profit. Occasionally an editor can slip in a book on 'merit' alone, but the occasions are few and far between. As conglomerates eat up the book business, the occasions will be even farther apart.

"Generally, publishing was a good experience for me. After the initial disillusionment about the artistic aspects of the job, I realized how foolish I had been in not learning, as a writer, more about the business aspects of my craft.

"I was fired from my job as an editor in 1977. I was crushed. Being fired was terrible. No matter how impersonal they try to make it seem it still feels as if you're being singled out as the resident leper. The company was going through a number of changes and heads were rolling left and right. I had signed up a number of books by Black authors and on Black subjects. That, to some extent, I felt didn't help my cause very much. At least, sales figures on the books didn't help my cause any.

"I was under contract to Viking to write a book at the time and that gave me some consolation. I finished the book and then went to Hong Kong to sulk. I'm good at sulking.

"In Hong Kong my wife and I discussed the possibility of my not looking for another job. By the time we reached Bangkok I was a full-time writer. Nervous, but a full-time writer.

"As my books for teenagers gained in popularity I sensed that my soul-searching for my place in the artistic world was taking on an added dimension. As a Black writer I had not only the personal desire to find myself, but the obligation to use my abilities to fill a void."[2]

"I enjoy writing for young people because the forms are less constricting, more forgiving to the stretched imagination. I particularly enjoy writing about the city life I know best. Ultimately what I want to do with my writing is make the connection—reach out and touch the lives of my characters and share them with a reader.

"I write to give hope to those kids who are like the ones I knew—poor, troubled, treated indifferently by society, sometimes bolstered by family and many times not. I was a high-school dropout, and I know how easy it is for them to lose their brightness in a web of drugs, gangs, and crime."

"I've been fortunate....My books have done reasonably well, I've sold them at a great rate, and I've been able to support myself and my family on the proceeds. I'm not all sure that I've hit upon my final destination, I suspect not.

"Any career, if it is to be successful, demands constant reassessment.

"I recognized, as all writers must, that man is not a singular entity. We are all many people, depending on whom we are dealing with, and who we happen to be on a particular day and in a particular circumstance. At various times, we play the role of parent, boss, employee, child, martyr, or hero. But usually we are not called upon to identify ourselves at any given moment. As a writer, however, I am constantly asked to identify myself.

"I learned something from the experience of other writers—like Frank Yerby, a superb Black writer. His early short stories are excellent examples of Black literature. Yerby soon discovered that his writing was boxed in by his race. He was expected to write of the Black condition (Write what you know!) but there were, and are, few market opportunities for the Black writer. Most of the popular magazines treat the Black story as a 'special category.' No one will announce this openly, but it is true nevertheless. A magazine with a predominantly White audience may well publish a story with Black characters, but will not consider another story with a Black theme or Black characters for the next year and a half. And there is no guarantee that a story will be published even if it is considered.

"Furthermore, it is much easier for a White writer to publish a theme about a Black than it is for a Black to publish a story about a Black. The reason is simple enough. The story by the White writer is more likely to take a White point of view which coincides with that of the magazine's projected readership. This is also true in children's literature."[2]

"What is there to be done? We must first acknowledge that in much of the black community reading as both a skill and as recreation is seriously undervalued. It is the urgent task of the black community to reinvest value in education and, specifically, in reading skills. If the market is created the books will come. Blacks are, arguably, the largest homogeneous group in the country. We should be able to command a great share of the market and fulfill much of our needs ourselves.

"If this seems unnecessarily harsh, or just not feasible, then we will simply have to wait for the next round of race riots, or the next interracial conflict, and the subsequent markets thus created. We can be sure, however, of one thing: if we continue to make black children nonpersons by excluding them from books and by degrading the black experience, and if we continue to neglect white children by not exposing them to any aspect of other racial and ethnic experiences in a meaningful way, we will have a next racial crisis. It will work, but it's a hard price for a transient market.

"In the meanwhile there will be black artists recording the stuff of our lives in rich and varied hues, and they will continue to do so. We will twist and smooth and turn our lines carefully to the sun and wait, as we have done before, to offer them to new travelers who pass this way."[1]

June, 1988. *Scorpions* published. The book features two boys from Harlem who join up with a gang. "They're involved in the narcotics trade. The members are young because when they are arrested, there is no penalty. The prestige for these kids is unbelievable....These things are real and they're happening more than we talk about. You can buy a gun in an hour or so. And a kid needs a reason not to have a gun."[3]

"I was writing...about a scene I know only too well, about a family like so many I grew up with—low-income families, headed by a single parent, a hard-working woman who leaves her young chil-

Dust jacket for Myers' novel about gang violence.

dren every morning and carries around with her all day long a fear that they may go wrong."[4]

Myers' most recent novel, *Fallen Angels* is the story of a young man in the Army from enlistment through his tour of duty. The book is based largely on Myer's own experience in the Army and was inspired by his brother's death in Vietnam. "No one really joined up because they wanted to fight or kill—people have different reasons for going.

"To me, the pivotal point was when they change from naive young people to understanding what war is about, that the currency of war is death, not ideals."[3]

"For me, this book also highlights the ironic fact that a generation ago, black kids with no place to go were welcome in the Army. These days, that's often closed to them, too, because they can't pass the tests."[4]

Both *Scorpions* and *Fallen Angels* marked a turning point in Myers' work. "[They] are a departure for me—very serious, probing work. Not that the others didn't address serious issues, too, but the new ones were more difficult to write."[3]

Those "departures" have brought his latest books favorable reviews. Mel Watkins of the *New York Times Book Review* said: "*Fallen Angels* is a candid young adult novel that engages the Vietnam experience squarely. It deals with violence and death as well as compassion and love, with deception and hypocrisy as well as honesty and virtue. It is a tale that is as thought-provoking as it is entertaining, touching and, on occasion, humorous."[5]

Myers lives in Jersey City, New Jersey and dedicates his time to helping kids in the Jersey City public schools. Twice a month he volunteers to teach a class of creative writing to seventh and eighth graders. "I have a younger brother, Horace, who teaches in the New York City school system. When he asked me to come and speak to his class, I realized how few resources are available for Black youngsters to open the world to them. I feel the need to show them the possibilities that exist for them that were never revealed to me as a youngster; possibilities that did not even exist for me then. I've taught Black literature and creative writing and I enjoyed working with high-school kids in the classroom. As much time as I spend alone, as I've always spent alone, I enjoy being with people immensely."[2]

With hopes of providing both children and adults with new avenues to trusting relationships, Myers has used his writing and teaching to bridge the often vast gap between the generations. "We trust children when they're first born. Perhaps it's because they respond so easily to our love and attention, and don't question us too closely. We lose that trust somewhere along the time they start talking. Then we tolerate them, most often love them still, and occasionally allow them to entertain us with their concerns. Trusting them is another matter.

"To begin with, we doubt the intellectual capability of the child who says that he or she wants a nuclear free world. When children suggest that we can, as rational beings in a rational, mostly civilized world, simply talk out our differences, we question their maturity. Nor do we trust their capacity for sustained logic when they say that if people on one side of the world don't want war and people on the other side don't want war there's really no need to have a war.

"What we end up doing is giving our wars with the regularity of Saturday night dances and casting suspicious glances at the children who think we're out of our minds.

"We're probably right not to trust children because basic to the child's world is the concept of free will. Free will is often embarrassing, if not downright unpleasant for adults to consider. Not so for children. Children tend to think that we, being adults, are perfectly free to exercise our wills to accomplish those things we say we believe in. It baffles them when we profess love but zealously guard our stores of hate; when we celebrate universal justice while talking of 'acceptable' levels of oppression.

"We confuse children even further when we tell them how fervently we want peace as we pass yet another huge military budget to insure it, knowing full well that the 'other side' will have to pass an equally huge military budget to keep their version of the 'peace.' We really confound children as we champion the cause of democracy by supplying arms to dictators.

"We've got one thing going for us, though. Somewhere between childhood and adulthood we teach a great many children to think like adults. We're even able to convince them that *their* children should not be trusted.

"As writers we face no more formidable task than to bring children and adults together. We need to see the world clearly and to explain it clearly to children so that they, in turn, can explain it back to us without our adult compromises, and without our adult excuses. To do less is to abandon our talents, perhaps even our universe. If we're lucky, we might even get children and adults to trust each other again. If we're lucky."[6]

Footnote Sources:

[1] Walter Dean Myers, "I Actually Thought We Would Revolutionize the Industry," *New York Times Book Review*, November 9, 1986.
[2] *Something about the Author Autobiography Series*, Volume 2, Gale, 1986.
[3] K.O.F., "Walter Dean Myers," *Publishers Weekly*, February 26, 1988.
[4] Shirley Horner, "Author Seeks to Inspire Black Youth," *New York Times*, August 21, 1988.
[5] Mel Watkins, "Fallen Angels," *New York Times Book Review*, January 22, 1989.
[6] W. D. Myers, "Earning Our Children's Trust," *Lion and the Unicorn*, Volume 10, 1986.

■ For More Information See

New York Times Book Review, April 9, 1972 (p. 8), May 4, 1975 (p. 28ff), January 6, 1980 (p. 20), November 9, 1980, July 12, 1981 (p. 30), June 13, 1982 (p. 26ff), September 13, 1987, January 22, 1989.

Theressa G. Rush and others, *Black American Writers: Past and Present*, Scarecrow Press, 1975.

Booklist, February, 1975 (p. 620), October 15, 1977 (p. 379).

School Library Journal, March, 1975 (p. 108), November, 1976 (p. 61), November, 1977 (p. 74), October, 1978 (p. 158), May, 1981 (p. 76), May, 1982 (p. 72ff), September, 1983 (p. 138), April, 1987.

Horn Book, August, 1975 (p. 388ff), April, 1978 (p. 166ff), October, 1979 (p. 535), August, 1981 (p. 434), March/April, 1985 (p. 186ff).

Ebony, September, 1975.

Interracial Books for Children Bulletin, Volume 10, number 4, 1979 (p. 18), Volume 10, number 6, 1979 (p. 14ff).

Children's Literature Review, Gale, Volume 4, 1982, Volume 16, 1989.

Shadow and Substance: Afro-American Experience in Contemporary Children's Fiction, National Council of Teachers of English, 1982.

Sally Holmes Holtze, *Fifth Book of Junior Authors and Illustrators*, H. W. Wilson, 1983.

Dictionary of Literary Biography, Volume XXXIII: *Afro-American Fiction Writers after 1955*, Gale, 1984.

Contemporary Literary Criticism, Volume XXXV, Gale, 1985.

Phyllis Reynolds Naylor

B orn January 4, 1933, in Anderson, Ind.; daughter of Eugene S. (a salesman) and Lura (a teacher; maiden name, Schield) Reynolds; married second husband, Rex V. Naylor (a speech pathologist), May 26, 1960; children: Jeffrey Alan, Michael Scott. *Education:* Joliet Junior College, diploma, 1953; American University, B.A., 1963. *Politics:* Independent. *Religion:* Unitarian Universalist. *Home and office:* 9910 Holmhurst Rd., Bethesda, Md. 20817. *Agent:* John Hawkins & Associates, Inc., 71 West 23rd St., Suite 1600, New York, N.Y. 10010.

■ Career

Billings Hospital, Chicago, Ill., clinical secretary, 1953-56; elementary school teacher in Hazelcrest, Ill., 1956; Montgomery County Education Association, Rockville, Md., assistant executive secretary, 1958-59; National Education Association, Washington, D.C., editorial assistant with *NEA Journal,* 1959-60; full-time writer, 1960—. Active in civil rights and peace organizations. *Member:* Society of Children's Book Writers, Authors Guild, PEN, Children's Book Guild (Washington, D.C.; president, 1974-75, 1983-84).

■ Awards, Honors

Wrestle the Mountain was selected one of Child Study Association of America's Children's Books of the Year, 1971, *How Lazy Can You Get?,* 1979, and *The Agony of Alice,* 1986; Golden Kite Award for Nonfiction from the Society of Children's Book Writers, 1978, and Children's Choice from the International Reading Association and the Children's Book Council, 1979, both for *How I Came to Be a Writer.*

Children's Choice, 1980, for *How Lazy Can You Get?,* and 1986, for *The Agony of Alice;* Best Book for Young Adults from the Young Adult Services Division of the American Library Association, and Notable Children's Book in the Field of Social Studies from the National Council for Social Studies and the Children's Book Council, both 1982, and South Carolina Young Adult Book Award, 1985-86, all for *A String of Chances;* Child Study Award from the Bank Street College of Education, 1983, for *The Solomon System;*

Edgar Allan Poe Award from the Mystery Writers of America, 1985, for *Night Cry;* Notable Children's Book in the Field of Social Studies, 1985, for *The Dark of the Tunnel;* Best Book for Young Adults from the Young Adult Services Division of the American Library Association, 1986, for *The Keeper,* and *Unexpected Pleasures,* and 1987, for *The Year of the Gopher;* Creative Writing Fellowship Grant from the National Endowment for the Arts, 1987; Society of School Librarians International Book Award, 1988, for *Maudie in the Middle;* Best Young Adult Book of the Year from the

Michigan Library Association, 1988, for *The Year of the Gopher.*

■ **Writings**

The Galloping Goat and Other Stories, Abingdon, 1965.

Grasshoppers in the Soup: Short Stories for Teen-agers, Fortress, 1965.

Knee Deep in Ice Cream and Other Stories, Fortress, 1967.

What the Gulls Were Singing, Follett, 1967.

Jennifer Jean, the Cross-Eyed Queen, Lerner, 1967.

To Shake a Shadow, Abingdon, 1967.

The New Schoolmaster, Silver Burdett, 1967.

A New Year's Surprise, Silver Burdett, 1967.

When Rivers Meet, Friendship, 1968.

The Dark Side of the Moon (short stories), Fortress, 1969.

Meet Murdock, Follett, 1969.

To Make a Wee Moon (illustrated by Beth Krush and Joe Krush), Follett, 1969.

The Private I and Other Stories, Fortress, 1969.

Making It Happen, Follett, 1970.

Ships in the Night, Fortress, 1970.

Wrestle the Mountain (Junior Literary Guild selection), Follett, 1971.

No Easy Circle, Follett, 1972.

How to Find Your Wonderful Someone, How to Keep Him/Her If You Do, How to Survive If You Don't, Fortress, 1972.

To Walk the Sky Path (Weekly Reader Book Club selection), Follett, 1973.

An Amish Family (illustrated by George Armstrong), J. Philip O'Hara, 1974.

Witch's Sister (first volume of "Witch" trilogy; illustrated by Gail Owens), Atheneum, 1975.

Walking through the Dark (Junior Literary Guild selection), Atheneum, 1976.

Getting Along in Your Family (illustrated by Rick Cooley), Abingdon, 1976.

Witch Water (second volume of "Witch" trilogy; illustrated by G. Owens), Atheneum, 1977.

Crazy Love: An Autobiographical Account of Marriage and Madness (adult nonfiction; Literary Guild selection), Morrow, 1977.

The Witch Herself (third volume of "Witch" trilogy; illustrated by G. Owens), Atheneum, 1978.

How I Came to Be a Writer, Atheneum, 1978, revised edition, Aladdin Books, 1987.

How Lazy Can You Get? (Weekly Reader Book Club selection; illustrated by Alan Daniel), Atheneum, 1979.

In Small Doses (adult humorous essays), Atheneum, 1979.

Revelations (adult novel), St. Martin's, 1979.

A Change in the Wind, Augsburg Press, 1980.

Eddie, Incorporated (illustrated by Blanche Sims), Atheneum, 1980.

Shadows on the Wall (first volume of "York" trilogy), Atheneum, 1980.

Getting Along with Your Friends (illustrated by R. Cooley), Abingdon, 1980.

Getting Along with Your Teachers, Abingdon, 1981.

All Because I'm Older (illustrated by Leslie Morrill), Atheneum, 1981.

Faces in the Water (second volume in "York" trilogy), Atheneum, 1981.

Footprints at the Window (third volume of "York" trilogy), Atheneum, 1981.

The Boy with the Helium Head (illustrated by Kay Chorao), Atheneum, 1982.

A String of Chances (ALA Notable Book), Atheneum, 1982.

Never Born a Hero (short stories), Augsburg Press, 1982.

The Solomon System, Atheneum, 1983.

The Mad Gasser of Bessledorf Street, Atheneum, 1983.

A Triangle Has Four Sides: True-to-Life Stories Show How Teens Deal with Feelings and Problems, Augsburg Press, 1984.

Night Cry, Atheneum, 1984.

Old Sadie and the Christmas Bear (illustrated by Patricia Montgomery Newton), Atheneum, 1984.

The Dark of the Tunnel, Atheneum, 1985.

The Agony of Alice (ALA Notable Book), Atheneum, 1985.

The Keeper (ALA Notable Book; Junior Literary Guild selection), Atheneum, 1986.

Unexpected Pleasures (adult novel), Putnam, 1986.

The Bodies in the Bessledorf Hotel, Atheneum, 1986.

The Baby, the Bed, and the Rose (illustrated by Mary Szilagyi), Clarion, 1987.

The Year of the Gopher, Atheneum, 1987.

Beetles, Lightly Toasted, Atheneum, 1987.

One of the Third Grade Thonkers (illustrated by Walter Gaffney Kessell), Atheneum, 1988.

(With mother, Lura Schield Reynolds) *Maudie in the Middle* (illustrated by Judith Gwyn Brown), Atheneum, 1988.

Alice in Rapture, Sort Of, Atheneum, 1989.

Keeping a Christmas Secret (illustrated by Lena Shiffman), Atheneum, 1989.

The Craft of Writing the Novel (adult
  nonfiction), Writer, 1989.
Bernie and the Bessledorf Ghost, Atheneum,
  1990.
Send No Blessings, Atheneum, 1990.
The Witch's Eye (first volume in the second
  "Witch" trilogy), Delacorte, 1990.

■ Adaptations

"My Dad Can't Be Crazy...Can He?" (based
  on *The Keeper*), starring Loretta Swit, Don
  Murray, and Wil Wheaton, "Afterschool
  Special," ABC-TV, September 14, 1989.

■ Work In Progress

Shiloh, King of the Playground, and *Josie's Troubles,*
all for Atheneum; *Witch Weed,* the second volume
in the second "Witch" trilogy; *The Witch Returns,*
the third volume in the second "Witch" trilogy;
Body Parts, a suspense novel for adults; *Reluctantly
Alice,* the third book in the "Alice" series; *Carrying
On,* a novel for adults.

■ Sidelights

Phyllis Reynolds Naylor began her prolific writing
career at the age of sixteen with her first published
short story. For twenty-five years she maintained a
humorous church newspaper column for teenagers,
and for ten years, a similar one for adults. Both
were concerned with philosophical questions, family life, and human relationships. She has also
written sixty-seven books and published over two
thousand short stories and articles.

Her work appeals to all ages. She has written
children's picture books and novels, young adult
novels, teenage advice books and adult novels. She
has also written an autobiography that details the
tragedy of her first marriage to a paranoid schizophrenic man and a second autobiographical account of how she became a writer.

Born Phyllis Dean Reynolds on January 4, 1933, in
Anderson, Indiana. "Mine was the most ordinary
family in the entire Midwest. Whenever people
wrote about middle-class values, mores, income, or
politics, that was my family they were talking
about. A walking Norman Rockwell portfolio, that
was us. We were descended on both sides from a
long line of teachers, preachers, and farmers. My
father worked as a salesman for various companies,
beginning with H. J. Heinz in the Depression,
symbolized by a giant pickle. All through our
childhood he was so loyal that I didn't discover

Campbell's soups until I was married. As he
changed jobs, we changed houses, and by the time
I entered high school, we had lived in eight
different neighborhoods, stretching across Indiana,
Illinois, and Iowa. And that's where our personalities developed. Like the roads in Iowa as seen from
a plane, all coming together at perfect right angles,
the men and women of American Gothic lived their
lives square and true.

"We were raised not to think but to be sensitive to
what we suspected everybody else was thinking.
We were the original other-directed family, with
supple spines ready to bend at a moment's notice.
What will the doctor think if you cry (that it hurts,
maybe)? What will the teacher think if your knees
are dirty? What will Grandma think if she doesn't
hear from us soon? What will the minister think if
we're late again? What will the neighbors think if
they see you and Ted kissing on the porch?

"We became master detectives of everyone's feelings but our own. We watched facial expressions
for the slightest hint of disapproval. We knew what

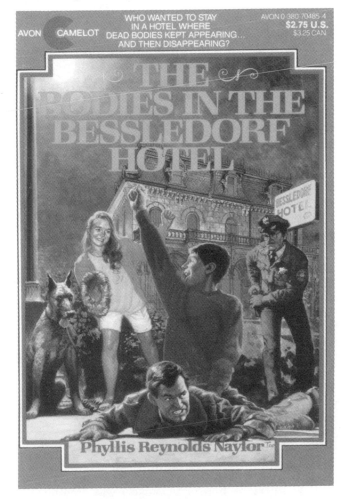

Cover from Naylor's comic murder mystery.

someone needed before he even asked. We were Pavlov's dogs, ready to snap to attention at the sound of the bell.

"As members of my mother's JOY club, which she organized for pre-teens, we bravely recited our slogan: '*Jesus* first, *Others* next, *Yourself* last.' We were always last. I grew up supremely confident of my own unimportance.

"The children thus raised in humility were consequently ravenous for praise and jealous of each other. We quarreled both openly and deviously for our parents' attention. Who does Daddy love most? Older sister? Younger sister? Little brother? None of the above. Daddy loves himself best.

"My father was the undisputed ruler of our home in things that mattered to him. If they did not matter, he left them to my mother. Perhaps the fact that the household revolved around him was not the result so much of male chauvinism as it was of the Depression. It was he, after all, whose salary determined where we lived and what we ate, and the income, in turn, depended entirely on whether he made a sale. Meals were scheduled at his convenience and were planned around his ulcer. An hour of quiet time was reserved each evening so that he could fill out his reports. His underwear and shirts were meticulously laundered, and when I was old enough to iron the handkerchief he wore in his breast pocket, I was told how important it was that the edges come together perfectly. Every potential customer, I was sure, accepted or declined on the basis of my father's pocket handkerchief, and ironing the edges gave me a feeling that I was doing my bit.

"My whole unverbalized hope in growing up was to match my sister's accomplishments and become as beloved as my brother. My sister made the honor roll, the madrigals, the operetta, and the senior play. I made the honor roll, the madrigals, the operetta, and the senior play. My sister took three years of art and painted in oils. I took three years of art and painted in oils. My sister talked the school into letting her drop home economics to take Latin instead. I went to the superintendent and asked to drop home economics and take Latin instead. (I have never yet met a person who greeted me with *Gallia est omnis divisa in partes tres*, but I have met several who wished I could cook.)

"I was never as pretty in my sister's hand-me-downs as she had been, and felt that I was destined forever to trying harder because I was Number 2. It never occurred to me that I had a choice, or that there were other things worth doing she might never have tried."[1]

"In those formative years...I frequently vacationed at either one of my grandparents' homes. If we drove west to Iowa, we drove through flat farmland. There was no way of telling Indiana from Illinois, or Illinois from Iowa. Peaceful horses and contented cows, endlessly chewing. When we got to the farm in Waverly, we would be met at the door by my maternal grandmother, who promptly fed us and put us to bed. Hugs were reserved for arrivals and departures, and in between was the practical no-nonsense business of the day to attend to, without emotion or fuss.

"This farm in Iowa was so remote from neighboring houses that we could see no other from the front steps. My world was bordered by cornfields and fences and by the one-room school, a mile away, where we traipsed when we stayed one winter. It formed the landscape for my book *To Make a Wee Moon.*

"Some summers, however, we did not go west for vacation, but headed east instead, where the land became mysterious and hilly about the time we reached Pittsburgh. From then on the terrain was rolling, the roads curving, and we would eagerly hang out the car windows, watching for the first sign of Maryland soil, each wanting to be the first child to screech, 'Purple dirt!'

"Again we arrived late in the evening and were fed and put to bed, but this was a different world from the one back in Iowa. My paternal grandparents, who insisted on being called Pappaw and Mammaw, had come up from Mississippi, and the humid, suffocating climate of inbred warmth and gossip had migrated north along wtih them. It was said that Pappaw's courtship of Mammaw began when he was a young boy and she just a baby. He would pick her up, carry her about in his arms, and announce proudly, 'This is the girl I'm going to marry.' And he did, when she was only fifteen. She was playing with her dolls right up to day of the wedding.

"In Iowa, by contrast, my maternal grandfather had started his courtship of my grandmother by sending her a formal letter, written painstakingly, with curled letters, on elegant stationery....A written invitation, two weeks in advance, to walk to church, with references provided!

"Although both sets of grandparents lived on farms, I was not isolated from other people on the one in Maryland. I found that I could walk almost anywhere I wanted to go—the one-room post office, the firehouse, a small grocery, the neighbors' house, or the church where my grandfather was pastor. For the first time in my life, I had a town I could encompass on foot, roads I could connect, faces that attached themselves to names I heard mentioned frequently over the supper table.

"My grandmother, the neighborhood midwife, knew almost everyone in Marbury, and claimed to have delivered most of its children. She knew the intimate secrets of innumerable families, and would talk about the marital problems of a young bride as readily as my grandmother back in Iowa might talk about house mice. On Sundays, my southern grandmother would pile us all in the car early and go traveling about the back roads of Charles County with a trunk full of donated clothes. At every home along her circuit, she would stop and see if the children were ready for Sunday School. If they were, they would climb aboard. If the excuse was no clothes to wear, Mammaw would simply open the trunk, find something the right size, and another child would be crammed in the backseat.

Cover of the 1983 paperback.

ALA's "Best Book for Young Adults."

"I never once thought of Maryland as my home, any more than I thought of all the other places we had lived as home but, quite without knowing it, I was soaking up the setting for future books.

"The idea of being a writer never entered my mind when I was growing up. An occupation, I knew, was something that took years of preparation and hard work, and writing was simply too much fun. So I decided to become a teacher, an actress, an opera singer, a tap dancer, or a missionary.

"My mother did not like the thought of my being an actress and told me I would probably faint under the bright lights. She also did not like the idea of my being a tap dancer, so I was never allowed to take lessons. Missionaries, as everyone knew, were sometimes eaten alive, so that left teaching and opera singing. Writing, which was the thing I loved most in the world, was only my hobby.

"My parents had always liked books, and they knew a good story when they heard one....So when we three children came along, we were born into a home that loved stories.

"When I arrived, the Depression was raging, but the picture of me in my baby book, dressed in hand-me-down clothes and shoes that were much too large, has this caption in my mother's handwriting: 'Phyllis Dean, a bright, happy little soul.' The truth is, I was too young to mind being poor. I remember the two checked dresses I wore to kindergarten, one red, the other blue, and Mother telling me that if I alternated colors, it would seem as though I had more clothes than I did. I simply thought how clever of Mother this was.

"And when Mother had to take in the neighbors' laundry in order to help pay our bills, and it was my duty and my sister's to return the finished clothes in a basket, I do remember Norma insisting that we take them back after dark, which I thought ridiculous, since I wasn't afraid of being seen, but I *was* afraid of the dark.

"One of the reasons I didn't know we were poor, however, was that we had books. Not many, but we heard them read over and over again—*Egermeier's Bible Story Book*, two volumes of *Grimm's Fairy Tales*, the complete works of Mark Twain, a set of *Collier's Encyclopedia*, a small collection of Sherlock Holmes books in red covers that the mice had nibbled, and a book with pictures of hell in it— demons cutting people in half and dousing their heads in boiling oil. I don't know what happened to that book, but I was glad when it disappeared.

"As we grew older, our book collection got bigger, and Mother often brought home books from the library. She read to us every night, almost until we were old enough to go out on dates, though we would never have admitted this to anyone.

"Our parents often sang to us, too, and many of their songs were really stories: 'The Preacher and the Bear,' another about a ship going down at sea, and even one about a homeless little girl whose mother was dead.

"Some of the best nights were the ones when my father did the reading. He could imitate all kinds of voices—the runaway Jim's in *Huckleberry Finn*, Injun Joe's in *Tom Sawyer*, and Marley's ghost in *A Christmas Carol*. And when Mother read 'Little Orphant Annie' from James Whitcomb Riley's *Child-Rhymes*, ending with 'Er the Gobble-uns'll git you/If you Don't Watch Out' (at which point she grabbed us), our hearts pounded. We worshiped those books that had the power to make us

shiver. I was never very curious about the authors, though. It was the *story* that was important."[2]

As soon as Naylor began school, she began writing her own stories. "My mother...saved the first one I brought home, probably in case I should ever need to show it to a psychiatrist:

"'Once upon a time there was a little boy and a little girl who lived in the woods with their mother. One day the little boy said, "Mother, I want an apple." The mother said, "Okay." The boy reached into the box and the mother closed the lid on him and cut off his head and set him out in the yard and tied a rag around his neck to keep his head on. The little girl came home. She cried a lot. She sneaked out and pasted his head back on with magic paste. Then she put her brother in her boy friend's house. She grew up and married her boy friend. The mother died. The end.'

"This story, I discovered years later, sounds suspiciously like 'The Juniper Tree,' by the Brothers Grimm, so not only was my first writing effort gory, it was plagiarism at that."[2]

Naylor became known in school for her writing talent. "I began to be 'on call' as an impromptu writer. In fifth grade, the teachers suddenly decided to throw a surprise party for the principal, and I was asked if I would mind staying in during recess to compose a birthday poem. I could write one in twenty minutes, couldn't I? Twenty minutes and one stomachache later, I had produced eight lines that were read over the microphone in the assembly room.

"I was now writing little books of my own. Each day I would rush home from school to see if the wastebasket held any discarded paper that had one side blank. We were not allowed to use new sheets of paper for our writing and drawing, so books had to be done on used paper. I would staple these sheets together and sometimes paste a strip of colored paper over the staples to give it the appearance of a bound book. Then I would grandly begin my story, writing the words at the top of each page and drawing an accompanying picture on the bottom. Sometimes I typed the story before stapling the pages. And sometimes I even cut old envelopes in half and pasted them on the inside covers as pockets, slipping an index card in each one, like a library book, so I could check it out to friends and neighbors. I was the author, illustrator, printer, binder, and librarian, all in one.

"I wrote about witches and little Dutch boys and animated fire engines. I wrote a series of mystery

The *ABC Afterschool Special* "My Dad Can't Be Crazy...Can He?" starred Loretta Swit and Don Murray, and was broadcast on September 14, 1989.

books about a gorgeous girl named Penny who was always being rescued by her boyfriend, and, because I had just learned to draw lace, somewhere in every 'Penny' book, my heroine lost her clothes just so I could draw her lacy underthings. I wrote of elves and fairies and talking refrigerators, and when my mother explained the facts of life to me, I even wrote a book called *Manual for Pregnant Women,* with illustrations by the author.

"But I never considered myself 'bookish.' There seemed to be something decidedly unhealthy about people who sat around in garrets fiddling with words instead of going out and living life in the flesh. I liked to make all kinds of things, not just books. I enjoyed having a finished product when I was through, whether it was a pot holder, a wagon, a house made of clay, or a poem. Summers were spent snitching ice off the back of the ice truck, sliding down a grassy hill on pieces of cardboard, building a clubhouse out of old coffin crates, and creating our own Tarzan movies by leaping off fences and walls. Reading was reserved for bedtime.

"When I reached junior high school, I enjoyed writing stories more than ever, but friends were important, too. Sometimes in the evenings, when I heard them calling out to me from the porch, I'd be torn between wanting to stay in my room and write and wanting to be with them. That was why I liked rainy nights and snowy weekends, when I knew that no one would be going out and I could write undisturbed."[2]

About this time, Naylor began going to revival meetings, a subject she later explored in several of her books. "We grew up in a very religious household, but we lived next door to a pentacostal family and every Sunday evening, their boys would climb up in our maple tree to avoid going to church, and their mother would come over with a clothes pole and poke at them. And they would climb higher and she would finally say to me and my sister 'Do you want to go?' And I would always say 'yes' because it was like a whole new world. We would go in this saw dust-filled tent where I had not been before and it was like a show in a way, a solemn show, and we would go down to repent, row by row. It was the drama of it, and the tears of it.

"I repented every single night, I was only nine or ten, and I would go through the tears and I was just absolutely fascinated with the songs that they sang...and everybody would get up and go down, knowing I was taking the place of the neighbor boys who for all I knew were still up in the maple tree.

"My mother didn't care whether I went....But she didn't entirely agree with this fundamentalist, so I was just sort of free to make up my own mind about it."[3]

By the time she reached high school, Naylor had published her first story. "When I was sixteen, a former Sunday School teacher, Arlene Stevens Hall, wrote to me. She said that she was now the editor of a church school paper, that she remembered how much I liked stories, and wondered if I would care to write one for her.

"I was delighted and began thinking about what I would write. I remembered reading something in the newspaper about a baseball player who lost some fingers on his right hand, and this gave me the idea for 'Mike's Hero,' a baseball story. I typed it up and sent it off.

"Because church school papers paid so little, they were always looking for material, and a few weeks later, I received a check for $4.67. I was thrilled. Imagine being paid for something that was so much fun! Where was the work? Where was the struggle? The words came effortlessly, and I simply wrote them down! What a life!

"Send me more, my teacher-turned-editor said. So I wrote all kinds of stories and poems and sent them off: poems for Halloween, Thanksgiving, and Christmas; adventure stories of dramatic rescue; tales of contests won and contests lost; and epics about unkind children who saw the error of their ways. Most of these stories were accepted, and when editing was needed, my kind teacher did it herself. Her criticisms were always gentle and accompanied by encouraging words.

"Why, I began to wonder, should I waste my talent on a church school paper when there were dozens and dozens of beautiful slick magazines out there just calling me? Why not write for *Children's Playmate, Jack and Jill, Highlights for Children, Boy's Life,* and *Seventeen?*

"I spent hours writing up stories with cute titles bound to win an editor's heart: 'Mrs. Wiggins' Walrus,' 'Willie, the Window Glass,' 'Snipper McSnean and His Flying Machine,' 'Barnabas, the Beagle,' 'Danny, the Drainpipe,' and 'Miranda, the Musical Mouse.' Then I wrote another batch of exotic stories for teenagers: 'The Cobra and Carol,' 'The Silent Treatment,' 'The Red Comb,' and 'Destination, Trouble.' I typed them neatly and sent them off with stamped, self-addressed return envelopes to magazines all over the country. Then I sat back and waited for the money to roll in.

"The first thing I discovered was that unknown editors did not reply as promptly as my loving former teacher. Weeks went by, sometimes months, before I began to hear from any of them.

"The second thing I discovered was that the stories came back with printed rejection slips, not page-long letters of apology with encouragement to try again.

"And the third thing I discovered was that all those big, beautiful magazines had been calling to someone else, not to me, because every story winged its way home. For two whole years I sent out stories, and for two years every single one of them came back.

"My dreams of fame and fortune had vanished along with all the money I had spent on stamps and envelopes over the last two years; they were replaced with a new respect for the business of writing. I merely had one toe in the door, I knew, and had not even begun to climb the stairs."[2]

Eventually, Naylor began a weekly column for a church story paper. "I decided to try a humor column for teenagers, which I'd write from the viewpoint of a fifteen-year-old boy. (I was afraid that if I wrote it from a girl's point of view, boys would never read it.) I took the pseudonym P. R. Tedesco and called the series 'First Person Singular.'

"The column lasted twenty-five years and appeared in a number of church magazines across the country. Readers wrote that they always looked forward to finding the column on the last page of their church school paper."[2]

In 1951 at the age of eighteen, she married a brilliant young man from her home town who was eight years older than she. She enrolled at Joliet Junior College and tried to be a model wife. "After graduation, I moved to Chicago with my husband, where he continued work on his Ph.D. While he was in school, I worked for several years as a clinical secretary in the university hospital. Then, because I had passed a state examination, I worked for six months as a third-grade teacher. My husband suggested books I might like to read, and I read most of the ones in his collection.

"My private education began with Thackeray's *Vanity Fair*, followed by several books by Dickens. There was *War and Peace* and the plays of Shakespeare, the collected works of Sigmund Freud, and *The Canterbury Tales* by Chaucer. We would read to each other from Balzac, Samuel Butler, or George Santayana.

"For several months I put myself on a steady diet of nineteenth-century novels by Dostoevski, Flaubert, Tolstoy, and Zola. Then I read more modern books by Sinclair Lewis, Upton Sinclair, John Steinbeck, and William Faulkner. Because these weren't school assignments, I could fling myself into the books, not having to worry about outlines and summaries and underlining the major themes. I could even read the last chapter first, if I wanted. But always, when I wasn't working and wasn't reading, I wrote.

"When I was twenty-three years old, something happened that was so sad and terrifying that many years passed before I was able to write about it at all. One day, while we were living in Chicago, my husband suddenly showed signs of severe mental

Paperback edition of the 1982 multi-award winner.

illness; he believed that the professors at the University were trying to kill him. For the next three years, while we moved from state to state, hospital to hospital, I wrote in earnest and in panic to support us. Sometimes I would take a whole afternoon and go off to a remote spot just to brainstorm—writing down ideas however they occurred to me until finally I had a list of plots to see me through the next few months.

"Not all of the ideas were workable, of course, but I was able to use enough of them to pay the rent and buy our food."[2]

"It's still very sad to me, but it also made me think, you know, I'm really stronger than I thought. There were times I thought 'I can't go through this, I can't even write a check. How can I go through this?' And yet I did. And sometimes when I'm facing something difficult I have to say to myself 'Hey, I went through that, I can go through this.' And so, there is something to be said for weathering storms and becoming stronger."[3]

It became evident that her husband required hospitalization and she took him to an exclusive sanitarium in Maryland that had been recommended by his doctor. His father agreed to pay half of the cost, but she was responsible for the rest, and consequently incurred a large debt for his treatment. For a while she lived near him, across the street from the sanitarium. "I discovered I was not really much good for anything. I couldn't teach in the county without a degree. I couldn't even substitute. I did not qualify as a secretary, accountant, nurse, beautician, or cab driver. Who would want a soft-spoken, anxiety-ridden young woman with a ten-thousand-dollar debt over her head, whose husband might, at any moment, hang himself? Who wanted an employee whose sole ability, it seemed, was writing weird little stories for magazines no one had ever heard of?

"I was hired finally by the psychology office in the Board of Education to type up clinical reports. The salary was laughable, but I was desperate."[1]

Eventually she found another job, spending 1958-1959 working for the Montgomery County Education Association. After eight years of marriage it was obvious that her husband would not recover, and she decided to divorce him. "I would immerse myself in my work, I decided. I would read the hundreds of books I had never had time to read, learn to love Shostakovich, make pottery, write a novel, sing, take a course in Chinese cuisine, travel, get a job in clinical psychology, finish my own psychoanalysis, and keep perpetually busy. And then I fell in love.

"Just when I had convinced myself that my career was all-important and I could adjust to the role of the single woman, I met a man who was intelligent, gentle, concerned.

"Panic set in. I began looking over law books to learn about the possibilities for divorce in various states. What I discovered, in this era before the no-fault divorce laws, was that insanity was grounds for divorce only under the most rigid conditions. In almost every state, the psychotic spouse must have been insane for a prescribed number of years, usually five, the years must have been consecutive, the spouse must have been confined during that time to an institution, and three doctors must have declared the person incurable.

"What would the judge say about a spouse who functioned reasonably well one week but went bananas another? What about a spouse who was in and out of hospitals at six-month intervals, or who was confined to an institution for four years and eleven months but was no better off when he left than when he entered? And where on earth would a lawyer find three psychiatrists—or two—or even one—who would pronounce a case incurable and hence rob that patient of hope? I was upset and anxious in the months that followed, and yet my marvelous friend was patient, and listened with amused tolerance to my elaborate plan to move to the Virgin Islands where one of the grounds for divorce was simply 'insanity occurring after marriage.'

During 1959-1960, Naylor commuted to Washington, D.C., to work as an editorial assistant at the *NEA Journal*. She was finally able to obtain a divorce. "After our divorce, I went back to college again for my bachelor's degree, studying to be a clinical psychologist. I was able to pay a large share of the tuition by writing and selling stories."[2]

On May 26, 1960, she married her "marvelous friend," Dr. Rex V. Naylor, a speech pathologist, and three years later graduated with a B.A. in clinical psychology from American University. "Finally, when I got the degree, I realized that I could never be satisfied unless I wrote full-time, so I gave up plans to go to graduate school and began writing five or six hours a day.

"After I married again and became a mother, I began another column about family life, called 'The Last Stanza,' for the adult church magazines. When I first started writing it, I discovered that

Naylor's 1987 novel about mental illness.

using the real names of my husband and children seemed to limit what I could say. I kept wondering if my family would be offended when I poked fun at them, so it was impossible to let my imagination run loose. I solved the problem by changing all our names except my own. My husband, Rex, became Ralph in the series, Jeff became Jack, Michael became Peter, and I invented an imaginary daughter named Susan to round out the family."[2]

In 1965 her first book was published. "One reason that writing a book frightened me was that I thought I would be bored with it long before I was through. I thought that all books took at least a year or two to write, and if they did not, they weren't any good. What if I spent two years on a book that never sold? What if halfway through I discovered that I simply could not stand the people I was writing about?

"Consequently, my first attempt at a book. . .was simply a collection of some of my short stories which had already been published in magazines. It was a safe investment of time. All I had to do was choose the ones I wanted to include and type them up in book form. The first publisher to whom I sent it accepted—miraculously—and the following year *The Galloping Goat and Other Stories* was published by Abingdon Press."[2]

Naylor's first novel for children, *What the Gulls Were Singing* was published in 1967. After that "I began writing one or two books a year. Some, such as *Wrestle the Mountain*, about a coal-mining family in West Virginia, or *To Walk the Sky Path*, about a Seminole Indian boy in Florida, took most of a year because they required a great deal of research, including travel to both these regions. Others, such as *Making It Happen* and *No Easy Circle*, both about teenagers who ran away, were so well formed in my mind when I started to write that they were completed within a few months."[2]

Naylor and her husband settled in Bethesda, Maryland and she was able to return often to her

Jacket from Atheneum's 1987 novel.

grandparents' home. "I went back occasionally to Marbury—sometimes just to visit, then to bury Pappaw, and finally to bury Mammaw. It wasn't until years later, on another nostalgic drive back, that I decided to place my next book there, a novel for adults called *Revelations*.

"By the time I placed a second novel, *A String of Chances*, in Marbury, and then a third, *Unexpected Pleasures*, I realized that this small southern Maryland town had worked its way into my blood."[2]

In 1977 Naylor published *Crazy Love: An Autobiographical Account of Marriage and Madness*, about her first marriage. "I knew that was a good story, beginning with the first insinuations that something was wrong and going through all the hell that you go through living with a paranoid schizophrenic....The big problem was how to write this without making it sound like violins were in the background, and had I written it before I'm sure it would have been a horrible book....I was so wrapped up in my own pain and the horror of what was happening to me that I think that's all that would have come out and it would have read like a soap opera.

"But when you get fifteen years down the road and you look back, there were funny parts of it. They weren't at the time, but there were things that he did which you could just sit back and laugh and say 'My god, that must have looked ridiculous, or what on earth did that salesclerk at Sears think?' And so those were in the book in a sort of sardonic way to give me relief as the writer and give the reader relief from this heavy, heavy material.

"I've heard from so many people that this was what they appreciated most, that trace of humor throughout that let them take a breath and think, well, we got a page of respite here....And I guess that made it a better book.

"I probably got more fan mail for *Crazy Love* than any other book I wrote....And I began to think, hey, if I couldn't cope with this so well as a twenty-three-year-old woman, how would a thirteen-year-old boy handle it? And, of course, that's how fiction begins: 'What if, what if?' And there was another book. I was glad I could do that because I think that speaks to young people."[3]

The second book on the subject was *The Keeper*, published in 1986, about a young boy whose father becomes paranoid schizophrenic. With the publication of *Crazy Love*, Naylor decided she needed an agent. "I published my first few children's books without an agent, quite a few in fact, though

when I wrote *Crazy Love* it was so much a part of me that I felt I just couldn't take it emotionally, sending myself out like that. A rejection of *Crazy Love* would be a rejection of me and my life, not just my writing, and it was just too embarrassing. I don't usually get that sensitive with writing but it just seemed too painful."[3]

"Most writers will agree that beginnings are perhaps the most important, and that beginning the beginning is the most difficult. Some say that theme or plot comes first, and that the characters follow. Others never start the actual writing until each character has developed an identity of his own. I usually begin a new book neither with theme nor characters, but with a mood, and this is difficult to define.

"Mood takes a lot of little details, blends them into a sauce, and pours it over the whole book, chapter by chapter, scene by scene, imparting its own special flavor.

"Mood depends partly on the plot, partly on the characters, partly on style—and on whether the story will be told in the first person, in flashbacks, or how. It is the overwhelming, atmosphere of the novel, and I never begin a book until I feel a tremendous sense of anticipation."[4]

Naylor dislikes doing research, but she does keep notebooks and files of information. "I have a notebook divided into sections—conversations—somebody says something and I rush home or I copy it on the back of a grocery receipt....Whenever I take a trip, I'm always eavesdropping and you hear such marvelous things and you wish that you could hear the whole conversation. I sometimes keep moving back, back, in a dining car so I can hear this marvelous conversation in bits and pieces."[3]

Currently, Naylor is involved with several writers' groups. "I live near Washington, D.C., and there's one of the largest groups of children's book writers in the country there. We meet once a month and share a lot of ideas. We're all published writers and illustrators.

"And then I meet once a week with a very small group of published writers who read their works aloud that are in progress. And this is very personal, very intimate, very emotionally charged, but very valuable. I love it. They're a great help because you can see your mistakes as you're doing them. I always have a book done before I read it to them, but it's still good to hear your own voice reading your work aloud and hearing their input immediately afterwards."[3]

Occasionally Naylor has aroused controversy. "I know that there are school systems that think some of my books have too much profanity in them. On *String of Chances,* a parent wrote to his school district and to all the members of the school board and the library and the superintendent of schools and demanded that *String of Chances* be taken off the shelf. But it was not for those things, it was for the religious question. He said that Evie Hutchins begins questioning her parents' religion and he waited. . .for her to return to the fold, and when she didn't he said that it promoted paganism and exposed his Christian children to ridicule.

"The library wrote to me and said that a committee had been formed. . . .The upshot was that the parent decided not to wait for the library's decision and he took the book off the shelf himself, refused to give it back and withdrew his children from the school.

"I suppose the biggest problem with this life, which I love very much, is balancing my personal needs with my family, with my husband, with my children. Truthfully, I would probably rather write than any other extra curricular activity that I can think of. But there are times. . .with a book when you don't know if you really have a book. . . .Until you get to that place, it's always on your mind, you're always upset. It's like a bank balance that never balances; your checkbook is always off. You're thinking about it all the time. . . .And you're thinking 'What kind of life is this? Am I living more in my characters? Am I running away from life?' Flannery O'Connor says no, that the writer is rushing headlong into life, they're investigating life. They're living life more than anybody else. But it's just very hard for me.

"I write to work out my own problems. I really don't write to teach. . . .I write about something that is bothering me and work it through. It's therapeutic, it really is. I write to find out where my strengths are, if I could cope with this, sort of rehearsing things so if it ever happens to me maybe I'll be stronger."[3]

"I can never imagine myself writing only for children or only for adults. I like to follow up a mystery story for the nine-to-twelve set with a contemporary novel for adults; after that perhaps I will do a picture book, or a realistic novel for teens, or possibly a humorous book for children. The marvelous thing about writing is that I may play the part of so many different people—an old grandmother on one page, a young boy the next; a middle-aged man or a girl of fifteen. I feel most whole when I can look at a scene through the eyes of several different people. My biggest problem is that there are always four or five books waiting in the wings. Scarcely am I halfway through one book than another begins to intrude. I'm happy, of course, that ideas come so easily, but it is like having a monkey on my back. I am never quite free of it. Almost everything that happens to me or to the people I know ends up in a book at some time, all mixed up, of course, with imaginings. I can't think of anything else in the world I would rather do than write."[5]

Footnote Sources:

[1] Phyllis Naylor, *Crazy Love: An Autobiographical Account of Marriage and Madness,* Morrow, 1977.
[2] P. R. Naylor, *How I Came to Be a Writer,* Macmillan, 1978.
[3] Kay Bonetti, "Interview with Phyllis Naylor," American Audio Prose Library, February, 1987.
[4] P. R. Naylor, "Mood Plot and Theme," *Writer,* March, 1986.
[5] *Contemporary Authors New Revision Series,* Volume 8, Gale, 1983.

■ For More Information See

Lion and the Unicorn, fall, 1977 (p. 111ff).
New York Times Book Review, December 2, 1979, November 2, 1986.
Martha E. Ward and Dorothy A. Marquardt, *Authors of Books for Young People,* supplement to the 2nd edition, Scarecrow, 1979.
Washington Post Book World, September 12, 1982, November 6, 1983, November 8, 1983, June 9, 1985, March 9, 1986, May 11, 1986, November 25, 1986, December 14, 1986 (p. 8), May 10, 1987.
Voice of Youth Advocates, April, 1983 (p. 40), August, 1985 (p. 188), June, 1987 (p. 81).
Chicago Tribune Book World, March 2, 1986.
Los Angeles Times, November 1, 1986.
Children's Literature Review, Volume 17, Gale, 1989.

Jane Yolen

Born February 11, 1939, in New York, N.Y.; daughter of Will Hyatt (author and in public relations) and Isabelle (Berlin) Yolen; married David W. Stemple (a professor of computer science), September 2, 1962; children: Heidi Elisabet, Adam Douglas, Jason Frederic. *Education:* Smith College, B.A., 1960; University of Massachusetts, M.Ed., 1976. *Politics:* Liberal Democrat. *Religion:* Jewish-Quaker. *Home and office:* Phoenix Farm, 31 School St., Box 27, Hatfield, Mass. 01038. *Agent:* Marilyn Marlow, Curtis Brown Ltd., 10 Astor Place, New York, N.Y. 10003.

■ Career

Saturday Review, New York, N.Y., production assistant, 1960-61; Gold Medal Books (publishers), New York, N.Y., assistant editor, 1961-62; Rutledge Books (publishers), New York, N.Y., associate editor, 1962-63; Alfred A. Knopf, Inc. (publishers), New York, N.Y., assistant juvenile editor, 1963-65; full-time professional writer, 1965—; teacher of writing, lecturer, 1966—. Chairman of board of library trustees, Hatfield, Mass., 1976-83; member of Arts Council, Hatfield, Mass. *Member:* Society of Children's Book Writers, Science-Fic-

tion Writers of America (president, 1986-88), Bay State Writers Guild, Children's Literature Association, Science Fiction Poetry Association, National Association for the Preservation and Perpetuation of Storytelling, Women's Popular Fiction Writers Network, Western New England Storyteller's Guild, International Kitefliers Association, Smith College Alumnae Association.

■ Awards, Honors

Boys' Club of America Junior Book Award, 1968, for *The Minstrel and the Mountain;* Lewis Carroll Shelf Award, 1968, for *The Emperor and the Kite,* and 1973, for *The Girl Who Loved the Wind; The Emperor and the Kite* was selected one of *New York Times* Best Books of the Year, and Caldecott Honor Book, both 1968; Chandler Book Talk Reward of Merit, 1970; *The Girl Who Loved the Wind* was selected for the Children's Book Showcase of the Children's Book Council, 1973, and *The Little Spotted Fish,* 1976; Golden Kite Award from the Society of Children's Book Writers, 1974, and National Book Award nomination, 1975, both for *The Girl Who Cried Flowers and Other Tales;* Golden Kite Honor Book, 1975, for *The Transfigured Hart,* and 1976, for *The Moon Ribbon and Other Tales;* Christopher Medal, 1978, for *The Seeing Stick.*

Children's Choice from the International Reading Association and the Children's Book Council, 1980, for *Mice on Ice,* and 1983, for *Dragon's Blood;* Honorary L.L.D. from College of Our Lady of the Elm, 1981; Parents' Choice Award from the

Parents' Choice Foundation, 1982, for *Dragon's Blood*, 1984, for *The Stone Silenus*, and 1989, for *Piggins*, and *The Three Bears Rhyme Book; The Gift of Sarah Barker* was selected one of *School Library Journal*'s Best Books for Young Adults, 1982, and *Heart's Blood*, 1985; Garden State Children's Book Award from the New Jersey Library Association, 1983, for *Commander Toad in Space*; Acton Public Library's CRABerry Award (Md.), 1983, for *Dragon's Blood; Heart's Blood* was selected one of American Library Association's Best Books for Young Adults, 1984.

Daedelus Award, 1986, for "a body of work—fantasy and short fiction"; *The Lullaby Songbook* and *The Sleeping Beauty* were each selected one of Child Study Association of America's Children's Books of the Year, 1987; World Fantasy Award, 1988, for *Favorite Folktales from around the World*; Kerlan Award for "singular achievements in the creation of children's literature," 1988; Parents' Choice Silver Seal Award, Jewish Book Council Award, and the Association of Jewish Libraries Award, all 1988, all for *The Devil's Arithmetic*; Golden Sower Award from the Nebraska Library Association, 1989, for *Piggins*.

■ Writings

Young Adult Fiction:

(Editor) *Shape Shifters: Fantasy and Science-Fiction Tales about Humans Who Can Change Their Shape*, Seabury, 1978.
The Gift of Sarah Barker, Viking, 1981.
Dragon's Blood: A Fantasy, Delacorte, 1982.
Neptune Rising: Songs and Tales of the Undersea Folk (story collection; illustrated by D. Wiesner), Philomel, 1982.
Heart's Blood, Delacorte, 1984.
The Stone Silenus, Philomel, 1984.
Commander Toad and the Dis-Asteroid (Junior Literary Guild selection; illustrated by B. Degen), Coward, 1985.
(Editor with others) *Dragons and Dreams: A Collection of New Fantasy and Science-Fiction Stories*, Harper, 1986.
Children of the Wolf, Viking, 1986.
Spaceships and Spells, Harper, 1987.
A Sending of Dragons (illustrated by Tom McKeveny), Delacorte, 1987.
The Devil's Arithmetic, Viking, 1988.
(Editor with Martin H. Greenberg) Werewolves: A Collection of Original Stories, Harper, 1988.

The Faery Flag: Stories and Poems of Fantasy and the Supernatural, Orchard Books, 1989.
(Editor with Martin H. Greenberg) *Things That Go Bump in the Night*, Harper, 1989.
(Editor) *2040 AD* (science-fiction anthology), Delacorte, 1990.

Adult Fiction:

Tales of Wonder (story collection), Schocken, 1983.
Cards of Grief (science-fiction), Ace Books, 1984.
Merlin's Booke, Steel Dragon Press, 1984.
Dragonfield and Other Stories (story collection), Ace Books, 1985.
(Editor) *Favorite Folktales from around the World*, Pantheon, 1988.
Sister Light, Sister Dark, Tor Books, 1988.
White Jenna, Tor Books, 1989.

Adult Nonfiction:

Writing Books for Children, Writer, 1973, revised edition, 1983.
Touch Magic: Fantasy, Faerie and Folklore in the Literature of Childhood, Philomel, 1981.
Guide to Writing for Children, Writer, 1989.

Juvenile Fiction:

The Witch Who Wasn't (illustrated by Arnold Roth), Macmillan, 1964.
Gwinellen, the Princess Who Could Not Sleep (illustrated by Ed Renfro), Macmillan, 1965.
(With Anne Huston) *Trust a City Kid* (illustrated by J. C. Kocsis), Lothrop, 1966.
The Emperor and the Kite (ALA Notable Book; illustrated by Ed Young), World Publishing, 1967, reissued, Philomel, 1988.
The Minstrel and the Mountain: A Tale of Peace (illustrated by Anne Rockwell), World Publishing, 1967.
"Robin Hood" (musical), first produced in Boston, Mass., 1967.
Isabel's Noel (illustrated by A. Roth), Funk, 1967.
Greyling: A Picture Story from the Islands of Shetland (Horn Book honor list; illustrated by William Stobbs), World Publishing, 1968.
The Longest Name on the Block (illustrated by Peter Madden), Funk, 1968.
The Wizard of Washington Square (illustrated by Ray Cruz), World Publishing, 1969.
The Inway Investigators; or, The Mystery at McCracken's Place (illustrated by Allan Eitzen), Seabury, 1969.

Hobo Toad and the Motorcycle Gang (illustrated by Emily McCully), World Publishing, 1970.

The Seventh Mandarin (Junior Literary Guild selection; illustrated by E. Young), Seabury, 1970.

The Bird of Time (illustrated by Mercer Mayer), Crowell, 1971.

The Girl Who Loved the Wind (illustrated by E. Young), Crowell, 1972.

(Editor)*Zoo 2000: Twelve Stories of Science Fiction and Fantasy Beasts*, Seabury, 1973.

The Girl Who Cried Flowers and Other Tales (ALA Notable Book; illustrated by David Palladini), Crowell, 1974.

The Boy Who Had Wings (illustrated by Helga Aichinger), Crowell, 1974.

The Adventures of Eeka Mouse (illustrated by Myra McKee), Xerox Education Publications, 1974.

The Magic Three of Solatia (illustrated by Julia Noonan), Crowell, 1974.

The Rainbow Rider (illustrated by Michael Foreman), Crowell, 1974.

The Little Spotted Fish (Junior Literary Guild selection; illustrated by Friso Henstra), Seabury, 1975.

The Transfigured Hart (illustrated by Donna Diamond), Crowell, 1975.

Milkweed Days (illustrated with photographs by Gabriel A. Cooney), Crowell, 1976.

The Moon Ribbon and Other Tales (illustrated by D. Palladini), Crowell, 1976.

The Seeing Stick (illustrated by Remy Charlip and Demetra Maraslis), Crowell, 1977.

The Sultan's Perfect Tree (illustrated by Barbara Garrison), Parents Magazine Press, 1977.

The Giants' Farm (*Weekly Reader* Book Club selection; illustrated by Tomie de Paola), Seabury, 1977.

The Hundredth Dove and Other Tales (illustrated by D. Palladini), Crowell, 1977.

The Lady and the Merman (adult; illustrated by Barry Moser), Pennyroyal, 1977.

Hannah Dreaming (illustrated with photographs by Alan R. Epstein), Museum of Fine Art (Springfield, Mass.), 1977.

Spider Jane (illustrated by Stefan Bernath), Coward, 1978.

The Simple Prince (illustrated by Jack Kent), Parents Magazine Press, 1978.

No Bath Tonight (Junior Literary Guild selection; illustrated by Nancy W. Parker), Crowell, 1978.

The Mermaid's Three Wisdoms (illustrated by Laura Rader), Collins, 1978.

Dream Weaver and Other Tales (illustrated by Michael Hague), Collins, 1979.

The Giants Go Camping (Junior Literary Guild selection; illustrated by T. de Paola), Seabury, 1979.

Commander Toad in Space (illustrated by B. Degen; Junior Literary Guild selection), Coward, 1980.

Spider Jane on the Move (illustrated by S. Bernath), Coward, 1980.

Mice on Ice (illustrated by Lawrence DiFiori), Dutton, 1980.

The Robot and Rebecca: The Mystery of the Code-Carrying Kids (illustrated by Jurg Obrist), Knopf, 1980, another edition (illustrated by Catherine Deeter), Random House, 1980.

Shirlick Holmes and the Case of the Wandering Wardrobe (illustrated by Anthony Rao), Coward, 1981.

The Robot and Rebecca and the Missing Owser (illustrated by Lady McCrady), Knopf, 1981.

The Acorn Quest (illustrated by Susanna Natti), Harper, 1981.

Brothers of the Wind (illustrated by Barbara Berger), Philomel, 1981.

Sleeping Ugly (Junior Literary Guild selection; illustrated by Diane Stanley), Coward, 1981.

The Boy Who Spoke Chimp (illustrated by David Wiesner), Knopf, 1981.

Uncle Lemon's Spring (illustrated by Glen Rounds), Dutton, 1981.

Commander Toad and the Planet of the Grapes (Junior Literary Guild selection; illustrated by B. Degen), Coward, 1982.

Commander Toad and the Big Black Hole (illustrated by B. Degen), Coward, 1983.

The Lullaby Songbook (musical arrangements by Adam Stemple; illustrated by Charles Mikolaycak), Harcourt, 1986.

Commander Toad and the Intergalactic Spy (Junior Literary Guild selection; illustrated by B. Degen), Coward, 1986.

Owl Moon (ALA Notable Book; illustrated by John Schoenherr), Philomel, 1987.

Commander Toad and the Space Pirates (illustrated by B. Degen), Putnam, 1987.

Piggins (Junior Literary Guild selection; illustrated by Jane Dyer), Harcourt, 1987.

(Reteller) *The Sleeping Beauty* (illustrated by Ruth Sanderson), Knopf, 1987.

Picnic with Piggins (illustrated by J. Dyer), Harcourt, 1988.

Piggins and the Royal Wedding (illustrated by J. Dyer), Harcourt, 1989.

Dove Isabeau (illustrated by Dennis Nolan), Harcourt, 1989.

Baby Bear's Bedtime Book (illustrated by J. Dyer), Harcourt, 1990.

Sky Dogs (illustrated by Barry Moser), Harcourt, 1990.

Tam Lin (illustrated by C. Mikolaycak), Harcourt, 1990.

The Dragon's Boy (novel), Harper, 1990.

Juvenile Nonfiction:

Pirates in Petticoats (illustrated by Leonard Vosburgh), McKay, 1963.

World on a String: The Story of Kites, World Publishing, 1968.

Friend: The Story of George Fox and the Quakers, Seabury, 1972.

(Editor with Barbara Green) *The Fireside Song Book of Birds and Beasts* (illustrated by Peter Parnall), Simon & Schuster, 1972.

The Wizard Islands (illustrated by Robert Quackenbush), Crowell, 1973.

Ring Out! A Book of Bells (Junior Literary Guild selection; illustrated by Richard Cuffari), Seabury, 1974.

Simple Gifts: The Story of the Shakers (illustrated by Betty Fraser), Viking, 1976.

(Compiler) *Rounds about Rounds* (illustrated by Gail Gibbons), F. Watts, 1977.

The Lap-Time Song and Play Book (musical arrangements by A. Stemple; illustrated by Margot Tomes), Harcourt, 1989.

Juvenile Poetry:

See This Little Line? (illustrated by Kathleen Elgin), McKay, 1963.

It All Depends (illustrated by Don Bolognese), Funk, 1970.

An Invitation to the Butterfly Ball: A Counting Rhyme (illustrated by Jane B. Zalben), Parents Magazine Press, 1976.

All in the Woodland Early: An ABC Book (Junior Literary Guild selection; illustrated by J. B. Zalben), Collins, 1979.

How Beastly! A Menagerie of Nonsense Poems (illustrated by James Marshall), Philomel, 1980.

Dragon Night and Other Lullabies (illustrated by Demi), Methuen, 1980.

Ring of Earth: A Child's Book of Seasons (illustrated by John Wallner), Harcourt, 1986.

The Three Bears Rhyme Book (illustrated by J. Dyer), Harcourt, 1987.

Best Witches: Poems for Halloween, (illustrated by Elise Primavera), Putnam, 1989.

Bird Watch (illustrated by Ted Lewin), Philomel, 1990.

Contributor:

Orson Scott Card, editor, *Dragons of Light*, Ace Books, 1981.

Terri Windling and Mark Alan Arnold, editors, *Elsewhere: Volume I*, Ace Books, 1981.

T. Windling and M. A. Arnold, editors, *Elsewhere: Volume II*, Ace Books, 1982.

Susan Schwartz, editor, *Hecate's Cauldron*, Daw Books, 1982.

Jessica Amanda Salmonson, editor, *Heroic Visions*, Ace Books, 1983.

T. Windling, editor, *Faery!*, Ace Books, 1985.

Will Shetterly and Emma Bull, editors, *Liavek*, Ace Books, 1985.

S. Schwartz, editor, *Moonsinger's Friends*, Bluejay, 1985.

Robin McKinley, editor, *Imaginary Lands*, Greenwillow, 1985.

Jack Zipes, *Don't Bet on the Prince: Contemporary Feminist Fairy Tales in North America and England*, Methuen, 1986.

W. Shetterly and E. Bull, editors, *Liavek: Players of Luck*, Ace Books, 1986.

W. Shetterly and E. Bull, editors, *Liavek: Wizard's Row*, Ace Books, 1987.

Donald R. Gallo, *Visions*, Delacorte, 1987.

W. Shetterly and E. Bull, editors, *Liavek: Spells of Binding*, Ace Books, 1988.

Parke Godwin, *Invitation to Camelot*, Ace Books, 1988.

Bruce Coville, *The Unicorn Treasury*, Doubleday, 1988.

Also author of *The Whitethorn Wood*, a chapbook. Author of column "Children's Bookfare," *Daily Hampshire Gazette*, 1970s. Contributor of articles, reviews, poems, and short stories to periodicals, including *Writer, Parabola, New York Times, Washington Post Book World, Los Angeles Times, Parents' Choice, New Advocate, Horn Book, Wilson Library Bulletin, Magazine of Fantasy and Science Fiction, Isaac Asimov's Science-Fiction Magazine,* and *Language Arts*. Some of Yolen's books have been published in England, France, Germany, Austria, Sweden, South Africa, Australia, Japan, Denmark, and Scandinavia. Member of editorial board, *Advocate* (now *New Advocate*), and *National Storytelling Journal*, until 1989.

■ Adaptations

"The Seventh Mandarin" (movie), Xerox Films, 1973.

"The Emperor and the Kite" (filmstrip with cassette), Listening Library, 1976.

"The Bird of Time" (play), first produced in Northampton, Mass., 1982.

"The Girl Who Cried Flowers and Other Tales" (cassette), Weston Woods, 1983.

"Dragon's Blood" (movie), CBS Storybreak, 1985.

"Commander Toad in Space" (cassette), Listening Library, 1986.

"Touch Magic...Pass It On" (cassette), Weston Woods, 1987.

"Owl Moon" (filmstrip with cassette), Weston Woods, 1988.

"Piggins and Picnic with Piggins" (cassette), Weston Woods, 1988.

■ Work In Progress

Elfabet ABC, a picture book, illustrated by Lauren Mill, and *Letting Swift River Go*, a picture book, illustrated by Barbara Cooney, both for Little Brown; *Greyling* to be reissued with new illustrations by David Ray, *Grandpa Bill's Song*, a rhymed picture book, editing an anthology, *Camelot!*, *The Seaman*, a picture book, and *Moon Songs*, poems illustrated by Ruth Councell, all for Philomel; *Briar Rose*, an adult novel, for Tor Books; *Dinosaur Dances*, poems, illustrated by Bruce Degen, for Putnam; *All Those Secrets of the World*, a picture book, illustrated by Leslie Baker; *Wings*, a picture book, illustrated by Denis Nolan, and *Encounter*, a picture book, both for Harcourt; *Merlin and the Dragons*, a book and video, and *Stories to Remember*, both for Dutton; editing an anthology with Martin H. Greenberg, *Mystery!*, for Delacorte; *Mouse's Birthday*, a picture book; with M. H. Greenberg editing an anthology, *Vampires*, for Harper; *The Traveler's Rose; Waves;* and *Wind.* Harcourt Brace Jovanovich plans to launch a Jane Yolen Book imprint in fall, 1990. Yolen will acquire and edit four to six books a year, including picture books and fantasy and science-fiction books for all ages.

■ Sidelights

Yolen is an American author of fiction, poetry, and plays for children and young adults, and a critic, essayist, and editor. Regarded as an outstanding prose stylist, she is perhaps best known for her literary folk and fairy tales. In these works Yolen combines familiar stories with modern twists or creates original stories which are reminiscent of the classic tales in structure and feeling. She often

The second, award-winning volume in the "Pit Dragon" trilogy.

writes metaphorically using symbols and allusions, and believes strongly in the value of folklore to shape one's awareness of language, art, and culture.

Yolen's work is characterized by a diversity of subject matter and style. She frequently writes tales of transformation, a beast becomes human or a human a beast, and stories about youthful detectives set in present and future times. While much of her writing utilizes wit and puns, the struggle between opposing moral forces displays itself in numerous folk tales and in works with a religious theme.

Yolen was born on February 11, 1939 in New York City into a family where reading and writing were considered valuable pursuits. "I remember practically nothing about my early childhood. Some of it was spent in New York City; about a year and a half was in California when my father was doing publicity for Warner Bros. We lived in a beautiful ranch house next door to Walter Brennan, the grizzled Western star. I have no memory of it. What I do remember, however, is the two years we lived with my Grandma Fanny and Grandpa Dan when my father was stationed in England during World War II. My father was head of the secret radio broadcasting to Europe, called **ABSIE.** So mother and [brother] Steve (who was only a baby) and I moved into the Hampton Roads house. The reason I recall that time so vividly was that my grandfather, whom I adored, died of a sudden and unexpected heart attack while we were there."[1]

The family returned to New York City when Yolen was ready for school. "I was in half a dozen schools by second grade, both public and private, as my mother looked for the best school for me. We lived on Central Park West, which was elegant, but on Ninety-seventh Street, which was not. The public school I was supposed to attend was dark, dirty, and to my mother's mind, totally inappropriate for me, so I was shifted from place to place. One time we even lied about where we lived to get into a better school, but I was too young to remember the pretend address, and so was found out. And kicked out.

"But I was also an early reader. When I read our semester's reading book overnight, the teacher had no alternative but to skip me into second grade. I spent the remainder of my elementary school days at PS 93 which is now only a parking lot on Ninety-third Street and Columbus Avenue. I walked to and from school with my best friend Diane Sheffield who lived in the apartment across the hall. She was skinny and blonde, I was plump and dark, but the boys seemed to pull my pigtails as often as hers. We were both tomboys, and we played rough-and-tumble games in the grass and rocks of Central Park.

"At PS 93 the teachers encouraged my reading and writing. I won gold stars and gold stars and more gold stars. I was the gold star star. And I was also pretty impossibly full of myself. In first or second grade I wrote the school musical, lyrics *and* music, in which everyone was some kind of vegetable. I played the lead carrot. Our finale was a salad. Another gold star."[1]

"When I was growing up, New York City was a much freer and more carefree place for a nine- and ten-year-old to roam in. I lived across the street from Central Park where I played alone or with friends. Now, I wouldn't even *walk* across the park alone; it has become very dangerous. The city has changed.

"When I wasn't in school or in ballet class (I studied at Balanchine's school for eight years, until I hit puberty), I played elaborate fantasy games in Central Park, such as Robin Hood and King Arthur, or I spent long hours traveling the subway which stopped right near my house. A nickel could buy hours of riding on the subway with changeovers. We'd all check the gum machines for pennies or dimes.

"We left New York City when I was thirteen and I did the rest of my growing up in Westport, Connecticut. Though we lived only an hour out of New York, we were focused on Westport which was, and still is, a very culturally exciting community. It was a hotbed of writers and artists, so I just assumed that when you grew up, you became a writer. For me that seemed a logical explanation for all the writers around."[2]

Yolen's father, besides being a champion kite flyer, was also a well-known author of books and radio scripts. Her mother wrote as well. "My mother was a not-very-successful short story writer. What she was successful at was making and creating crossword puzzles and acrostics. She would have graph paper and plot out the words and clues. She used to be able to do the *New York Times* Sunday crossword—in pen—in an hour! She had an incredible vocabulary. It wasn't a speaking vocabulary but, rather, a reading and crossword puzzle vocabulary. She spoke very well but I never heard enormous words in her everyday speech.

"I was very involved in high school as captain of the girls' basketball team, staff member of the newspaper, and member of the Jazz, Spanish, and Latin clubs. We had one of the best choirs in the country, touring and performing.

"I would often write my term papers in verse. I'm more at ease with verse than prose. It's a party trick."[2]

"My first best friend in Westport was Stella Colandrea who was Catholic. I had never really been close to anyone but Jews and Quakers before. But I began going to church—and Christmas Midnight Mass—with Stella who sang in the choir with the loveliest soprano voice I had ever heard. She had a wicked sense of humor, too. We used to do our homework on the roof of her porch, right outside her bedroom window, on warm evenings. We'd also make up naughty limericks about the boys in our class, being terrible flirts the both of us.

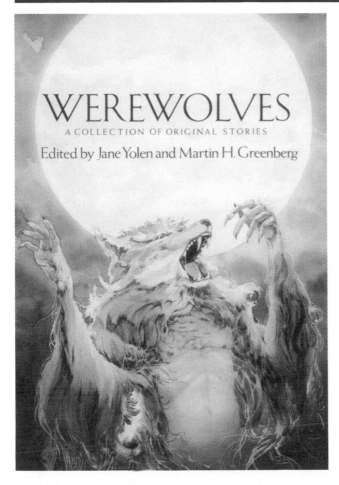

Jane Yolen examined werewolves through the eyes of fifteen writers.

Yolen co-edited this 1987 anthology of short stories.

It was because of Stella's influence that I became enamored of different religions. My own Judaism and camp-discovered Quakerism were the most morally appealing, but the panoply of Catholic rites seem to have taken hold of my imagination and wind in and out of many of the elaborate religious rituals I write about in my fantasy tales. And, since I am an Arthurian buff and a lover of things medieval, knowing a bit about the church helps. In *The Magic Three of Solatia*, the ceremony of Thrittem is a kind of bar mitzvah crossed with a silent Quaker meeting. In *Cards of Grief*, I worked in storytelling, seders, and the Mass, along with Communion, Confession, and the Viaticum.

"I was only marginally popular in high school, running around with two very different crowds: the intellectuals and the fast social crowd. I was a nondrinker and too slow for the latter, too fast and flirty and insubstantial for the former. I developed a wisecracking, cynical patter and an ability to tell funny stories which was, I think, why I was kept around in each.

"Later on in high school my two closest girlfriends were LeeAnn Walker and Mariette Hartley, the one an artist, the other an actress—the two careers I would have loved if I had not been a writer. Mariette and I especially have kept in touch over the years. I had her in mind to play the part of Sister Agatha in *The Gift of Sarah Barker*, writing the description to fit her. Unfortunately it has not been made into a movie.

"The greatest influence on me in high school was neither parents nor friends but my cousin-in-law Honey Knopp. A pacifist, a peace activist, who held hootenannies (music fests) at her home, Honey gave me my first copy of George Fox's *Journal*. (Fox was the founder of Quakerism and I wrote a biography of him, *Friend: The Story of George Fox and the Quakers*.) This secret, alien, meditative, poetic side I kept well hidden throughout much of high school except from Honey and some of the people I met at her house. This was in the mid-1950s, when to be interested in such things branded one an outsider, a beatnik, a left-winger. I adored Honey and her husband Burt, and their home became my haven. Oh, I still went to basketball games and dances and parties, wisecracking with my friends and being outrageous. But Honey called out another side of me. Her influence can be seen in many of my books: *The Minstrel and the Mountain, The Transfigured Hart, The Hundredth Dove, The Gift of Sarah Barker* among them. My poetry, much of which I shared only with Honey and my mother, was filled with the imagery of life/death, light/dark, and cadences of the folk songs I learned at the hoots.''[1]

From high school Yolen went to Smith College, an all-girls school in western Massachusetts, one of the famous Ivy League's sister schools. It had a profound effect on her development as a writer. "In college I started publishing in magazines and newspapers. Between junior and senior year, I had my first poem published in a 'real' poetry magazine.

"First I thought I'd be a journalist, but found out that I made up facts. When I had to interview poor people in terrible straits. I'd get so upset I'd start crying. I ended up writing stories off the top of my head, which these days could win you a Pulitzer Prize, but in those days was frowned upon if you wanted to be a journalist. It became clear that I was a fiction writer.

"I wrote a lot of poetry. At that time, I made a distinction between poetry and journalism. I didn't think the two could ever meet. I won all the poetry prizes at Smith as well as the journalism prize. I saw poetry and journalism as two very separate strands of my writing. Although both of them run very strongly within me, the poetry has really won out. When I write fantasy books, I like to think that I see my fantasy world with a journalist's eye, as well as a poet's eye. I know how the imaginary country runs, what the gross national product is, even if I don't write it down. That's where the journalist eye comes into my writing.

"My first adult fantasy book, *Cards of Grief*, was chosen for the Science Fiction Book Club, so I feel very good about it. It is a combination of science fiction and fantasy and is very poetic. It's about the life of art in a culture on a planet in which grieving is the highest art, and about the religion and the structure around which the entire society is ordered. Grieving really is an art form; perhaps *Cards of Grief* is my manifesto.''[2]

"My real life work began when I graduated, broke up with my fiance because—as I told him—'I have to find out if I can be a writer,' and moved to New York City for good. Or so I thought. I got...[a]

summer internship, this time with *This Week* magazine, on the strength of my scrapbook of bylined magazine and newspaper articles from such diverse places as the *Bridgeport Sunday Herald*, the *New Haven Register* (about Smith College activities), and *Popular Mechanics* (about kites). I stayed there until halfway through the fall, in the research department, mail room, and facts-checking department, and then all the editors returned from vacation and there was no room for me. Knowing that would probably happen, I had already lined up another job, with *Saturday Review*.

"At *SR*, I was in the production department, a job which meant I had to help lay out the magazine, as well as choose the cartoons and let the poetry editor know how much room we had for a poem. To my horror, poetry was seen as 'filler' material. We would need a three-inch poem, or a seven-inch poem. However, the production manager and I did not get along, and a few days before Christmas I was fired. In fact, I was the seventh person she had fired within two years, and I had already been warned by friends at *This Week* that life for the underlings at *SR* was usually short and not so sweet.

"I spent the first few months of 1961 trying to make a living as a free-lance writer. I researched and helped write a book for my father who had been asked to do *The Young Sportsman's Guide to Kite Flying*. Since he loved signing contracts, signing autographs, and countersigning checks, but not writing books, he hired me to put it together. And I loved—and still love—the writing part best of all. It was no hardship, but the pay was very low! With the help of my father's best friend, Will Oursler (author of *The Greatest Story Ever Told*), I also got a number of small free-lance assignments, including writing short, pithy bios for Cleveland Amory's *Celebrity Register*. My best line was about the then-Senator from Connecticut, Thomas Dodd, a silver-toned orator of the old school. I wrote that he 'had one of the finest voices to ever vox the populi.' That was my first in print pun. Later such things were to show up regularly in books like *The Witch Who Wasn't*, in short stories like 'The Five Points of Roguery' and 'Inn of the Demon Camel,' and in my 'Commander Toad' series.

"But the life of a free-lancer is long on searching and short on payment. I was literally living in a garret, a skylit studio apartment in the attic of a three-story house on Commerce Street in Greenwich Village, next to the Cherry Lane Theater. And I was beginning to write books.

"The Commerce Street garret was actually my second venture in living in the city. The first, a groundfloor 'shotgun' or 'railroad' apartment where the rooms are laid out all in a row and connected by sliding doors, had not been as successful. I lived there with two roommates, young women I had met that summer when I had been commuting from my parents' home in New Rochelle. One woman was to remain my roommate for another six months, the other (who was a friend of the singing group called The Clancy Brothers and Tommy Makem) lasted only two. The problem was partly the Clancys who used to spend a lot of time at our apartment with their friends and hangers-on (who were legion in those days), and partly the layout of the apartment. But that place was special for a different reason.

"Between the three roommates, we knew about half of the young artists, writers, musicians, and radical politicians in the Village the summer of 1960. We invited everyone we could think of to our housewarming party, and the Clancys brought even more. There were so many people coming in the front door of our ground-floor apartment, that one handsome moustached young man decided not to wait any longer and climbed through the window. He saw me standing in the crowd, my long dark braid over one shoulder, and came over, kissed me on the nape of the neck, and introduced himself.

"'I'm David Stemple,' he said, with a slow smile. 'I'm a friend of one of the girls who lives here.'

"'I'm Jane Yolen,' was my icy reply. 'And I'm one of those girls. You're not *my* friend!'"[1]

In 1962 Yolen married David Stemple, a photographer and computer expert. She also began writing children's books; *See This Little Line?*, a concept book in rhyme, appeared in 1963. "Literature should begin in the cradle. If we didn't have literature in childhood, we wouldn't have an adult literature or adult readers. The best readers are those who develop a love of reading early from the strong, beautiful, moving books of childhood.

"The only time I *don't* like to be identified as a 'children's writer' is when people try to put me in a box with, 'Oh, you write kids books. . . .' or 'Oh, you write science fiction,' or 'poetry' or 'fantasy.' I'm a storyteller. I tell a story, then someone else decides how it should be packaged—for children or adults. That is a blurry line in many of my works.

"It is very rewarding to read how my stories have affected readers. But I am very embarrassed when it happens in public because it puts emphasis on me, not the story. I'm a conduit for the story, but the reader invests that story with power. The story by itself has only the power that one allows it to have. A little boy once wrote me, 'Your stories will live forever. I hope you live to be 99 or 100, but who cares!' He was right. I think the problem, especially in this country, is that the storyteller, the writer, becomes more important than the writing itself. We have a 'cult' of the writer, just as we do for rock singers. Their followers shout and scream so loudly you can't hear the songs. That's ridiculous. I feel if one is not really listening, one is, in a sense, cursing the singer, denying his power.

"One of the problems people have with me is that they can't label me. Librarians sometimes say 'We don't know where to shelve you. . . .' That's not my problem. I just tell stories. I hope my stories amuse

The first volume of Yolen's trilogy about dragons.

and entertain and move people. But in truth, I'm just telling a story and what happens between the story and the listener is between the story and the listener.

"Many of my stories are about a girl trying to please her father. That's me. But my father didn't know. He really never read anything that I'd written. He was an international kite flying champion who singlehandedly created a renaissance for kites in this country. He'd written several books on kites as well as edited many others for the Overseas Press Club, of which he was president for a while. He was a journalist for a number of years and a public relations man. He knew the value of books and reading. He liked to tell people I'm a writer; he liked to see my books on display, but he never read them, because he felt they were not 'real' books because they were kids books. My brother on the other hand has been a journalist, an economic and political reporter about South America, and he was considered a 'real' writer by my father."[2]

About her writing technique, Yolen admits: "I have no idea where the first draft which comes pouring off my fingers comes from. I'm often surprised during the first draft, and think, 'Oh! Is *that* how the story ends!' But in revision I know that I have a hand in it. I tidy it up and I look for the right word and I rephrase. I truly enjoy that part. On a book or a story I might do up to twenty revisions—sometimes simply going through and polishing, sometimes tearing apart and putting back together again. I would say that each book I ever worked on has had at least three or four major revisions. I take things out, throw them away and re-shape. That comes from being a poet. I read everything aloud and when you read aloud you hear it again, the way you would a poem. People are amazed that someone as prolific as I am would be able to do that many revisions, but when I'm writing I am totally involved. There are times when I don't even hear the phone ring.

"I compose on the typewriter because I visualize better in print, but the revision process is both by hand and typewriter. We have a word processor— my husband is a computer scientist and my children all use it—but one of the things I have to do is run drafts through the typewriter again and again. I am a 'skim reader.' I need to hear it again. Also, I'm faintly annoyed at something called a 'word processor.' It smells of nitrates.

"In the beginning I didn't know much about children's books. I started reading them when I started writing them. I don't think you should ever write something without having some knowledge of the field. It's as if to say 'I don't need to know this stuff, what I write is good enough.' That attitude betrays an absurd lack of self-knowledge.

"I really started to learn more about children's books when people began asking me to give speeches. I wanted to be able to say something fundamental, something about the whole process of writing, but I also wanted to be able to link it to what people throughout the ages had written. I looked through books about children's literature and I discovered I knew very little. Then I started reading the books themselves. As it turned out, I am a good lecturer, so I have become more and more in demand. The more I was in demand the more I had to find out about the various genres that I was writing in. When I began working on my book, [*Writing Books for Children*], which came out of a number of those lectures, I had to do even more research to find out about those topics which I didn't spend a lot of time writing myself."[2]

Besides writing, Yolen taught children's literature at Smith College for six years. "There are different periods in children's literature, different specialties, genres....It's absurd to try and teach children's literature in one semester....It's like trying to teach World Literature in one semester. I mention a few signpost books, look at some trends and give people ways of evaluating the literature that's there. You can't possibly choose three fantasy books for students to read. I could choose thirty-three more easily than I could choose three."[2]

Yolen feels her most significant contribution to literature for children has been her fairy tales. "There was a heyday for literary fairy tales around the time of Laurence Housman and Howard Pyle. Before that, there was Oscar Wilde and the Rossetti crew (who were trying to live like fairy tales as well as create them!), Hans Christian Andersen, and then back further to the French Comtesse d'Aulnoy. But literary fairy tales were not something that had been done much in this century. There have been single picture books, but no collection of romantic fairy tales that grew out of the folk mode, and yet were original stories, until *The Girl Who Cried Flowers.*

"*The Girl Who Cried Flowers* continues to be a good seller, and it is the collection I am most known for. I have written others which I feel are better collections, such as *Dream Weaver, Neptune Rising,* and *The Faery Flag,* but they haven't done as well. I think people say, 'I already have one

Yolen near her farmhouse in Massachusetts, 1981.

collection, I don't need another,' as if there is a finite number of fairy tales you can have.

"I am an incorrigible punster. I am probably the best punster writing for children today since I make the *worst* puns. Big distinction. I read the last *Commander Toad* book to my two sons. Adam rolled his eyes and said 'Oh, God, I hope nobody knows she's my mother.' Jason put his head down on the table. David, my husband, laughed out loud. When you are over forty-five you can laugh aloud at silly puns. Heidi, my daughter who is eighteen, refused to come in and listen. But the next day I got a note from her that said, 'I read the manuscript last night and I laughed out loud.' That was wonderful."[2]

One of Yolen's books, *The Bird of Time*, is dedicated to the memory of her mother. "Ostensibly, the book was started when I misheard the lyrics of a Righteous Brothers song on the car radio. I thought the words were 'time bird,' since the singers mumbled a lot. Before I had quite caught the real lyrics (which had nothing to do with either a bird or time), I found myself consciously thinking about

a time bird. I started writing the first paragraph of *The Bird of Time* on the day that I was told my mother had incurable cancer. The story, a classic fairy tale, is about a miller's son who finds a bird that can speed up time or slow it down.

"When the book was accepted for publication, I gave the manuscript to my mother. It was the last time I saw her alive. She had come up to visit us. She knew she had cancer but we didn't talk about it because my father didn't want her 'to know.' My mother was a very bright woman with a master's degree in social work. *She knew.* She was respecting his wishes not to talk about it. I, on the other hand, was desperate to talk about it. Heidi was almost four, Adam was two, and I was very pregnant with Jason. Mother sat in a big chair (she was a very tiny woman), finished reading the story, looked up at me as if to say, 'It's all right. I know I have cancer; I know I don't have long to live.' What she said was: 'Intimations of mortality—eh?' And then I knew where the book came from. I had loved to read the *Rubaiyat of Omar Khayyam.* I hadn't thought of that book in years, but my favorite quotation from it was 'Lo into the fire of spring, the winter garment of repentance bring, the Bird of Time has but a little way to flutter, and Lo the Bird is on the Wing.' Which, like my story, evokes a sense of time passing and seems to say,

Dust jacket from the 1989 collection of Yolen's work.

'Don't worry, there will be a renewal.' And I knew at once that she knew she was dying. The story was a bridge between us.

"Jason was born nine days before my mother died. It was about a year later, after the book was published and dedicated to my mother's memory, that I began to understand that it was a book for her, about my desire to stop time. That happens often with my stories. I find out long after that they were about more than the story itself. For example, one morning, eight years after my mother died, I was reading out loud a story in *Dream Weaver* called 'The Boy Who Sang for Death.' There is a line in which the boy says, 'Any gift I have I would give to get my mother back.' I started to sob. I realized that 'The Boy Who Sang for Death,' written eight years after her death, was a story in which I was still mourning my mother. I hadn't realized it when I wrote it; I only realized it when I spoke it out loud. Stories do give us permission to have feelings; not only do they give permission to the author, but they also give it to the reader. Stories help people, heal people."[2]

Dream Weaver is a collection of surrealistic tales. In a 1979 *Children's Book Service* book review, Violet H. Harada described it as, "a collection of tales which combines threads of classic folklores with modern strains of psychological insight into a rich tapestry of fantasy....[These are] bittersweet stories....Death, love, faith, and greed are the themes woven through these sensitively drawn portraits of human sorrow and joy. Adult readers will probably enjoy the truths in them as they share them with their children."

Yolen, who keeps an idea file filled with anything that comes along, believes that her characters often dictate new ideas to their authors. Such was the case in her historical book *The Gift of Sarah Barker*. "The crafts of the Shakers had...interested me, but I didn't know much about their culture. Though the Shakers did grow out of the Quakers, they have totally different religious beliefs. The Shakers are a millennium religion, and believe that Mother Anne is the female incarnation of Christ. After a visit with the few remaining Shakers, I felt I could go ahead and write the book.

"My only daughter was becoming interested in boys right about the time I was writing the book. I kept wondering how, in a Shaker community, you could keep the boys away from a girl like Heidi or keep Heidi away from the boys. I imagined a Romeo and Juliet story within the Shaker setting."

Yolen took two to three years to think about the story before coming up with the right theme.

"It later occurred to me that *Dragon's Blood* and *The Gift of Sarah Barker* are in some ways the same book. They are both set in farm communities where men and women are separated with rigidly set roles within the communities. There is even a large central mow in the big Dragon barn which comes right out of a description of the Shaker mow in *The Gift of Sarah Barker*. A boy and a girl fall in love, without really understanding what's happening to them or that they will eventually be thrust out of the community. In some ways the two books lean on each other. I've noticed the same phenomenon with my third 'Dragon' book and my *Children of the Wolf*—the idea of muteness and language is very important in both. It's interesting to find out about these similarities afterwards, but while I'm right in the middle of writing I don't think about it. Once a class of sixth graders said to me, 'Why do you have so many walls in your stories?' We started exploring the possible meanings together. I said, 'Walls could mean the difference between freedom and imprisonment...the difference between cozy and comfortable. Walls could mean being out in the scary but real world.' *The Girl Who Loved the Wind* and *The Seventh Mandarin* are both about what's beyond the wall, as is *The Seeing Stick*, in which a girl goes beyond the walls of the city. I had never thought of walls as a kind of thematic tic, but those kids were right."[2]

"It was in the 1980s that I was discovered! Adults as well as children were suddenly reading my tales. Or perhaps it was just that the boys and girls who had loved my stories were growing up and remembering them. My stories started appearing regularly in adult magazines like *Fantasy and Science Fiction* and *Isaac Asimov's SF Magazine*. I became a much-anthologized short story writer, in such collections as *The Year's Best Fantasy Stories*, *The Hundred Greatest Fantasy Short Shorts* (in which I had *three* tales), *Heroic Visions*, *Hecate's Cauldron*, and many, many textbooks. Storytellers had begun a renaissance in America and they were coming upon my work. I now receive about one letter a month from storytellers requesting permission to tell one or more of my stories. And there is no guessing what things they will tell. One told 'Dawn Strider' at a wedding, another told 'The White Seal Maid' at feminist gatherings. One teller even told a shortened hand-signed/spoken version of my novel *The Mermaid's Three Wisdoms*, which is about a hearing-impaired child."[1]

"I have two pieces of advice for young people interested in writing: read and write. Read and read and read. It's the only way you will discover what great stories have been told, and what stories you want to tell better. Write every day because writing is like a muscle that needs to be flexed. I don't [physically] exercise as much as I should, but I do exercise my writing every day. Faulkner said, 'I only write when I'm inspired. Fortunately, I'm inspired at nine o'clock every morning.' That's so true. You can't wait around for inspiration. You just have to get up and go to your desk and write."[2]

"I can't start my writing day until I get my mail. There are times when I'll work for just one or two hours in a day, but when I was finishing each of the 'Dragon' books, and *Cards of Grief*, I worked for about two weeks for ten solid hours a day. The rest of the time, I was thinking about the book. In fact, I was probably very bad company, not responding to anyone because I was so busy thinking and running upstairs to my studio whenever I could.

"I also feel very strongly that nobody gets to be a writer without help. I feel that one of our responsibilities as established writers is to reach out and pass our knowledge, passion, and information on to others. That's why I teach and conduct workshops. You don't become who you are without a helping hand from somewhere, even if it's just from reading other people's work. I run a monthly Society of Children's Books workshop and go to children's literature conferences. I am an editor. I know many people have more talent than I do, but they often don't know how to focus or how to start; they don't know the right questions to ask, so they're afraid to ask questions at all. I feel it's vital for aspiring writers to get the answers early so they won't have to spend years and years making the same mistakes."[2]

Footnote Sources:

[1] Adele Sarkissian, *Something about the Author Autobiography Series*, Volume 1, Gale, 1986.

[2] Anne Commire, *Something about the Author*, Volume 40, Gale, 1985.

■ For More Information See

Horn Book, August, 1970 (p. 391ff), October, 1975, June, 1984, January/February, 1986 (p. 123ff), November/December, 1986 (p. 790).

Publishers Weekly, February 22, 1971, May 7, 1979, May 20, 1988 (p. 44).

New York Times Book Review, September 10, 1972 (p. 8ff), May 15, 1974 (p. 43), September 19, 1976 (p. 16), November 20, 1977 (p. 30), January 1, 1978 (p. 20), February 18, 1979, October 28, 1979 (p. 18ff), May 23, 1982, June 26, 1988 (p. 28), November 13, 1988.

Library Journal, March 15, 1973.

Wilson Library Bulletin, October, 1973, September, 1986 (p. 9), September, 1987 (p. 66), May, 1988 (p. 72).

Jane H. Yolen, *Writing Books for Children*, Writer, 1973, revised edition, 1983.

Writer, April, 1975, December, 1978, January, 1981, August, 1983 (p. 15ff), May, 1984, May, 1986 (p. 5), January, 1987 (p. 7).

Cricket, September, 1975.

Doris de Montreville and Elizabeth D. Crawford, editors, *The Fourth Book of Junior Authors and Illustrators*, H. W. Wilson, 1978.

D. L. Kirkpatrick, *Twentieth-Century Children's Writers*, St. Martin's, 1978, new edition, 1983.

Children's Literature in Education, Volume II, number 3, 1980.

Washington Post Book World, February 8, 1981.

J. H. Yolen, *Touch Magic: Fantasy, Faerie and Folklore in the Literature of Childhood*, Philomel, 1981.

Children's Literature Review, Volume IV, Gale, 1982.

Language Arts, May, 1982.

Chicago Tribune Book World, November 7, 1982.

Fantasy Newsletter, September, 1983.

Jim Roginski, *Behind the Covers: Interviews with Authors and Illustrators of Books for Children and Young Adults*, Libraries Unlimited, 1985.

New Orleans Times Picayune, March 30, 1986 (p. C4).

Penelope Moffet, "Writers Discuss Their Creativity," *Los Angeles Times*, November 27, 1986.

Boston Globe, October 12, 1987 (p. 57).

Dictionary of Literary Biography, Volume 52, Gale, 1986.

Collections:

De Grummond Collection at the University of Southern Mississippi.

Kerlan Collection at the University of Minnesota.

Cumulative Index

Author/Artist Index

The following index gives the number of the volume
in which an author/artist's biographical sketch appears.

Adams, Douglas 1952- 4
Adler, C. S. 1932- 4
Adoff, Arnold 1935- 3
Aiken, Joan 1924- 1
Alexander, Lloyd 1924- 1
Andrews, V. C. 1986- 4
Baldwin, James 1924-1987 4
Ballard, J. G. 1930- 3
Blume, Judy 1938- 3
Bonham, Frank 1914- 1
Boorman, John 1933- 3
Campbell, Joseph 1904-1987 3
Carpenter, John 1948- 2
Chatwin, Bruce 1940- 4
Clarke, Arthur C. 1917- 4
Colman, Hila 1
Cormier, Robert 1925- 3
Danziger, Paula 1944- 4
Duncan, Lois 1934- 4
Ellis, Bret Easton 1964- 2
Feiffer, Jules 1929- 3
Forster, E. M. 1879-1970 2
Fox, Paula 1923- 3
Freedman, Russell 1929- 4
Fuentes, Carlos 1928- 4
Garcia Marquez, Gabriel 1928- 3

Guisewite, Cathy 1950- 2
Guy, Rosa 1925- 4
Hall, Lynn 1937- 4
Hamilton, Virginia 1936- 2
Hentoff, Nat 1925- 4
Herriot, James 1916- 1
Hinton, S. E. 1950- 2
Jones, Chuck 1912- 2
Jordan, June 1936- 2
Kaufman, Bel 4
Keillor, Garrison 1942- 2
Kennedy, William 1928- 1
Kerr, M. E. 1927- 2
King, Stephen 1947- 1
Klein, Norma 1938- 2
Konigsburg, E. L. 3
Kundera, Milan 1929- 2
Larson, Gary 1950- 1
Lee, Spike 1957- 4
L'Engle, Madeleine 1918- 1
Lewis, C. S. 1898-1963 3
Lloyd Webber, Andrew 1948- 1
Lucas, George 1944- 1
Lustig, Arnost 1926- 3
Mamet, David 1947- 3
Marshall, Garry 1934- 3

Mathabane, Mark 1976- 4
McKinley, Robin 1952- 4
Morrison, Toni 1931- 1
Mowat, Farley 1921- 1
Myers, Walter Dean 1937- 4
Naylor, Phyllis Reynolds 1933- 4
O'Dell, Scott 1898- 3
Pascal, Francine 1938- 1
Paterson, Katherine 1932- 1
Paulsen, Gary 1939- 2
Peck, Richard 1934- 1
Peck, Robert Newton 1928- 3
Pinkwater, Daniel Manus 1941- 1
Sachs, Marilyn 1927- 2
Sagan, Carl 1934- 2
Salinger, J. D. 1919- 2
Shepard, Sam 1943- 1
Strasser, Todd 1950- 2
Taylor, Theodore 1921- 2
Voigt, Cynthia 1942- 3
Walker, Alice 1944- 3
Wersba, Barbara 1932- 2
Yolen, Jane 1939- 4
Zindel, Paul 1936- 2